D0897074

Mexican Americans and World War II

Mexican Americans & World War II

EDITED BY

MAGGIE RIVAS-RODRIGUEZ

University of Texas Press
Austin

Copyright © 2005 by the University of Texas Press

All rights reserved
Printed in the United States of America

First edition, 2005

Requests for permission to reproduce material from this work should be sent to
Permissions, University of Texas Press, Box 7819, Austin, TX 78713-7819.

∞ The paper used in this book meets the minimum requirements of ANSI.NISO
Z39.48-1992 (R1997) (Permanence of Paper).

Library of Congress Cataloging-in-Publication Data

Mexican Americans and World War II / edited by Maggie Rivas-Rodriguez.—
1st ed.
   p.   cm.
  Includes bibliographical references and index.
   ISBN 0-292-70651-0 (alk. paper)—ISBN 0-292-70681-2 (pbk. : alk. paper)
   1. Mexican Americans—Social conditions—20th century. 2. United States—
Social conditions—1933–1945. 3. United States—Race relations. 4. World
War, 1939–1945—Social aspects—United States. I. Rivas-Rodriguez, Maggie.
E184.M5M513 2005
940.53'089'6872073—dc22

                                                   2004024343

To the Latinos and Latinas of the World War II generation

Contents

Preface

This volume owes its beginnings to a conference that took place over the Memorial Day weekend of the year 2000, titled "U.S. Latinos and Latinas and World War II: Changes Seen, Changes Wrought."

However, this is not a book of conference proceedings. In fact, in order to make a coherent whole, several very worthwhile essays were left out. Even so, the conference has imbued this book with a special spirit, a sense of importance that has certainly transcended any one individual effort. For one thing, we were fortunate to include two roundtable discussions by the Latinas and Latinos of the World War II generation (Mary Murillo, Elisa Rodriguez, and Marta Cotera of Austin; Ed Idar of San Antonio, Albert Armendariz of El Paso, and Virgilio Roel of Austin). Many more attended the conference, sitting in on panel discussions of events they actually witnessed or took part in. For the academics, it was a rare opportunity to meet face-to-face with the people we research, comparing our perceptions with those of the actual participants. On a few occasions over the two-day period, our conclusions were challenged by these men and women. Besides the roundtable discussion with this generation of people, we also had readings of nonacademic papers and informal discourses on World War II and Latinos, including one by a high school student who wrote about her father translating Japanese in the war.

And lastly, for this generation of Latino academics, in their fifties and mid- to late forties, the theme resonated in a very personal way. We are, in effect, the children of this generation. Professor Rico Ainslie's own father, Roberto Francisco Ainslie, was a Mexican citizen who served in the U.S. Navy and saw action throughout the Pacific; Rico wore his father's dog tags throughout the conference.

David Montejano pinned on our exhibit bulletin board a 1995 obituary of his father, Juan H. Montejano, which included the elder Montejano's participation as a B-25 machine gunner in Borneo, Japan, and the southern Philippines offensives. Rafael Chabrán of Whittier College in California and Rita Sanchez of San Diego Mesa College presented papers on their own family's experiences in the war effort. Noted scholar Rolando Hinojosa-Smith of the University of Texas at Austin presented a paper about how the war changed his hometown of Mercedes, Texas.

Over the course of the two days, we organizers realized the great yearning—on the part of the general public, as well as the academic community—to consider, evaluate, and analyze the contributions of this generation of Latinos. And simultaneously, there was a bittersweet reminder that these stories have too often been omitted from other general historical treatments of World War II.

As a one-time, stand-alone conference, one not associated with an organization or one particular discipline, we had the freedom to try new things. Our dedicated conference planning committee was composed of professors at the University of Texas at Austin: Lisa Montoya, a government professor; Ricardo Ainslie, in educational psychology; Neil Foley, history; David Montejano, history; and this writer, in journalism. Professor Montejano, then the director of the Center for Mexican American Studies, served as a conference co-chair.

In a very real sense this book, and in fact, the larger U.S. Latino and Latina WWII Oral History Project of which it is a component, had its start eight years earlier, when I was working on a story for the December 6, 1992, issue of *Dallas Life* magazine, the now-defunct magazine of *The Dallas Morning News*, where I worked as a reporter for about twelve years. The story, which ran on the cover, was titled "Brothers in Arms," and it explored the World War II generation of Mexican Americans in Texas. It was that generation that went on to make significant contributions to Latino civil rights. From that generation came such heroes as Hector P. García, the founder and legendary leader of the American G.I. Forum, the people who created the Mexican American Legal Defense and Educational Fund (MALDEF), men like Pete Tijerina, Ed Idar, Albert Armendariz, and scores of others who made their mark in less public, but nonetheless important, ways in order to desegregate the state's schools and other public institutions.

In the course of researching that story, I found a few excellent articles and books—those by David Montejano, Guadalupe San Miguel, Mario T. García, and Rodolfo Acuña, to name just a few—but hungered for more. Among my sources for that magazine piece were University of Texas college history professor David Montejano (now at the University of California at Berkeley) and Carlos Velez-Ibañez, then an anthropology professor at the University of Arizona in Tucson (now at the University of California at Riverside's Ernesto Galarza Applied Research Center). When I asked them for further references, they both responded that the effect of World War II on Texas's Mexican Americans was just one of many, many underresearched topics. The three of us briefly attempted to establish an oral history project, working with members of the National Association of Hispanic Journalists. The idea was for us to join forces—Latino academics and Latino journalists—to record the untold stories of these men and women. The result would be an archive of oral histories. None of us had the time to devote to the effort back then. But I credit professors Montejano and Velez-Ibañez with helping me think through some problems and helping to set up a framework back in 1993. Six years later, after I had arrived at Austin and was allowed to teach a class that would be dedicated to developing oral histories of Latinos and Latinas of the World War II generation, I came armed with ideas that had been evolving over the years.

One component of this budding new oral history project was a conference that would lead to an edited volume such as you have here; for us as academics, it would be useful to get publications out and to jump-start some research on the subject.

My first call was to my friends at the Belo Foundation. The A. H. Belo Corporation owns the *Dallas Morning News*, where I worked for twelve years, until 1996. I had worked closely with Belo's philanthropic arm, in particular with Judith Garrett-Segura, on projects to recruit and encourage young Latinos to pursue writing careers. Belo eventually agreed to provide a $36,500 grant for the conference. With that sizeable donation, the game was afoot. The conference got a small office, a cast-off computer, and a telephone line. With that, we established an e-mail account, put up a skeleton of a Web site, and had enough information to develop a nice brochure.

Since 1999, the larger project has come a long way—we have videotaped interviews with more than four hundred men and women across the country, digitizing, at a high resolution, several hundred more beautiful photographs. Each interview has been featured in a semiannual publication called *Narratives*—with the generous in-kind support of the *Austin American-Statesman* and the *San Antonio Express-News*, which alternated providing production assistance and printing.

The project will spin off several more books and other components: a book of excerpts from interviews, another that showcases the beautiful digitized photographs mentioned above, and finally, another edited volume, this one relying heavily on the interviews, coalescing around various themes, including issues of race and identity, Spanish-language radio in World War II, Mexican citizens serving in the U.S. military, the changing roles of Latina women on the home front, the challenges of young men returning from the battlefields with cases of "nerves," or what today is called post-traumatic stress disorder. There are also plans for a play based in large part on our interviews, as well as a documentary, with related educational materials. Starting in 2005, the archives themselves will start opening to the public at the Nettie Lee Benson Latin American Collection and at the Center for American History, both at the University of Texas at Austin.

And it all started with that Memorial Day weekend conference in 2000. My deepest thanks to the A. H. Belo Corporation Foundation for its support, which got this ball rolling forward and gaining momentum, rather than rolling back on top of me. Thank you, too, to the University of Texas School of Journalism (then under chair Steve Reese and now under Lorraine Branham), the College of Communication (then under Dean Ellen Wartella), and the Center for Mexican American Studies (first under David Montejano and now under José Limón) for support of the conference, as well as subsequent support. I often say it has taken lots of people up and down the food chain to make this happen—and to make it keep happening.

And some of those other folks are the ones who lent their time— the volunteers at that Memorial Day weekend conference in 2000 who videotaped all the panels and discussions, as well as assisted in myriad ways—in particular, Grace Rocha, Chris Shanahan, Cheryl Smith, Dolores Garcia, and Virginia Raymond. And a special bow to my longtime buddy Pat Vazquez, who had worked with me on other ambitious projects and who drove in from Houston, armed with customized T-shirts and buttons—as a donation to the project—and doing all the glamourless things that had to be done. Finally, the show could not have proceeded without the careful attention of Denise Rocha, who was our conference coordinator and has now moved on to other work but remains a dear friend.

Thank you to our friends at the University of Texas Press—Theresa May for seeing its potential, Lynne F. Chapman for steering it through the final stages, and Salena Krug, who was meticulous so that the whole was as good as it could be. Thank you, too, to our external reviewers for their very helpful suggestions.

As the editor of this volume, I was forced to make difficult decisions. One of the most drastic was to focus strictly on Mexican Americans, with two chapters on Mexican citizens in the United States during the period. Our 2000 conference sought to encompass all U.S. Latinos and Latinas and had several excellent papers about Puerto Ricans. But without adequate representations of other groups, this volume could not claim to represent all U.S. Latinos. In order to get the volume out in as timely a fashion as possible, I decided to narrow the focus to only Mexicans and Mexican Americans, rather than broaden the focus to include more groups—and find new contributors, edit new first drafts, and so on. I do remain personally committed to seeing a future volume that will tell that broader story—of Puerto Ricans both on the mainland and on the island, of Cuban Americans in Ybor City, and of other groups.

It is my hope, and I believe the collective hope of all the contributors to this book, that this volume will provide a strong foundation for future work on the larger picture of U.S. Latinos and Latinas and World War II.

Introduction

Sixty years after the conclusion of the Second World War, a distinct sense of awe of the period remains undiminished. It was a time of high drama, as our country displayed a remarkable ability to rise to a daunting challenge—the Germans and the Japanese had already demonstrated their military cunning, as well as their resolve to ruthlessly vanquish their foes. Even today, in analyzing contemporary international wars and events, World War II is frequently used as the vantage point, the compass that grounds us, that situates the international community in somewhat of a unified history. The war served as the great turning point for many countries, and for their peoples.

To gauge the continued fascination with the war, one need look no further than the continued output of books and documentaries related to World War II, works which seek to apply new information or new perspectives to historical events—how aware were Catholic Church officials about atrocities toward the Jews in Germany, and could the Church have protested more vigorously? Were the commanders at Pearl Harbor unfairly scapegoated for being caught off guard on that "day that will live in infamy"? Did British Prime Minister Neville Chamberlain's controversial policy of appeasement toward Germany in the late 1930s actually work to his country's advantage in the long run?

And in our country, we saw how that one war struck our own social structures like a meteor; the dust is settling. American women's longtime participation in the lower levels of the nation's workforce had been largely ignored—until their labor became necessary to meet the gargantuan need for labor to build the thousands of ships, airplanes, and other armaments. The government responded with colorful posters depicting women factory workers as patriots doing their share for their country. By the end of World War II, nearly nineteen million American women were working outside the home—an unprecedented number.[1]

African American men, serving in segregated units, distinguished themselves for their valor, although they were often relegated to the less desirable duties, such as loading explosives aboard ships. The 996 pilots and support staff of the Tuskegee Airmen, who served as pilots in the 332nd Fighter Group, escorted Allied bombers in the European theater.[2] Back home the African American community galvanized a "Double-V" campaign—Victory overseas and Victory at home—victory, that is, against the racism that continued to oppress some Americans.

On the West Coast, 120,000 Japanese Americans were herded into internment camps, as alarmists worried that these Americans would sooner side with the Pacific Rim nation than with the United States.[3]

And for Mexican Americans, World War II would indeed prove to be the war that led to substantial headway in the fight toward desegregating public institutions, and lessening, if not eliminating, the intransigent discrimination that had existed since the end of the Texas-Mexico war. Even in early 1940, there were small communities of Mexicans and Mexican Americans in the Midwest, the Northwest, and elsewhere in the United States. The largest concentrations were in the Southwest, home to 90 percent of Americans of Mexican descent.[4] And it was in the Southwest, perhaps most notably in Texas, where discrimination and prejudice were rampant. Socially segregated schools were commonplace, in particular in the smaller, rural areas; it was not uncommon to see placards in restaurant windows stating that the proprietors would serve neither dogs nor Mexicans.

Consider an anecdote related by Armando Flores of Corpus Christi, Texas. Mr. Flores vividly recalled a chilly winter day in 1942, standing with a group of soldiers in Sheppard Field, Texas. The men had jammed their fists into their pockets against the frigid cold. Noticing it, a lieutenant rebuked them: "American soldiers stand at attention, on a cold day, or a hot day. They never keep their hands in their pockets."

Private Flores marveled at the officer's choice of words.

"The funny thing about it—and the reason that I remember that—was because nobody had ever called me an American until that time," he recalled many years later.

"I had been called a lot of things . . . wetback and spic, and greaser. . . . That was the first time in my life that I had been called an American," he said.[5]

Mr. Flores's family, in fact, had lived in Texas since before 1846, when Texas became a state. And yet . . . and yet, no one had called Armando Flores an American until 1941. And, it might be noted, the citizenship of U.S. Latinos is still routinely challenged. World War II, then, imparted to Mr. Flores and other Mexican Americans a sense of belonging. For once, there was inclusion, although it was fleeting and it would require the strongest efforts of this World War II generation of Latinos to reclaim any part of that inclusion.

General treatments of World War II, of the Great Depression, and of the postwar years in America generally exclude stories of U.S. Latinos and Latinas. There is, in fact, even today, a lingering and curious dismissal of U.S. Latinos, as if Latinos had not lived here, had not served the country, had not, as a matter of fact, made the ultimate sacrifice for inclusion.[6] It is as if, to apply Ralph Ellison's analogy to Mexican Americans, they were invisible men and women— part of the landscape, supporting actors in a drama that purported only to affect them, not to be affected by them, a history that denies them the recognition of the very agency they courageously demonstrated time and again.

It was not the actual battlefield experiences that set apart the Mexican American World War II experience, although Mexican Americans did have more Medals of Honor than any other ethnic group. Tens of thousands of Mexican American men—and some women—accepted military service as a way to a regular paycheck, just as tens of thousands of other American men did. Mexican American women on the home front likewise got good jobs with good wages and experienced the liberating effects of self-sufficiency, as did other American women.

What did separate the war-years experience for Mexican Americans, however, was that it would be the first time that they were participating fully in mainstream society, even working alongside Anglos as equals. They discovered, if there was any doubt, that white Americans were, after all, only humans, no worse and no better. Also, with the introduction of the G.I. Bill of Rights, many returning veterans were able to afford training and other schooling that would have been impossible otherwise. It is no coincidence that many of the founders of the Mexican American Legal Defense and Educational Fund—men like Pete Tijerina, Albert Armendariz, and Ed Idar—were themselves returning World War II G.I.'s who availed themselves of the G.I. Bill.

World War II, then, imbued the ongoing Mexican American civil rights movement with new leadership and a new attitude of entitlement—Mexican American men had, in large numbers, served their country as Americans; now it was time to reap the benefits of full citizenship rights.[7]

Not that there was a shortage of activism before World War II. One early chronicler—and battler—of the dual system was Alonso Perales, a veteran of World War I and a member of the League of United Latin American Citizens (LULAC). Perales collected depositions, letters, and newspaper clippings that documented instances of discrimination.[8] His book, published just after World War II, gave voice to the many men and women, Mexican and Anglo, who were outraged by a system rife with unfair treatment for Mexican Americans. However, the persistence of the inequities indicates how futile those protests were.

This book considers the effect of World War II on Mexican Americans and Mexicans living in the United States, on several levels: the family level, within locales, and in perceptions of how the world viewed Mexican Americans and how Mexican Americans viewed themselves.

The essays presented here endeavor to appeal to a general audience, as well as an academic one; it is hoped that this volume will be of interest to the broadest possible readership. This is not the complete Mexican American World War II experience, but it is an effort to gather this group of writers and academics around this very important topic. It is hoped that future treatments—by these and other writers—will be representative of the larger Latino experience, as we compare and contrast this American Latino experience.

This volume opens up with the scene-setting essay by Rita Sanchez in which she writes about her own family's experience. Sanchez's essay centers on one Mexican American family's involvement in the war effort and how that was understood by a young child, now a woman. The Sanchez family journeyed from northern New Mexico to southern California for steady work after the Great Depression. But the distance between Bernalillo and San Bernardino amounted to more than 760 miles—it crossed the rural homestead with adobe buildings and *Matachines* dancing in the street, Christmas gifts of food, young boys riding horses, the clear, diffuse light that has enchanted generations of artists and photographers. The destination was urban, less welcoming to them. But the Sanchez family persevered, holding tight to those customs they had grown up with—the big busy Sunday dinner, with *chiles* serving as a staple. That generation of Sanchezes would not be self-conscious about its heritage: it was simply a fact of life. But in writing about that everyday existence, Rita shows us the ordinariness of this type of Americanness—families who felt they were Americans, who did all the things that many other Americans did, including grieve for a son who would not return from the war.

David Montejano's essay on his uncle illustrates a very different family legend—one awash in the ugliness of discrimination and division of that period. Montejano's family lore included an incident in the final days of the war involving Ben Aguirre, a young soldier beaten nearly to death by a gang of white teenagers. Montejano's fascination with this tale leads him to travel back to Midland with his uncle, Fred "Lico" Enriquez, to search out the victim of the attack. What Montejano finds is different from the lore—in many ways, the embellishments make the story far worse than it was to begin with, the brutality even uglier. But in other ways, the reality he uncovers is even crueler, the injustice more outrageous. Montejano leaves it to the reader to decide whether justice was meted out by a Higher Power. In another sense, however, Montejano's piece reveals a social order that resisted change, that was threatened by these young brown men who were poised, perhaps, to make their own mark on the world.

Education, the mighty fulcrum to greater job opportunities, and generally higher incomes, looms large in three chapters within this volume. One, Julio Noboa's look at Sidney S. Lanier High School on the predominantly Mexican American West Side of San Antonio, paints a picture of prewar San Antonio's West Side that has little to recommend it as a beacon of patriotism. As part of that picture, he introduces the reader to a housing project that at once draws sharp attention to the poverty of the West Side, as well as the role of the

Catholic Church in the lives of many of those residents. Noboa also examines Lanier's strongly vocational curriculum, and traces the educational theory that led many educators to adopt it as a savior for those young people apparently destined to follow their parents to blue-collar jobs. Lanier, for all the strikes against it, responded with a patriotic fervor. This was the school from which many of San Antonio's Mexican American boys left to contribute to the war effort and the community to which they returned. As such, it speaks volumes about the expectations—and about the transcendence of those expectations—the young Mexican Americans faced.

In neighboring New Mexico, where Mexican Americans enjoyed a relatively higher level of participation in civic life, changes were begun before the war to increase educational opportunities for Mexican American children. Lynne Marie Getz argues that the war retarded progress for Hispanic children's education in New Mexico. As Getz points out, caring educators had attempted to tailor an educational system that would be respectful of the Hispano culture and provide them skills that would prepare them for better employment. Those advances, carefully studied and planned for years before the onset of U.S. involvement in World War II, were derailed because of a powerful redirection of priorities and resources. So marked was the change that where once the Hispano culture was considered front and center an important cultural asset for the state, during the war, it was taught as a "foreign culture." In many cases, Getz notes, that "lost momentum" would never be regained. So it is that the New Mexico educational story runs counter to the prevailing understanding of World War II having leveled barriers for Mexican Americans. In this case, the war did not lead to better conditions, but actually halted improvements dead in their tracks.

Dionicio Valdés also points to a war experience that brought hardship to at least one group of Mexican Americans, the early newcomers to the Midwest. Valdés writes of the Mexican American community of St. Paul, Minnesota, a community of about two thousand in 1940, that was the target of local social workers' assimilation efforts. Whereas in other parts of the country Mexican Americans were able to take advantage of better job opportunities tied to the war effort, in St. Paul, that was not the case. For various reasons, the better jobs did not materialize for many St. Paul residents. Valdés writes that many Midwest Mexican American families turned to local social agencies for help, thus becoming subject to probing, undignified home visits that, as reflected in the social workers' own writings, had little regard for the clients' culture. As in the Southwest, expectations of these men and women were low; schoolgirls, in fact, were strongly steered to learn skills that would serve them well as maids, or baby-sitters, regardless of their intelligence; white-collar jobs were not considered possibilities for these young girls. Valdés's essay provides the prewar context of these men and women, which offers readers a better understanding of how the war experience, so celebrated as the opening to unprecedented job opportunities, was not realized in that manner everywhere.

All was not rosy in other parts of the country for other Mexican Americans. In Los Angeles and other major metropolitan areas, the war drew into sharp relief the divisions between Mexican Americans, blacks, and the dominant Anglo society. In his essay, Luis Alvarez considers the Zoot Suit Riots of 1943 in Los Angeles as a clash between a home front that called for homogeneity and a subculture of minority youth that was developing its own notions of self-identity. Alvarez calls the beatings and other humiliations heaped on the zoot-suiters a "figurative and literal slap in the faces of youth of color."

Before World War II in the Southwest, it was unusual for mainstream newspapers to carry stories about the common Mexican Americans, or the everyday experiences of that group. That changed during the war, as news from the battlefront often included Mexican Americans. Two chapters rely heavily on that newspaper coverage. The first, by Maria Eva Flores, concerns the societal changes in Fort Stockton, a deeply divided community in West Texas. Flores uses the newspaper as a gauge of the opening of the town to its Mexican American population. The local newspaper, as the chronicler of life in that community, in a flush of patriotic pride, carried several stories about Mexican American "boys" who were overseas, many distinguishing themselves on the battlefield. This would be the first time that Mexicans were included in regular coverage in the *Fort Stockton Pioneer*, a sign that perhaps the dominant society might adopt a similar inclusiveness. In Fort Stockton, the Anglos and Mexican Americans rarely mixed; yet overseas, young men from the two groups—from opposite sides of the tracks—would meet one another on equal terms. Flores provides the background on the dual treatment of Anglos and Mexican Americans, so the irony is thick when the *Fort Stockton Pioneer* notes that "Tiodoro Moreno and W. R. McKay have met at their new station in Camp Breckenridge, Ky."[9] Those wartime experiences would embolden them to fight hard after the war for equal rights. It would be, Flores notes, several years before the actual desegregation would take root.

The other chapter that relies heavily on newspaper accounts is one by this writer that considers the way newspapers in Texas and outside the state reported on the case of Private Felix Longoria, killed in the Philippines in the closing days of the war, in June 1944. The case made national headlines when his relatives were not allowed to use funeral home facilities in his South Texas hometown because of supposed objections by whites. The Three Rivers story—the first time that Mexican American civil rights were the subject of a national news story—has been examined time and again. In this essay, the framing of the news story is the focus. Rereading the newspaper accounts in Texas newspapers, sixty years later, in which both Hector Garcia and the dead soldier's wife and family are vilified, is a reminder of the deep roots of racism in many Texas newspapers as they resisted a segue into a fairer, more inclusive world. It is also, to a large measure, a reminder of how outraged major outside news media (Walter Winchell came out swinging and the *New York Times*, while calmer, painted a powerful picture of the outrage) can wield a powerful gavel in the court of public opinion—and begin to effect change in attitudes.

Emilio Zamora also looks at public opinion, but as it applied to Texas and the United States in the eyes of Mexico and other Latin American countries. Zamora considers the Good Neighbor Policy, established by the United States in the late 1930s to draw Latin American nations close and away from the Axis Powers, as the beginning of a tidal change in relations between the economically powerful United States and its poorer southern neighbor. News of the discrimination faced by Mexicans and Mexican Americans made headlines in Mexican newspapers; indeed, some of those incidents happened to Mexican government officials. Mexico, Zamora argues, successfully made Mexicans and Mexican Americans key players in that relationship—bringing pressure to bear on the problems of discrimination. With the U.S. need for braceros, or guest workers, Mexico's ability to make demands grew stronger, although that came to an end after the war.

Two writers look at the jobs created by the war effort: Naomi Quiñonez looks at the Mexican American women who were given entrée into the defense manufacturing plants, while Erasmo Gamboa considers the Mexican guest workers who were recruited as laborers to replace the worker-turned-soldier.

In the first essay, Quiñonez relies on oral history interviews with five Mexican American women who worked in defense plants in Southern California, about how that experience transformed their worlds. Gone were the chaperones, the docility of young women looking for husbands who would support them. Replacing them were self-reliant women with ambitions of their own. As a result, the Rosita the Riveters acquired new expectations of marriage and of men. This generation of Chicana workers, Quiñonez says, replaced old social constructions with new ones that better reflected where they had been and what they had done.

Last, Erasmo Gamboa introduces the reader to the Northwest Mexican American experience, particularly as it dates to World War II, when Mexican guest workers, or braceros, were brought in. The workers, many of whom remained in the Pacific Northwest after the war and formed a new community of Mexican Americans, faced a broad range of living conditions: the best were similar to dormitories for factory workers, the worst were akin to chicken coops. Gamboa also notes how Mexican officials, charged with visiting those camps to ensure sanitary living conditions, sometimes painted a far more positive picture than the reality dictated. Gamboa notes the hardships of these braceros, separated from family, living under sometimes undesirable conditions, subjected to discrimination. But he also allows that Chinese Mexican cooks hired to prepare meals were themselves sometimes subjected to the ridicule of these braceros; records show that some of these cooks walked off the job.

It is said that all research is personal at some level. And this is true, in large measure, for these essays. To many scholars whose work appears in the following pages, World War II was not strictly an academic subject. These scholars, now in their forties and older, are the daughters, sons, nieces, nephews, of the World War II generation. Because of that, many of us are entering into this research area with the advantage of having witnessed firsthand the changes and the advantages made possible by the war effort; we are also cognizant of the challenges faced by this World War II generation of Mexican

Americans. Because of that, we are able to imbue our efforts with a certain passion that is born of personal investment; I believe that passion is evident throughout.

Notes

1. David M. Kennedy, *Freedom from Fear: The American People in Depression and War, 1929–1945* (New York: Oxford University Press, 1999), 778.

2. J. Todd Moye, "The Tuskegee Airmen Oral History Project and Oral History in the National Park Service," *Journal of American History*, September 2002 <http://www.historycooperative.org/journals/jah/89.2/moye.html> (January 30, 2004).

3. Ronald Takaki, *Double Victory: A Multicultural History of America in World War II* (Boston: Little, Brown, 2000), 137.

4. Richard Griswold del Castillo and Arnoldo De León's *North to Aztlán: A History of Mexican Americans in the United States* (New York: Twayne, 1997), 85.

5. Armando Flores, interview by Bettina Luis, videotaped recording, Corpus Christi, Texas, May 24, 2001, U.S. Latino and Latina WWII Oral History Archives, Austin.

6. There are, fortunately, exceptions; among the mainstream historians who have done an admirable job of including Latinos' experiences in World War II and the Great Depression is the award-winning David Kennedy, cited above.

7. For a few examples, see Griswold del Castillo and De León's *North to Aztlán*, particularly chapters 6 and 7. The writers note that in 1940, the vast majority—90 percent—of the "Mexican-stock population . . . lived overwhelmingly in the states of the American Southwest." Griswold del Castillo and De León write: "This 'G.I. generation' would lead the cause for Mexican-American equality between 1945 and the 1960s" (103). Historian Mario T. García refers to the Great Depression and World War II as the coming of age for Mexican Americans: "Both the Great Depression and WWII can be seen together as the twin historical experiences for a political generation committed to actively struggling for civil rights and first-class citizenship for Mexican Americans." Mario T. García, *Mexican Americans: Leadership, Ideology and Identity, 1930–1960* (New Haven, Conn.: Yale University Press, 1989), 18. Also, Richard A. Garcia, *Rise of the Mexican American Middle Class: San Antonio, 1929–1941* (College Station: Texas A&M University Press, 1991) writes that World War II "increased [Mexican Americans'] sense of rising expectations" (302). Montejano also credits World War II with bringing to an end the segregated social order in Texas: "The war created a generation of Mexican American veterans prepared to press for their rights and privileges. The cracks in the segregated order appeared to be irreparable." David Montejano, *Anglos and Mexicans in the Making of Texas, 1836–1986* (Austin: University of Texas Press, 1987), 264.

8. Alonso Perales, *Are We Good Neighbors?* (San Antonio: Artes Gráficas, 1948).

9. *Fort Stockton Pioneer*, July 7, 1944.

Mexican Americans and World War II

CHAPTER I

The Five Sanchez Brothers in World War II

Remembrance and Discovery

RITA SANCHEZ

O Beautiful for heroes proved in liberating strife,
Who more than self their country loved,
And mercy more than life!

This is a story of five brothers who faced a world war: the Sanchez brothers in World War II. Descendants of a family from a little town called Bernalillo, one of the oldest Spanish land grants in New Mexico, they left behind a story that inspires courage and hope. They deserve to be remembered.

I was four years old when the war broke out. Yet my memories of the war years are clear. I remember the news of the battles and the soldiers in uniform. But most of all, I remember these brothers. They were my father, Leonidas Nicolas, and my vibrant young uncles, Emiliano, Santiago, Severo, and John Edward, who went overseas. I also remember the sentiments of those who were left at home to wait and wonder. To all of them, especially to one brother who did not return, I dedicate this essay.

As a child steeped in World War II, I saw my parents turn on the radio to listen to the war news every evening. I remember the times my father would point out on maps the places where his four brothers were fighting: the Aleutians, the Rhine, and the Battle of the Bulge. Names like Attu, Kwajalein, and Leyte became household words.

I listened to the air-raid siren at night with my brothers and sisters. We huddled in the dark during these terrifying blackouts. I knew what these alerts meant because we went to war movies together. We watched as bombs rattled neighborhoods like ours in black-and-white films. And so the war became even more real.

Many like us were affected by the war. In 1942 the United States drafted hundreds of thousands of young men into the armed services to fight in World War II.[1] The Sanchezes had already decided to take some profound action, "to end this war," they said. Many Mexican American families like ours stepped forward willingly as Americans to join the cause.

To understand the story of the five Sanchez brothers, one must know a little bit about Bernalillo, New Mexico, their ancestral home. Four hundred years ago, New Mexico was uncharted territory in the northern part of *La Nueva España*. In 1848 it belonged to the United States. What survived were the family names, Sanchez, Gurulé, and Valdés on one side, and Sánchez de Yñigo and Durán y Chaves on the other, *primeras familias* of New Mexico.[2]

A tiny colonial adobe chapel still stands between Santa Fe and Albuquerque. And from the choir loft one can look out and see the cloud-covered Sandia Mountains. The spectacular view elicits memories of time past. To add to that, the weatherworn village cemetery headstones nearby attest to the extent of its long history. This is where the brothers grew up.

Their parents were Emiliano and Dolores Sanchez. Walking through the historical town in the summer when the sun-drenched mountains and trees sparkle with light, it is easy to imagine the horse and carriage that brought the hopeful couple to the altar of Nuestra Señora de Dolores chapel for their August 19 wedding in 1895.

On that day Emiliano, twenty-two, and Dolores, fifteen, married. The groom's parents, José de Jesús Santiago Sánchez and María Soledad Valdés, gave the newlyweds ten acres of Bernalillo land as a wedding gift to help them start their new life. There they set out to raise twelve children, losing two as babies, both sons named Leopoldo. Ten survived. On their land they learned to cherish the ancient ways. These were the values that prepared five brothers to serve in the war.

Emiliano and Dolores Sanchez, in a photo taken about 1910 in San Bernardino, California. Courtesy of Cathy Sanchez Bates.

The oldest, Leonidas, and his brother Emiliano—his father's namesake—described some of the cultural events. They remembered the holy days, the music, the food, and the distinctive *Matachines* dances. These came with the Feast of San Lorenzo every August 10.[3] That day was considered one of deliverance for their ancestors who survived the Pueblo Revolt in 1680. These customs had gone on long before the Sanchez brothers and sisters were born. The U.S. takeover and the railroad also disrupted the old ways on the land. More changes were in store.

The Sanchez family faced change courageously. A new economy demanded wage labor. About 1910 their Papa Emiliano began to work for Southern Pacific Railroad as a repairman, traveling back and forth between New Mexico and California. My father, Leo, said, "We had two homes then, one in Bernalillo and one in San Bernardino near the train station. When my mother was expecting, we traveled home to New Mexico so the new baby could be born there."[4] In this way, allegiance to the homeland prevailed.

Listening to my father, I could sense that life in New Mexico had a different rhythm. Age-old traditions were guided by the Catholic liturgical calendar. He recalled the open houses on *La Noche Buena*, Christmas Eve. His brother Emiliano, my Uncle Elmer, remembered all the lighted adobes and Indian dancing in the streets.[5] "The people prepared many special dishes and then welcomed one another to their homes. We didn't wrap presents, but the people brought and took home armfuls of food. These were our gifts," he said.[6]

One of their five sisters, Angelica, recalls another story. Their grandfather Santiago took her by the hand and walked her to the mercantile store to buy her a little blue suit. She said, "Our grand-parents lived near us in adobes." When I asked her where our ancestors were born, she answered, "Bernalillo. And from there we traced our Valdés roots to Spain. But we are also Indian you know."

My father's fondest, yet saddest, memories were of their mother, Dolores, who married at fifteen, and then died at age thirty-eight, giving birth to her twelfth child. When their mother died in 1919, their Papa Emiliano, grief-stricken, "immediately sold our Bernalillo home and took us to Albuquerque," Elmer said. The story goes, my grandfather proposed to Dolores's sister, Lorenza, asking her to take care of his children. She refused his offer, but agreed to adopt baby Dolores.[7]

Sanchez family portrait, taken in 1918, in San Bernardino, California, one year before Dolores died in childbirth with her last child, also named Dolores. Her youngest son, John Edward (Eddie), is in her arms. Pictured, back row, left to right, are the father, Emiliano Sanchez, next to his daughter Amalia (Molly); Emilio Medel, husband of Angelica, who is below him holding their baby, Louis Medel; and Antonia (Toni). Second row, left to right, are Leonidas (Leo), Emiliano (Elmer), and Santiago (Jimmie), seated. Front row, left to right, are Severo and mother Dolores, holding John Edward. Courtesy of Josephine Sanchez Zanone.

Uncle Elmer explains what happened as a time of struggle and transition. "We stayed with our Lucero cousins in Albuquerque while Papa worked in Los Angeles.[8] Leo, at fourteen, searched for work right way." Elmer said, "He got a job busing dishes at the Harvey House, a hotel train stop in Albuquerque."[9] But eventually, their papa had to move the family back to California. And what a lonely trip that was, for this time it was without their mother.

Their father could not remain in the place that held so many memories. Then in 1923, four years after their mother died, their papa was in a terrible accident in Los Angeles. "He was on his way home, rushing through the freight yard," Elmer said. His daughter Josephine was about to give birth. My Aunt Fina, twenty-five, married to Jacobo Gonzalez, was expecting their third son, Benjamin. He never met his grandfather. Papa Emiliano was hit by a train and died within a short while. Now two births had been surrounded by tragedy. The Sanchez children were completely orphaned: my father, Leo, at nineteen; Elmer, fourteen; Jimmie, eleven; Severo, eight; and the youngest, Eddie, six.

Another story proves the young family's determination. After their father died, they challenged Southern Pacific in court. The railroad offered the orphaned children a $1,000 accident settlement, but the older sisters, Josephine, Angelica, and Amalia (Molly), just in their early twenties, refused it. They fought their case, but lost. The younger sisters were Antonia, ten, and Dolores, three. With no help from the railroad, older sisters acted as parents for the generation of young men who would one day go to war.

In Los Angeles, the traditions of New Mexico sustained them. There they began to establish their own families. The Sanchez family had managed to transplant Bernalillo to California. Their actions said, "We are here. This is where we will rebuild." Their treasured homeland was now a memory for them to pass down to their children.

Celebrations and weddings brought family closer together. My father and mother, Leo Sanchez and Macedonia Acuña, married on October 16, 1927, at St. Bernardine's Catholic Church in San Bernardino.[10] My mother's best friend, Lena, was maid of honor, and Leo's brother Elmer, best man. Elmer was just seventeen and Lena sixteen when my mother introduced them; soon after—another wedding. In 1929, Elmer and Lena—Emiliano Sanchez and Magdalena Salazar—got married. Best friends had married brothers.

Leo and Macedonia soon began to have children of their own. My father became something of a family patriarch, not only for his own family, but also for his siblings. His younger brothers were not much older than his oldest children. The outcome—brothers and sisters cared for one another, creating a dynamic extended family in the prewar years.

I remember my mother cooking a huge pot of green chili con carne or red enchiladas, the long table set as if for a banquet when relatives came. Music and laughter often accompanied stories of Bernalillo. These close-knit get-togethers filled the house with remembrances of the past. We children played in the background. We learned by listening, sometimes to things the adults did not want us to hear. I think that is how I first learned about my grandparents' deaths.

At first, Los Angeles in the twenties seemed a far cry from Bernalillo of old, with its family loyalty and communal support. At one time, the Sanchez brothers ran through the tall grass of Bernalillo, swam in the nearby Rio Grande, rode horses on the plain, and gathered wood for the family hearth. They shared with each other in good times and bad. Soon, Los Angeles began to feel like one big happy family too.

The people from New Mexico did not consider themselves immigrants, nor were they. Their ancestors were here before the Pilgrims. Yet they saw how immigrants from Mexico were treated. With economic crises, discrimination escalated, becoming rampant in the big city.

History now records how these conditions escalated. Immigrants provided cheap labor, the working poor. Strikes became common as the people sought better wages and working conditions. Since many Mexican immigrants were also strikers, labor activism became associated with the Mexican people. Soon deportations became an easy substitute for providing resources, as prejudice grew.[11]

New Mexico residents and other U.S. citizens watched in horror as neighbors, friends, or relatives were deported.[12] During the Repatriation Movement of the 1930s, more than half a million immigrants would be forced out of the country. This era was one of U.S. economic insecurity and nativism.[13]

No one was exempt from these attitudes. All the brothers were affected in one way or another by the Depression that followed. Leo worked for the Santa Fe Railroad and had been used to speaking out. However, he lost his job with the railroad when he stood up at an open union meeting. He questioned whether it was required of workers to buy from the company store. "Money," he recalled, "was taken right out of our paychecks and we were given credit vouchers for purchases. After I spoke up at the union meeting we no longer had to buy at the company store. But the next day the railroad gave me my walking papers."[14] Papa was fired.

The older brothers, Leo and Elmer, faced their own struggles with work. During the Depression the youth were also affected by the nation's hurting economy. Masses of jobless youth had depended on wage labor. With two brothers married, the three younger ones had to figure out how to make a living.

By 1936, Santiago—"Jimmie," the oldest of the three younger men—had to survive on his own in Los Angeles at a time when a new kind of discrimination had become apparent. Jimmie made friends with the Los Angeles youth. Some of these boys were forerunners of the zoot-suiters. He liked the way they dressed. They liked music. They liked to dance and so did he. He easily fit in with them. But at that time, these youth were suspect.[15]

The Hearst papers at the time began making a case against these Los Angeles teenagers. They sensationalized stories about them to promote the sale of newspapers. They heightened the drama, capitalizing on youth styles as gang-related. The family witnessed this current of anti-Mexican sentiment in Los Angeles. Leo thought Jimmie could take care of himself. But he worried that the two younger brothers might be easy targets for trouble on their own. So with his help, Severo and Eddie were sent out of state to get work to keep them out of trouble.

Papa said, "To have a job is a blessing." And he was right. The brothers were used to working, but the Depression was in full sway. Eddie, at eighteen, was fortunate to get work in the Civilian Conservation Corps. In 1936 he went to Utah to fight fires; Severo went to work with a friend of Leo's in Nebraska while Jimmie remained in Los Angeles.[16] My sister Jo still has letters and photos of Severo enthusiastically shucking corn. When they returned to Los Angeles,

Photo of the wedding of Leonidas and Macedonia Sanchez, taken on October 16, 1927, in San Bernardino, California. Courtesy of Josephine Sanchez Zanone.

two handsome young men, Severo and Eddie, got an apartment together. The year was 1937.

In Los Angeles, Eddie, twenty, soon met Helen Tapia, a tall green-eyed beauty from Socorro, New Mexico. Helen was my Aunt Lena's cousin. Now it was Helen and Eddie's turn for love, and time for another Sanchez celebration. Eddie and Helen got married in 1938 at the Placita Church on Olvera Street, Our Lady Queen of Angels. Today this lovely memory is captured in a photo at their wedding

Emiliano and Magdalena Salazar Sanchez (center) in a group wedding photo, 1929. Courtesy of Cathy Sanchez Bates.

reception in Echo Park. The photo now sits on the mantel in the family home. During the war it provided a warm reminder of that special day.

Severo, a heartbreaker at twenty-two, was not ready for marriage. Then World War II broke out in Europe. Hitler invaded Poland in 1939. The brothers knew that if the United States went to war, they would be expected to serve. Severo did not wait. He was the first brother to enlist in the Army. Against any and all objections he said,

"They're going to take me anyway; I want to join." In January 1940, Severo Sanchez enlisted in the Army.

Five months later, in May 1940, our Uncle Jimmie—Santiago Sanchez—enlisted too.

On December 7, 1941, Pearl Harbor was attacked. War was declared. The United States had to defend itself from the Japanese. December 7 was to become a particularly significant date in our family. At that time no one really knew the extent. Exactly three years to the day, December 7, 1944, would bring to our home a dreaded telegram from the War Department with sad news about one brother. Meanwhile, the Sanchez family prepared for the worst as all five brothers readied for war.

Their sisters contributed to the war effort. "We are also doing our bit to help end this war," my Aunt Angie wrote on the back of a photo she sent to her brother Severo. Three sisters, Angelica, Antonia, and Molly, worked in the war industries as riveters.[17]

With two brothers, Severo and Jimmie, in the service, Eddie and Helen both decided to join the war effort too. Their children were small. Little Eddie Jr. was four and their baby, Dolores, was two. Helen talked about those days: "Eddie got a job in a shipyard in San Pedro and after standing in lines of people looking for employment, I got a job as a riveter and a buckler in a Lockheed defense plant where I went to work making molds for wing sections." One parent cared for the children while the other worked. "Sometimes if I missed my connection, I didn't get home until 1:30 in the morning," Helen said. "If I missed the streetcar, I had to go all the way to Temple Street, get off at First Street, and walk through the dark tunnel," which she described as a frightening and dangerous stretch. "How did you do it?" I asked. "I just prayed to God to get me through it," she recalled.

Our family was beginning to be separated by war. One consolation was that the letters and furloughs kept us connected. My older brothers and sisters were expected to write, and so I tried too. Reading these letters now reminds me of how much the loving letter-writing ritual was a part of my childhood.

Letters from Severo describe the extent of his training in the Army. His tone also reveals a determination to be chosen to go over.

He wrote home on January 11, 1943, from San Luis Obispo. "They are really giving it to us now for they are trying to see who are the boys who can't take it for they want to get rid of them. For all they want are guys who can take it and who can fight." From his descriptions, we could picture how rough it was. Sometimes my brothers, Leo, Chris, Emiliano, and Joseph, imitated his actions. "Two to three times a week we go on forced marches for five miles at a time—but five miles in sixty-three minutes with full field packs!"

It only got worse.

Severo wrote, "We had a five-mile forced march and the next day we went on a 16-mile hike in four and a half hours also with full field packs on." His best efforts were exerted to get himself into battle. But not soon enough for him. He was getting tired of moving around the country. Disappointed, he adds, "But I guess all we can do is wait until the big shots send us over."[18]

His wish would soon come true. As his training intensified, Severo's letters began to describe his even more determined preparation for battle. "As soon as we got here we went on a night problem. We went out at eight A.M. and didn't come back until about ten in the evening. There we were getting all wet but do you think they would bring us in? No. I tell you we were as wet as a rat. You know how a rat looks when it's wet? Well that's about the way we looked." No matter how difficult the moment, he made us laugh.

Homecomings were special.

"Sometimes when Uncle Severo came home, we were in school. But that did not stop him. He would not wait until school was out. He would walk over to the school yard to collect us," my sister Theresa recalls. "I remember one time he came to the school, swept me up onto his shoulders, and walked me home. I was paraded for the several blocks from the school to our home, high on the shoulders of this U.S. soldier in uniform. I was more embarrassed than proud. But that is how we remember Uncle Severo. He was extravagant and outrageous. We loved him so much."[19]

Theresa remembers how upbeat he tried to keep the day before he left for overseas:

I watched him getting ready to go out. He walked from the bathroom to the bedroom, dressing and grooming himself.

Severo Sanchez, S. Sgt., the second youngest brother, as a private first class with the 7th Division, 32nd Infantry, Company E, at the age of twenty-four. Killed in action in Leyte, Philippines, on October 21, 1943. Courtesy of James Arthur Sanchez.

He sang his favorite song. ("South of the Border, down Mexico way. That's where I fell in love when stars above came out to play.") He combed each little hair over and over to get it in the right place. He looked in the mirror, checked his teeth, recombed his hair, and finished the song (". . . but our tomorrow never came"). And he went out.

The next day it was time for him to go. Severo looked hopeful and excited before he left for overseas. He hugged each one of us and received a blessing from my mother and father. Then he was gone.

"But not long after he left, the neighborhood children called us outside," Theresa recalls. On E Street in the center of town was a ticker-tape farewell and send-off for the soldiers going to war. Confetti

Angelica (Angie) Sanchez Miller wrote of working as a riveter, "We are also doing our bit to end this war." Courtesy of Josephine Sanchez Zanone.

Amalia (Molly) Sanchez Carpenter, one of three sisters who served during the war as a riveter. Courtesy of Josephine Sanchez Zanone.

Antonia (Toni) Sanchez Mehl worked with her two sisters as a riveter during the war. Courtesy of Randal Mehl and Carol Ann Fare.

filled the streets. Convoys of soldiers rode through the town of San Bernardino where we lived.

"We didn't want to miss this. But how would we get there? The parade had already started." Theresa remembers that the only way we ever got around was on foot. "None of us had bikes. We didn't have a ride there either. So we started running as fast as we could the eight long blocks down E Street to downtown San Bernardino. We watched as the convoy of soldiers rode through the streets, thinking we had already missed them.

"Then we spotted him. 'There he is! There he is! That's our Uncle Severo,' we shouted. He was in one of the several combat trucks. And he was waving. We hoped he had seen us too. Elated as we were, we ran all the way back home to tell everyone. The memory will forever be etched in our minds. That was the last time we saw him."[20]

Letters from home became important to Severo. "Please write, even if it is just a few lines," he would say. He also asked the family not to worry about him. "I am fine, and besides," he added, "I'm aching for some action."

Severo would not have to wait long, for the 7th Division would soon embark on a troop ship for Alaska to confront the Japanese. As an adult I researched the places he went and saw what he faced. As a child I only heard things from the sidelines. I learned years later that the Japanese had been entrenched in the hilly, frozen island of Attu. Documents reveal that Severo shipped out on April 13, 1943, to the Aleutian Isles. The Japanese had occupied two islands there, Attu and Kiska, since the middle of 1942. The 7th Division would soon be battle-tested.

Two weeks before he shipped out he wrote, "I asked for a pass, but they are not giving any." As excited as he had been about going to war, his letters now took on an ominous tone. "But I hope to be home someday, if I am one of the lucky ones to come back from wherever we go," he added hopefully.

Reality had raised the clear possibility of death. On April 16, 1943, he sent home a discomforting letter and serious legal paper. The surprising words continue, "If I'm gone and don't come back, then you have the right to claim whatever is coming to me." He added softly, "But who knows, I might be one of the ones to come through." My sister Josephine remembers as a young girl, fourteen at the time, being very troubled by her uncle's words. He was trying to tell us that wherever he was going, he might not be back.

In August he wrote to Josephine, who kept asking where he was; he answered, "It's impossible for now, but someday you will know where I've been, I hope." He finally told her to "please stop asking."

It was a while before we heard that Severo was a survivor of one of the first World War II American land victories. His letters did not sound at all victorious. But it was always a relief when my father got the news that Severo was okay. "I really don't like to discuss these experiences, but someday I will be able to talk about it. Now I would just like to forget it, if I can help it, but I guess that will be something I will never forget."

For Severo, "seeing action" was no longer a priority; instead, coming home was. He had now seen war.

Much later Severo tries to describe for Leo what he had endured in Attu. "You can only imagine how rugged it is. The mountains here are plenty high. I tell you those things are so steep that you go up and drop right down. The swamp ground is bad enough," he explains.

Finally he just says, "I don't see how anybody could take what we went through."

In reality, he and his 7th Division buddies had trudged the high ice-covered mountains, felt the knee-deep snow, seen the enduring horrors of death everywhere, and witnessed the Japanese banzai charges. Severo's letters invariably ended with his greatest desire. "All I can do is pray that we come home soon. Then we could be back with our dear ones again."[21]

Despite the tough battles Severo had just been through, he worried about his brothers. While he was hoping to come home, Eddie was trying to go in. Severo also wondered why he had not heard from Jimmie in so long. "I wish we could know where he is so we wouldn't be in suspense." In June he wrote, knowing Jimmie might get a leave, "I wish he would take his furlough to see the family in Los Angeles before he goes overseas, instead of going to New Mexico." Jimmie loved to visit Albuquerque. He wanted to see his sister Dolores and her husband, John "Bud" Lyons, every chance he got. But one day Jimmie came home.

Severo heard about it and you can hear the excitement in his letter. "I hear Jimmie came to see you. I bet you were surprised to see him. Did you know he was coming? I sure would like to see him. Did he look good in his uniform? I bet he did." What he was really saying was, "I miss my brother." One day Jimmie would also be shipped overseas.

Seeing Severo and Jimmie serve, Eddie wanted to join too, but he had been classified 4-F because he was color-blind and married with two small children. In August 1943, his 4-F draft status was modified on appeal and John Edward—Eddie, the youngest—became the third Sanchez brother to enlist. Unable to serve in the regular Army or Navy, he joined the Seabees, the U.S. Navy Construction Battalion. Three Sanchez brothers, soon four, would go overseas. In the U.S. Navy Seabees, Eddie was still trained for war. He served in the Company C-6 15th Super Battalion. Helen remembers the day she said goodbye to Eddie at the train depot. "Many other soldiers in uniform were saying goodbye too," she said. "I wasn't alone. Lots of goodbyes were happening all around us."

Helen recalls how she felt after Eddie left. "The only way the service would take him was if I signed a letter of approval." She did. Today she looks back at her decision and wonders how she could have done it. "At that time we were so young. Neither one of us realized what we were getting into. We had no idea what the war was about or how long it would last."

Stationed in the South Pacific, Eddie faced the dangers of battle along with his buddies. The construction battalion was assigned to build airstrips and landing docks in the war zones. They were also trained as soldiers for combat. And so they were dubbed the Fighting Seabees.

In one letter, Eddie writes from Virginia, "I certainly wish that this war was over. . . . But I can just imagine how the guys are doing that are really fighting and going through the mill." By the end of the war Eddie had seen battle himself. He was awarded the Pacific Theater Medal, the Good Conduct Medal, and a Bronze Star. While two brothers served in the South Pacific, each in different capacities, both were our heroes; both had chosen to go.

Soon it would be Christmas without our uncles Jimmie, Severo, and Eddie. We especially missed our Uncle Severo, who brought home a sense of humor in the hardest times. My sister Josephine remembers one special Christmas before the war. "He surprised all of us with lots of gift-wrapped packages we weren't used to receiving. One big box contained a Monopoly game." Years after, we spent countless hours enjoying it. My sister remembers that day, now long past, as "the best Christmas ever."

Emiliano Sanchez, my Uncle Elmer, was the fourth brother to go into the service. He was drafted into the Army in August 1943 and became a medic. My father laughed as he recalled how "Elmer would nearly faint at the sight of blood. And now he's a medic." But Elmer had chosen to be a corpsman rather than pick up a gun.

An essential man is a good way to describe my Uncle Elmer. That was the term used for those contributing to the war effort on the home front. Emiliano Sanchez lost his "essential man" draft deferment that had been conferred upon him when he worked for the war industry. "I knew my days at home with Lena were numbered, and not long after, I was drafted," my uncle remembers. He went into training to be a medic before getting shipped overseas.

Santiago (Jimmie) Sanchez, the third oldest of the Sanchez brothers, with the 27th Armored Infantry, Company B, in 1944. Courtesy of James Arthur Sanchez.

Years later I asked him about it. He told this story. "Before shipping out I trained in the United States." He described the day he and Lena parted as "one of the saddest days of my life." He recalled the convoy of soldiers with whom he was driving as they went into a cold dense fog, so far removed from the warm climate of Los Angeles, going further and further away. He remembered when he arrived at the desolate camp in Oregon. "We were given a tin cup, a cold plate of Spam, and two slices of white bread."[22] So far from home.

As a child, I remember the wartime dramas we saw at the movies and how they seemed so close to what was happening in our own lives. My sister Mary reminded me that we went every other Sunday, "the girls one week, the boys the next." Love stories romanticized families like ours separated by war. So it never occurred to me that our family was any different from the ones we saw in the movies. The stories were not about Mexican American families, but the sentiment was the same. And so we sympathized, feeling connected to other Americans during wartime.

I thought our Uncle Elmer and Aunt Lena's story was the most romantic of all. Lena joined her husband during his tour of duty in the United States. To be near him she took the train to his initial assignment. It was her first time away from home alone. In Salem, Oregon, she rented a room in a boardinghouse. "It was run by a one-hundred-year-old lady, Mrs. Spoor," Lena said. At age ninety, Lena still recalled those memorable times: "I met another woman and her husband, who was also waiting to ship out, Ann and Joe Caminetti, a classy couple from New York." In Oregon, the two women got jobs plucking chickens in a butcher shop. "I didn't mind," Lena said. She took courage from her new friend. "If a New York secretary could do it, so could I."[23] So Lena ended up staying just a little while longer.

Lena then followed Elmer to Missouri, where she lived in a small cabin near the base. When he was transferred to Pennsylvania for medic training, Lena went there too. She rented an apartment nearby from a war widow who lived with her mother. Soon enough it was all over. They both remember that last day. "We said goodbye in a Pennsylvania train depot overflowing with soldiers." After Elmer left, this delicate lady found work in a Los Angeles cigar factory called Braunswig Company. All for the cause to end the war.

Now the oldest, Leonidas Nicolas, my father, could not stand by as his younger brothers, Elmer, Jimmie, Severo, and Eddie, went to war. Leo decided to enlist also. I remember the day it happened. When he returned home, my father walked in the back door and said, "They wouldn't take me." They told him, "You can do more for the war effort at home than overseas." Seeing his disappointment, they responded with humor: "You want us to win this war, don't you?" Leo was forty years old, color-blind, and married, with nine children.

Severo had written, "Well, Bud, all of us are in the service except you. Gosh, I hope they won't have to take you. After all, you have a big family to take care of. Besides, I think enough of our family are in, don't you?" Papa heard only the part that said, "All of us are in except you." Severo was referring to his brothers and the cousins and nephews he grew up with, his sister Angelica's son Louis Medel, and

John Edward (Eddie) Sanchez, the youngest of the Sanchez brothers, at the age of twenty-three; Private First Class, U.S. Navy Seabees. Courtesy of Cathy Sanchez Bates.

his sister Josefina's son Benjamin Gonzales, who was also serving. They were all about the same age. As kids they were inseparable. Now they were scattered by war.

Once they all went to go swimming at Perris Hill Plunge in San Bernardino—brothers, nephews, and cousins together. My mother told us, "The darker-skinned ones were refused admission." They were told, "No Mexicans allowed." My mother said, "Brothers were separated from brothers because of the color of their skin." I learned at an early age after listening to this story how shame is produced because of racism.[24] Severo and his brothers had suffered prejudice, yet they were still willing to serve their country.

My father, Leo, like his little brother Eddie, had found his own way to enter the fight. Papa became an air-raid warden. He soon had to realize that this war was not only for soldiers in uniform. The fighting was not just on battlefields. It was also on the home front.

Emiliano (Elmer) Sanchez, the second oldest of the Sanchez brothers, as a medic during World War II with the 370th Medical Battalion, 70th Division, Company C, in 1944. Courtesy of Cathy Sanchez Bates.

With four brothers going overseas, this job meant a lot to my father. My sister Mary remembers, "Papa was responsible for patrolling the neighborhoods during blackouts. He had to wear a helmet like a soldier in the Army and carry a whistle that he used to give an all-clear signal." And more than that, it was a dangerous assignment in the event of a real attack.

I remember those air raids too. The sirens began their eerie cry and the family rushed around turning off lights. We huddled together in the dark waiting for what might happen next. I felt some of the terrors of war, thinking the worst. If our family was at all like the ones I had seen in the movies, our home could also be bombed. My brothers said that if any of those sirens ever stopped, a bomb was about to explode. Their graphic descriptions did not help. We all acted bravely. Nevertheless, I was scared and then relieved when the all-clear signal came and the alert was over. Somehow the crises brought us even closer. That Papa was a Civil Defense soldier helped.

Of all the uncles, Severo is the one whose letters have survived to tell us of his experiences in the war. They became vivid memories for all of us at home who read them, and they made us a part of this horrible conflict. These letters helped us remain a family, sharing our hopes and fears.

Severo wrote from the South Pacific, "I wish I could be home for Christmas." Since September 1943 his unit had been sent to Hawaii to rest up before the next battle. Yet he never gave up the dream of going home. He wrote, "We still have a lot to be thankful for—our lives, and the hope of coming back home someday, after we clean up. It's going to be a hard job, but that's what we have to do before we can live in peace again."

In Oahu, Severo compiled a photo album autographed by his buddies. Their words attest to the admiration he received from his men. "To a swell sergeant who made a good man out of me," writes Private First Class Bill Fredericks from Massillon, Ohio. "To a grand sergeant and a better friend," signs Harold Ebell, Kenosha, Wisconsin. Another signs, "David Benquiat, a *chuco* from L.A." Each signature comes from one soldier asking another to make sure he is not forgotten: "Think of me when you see these pictures after the war."

Severo sailed from Pearl Harbor on January 22, 1944, for Kwajalein. A letter postmarked February 1944, "somewhere in the Marshals [*sic*]," slipped by the censors. He doesn't talk about battles. He only wants to hear more about the new home Papa and Mama bought.[25] "Please tell me more about the house. What do the rooms look like? Does it have a backyard? Describe it to me,"[26] he writes, as Operation Flintrock included the 7th Division with 54,000 men to invade Kwajalein Island.[27]

While the operation resistance was brutal, the actual struggles that Severo and his buddies went through were not detailed in the news at home. The true accounts reveal that they faced almost guerrilla-like warfare. First of all, the troops walked into massive destruction from the intensive bombing that preceded their stepping onto the island. They waded through swamps that filled craters left behind by the bombardment. It appeared that nothing could have survived this hellhole.[28]

At home we read the *Los Angeles Examiner* headlines on Sunday, February 6, 1944: "Kwajalein Crushed, Isle Captured." The battle lasted six days and annihilated all but a few Japanese. "Four thousand Japanese fought to their deaths. American casualties mounted to 2,000." Still the war did not end.

Severo lived to tell about it in a letter to his brother Leo. On February 22 he wrote, "I came out okay, so don't worry about me. I know how much you worry when you don't hear from me. Love and kisses to the kids." He wrote about his officers, "They really know their stuff. Will follow them anywhere. But I've seen so much action now. I don't care to see any more. It's beyond explaining. I hope I can come back home where I belong. This is something we will never forget. But we have a job to do and we have to do it."

Then he asked my dad this question, as if searching for an answer: "The harder we work, the sooner it will be over, no?"

Again, the 7th Division was shipped back to Schofield Barracks at Oahu, giving the soldiers a false sense of security once more. Severo wrote home, "Some of us may come back and will have something to talk about to the young ones. It will be history for them. But it was hell for the ones that were in it."[29]

Severo also begins to see life slipping by as he hears that his nephew Louis Medel got married. "Everybody's getting married except me, but how can I with this war?" Cousin Lou, Angelica's son, was Severo's nephew although they were nearly the same age. Lou was in Intelligence Operations serving under General Eisenhower in a special contingent in Paris after the landing of Normandy. He married his sweetheart, Elsie Tully, while on furlough in California. Severo adds a warm thought for his sister. "Angie must be thrilled. I'm so happy for Lou certainly deserves it."[30]

Any struggle one may interpret today in Severo's letters, we did not detect as children. He passed over the troubles fast and paid more attention to us, to family, and to holidays. In March he wished us a happy Easter. "I went to Mass," he said, "and to the three hour devotion on Good Friday." His words still bless us.

Then he added a kind of apology to my father, recalling his youth.

Leonidas Nicolas Sanchez, a Civil Defense volunteer during World War II, at the age of forty, in San Bernardino, California. Courtesy of Josephine Sanchez Zanone.

"I was drinking quite a bit there before I left, no? Those days don't exist anymore, and thank God . . . I'm all over that now." His present actions had more than redeemed him.

Soon Severo's time moves quickly in preparation for the next campaign. His days only get closer to the next battle. At the same time my father continues to believe that the war might be over soon. Hope fills the air.

Then in August 1944, Severo sent home the photo album he had been keeping in Oahu, as if to put it in his brother's safekeeping. He also expressed his deepest desire. "According to the news it looks like this war will end soon. Could this be a victory year?" He then adds, "I haven't heard from Eddie and Jimmie. Gosh it seems like they're sending us further and further apart. Why can't they put us brothers closer together?" His letter seems mixed with hope and desperation.

At almost the very same time as Severo was preparing to ship out for more fighting in the South Pacific, his brother Jimmie was being shipped to Europe. Jimmie went on the *Queen Mary*, the ocean liner used as a troop transport during wartime.[31] In his letter he said the voyage was "swell," a clue that he had no idea what he was getting into when he arrived. Jimmie wrote to Leo in a letter postmarked September 7, 1944.

"Well Bud, we finally made it overseas. And we sure enjoyed the trip. We're somewhere in England. Pretty far from home, no?" Jimmie asked about his brother. "Have you heard from Severo? I haven't received any answer to my letters." Severo would ship out September 13, 1944, only five days later. Their letters to one another had crossed in the mail.

On September 13, 1944, Severo journeyed to Leyte, the first of the Philippine Islands to be invaded. It began early one ominous morning long before dawn.

Up by 3:00 A.M., the soldiers had only been told that they were selected for a top-secret mission. They knew what that meant: You have no idea where you are going, and you might not come back.

At 7:00 A.M. they began their uncertain journey by boarding a troopship, the *George F. Clymer*, to enter a huge convoy. All they knew was that they would be landing in a place called Dulag on Leyte. Soon that day arrived. A-Day, October 20, outside their transport, the skies roared with guns and bombs as the first wave prepared to land.[32]

To walk this journey with my Uncle Severo, who was in the midst of it, is both redeeming and horrifying. It is redeeming to know the truth of what happened that fateful day. But it is awful to know the horrors of war and to see what he and the others went through. Severo wanted to be able to tell the story someday, "but there's a time and a place for that," he wrote. That was more than sixty years ago.

At 8:00 A.M. the assault troops of the 7th Division began to clamber down the nets of their transports into landing barges that were to carry them to shore. Severo and the troops had rehearsed this moment many times before on the island paradise of Maui. And now it was upon them.

By 8:15 they had boarded and were in line for departure. The first tractors began to hit shore. The infantrymen scrambled over the sides.[33] The 7th wave proceeded against active enemy opposition.

At 10:22, they encountered enemy shell fire, suffering casualties even before they reached shore.[34] The devastation persisted all around them. As "great fires burned from the bombardment, naval shells and aerial bombs exploded." The Japanese positions just off the beach included a 70-millimeter field piece. It poured a heavy fire on the approaching landing craft. Then one of the big tractors suffered a direct hit. Four of the men from Company E, 32nd Infantry, were killed and twelve wounded.[35]

The disasters were played down in the news at home: "At Leyte the 7th Division made another perfect landing." In reality, operations in the zone of the 32nd Infantry, Company E, lost half of one platoon before it set foot on land. Casualties mounted to 49 men killed, 192 wounded, and 6 missing in action.[36] Severo, the brother most eager to enter battle, was one of the missing. On that lonely day in Dulag, the heavens, barely hidden by a rising blanket of smoke and fumes, were the only true witness to what happened.

A telegram reached my parents' home at 1471 West 9th Street in San Bernardino, California, notifying the family. "Staff Sergeant Severo Sanchez is missing in action." As a child of six I listened and waited along with the rest of my family. I understood *missing in action* the way my father explained it: "Maybe Severo was just lost, and could not find his way back." With Severo's presence unaccounted for, my mother called us to pray the rosary. I prayed, along with my family, that somehow everything would be all right. One thing was certain, we all hurt for our Uncle Severo and wished this long and terrible war would end.

As our family waited for more news about Severo in one part of the world, war raged for two more brothers in another part. For Elmer and Jimmie, in the Rhineland of Germany, the dark clouds of October set the mood for what was to come. The U.S. troops advanced under obscure skies, lashed by wind, rain, and showers of snow. In the midst of this desolation lingered a hope that the troops might be home by Christmas.

Meanwhile the ambulance drivers like Elmer kept bringing in more and more wounded. There were more than 140,000 casualties during the fighting which led up to the Battle of the Bulge, and Elmer's brother Jimmie would be one of them.[37] Two Purple Hearts would be awarded in the Sanchez family before this war was over.

Before the word *medic* became synonymous with *hero*, my uncles Elmer, Jimmie, Eddie, and Severo were already our heroes. And America's heroes. They had gone to war courageously. They were separated from their families, leaving behind those most precious to them. They were also separated from one another—brother from brother. And we knew they had done it for us.

Knowing each other's struggle, Elmer and Severo one day made a pact to name each other as beneficiaries. Elmer was a T-5 station medic and ambulance driver for Company C, 370th Medical Battalion, 70th Infantry Division. He served in the Ardennes, Alsace, and Rhineland where his brother Jimmie crossed. Not until after the war did Elmer discover how close he was to Jimmie. Without his brothers beside him, he depended on the responsibilities learned in his youth, as one of ten surviving children in New Mexico, to get him through. These lessons helped him understand the seriousness of being the one in charge of the vehicle and other people's lives.

He saw too much to be able to talk easily about it later. After witnessing the horrors of war, he couldn't articulate what many of us wanted to hear. History helps document some of it. The "Trailblazers" lived with "machine gun fire . . . snow up to our armpits, severe unbelievable cold, living in foxholes like rats."[38] Medics, the easiest targets, drove marked trucks and their helmets were labeled with red crosses. When the enemy killed a medic or destroyed an ambulance they deprived the wounded of help and made capturing them easier. To kill the ambulance driver meant to deprive the Army of its most essential man.[39]

Medics like Elmer were persistently on the front lines. The only consolation for the long hours probably came from what they saw in the wounded who counted on them. Their efforts meant the difference between life and death. Elmer faced death himself as he transported the wounded where the 70th served. His discharge papers say, "Through mountainous forests, twisting country roads through mud, rain and snow." One wonders how the driver could keep going in his endless battle to retrieve the wounded and return for more during the coldest winter in history. All of this was to answer the call "Medic!" After all, each soldier's desperate cry for help could be from one of Elmer's own brothers.

As our family at home waited to receive news about one missing brother, Severo, we also waited for the arrival of a new baby. My mother had tiny silver-blue booties ready; the satin tassels looked elegant enough for a little prince.

December 3, 1944, was a day filled with anticipation and for a brief time the news of the war was postponed. My mother was expecting her tenth child. My father and my brothers and sisters welcomed our Aunt Angie, who came to the house to help. As she arranged everything for a home delivery, we children were sent outside to play. We lurked behind the scenes, waiting and wishing we could be included.

Hours later we could hear the distinctive squeals of new life. At last we were invited in, relieved to see that our mother was fine. She gave birth to an eight-pound boy "to even the score," Papa said. We were now five sisters and five brothers. We saw the long thick eyelashes and the dark curly hair. We got to touch the tiny little feet. We celebrated that day. My father named their new son Severo, after his missing brother. My mother added Francis Xavier, his patron saint. Three days later we got the sad news.

On December 7 the telephone rang. My sister Josephine was the one to answer it. "Aunt Angie was crying hard," Jo later told us. "Your Uncle Severo is dead. He was killed in action." Aunt Angie wept. Those words ended our hope. "I started crying out loud too," Jo recalls. Aunt Angie said, "Honey, please be quiet, your mother is still recovering and we don't want to upset her." But my sister said Mama already heard her and came out. My father's heart broke that day. At first he never let us know how much. But one dark night, my sister Mary remembers, we heard him cry out against this great loss of a younger brother.

Our Uncle Severo would not be returning. No more letters from overseas arrived. No more waiting. Now letters of condolence came. On Pearl Harbor Day, December 7, 1944, three years to the day after the war began, the telegram read, "We regret to inform you . . ." My family already knew what that meant.

One after the other more letters came, first from official offices, and then from Severo's commanding officer. Lieutenant Fred Capp wrote glowingly about him:

> Severo was a squad leader, and, as such, controlled the actions of twelve men. He was killed during the Leyte Island operations where the vehicle in which he was landing was struck by a high explosive shell from a Japanese gun. He died instantly.
>
> Severo's sincerity, his high ideals and unfailing good humor made him one of the best liked and admired squad leaders of this organization. His loss leaves a gap in our lives that cannot be filled.[40]

Lieutenant Capp would himself become one of the casualties of the war. In Okinawa, near the end of a grueling six months of battle, Capp, just rocks away from reaching the top of Hill 114, died after being struck down by a bullet from a Japanese sniper. The battle ended days later.[41]

By May 1945, letters continued to come from the highest command. But not even the one from General MacArthur himself could console my father. It offered "deepest sympathy in the death of your brother. . . . His service under me in our fight for liberty in the Pacific was characterized by his unswerving devotion to our country. We have lost a gallant comrade in arms and mourn with you."[42]

On December 8, my father had read to us from the front-page headlines of the *San Bernardino Sun-Telegram*. "First Casualty of the South Pacific: Severo Sanchez Killed at Leyte." Today I look at the handsome features and remember what I saw then, our uncle in his uniform with the red and black hourglass insignia on his arm, his thick black hair curling out from his Army cap, the sweet mischievous smile of youth still glowing under his thin black mustache, the tragedy of war.

My sisters say that we did not want to go to school that day. But Mama said we had to go. I was only in the first grade, but I remember my father as he bent down on one knee. He looked into my eyes and asked me to tell my class that my uncle died for his country. Now I had this mandate. I remember not wanting to do it. I was scared. But at the young age of six I learned to draw from the courage of my brave Uncle Severo. I also saw something in my father's eyes, asking me to do what was very important to him. That much I understood, enough to walk forward to show my class the clipping and the photo.

"My Uncle Severo gave his life for his country." Saying those words out loud in front of my class impressed it in my memory. Only today, after knowing the history, the battles, and his letters, have I come to truly understand how much he gave. But even now, I realize I will never fully comprehend.

Christmas Eve 1944 was a lonely one. One brother was dead and three others remained in the midst of battle. We had only memories of one special Christmas that seemed so long ago when Severo brought home gifts and laughter. Still the fighting did not end. Eddie, in the Pacific, had lost contact with the other two, Elmer and Jimmie, in Europe.

Jimmie was spending a cold Christmas Eve somewhere in the Ardennes, a stranger in a strange land. Los Angeles and youth seemed far away. At home we remembered all the music and laughter of other Christmases when the Sanchez brothers and sisters were together. When we heard a popular wartime song on the radio that we learned to sing as children, it reminded us of Jimmie. It was a kind of sad lament for him, especially because his name was in it. It went, "The shepherd will tend his sheep/ the valley will bloom again/ and Jimmie will go to sleep/ in his own little room again." This song was our prayer that the war would end soon.[43]

The family lost track of Jimmie as no letters came. Would Jimmie, like Severo, not come home? We wondered. Two days before Christmas, amid the cruel fighting called the Battle of the Bulge, a hand grenade exploded near Jimmie, close enough to fill his back and leg with shrapnel. My Aunt Mary, his wife, told me after the war, "He kept on fighting until a medic could attend to his wounds." After two weeks he was back in battle.

By March 1945 Jimmie's unit was in Germany during another historic event: the crossing of the Rhine River. At home, big headlines splashed across the newspapers on March 8, "Yanks Smash across the Rhine." In the town of Remagen, Company A 27th Armored Infantry Battalion was ordered to defuse the wires that the Germans had strung across the bridge to blow it up. They succeeded in defusing the explosives and Jimmie, along with his buddies in Company B, was among the first to set foot in Germany, a step toward bringing the war in Europe to an end.

The official history of this battle tells us a little of what Jimmie and his unit faced. The taking of the only surviving bridge across the Rhine was an important event, shortening the war by months. And the strategy to take the bridge was built around the 27th Armored Infantry, of which Jimmie was a part. The Germans had devised an elaborate detonation scheme for blowing up the bridge. But after what seemed like an eternity to the U.S. troops, the bridge was still standing. Then a group of American soldiers began to cross. "Bobbing and weaving, dashing from the corner of one metal girder to another, the men of the 27th Infantry made their way onto the bridge dodging machine gun fire." Soon American troops appeared at both ends of the tunnel at the other end of the bridge. The Germans defending it then surrendered.[44]

Jimmie's crossing with the 27th Armored Infantry Battalion was a drama he hardly discussed. I learned only later that he had been in one of the key turning points of the war in Europe, the crossing of the Rhine and the taking of the bridge at Remagen. This event took on greater meaning for me as I got older. All I remembered as a child were Papa's words, "Jimmie crossed the Rhine!" And I knew he did something important.

In May 1945, V-E Day, streets all over America were covered with ticker tape. Not everyone wanted to celebrate this victory. I remember my father refused to go into the streets, still saddened by the death of his brother Severo. Elmer, Jimmie, and Eddie were not at home to reunite with their oldest brother, Leo. Together they could have celebrated their homecoming and mourned the death of Severo. They would not return until nearly the end of the year. Jimmie had enlisted in May 1940. Five years had gone by. He was soon to be thirty-five. In August, V-J Day came and went. Jimmie finally came home in October 1945.[45] Like Severo, he had been awarded the Purple Heart. The war had finally ended.

Jimmie had one stop to make before he went home—New Mexico. He went to see his sister Dolores and her husband, John "Bud" Lyons. The two buddies chanced upon each other in a crowded saloon filled with soldiers, Bud Lyons recalled. "I knew Jimmie was in there when I heard the distinctive Sanchez laugh. So I yelled, 'Jimmie Sanchez, stand up!'" They spent the next three days trying to catch up on what had happened since their last goodbye, years before.[46]

In the meantime, Aunt Lena's sister-in-law, Mary Sigala, admired a photograph in Elmer and Lena's home. "Who is the handsome man in uniform?" she inquired. "He's my brother," Elmer answered. "And he's single," Lena offered.

Before long, a meeting was arranged. Mary, then thirty-five like Jimmie, later recalled, "I had never met a man I wanted to marry. My family had moved to the United States when I was a little girl to escape the Mexican Revolution. They took me to Anthony, Texas, the year I was born in 1910. After that we traveled to El Paso and then to California. I looked forward to the day I would meet my true love. It was a long time, but it was worth the wait," sighed Mary, a true daughter of the revolution.

On November 24, 1946, Jimmie and Mary were married at Nuestra Señora de Soledad on Brooklyn Avenue in Los Angeles. They bought a home in Pico Rivera and raised three children there, Anna, Maxine, and James Arthur.

Some who made it home adjusted; others suffered the effects of the war. My Uncle Elmer seemed troubled. I saw my Aunt Lena's grief and asked, "What's wrong with Uncle Elmer, Mama?" "He had a hard time in the war," my mother answered. "They call it shell shock or battle fatigue." As a child I understood that my uncle must have suffered. But of all the pain and suffering our Uncle Elmer went through, none would be so great for him as the loss of his brother Severo, the one he could not reach on the battlefield, and the loss of his dream to reunite the five brothers after the war.

Elmer had also dreamed of getting the education his father had promised him. After the war he was happy just to be home, feeling privileged to have a job. At age thirty-six he thought he was too old for school. He went to work for Norris Machine Shop, and there he remained in good standing for forty years.

Elmer and Lena, Eddie and Helen also saved enough to be able to buy their own homes in Downey, a suburb of Los Angeles—once only a possibility, now a dream fulfilled, thanks to the G.I. Bill. Helen and Eddie had two more children, Cathy and Daniel.

In February 1949 the family gathered one more time to say a final farewell to their brother Severo. No one would feel complete without this one homecoming. My father decided to honor his sisters' wishes and ask the United States Army to return the remains of their brother who was killed in Leyte. Severo had been buried in the Philippines. His chaplain described it as a Christian burial on sacred ground surrounded by tropical flowers. Still, nothing sufficed but to have Severo's casket returned home to the United States.

When the day arrived, we met the train at the Santa Fe Depot in San Bernardino. An armed serviceman, or honor guard, accompanied the casket of Staff Sergeant Severo Sanchez. I remember my aunts running alongside the train, tears streaming down their cheeks, to receive their brother and to provide the burial they wanted for him at home. The honor guard stood at attention and saluted my father. We saw Severo's flag-covered casket. My whole family gathered to honor our uncle and brother, our hero.

Together, my mother and father, my brothers, sisters, aunts, uncles, and cousins, drove to Mountain View Cemetery in San Bernardino. The place once known for segregation became Severo's final resting place. The town where he and his brothers, nephews, and cousins had been refused entry to the local plunge now paid him its respects. There he was laid to rest.

As children, a little older now, we appreciated this final ritual. As Severo's body was placed in the California earth we understood the seriousness of the moment. We heard the sad sound of "Taps." My little sister Angelica jumped at the sound of the solemn gun salute. We watched as the officers briskly folded the American flag into a neat triangle. They handed it to my father, Leo, the oldest, who stood beside his three younger brothers, Elmer, Jimmie, and Eddie. He received it with tears but fortitude.

Peace had come at last. A beloved brother, and our Uncle Severo, was now safely home, his fondest dream. The five Sanchez brothers were reunited at last.

After surviving a world war, three brothers succumbed to cancer. In 1981, Jimmie died at seventy of kidney cancer; in 1983 my father, Leo, died of lung cancer at seventy-nine; and in 1997, at eighty, Eddie lost a five-year battle with prostate cancer.

In 1997 I went to visit the only surviving brother, my uncle Elmer, Emiliano Sanchez. He was ninety years old. I had not seen him for many years. He was the last of the Sanchez family. He had survived the deaths of his sisters and brothers. To the end, Elmer could vividly recall his initial induction into the Army. He remembered his brothers by displaying their pictures in wartime uniforms. He recalled all the details of his visits from Lena. He could almost relive that sad memory of leaving his bride. And he never forgot those he could not reach on the front lines.

I wondered how he made it as a medic under these conditions. He attributed his strength to his mother, María Dolores Sanchez. He remembered what it was like as a child growing up on the plain of Bernalillo. "I remember how hard she worked," he said. "I am amazed by the courage she had. In an adobe with no electricity, gas, or plumbing, she made us a warm and smooth-running home." He asked, "How could I not do as much?"

He would not talk about his war experiences in France and Germany, so those untold stories would die with him. He held onto one artifact, however, that spoke volumes; he found it somewhere in Europe—a crucifix. It had great meaning for him. My cousin Cathy recalls him praying before it each night.

The last surviving brother, Emiliano Sanchez, entered the Downey Community Hospital in November 1999. Lena was by his side. So were Aunt Helen and cousins Cathy and Dolores. My youngest sister Emily and I paid our last respects. Elmer and Lena celebrated their seventieth wedding anniversary there. On December 1, 1999, after surviving a major economic depression, a world war, and prostate cancer, Elmer died peacefully of pneumonia. At his burial he held in his hands the German cross he had carried with him during and after the war.

Five brothers said yes to serving their country. They grew up with a pride in a distinctive heritage nurtured in Bernalillo, New Mexico.

Photo of the wedding of Santiago (Jimmie) and Mary Sigala Sanchez, 1946.
Courtesy of James Arthur Sanchez.

Proud to be Sánchez, Gurulé, and Valdés on one side, and Sánchez de Yñigo and Duran y Chaves on the other, and always faithful to their traditions, they were loyal Americans. They were among the first to stand up for a nation hit by a surprise enemy attack. What they entered into they never could have imagined, and yet they never gave up.

Since I was a child I was affected by their generous actions. I must have carried them in my heart because as a young adult, I realized that they helped shape the way I thought and felt about America. During the civil rights movements I understood why they went to war. They stood up for the promise of true justice. Because of them I realized that I must learn to do the same. I thought of what they taught us about courage and self-sacrifice.

Sometimes when family duty seemed too difficult to follow, I remembered them. After the war, I watched my father put out the American flag on Memorial Day. At first I thought what he did was only about patriotism. In the seventies, I judged the imperfections I saw in our own country; then during the many World War II commemorations of the 1990s, I noticed that no one mentioned the extensive contributions made by Mexican Americans. In this I saw evidence of ongoing discrimination. My uncles went to war believing they were fighting against that, I thought. And would their efforts now be diminished?

Then I realized why my father raised the flag, not just as a patriotic gesture, but to make sure that his brothers and the actions they took against injustice were never forgotten. His action inspired me. As an adult, I began to write about these brothers, to remember them and what they fought for. I also knew that those of us left behind were the only ones who could tell their stories.

Sometimes the war memories can be painful because war is not always equated with glory. However, to remember and write is to heal the wounds of war and discrimination. The noted author, Tomás Rivera, once said, "Remembering reminds us of our humanity in the face of even the most inhumane annihilation, as long as we hold on to those things most treasured, love of family, love of neighbor, and love of God." These humanitarian words echo in the lives of the five brothers who fought and died for those precious values.

I was in the next generation, along with my brothers and sisters and cousins, and so was inspired by them to continue to strive for these things. As a result, our children and their cousins, too, have drawn on the heritage of these brothers. They have resisted injustice, valued family, honored duty. But most of all, they have remembered. This is the five Sanchez brothers' greatest legacy.

Notes

Words and music to *America the Beautiful* by Katherine L. Bates and Samuel A. Ward (Portland: Oregon Catholic Press, 2001). My daughter, Lisa Fink La Rossa, wishes to dedicate verse three to the Sanchez brothers.

1. "Selective Service," *Columbia Encyclopedia*, 6th ed. (New York: Columbia University Press, 2001). Draft statistics went from 900,000 in 1940 to ten million by 1947.

2. Sánches paternal ancestry: Santiago Sánches m. Manuela Gurulé; Pablo Sánches m. Paula Lovato; Jose Santiago Sánches m. Soledad Valdés; Emiliano Sánches m. Dolores Sánchez.

Sánchez maternal ancestry: Jacinto Sánchez de Yñigo m. María de Castro Xabalera; Francisco Sánchez m. Josefa Chaves; Juan Cristobal Sánchez m. Juana Chaves; Pedro Juan Baptista Sánchez m. Manuela Sánchez y Chaves; Mariano Sánchez m. María Gutierrez; Severiano Sánchez m. Barbara Lucero; Dolores Sánchez m. Emiliano Sánchez.

3. Flavia Waters Champe, *The Matachines Dance of the Upper Rio Grande: History, Music, and Choreography* (Lincoln: University of Nebraska Press, 1983).

4. Leo N. Sanchez, taped interview by Lisa Fink, San Bernardino, California, May 11, 1980.

5. Arthur L. Campa, *Los Comanches: A New Mexico Folk Drama* (Albuquerque: University of New Mexico Press, 1942).

6. Emiliano "Elmer" Sanchez, interview by author, Downey, California, June 15, 1998.

7. Story told to Robert and Theresa Ybarra by Dolores Sanchez Lyons, Albuquerque, New Mexico, May 1977.

8. Santiago Lucero, or cousin Willie, owned a dress shop in Bernalillo until his wife Josefa Gonzalez died after childbirth, May 15, 1925, leaving fourteen children in his and his older children's care, one of them my cousin Paulita, whose life story was written and presented for her on her ninetieth birthday, July 1, 1998, by her daughter, Dorothy Borrego Villalobos.

9. Elmer Sanchez interview.

10. For Macedonia Acuña's ancestry see two works by Rita Sanchez, "Charles H. Coleman and Macedonia Cruz: A Southern New Mexico Legacy," *Southern New Mexico Historical Review* VIII, no. 1 (January 2001): 7–13, and *Cochise Remembers Our Great-Grandfather: A Primary Document in New Mexico History* (San Diego: R and R, 2000), 13–14.

11. Zaragosa Vargas, ed., *Major Problems in Mexican American History* (New York: Houghton Mifflin, 1999), 233–234.

12. Vargas, "Mexican Americans in the Great Depression," Chapter 9 in ibid., includes "Carey McWilliams Assails Mexican Repatriation from California, 1933,"

274–275, from a reprint of his essay, "Getting Rid of Mexicans," *American Mercury* 28 (March 1933).

13. Vargas, U.S. Commissioner General of Immigration Reports on Mexican Immigration, 1931, 272. Originally published as House Committee on Immigration and Naturalization, 71st Cong., 2d Sess., *Annual Report of the Commissioner General of Immigration to the Secretary of Labor for the Fiscal Year Ended June 30, 1931*, Washington, D.C., 24–25.

14. Leonidas Sanchez, interview by Lisa Fink, tape recording, San Bernardino, California, May 11, 1980.

15. Violent anti-Mexican sentiment aimed at young boys in drapes, pachuco-style dress, while not instigated, was certainly inflamed by the Hearst newspapers in Los Angeles in the 1940s. Such sensationalism, or "yellow journalism," contributed to the escalation of the Zoot Suit Riots in 1943. Carey McWilliams, *North from Mexico: The Spanish-Speaking People of the United States* (1949; New York: Greenwood Press, 1968), 247–251.

16. Helen Tapia Sanchez, interview by author, Downey, California, June 15, 1998.

17. Three sisters and one of their sisters-in-law worked at Lockheed in 1943 in Los Angeles, California.

18. Severo Sanchez, letter to Leo and Maxine Sanchez, January 11, 1943.

19. Theresa Sanchez Ybarra, telephone interview with author, February 15, 2000.

20. Ibid.

21. Severo Sanchez, letter to Leo and Maxine Sanchez, August 21, 1943.

22. Elmer Sanchez interview.

23. Lena Sanchez, interview by author, Downey, California, June 15, 1998.

24. Vicki L. Ruiz, "The Acculturation of Young Mexican American Women," in Vargas, ed., *Major Problems in Mexican American History*, 265–271. Ruiz examines Americanization and discrimination in the 1920s and 1930s. "Many restaurants, theaters, and public swimming pools discriminated. . . . In southern California, for example, Mexicans could swim at the public plunges only one day out of the week, just before they drained the pool." Los Angeles–area municipalities had covenants that discriminated in housing and other ways.

25. The Sanchez home at 1471 West 9th St., San Bernardino, California, stayed in the family from 1944 to 1999. Those fifty-five years saw countless Christmases and other significant family events such as births, baptisms, marriages, and deaths. The house was sold when Mama, Macedonia Acuña Sanchez, died August 7, 1998.

26. Severo Sanchez, letter to Leo and Maxine Sanchez, January 9, 1944.

27. "Seventh Infantry Division, Operation Flintrock," National Archives and Records Administration (NARA), Washington, D.C.

28. Edmund G. Love, *The Hourglass: A History of the 7th Infantry Division in World War II* (Nashville: Battery Press, 1988), 137.

29. My daughter Teyana L. Viscarra has since visited Oahu and Maui, where her great-uncle served.

30. Severo Sanchez, letter to Leo and Maxine Sanchez, March 24, 1944. Also, Ken Medel, Maureen Medel, and Pattee Medel Barta, grandchildren of Angelica Sanchez Miller, contributed notes from their father Louis Medel's letters to his wife Elsie Tully.

31. "Queen Mary at War," *Press Enterprise* (Riverside, Calif.), July 6, 2001.

"The Queen Mary carried 800,000 service people during World War II . . . and a record 16,683 in one 1943 crossing."

32. M. Hamlin Cannon, *The War in the Pacific: Leyte: The Return to the Philippines* (Washington, D.C.: Office of the Chief of Military History, Department of the Army, 1954), 40–41.

33. Ibid., 41.

34. "Leyte Operations Report," *G3 Journal*, NARA, Washington, D.C.

35. Love, *The Hourglass*, 208, 212.

36. Cannon, *The War in the Pacific*, 41.

37. Albert E. Cowdrey, *Fighting for Life: American Military Medicine in World War II* (New York: Macmillan, 1994), 128.

38. Les Habegger, "274th Regiment Medic," 70th Infantry Division Website: www.trailblazersww2.org.

39. See Cowdrey, *Fighting for Life*.

40. Fred Capp, First Lieutenant, Commanding Officer, Company E, 32nd Infantry, personal letter to Leo N. Sanchez, February 13, 1945.

41. Love, *The Hourglass*, 463.

42. General Douglas MacArthur, General Headquarters, Southwest Pacific, condolence letter to Leo N. Sanchez, Washington, D.C., May 22, 1945. Personal papers of the Sanchez family.

43. "There'll Be Bluebirds over the White Cliffs of Dover," 1942 pop classic by Nat Burton.

44. Charles B. Macdonald, *U.S. Army in World War II: The European Theater of Operations: The Last Offensive* (Washington D.C.: Office of the Chief of Military History, 1973), 212–217.

45. Information from the papers giving honorable discharges from the U.S. Army to Jimmie Sanchez Elmer Sanchez, October 1945; and John Edward Sanchez, U.S. Navy, November 1945. The Sanchez family papers are in the possession of Josephine Zanone, Cathy Sanchez Bates, Carol Ann Fare, Randall Mehl, James Arthur Sanchez, and Helen Tapia Sanchez, and also NARA, Personnel Records, St. Louis, Missouri.

46. John "Bud" Lyons, interview by author, Albuquerque, New Mexico, April 2001.

CHAPTER 2

The Beating of Private Aguirre

A Story about West Texas during World War II

DAVID MONTEJANO

This gang of white rednecks beat up Ben Aguirre while [he was] in uniform. They left him for dead. The Mexican community got upset. The community started a collection but the white businesses refused to donate. They put up signs that said "Aguirre is Mexican. Ask Mexicans for help." Many years later a tornado was going to hit the colonia but at the last moment, it veered away and jumped the Concho River. It swept away the Anglo neighborhood. They started a collection but the Mexican businesses put up signs, "Remember Ben Aguirre. The tornado was an act of God. Ask God for help."

So went one of the stories that my uncle, Fred (Lico) Enriquez, would relate about life in San Angelo, Texas, in the 1940s. He told me that Ben Aguirre was still walking around with a metal plate in his head. A few summers ago, I finally responded and said, "Let's go find Ben Aguirre and talk to him." The result was a fascinating trip to West Texas that led to the recovery of an episode of San Angelo history and of personal family history as well. This account is a sketch of that trip.[1]

Starting Out

We leave San Antonio early and head west on U.S. 90 toward Del Rio. Although my brothers, sister, and I have grown up in San Antonio, we have always regarded Del Rio as our family home. The families of our parents settled there; or better put, they used this desert oasis as a base for frequent migrations. My paternal grandfather was a sheep shearer (or *trasquilador*) who followed a well-worn migratory route. The Mexican sheep shearers would begin their annual trek in the Del Rio area and work their way northward, through San Angelo and up into Montana. I recall seeing a photo of "Papi" standing next to railroad tracks in Montana. I have memories of myself as a child trying to hold his heavy shears. I also remember that he was proud of his skill.

On my mother's side, the grandfather I knew, "Papá Telésforo," was a storyteller, a violinist, and a master domino player. Over the years, I came to understand that he had been the head of a large extended family of migrant workers. My grandfather's family followed the crops to Colorado and Idaho, and to Iowa, Minnesota, and Wisconsin. As the children became adults and started their own families, they added to the family labor pool. As a result of these migrations, today we have cousins in places like Conesville, Iowa, and Pierceton, Indiana. But in the 1940s, when my mother, her four sisters, and her only surviving brother, Lico, were teenagers, San Angelo, with its cotton fields, and only 150 miles from Del Rio, was a frequent second home. Thus it makes sense that our trip from San Antonio to San Angelo should take us through Del Rio. We intend to retrace the route that Papá Telésforo's family followed between Del Rio and San Angelo.

In my family, the art of storytelling was passed from Papá to my mother and my Uncle Lico. As children, we heard stories about life *en las piscas* (picking cotton). I remember one story about how my mother, as the lightest-complected of her siblings, would be sent to buy food because she could pass as white; and another about the need to travel in West Texas with two spare tires, so as not to be stranded in a hostile place. These family stories were part of my experience growing up, and in a fashion they raised some of the questions that moved me to examine Anglo-Mexican relations in my previous work.[2] In some sense, that work was an effort to provide a general historical context for the many stories and jokes I had heard as a child and teenager. Now, in the search for Ben Aguirre, I was attempting to document a specific family story.

The general context for the 1940s can be outlined here only in the barest terms. In the Texas farm areas, segregation remained virtually unaffected by the war against Hitler and race supremacy. This created complications of all sorts. At the highest diplomatic level, the harsh treatment of Mexicans and Mexican Americans prompted Mexico to exclude Texas from its binational agreement regarding the guest worker (bracero) program. In response to Mexico's blacklisting, Governor Coke Stevenson had the legislature approve, in 1943, the "Caucasian Race Resolution," which forbade discrimination against "Caucasians." But since the definition of *Caucasian* (or "whiteness") was based on local practice, the resolution was meaningless, even as a symbolic gesture.[3] Nothing, of course, changed on the ground. On occasion, the excesses of Jim Crow moved Texas Mexican laborers to avoid entire counties. To provide one West Texas example: In October 1944, the farmers of the Big Spring area experienced great difficulty in harvesting their crops because a local constable had flagged down all migrant-filled trucks on the highway, instructing them not to stop in town under threat of arrest.[4] In spite of these conditions, World War II was a watershed period for the Texas Mexican community. Servicemen and their families, citing their loyalty and sacrifice for the country in wartime, began to challenge Jim Crow segregation aggressively.[5] They would lay the basis for the civil rights movement of the late 1940s and early 1950s. This in brief, then, suggests the Texas world of my grandparents and parents back in the 1940s. It also provides the backdrop for my uncle's story about Ben Aguirre.

I had prepared for the trip by rereading two books from the period. Both served as reference guides to Texas in the 1940s. The first book was a 1940 travelogue titled *Texas: A Guide to the Lone Star State*.[6] Compiled by the Writers' Program of the Works Projects Administration, this New Deal project contained descriptive tours of the major routes in the state. Considerable attention was paid to the animal and plant life as well as to the "social landscape" that one might see along the road. Read sixty years later, these descriptive tours provide not just road maps; they provide revealing observations and sentiments of that time, especially when they focus on the "racial elements" of the state.

The second reference book, titled *Are We Good Neighbors?*, was a compilation by civil rights lawyer Alonso Perales of affidavits, letters, telegrams, articles, editorials, congressional testimony, and government reports regarding the ill-treatment of Mexican Americans.[7] This was my sociological map of Anglo-Mexican relations for the World War II period. In March 1945, Perales had testified before a U.S. Senate committee that the three million "Americans of Mexican extraction" in Texas and the Southwest "are more discriminated against more widely today than 25 years ago."[8] He introduced a list of 150 towns and cities in Texas "where Mexicans are denied service, or entrance" in public places of business or amusement. In nearly every town and city, Perales noted, Mexican Americans were segregated in schools and neighborhoods. In Perales's words, "American citizens of Mexican extraction, whether in uniform or in civilian attire, are not allowed in public places, cannot buy food or clothes except in certain designated areas, cannot secure employment in any industry except as common or semi-skilled labor, cannot receive the same wages as other Americans in the same area."[9]

Perales provided detailed affidavits of uniformed Latin American servicemen being refused service in cafés, barbershops, theaters, and so on. In one instance (in Ozona), the complainant, Private Arturo Ramirez, had died in action a few months after filing his affidavit. In another, Sergeant Macario Garcia, who had been awarded the Congressional Medal of Honor, had been chased from a restaurant (in Richmond) that did not serve "Mexicans." Servicemen were not the only ones to file sworn complaints of discrimination. A good number of affidavits (25 of 116) were filed by mothers, wives, and sisters of servicemen. Virtually all cases made reference to service to the country in time of war.[10]

As I look at the road map, I see that all the major towns on our trip—Hondo, Uvalde, Bracketville, Del Rio, Sonora, and San Angelo—are mentioned in the affidavits collected by Perales.

On the Road

The topography of the route from San Antonio to Del Rio has not changed significantly from the travelogue description given in 1940: "San Antonio to Del Rio; 154 m. U.S. 90 enters the wooded hills of the Edwards Plateau, passes through the brush country, then over alkaline plains and low mesas dotted with chaparral."[11] Forty miles from San Antonio, we reach the small town of Hondo, a nineteenth-century German settlement best known to motorists today for its prominent sign: "This Is God's Country. Don't Drive Thru It Like Hell." In the 1940s, according to several affidavits, the cafés and theaters of "God's Country" were off-limits to Mexicans. We cruise through the town.

The old travel guide offers an interesting observation of the surrounding countryside: "Throughout the area, tiny jacales with accompanying patches of chili peppers and beans bespeak the presence of Latin Americans."[12] As my uncle and I drive past roadside shacks in hamlets called Knippa and D'Hanis, I wonder how much has really changed.

We reach Uvalde, the midway point between San Antonio and Del Rio. Uvalde's claim to fame is that it is the hometown of movie star Dale Evans (wife of Roy Rogers) and former governor Dolph Briscoe. In 1940, Uvalde had a population of 5,286 and one hundred businesses.[13] At that time, most of these businesses, or those belonging to Anglos, did not serve Mexicans. According to Perales's 1945 testimony, Mexicans, including "American soldiers of Mexican descent," were denied service at all Anglo-American barber shops and at the following Anglo-American business establishments: "Dinette Café. Newport Café . . . Shadowland Café and Beer Parlors . . . Walgreen's Drug Store . . . Hanger Six Café. Palace Drug Store. Uvalde Candy Shoppe. Manhattan Café. Casey Jones Café and Beer Parlors . . . Casal Cave."[14] Had Lico and I been traveling in the 1940s, it would not have been advisable to stop here.

Among Texas Mexicans, Uvalde had long acquired fame as a stronghold of the old segregated order. In the 1950s and 1960s, as I was gaining consciousness of these things, I recall that my parents were always careful to stop on the Mexican side of town. In the 1970s, Uvalde was a major site of Anglo reaction to the Chicano civil rights movement that was then challenging segregation and discrimination throughout the region. Rancher-businessman Dolph Briscoe was governor of Texas at the time. Worried in particular by the Chicano electoral victories in nearby Crystal City, Governor Briscoe denounced Crystal City as a "little Cuba." At the time, those of us in the *movimiento*—I was a college student then—took that as a compliment. As we pass near the First State Bank, where the Briscoe art collection—"from Rembrandt to western American artists," reads the promotional brochure—is proudly exhibited, these events seem to belong to some blurry past.

Seven miles outside of Uvalde we cross over the dry Nueces River—dry probably because of irrigation as well as drought. The scenery looks pretty much like it did in 1940: "The route now winds around and over brush- and timber-covered hills. Cenizo, greasewood, huajillo, catclaw, and Spanish dagger are abundant. . . . This is chiefly goat ranching country."[15] Looking at the scrubland that surrounds us, which can only sustain goats, I find it difficult to understand how the boundary dispute over the Nueces could have been the immediate cause of the Mexican American War a century and a half ago. The thought reminds me that we are following an old frontier line of defense—Ft. Inge in Uvalde, Ft. Clark in Bracketville, and Camp Del Rio. These U.S. Cavalry posts were built to guard the border and protect the San Antonio–San Diego stagecoach road. All are now historical museums or parks.

On passing Bracketville and Ft. Clark, Lico recounts a story of a good experience with *gabachos*, or Anglos, in the late 1940s. He was working as a carpenter's helper with some young vets on a roofing job at a restaurant. When they took the lunch break, the guys asked him to join them for a hamburger. "Sure enough, the restaurant owner refused to serve me inside. I said 'I could eat outside,' but the guys insisted that we all eat together or not at all." So they got up and left the restaurant, and they never returned. They left the unfinished roofing job behind. "That was something," Lico says, smiling. "We left a big gaping hole in the roof. And you know how out here," Lico gestures to the land around us, "storms can come up easily."

Of course, I have heard this story many times before. Usually it is a prelude to other stories, none of which have any cheery element. The "hamburger story" establishes the premise that some *gabachos*

Benigno Aguirre (left) and Fred Enriquez (right), in a photo taken in July 1995 outside of Aguirre's home in San Angelo, Texas.

were okay in their relations with Mexicans. With that taken care of, my uncle would generally proceed to the darker stories about race relations.

Three hours into the trip, we reach Laughlin Air Force Base on the outskirts of Del Rio. Created in the 1940s for the purpose of pilot training, Laughlin Field was once the home base for a squadron of U2 spy planes. Today, with the end of cold-war tensions and the development of satellite spy technology, the base seems like an aging fort, defending a twentieth-century frontier that no longer exists. We enter Del Rio and pass San Felipe Springs, the key to life in this semi-desert. As the family home place, Del Rio and its sister city on the Mexican side, Ciudad Acuña, are associated in my mind with many warm childhood memories. But I also remember, without understanding at the time, the odd mixture of "Texas country" and northern Mexican ranch life. The WPA travel guide of 1940 suggested such contrasts, describing Del Rio, population 11,693, as a "blend of modern hotels and aged adobe jacales, of Americano ranchmen and copper-colored peones, of sleek automobiles and plodding burros—a city on the Rio Grande."[16] But the strangeness of border life that I sensed—I realize in retrospect—came not from straightforward cultural contact, but from the exaggerated and distorted expressions of this contact. I understand now: the border has historically accommodated eccentric or deviant personalities and practices, or what some would explain as "frontier" behavior. Prominent examples from the Del Rio section of the border would include Judge Roy Bean or the "Law West of the Pecos," the red-light district known as "Boys' Town" in Ciudad Acuña, and Wolfman Jack with his "border-blasting" music from Acuña. I recall, as a child, playing with my grandparents' radio (what is now called "surfing"), listening first to Baptist fundamentalist preaching, then to Wolfman Jack, and then to Mexican rancheras, after which I would start the whole cycle again. I recall seeing the drunk cowboys in Acuña with their Mexican "girlfriends." In my child's mind, Del Rio and Ciudad Acuña at times took on a surreal setting. Orson Welles in *Touch of Evil* (1958) had a memorable line about border towns bringing out "the worst in a country." This was dramatic exaggeration, but as a child I probably would have agreed.

West of Del Rio, U.S. 90 "winds up into barren hills. The long blue ridge of mountains low on the horizon to the left is in northern Mexico, across the Rio Grande."[17] Five miles outside of Del Rio, we turn right, northward, onto U.S. 277, which will take us to San Angelo. The harshness of this arid land of cactus, chaparral, and mesquite dominates the senses. Even goats may find it difficult to survive here. The old travel guide notes, "In these western solitudes, the ranchman who drives 50 miles for his mail or a loaf of bread is the rule rather than the exception."[18] In 1940, this particular section of the road was dangerous. The paving stopped ten miles after the turnoff to San Angelo. "This section of the route is hazardous in wet weather and local inquiry should be made before attempting to travel it," warned the travel guide.[19] Even in dry weather, this desolate stretch of some seventy miles involved some risk.

As we drive through the desert, Lico and I talk about San Angelo during World War II. The city had a well-established racial order.[20] School segregation, residential segregation, public displays of racism, and police brutality were all part of the everyday experience of Mexicans. Mexicanos were routinely denied service at cafés and drugstores; nor were they allowed to use the city swimming pool or the gymnasium. Even when in military uniform, they were denied service in most downtown restaurants during the war years. Lico, noting that hazing by Anglo teenagers was commonplace, tells me the story about "Shorty," a slightly built Mexican teenager who knifed an Anglo football player when cornered by the team in the high school boys' room. Shorty, who disappeared after the incident, became an instant hero for the Mexican youth of San Angelo. "Conditions were bad," Lico adds as a summary note.

In 1940, the paving on U.S. 277 resumed at mile 65, some twenty miles before Sonora, a small sheep- and goat-ranching center. In Sonora my uncle unexpectedly pulls over to look at vacant land next to the creek (the "dry fork of the Devil's River"). He tells me that there used to be a one-room house on the site, and that the family—all eight of them, including my mother—used to live there. I know that in the 1930s and 1940s Sonora and its neighbor city of Ozona were inhospitable places for Mexican workers. I want to tell my uncle that Sonora had a standing school policy of not allowing Mexicans beyond the sixth grade, but I silence myself.[21] He lived through this period. At age thirteen, Lico had dropped out of Sam Houston Elementary in San Angelo in order to help the family in the fields.

North of Sonora, U.S. 277 follows the winding course of the South Concho River past some of the "finest ranching land" in Texas.[22] Six hours into our trip, we approach the San Angelo area, one of the largest primary wool markets in the country. Irrigated farming is fairly extensive, but ranching is the largest industry. In 1940, San Angelo had a population of 25,308; about a quarter of the population was Mexican American. The travel guide poetically described the Mexican presence of that time as follows: "Here the Mexican vaquero, half Indian and half Spanish in origin, has a folklore rich in religious symbolism and pagan superstition. He tells how the paisano, once a proud and haughty bird, was punished . . . for his vanity, being condemned to walk instead of fly; thus was the lowly 'road-runner' created."[23]

As I read and react to this archaic description of Mexican ranch hands, I am chagrined to think that I may be engaged in folkloric study. After all, I am checking out a story that has been circulating for fifty years. There are intriguing elements of protest, collective memory, and religious symbolism in the narrative that call for an assessment. All popular oral histories run the risk of becoming "folklore," in the sense that exaggerations, half-truths, and even "superstition" become part of the narrative as the story is told and retold. My uncle understands this difference between oral folklore and written history—that is why he has brought his nephew the historian to find Ben Aguirre. This trip is clearly meant to ground the narrative in details. But one thing is already clear: there are no meek "road-runners" in my uncle's story. Indeed, this story suggests a galvanized Mexican community with a long memory.

"Conditions were bad," Lico says again, picking up the loose ends of the past hour. But the soldiers who came back weren't afraid of the *gabachos*. "We're not afraid anymore," said Lico. "We were in a war over there, and now we're in a war over here. *Qué siga la guerra*. [Let the war continue.]"

The Mexican community of San Angelo was quite active in the 1930s and 1940s. In 1930, a local chapter of the League of United Latin American Citizens (LULAC) was formed in order to promote Americanism and first-class citizenship among "Latin Americans." Over the next two decades, LULAC, allied with other social and cultural organizations, protested segregation at movie houses and public events, the classification of Mexicans as "non-white," and so on. When World War II broke out, LULAC led the way in expressing support for the military draft. The sons of many local families saw combat and were killed in action.[24]

Such sacrifice and loyalty to the country intensified the campaign of the Mexican American community for changes in local conditions. One eloquent letter to the *San Angelo Standard-Times* voiced the sentiment of many "Latin-American citizens," noting that "our Latin-American boys are not segregated at the front line. They are fighting right beside the Anglo American boys. They are dying beside the Anglo boys for a most worthy cause—that democracy may live and so that people may have all the privileges of a democracy."[25]

The letter-writer then asked some pointed rhetorical questions:

after their service, how will the Latin American soldiers react when they return home and "find that they are not considered good enough to go into a café because they happen to be of Mexican origin . . . ?" Moreover, how do the mothers and wives of these soldiers feel about these humiliations? "The mothers and wives who have sacrificed the lives of their loved ones to win the war—how do they feel when they are refused a glass of water in a café? Their children are not good enough to enjoy the rights of American citizens, but they are good enough to die defending their country. The Latins will feel just like the Jews in Germany."

The letter-writer concluded by noting that "if Latin-Americans in Texas are not to be 'The Jews of Germany' then discrimination should be completely abolished and Latin-American citizens should be allowed to exercise all their privileges as given to all citizens by the Constitution of America."

As I read this letter, I wonder whether this striking comparison to "Jews in Germany" is a not-so-subtle reference to the sizable Texas German community among West Texas Anglos. The Texas German towns were infamous for their segregationist practices. Mexican Americans in their sworn testimonies about discrimination often identified the offenders as Germans.[26] An implied irony in these documents was the suggestion that Texas Mexicans were fighting Germans abroad and at home. The way Lico put it was, "Anglos are the children of Germans. Their parents taught them to hate Mexicans."

The author of the remarkable letter was Aurora García (Jáquez), whose brother, brother-in-law, and husband were at the time stationed in South Asia. The letter of Mrs. García, a well-known community activist, suggests the type of informed and critical commentary then circulating in the barrios of San Angelo.[27] The letter was written July 27, 1945, only a month before the beating of Benigno Aguirre.

The Benigno Aguirre Beating

It is mid-afternoon when we pull into San Angelo. We stop at a relative's house. We look through the San Angelo telephone directory, find the listing for Benigno Aguirre, and call. I briefly explain the purpose of my call, and Mr. Aguirre immediately invites us over to talk.

I review my notes of the newspaper articles I had previously surveyed.[28] I realize that without these articles my uncle's story could have remained largely unverifiable; it could have remained an interesting "folktale." For the incident almost went unnoticed outside the Mexican barrios of San Angelo. The *San Angelo Standard-Times* and its companion newspaper, the *Evening Standard*, reported on the beating and hospitalization a week after it had happened, and only because Mrs. Aurora García, the eloquent letter writer and activist, had insisted that the editors look into the matter. The editors found Benigno Aguirre, comatose and in critical condition, in a basement room of the San Angelo hospital. Then they found that the police had apparently made no attempts to investigate the incident. Although the police had filed a report, they had never asked Aguirre's companions about the assailants. Police Chief Lowe said he never saw the police report on the beating; the desk sergeant said "he didn't know how it had missed being brought to Lowe's attention."[29] However, the initial story of September 9—with the headline "Ex-Soldier Still Unconscious Week after Assault; None of Assailants Apprehended"—provoked a storm of protest, and within days the city police had charged twelve boys, most of them sixteen and seventeen years old, with the assault. The newspaper reporting on the beating and subsequent legal proceedings suggests that the Aguirre incident shook the old racial order of San Angelo.

Solely on the basis of the newspaper articles, I had reconstructed the history of the Aguirre incident as follows. On Saturday night (September 1, 1945), according to court testimony by several of the Anglo teenagers, policeman Bill White had "carried a bunch of the boys out" to a local nightclub where they drank until 1 a.m. Later, while driving down Washington Drive, the group decided to "Go over into Mexican town and beat up some Mexicans." They saw two near Ben Ficklin Road, but those two disappeared while they turned the pickup around. They "piled out of the pick-up" when they saw two more on Avenue K, but those two also "got away." At Washington Drive and South Chadbourne, "the boys" confronted Benigno Aguirre, twenty, Pete Gonzales, sixteen, and Rudy Salazar, nineteen. They claimed that the trio had cursed and thrown something at them as they drove by. But Pete Gonzales was emphatic in noting that "we sure didn't start it." In his statement, Gonzales said that he, Ben, and

Rudy were returning from a Latin American club where "some television thing with recordings" was being demonstrated. On the way home, some "white boys" saw them and shouted "There are three Mexicans!" "Ben and I were going down Chadbourne, trying to get away, when they drove up in a pick-up and piled out." There is agreement on what happened next. Gonzales and Salazar got away, but Aguirre was caught after a short chase. Aguirre, 115 pounds, was beaten unconscious.[30]

When the *Standard-Times* broke the story a week later, Aguirre, with "both eyes blackened and bloody, and with a cut inches long X-ed above his left ear," was semiconscious and in critical condition at the hospital: "His lips moved without speaking, as his eyes opened without seeing. His quiet-spoken father, Manuel J. Aguirre . . . could [speak]. Not without bitterness. 'No, I don't know who beat my boy. It is bad.'" Speaking "in broken sentences," his father said that "Ben had a medical discharge [from the Army] . . . he was not a strong boy. He never drank. He never had a fight before in his life that I know of. He was a good boy."[31]

The Mexican community of San Angelo, which had long complained of hazing and other acts of provocation by Anglo teenagers, was outraged by the assault. Community leaders noted that the Anglo boys were out "hunting greasers" in the barrio just for fun, and that the beating was unprovoked. The incident further demonstrated that these Anglo gangs were encouraged, and sometimes escorted, by the Anglo police as they harassed Mexican youth. Within a few days of the first published report, a group of prominent community members had joined together and sent telegrams to Governor Coke Stevenson, the Mexican Consul in Austin, and the Mexican Secretary of Foreign Affairs, asking for some redress, since local authorities had ignored the situation. The telegram read in part: "For some months past there has been an organized gang operating in San Angelo, Texas, composed of Anglo-Americans who have been and continue to threaten, abuse, beat, maltreat and waylay Latin-Americans."[32] Of the governor, they asked that Texas Rangers be dispatched forthwith to "put a stop to this practice." As an indication of the tension in the city, they warned that "delay in bringing this condition under control will undoubtedly be fatally serious." Cursing and fights between Anglo and Latin American youths had already taken place outside a downtown theater and the Standard-Times Building the day before.[33]

The signatories of the telegram were three pastors—Reverend G. C. Rodríguez of the Mexican Baptist Church, Reverend Antonio Guillen of the Mexican Methodist Church, and Reverend Raymond Soper of St. Mary's Catholic Church—and three prominent businesspeople, J. M. Jáquez of the Mexican Grill, José Figueroa of Figueroa's Grocery, and Albert Cano of the Little Mexico Café. These pastors and businessmen constituted the leadership of the ad hoc committee that formed in response to the Aguirre beating. They also provided the network for the Ben Aguirre hospital fund. Two days after the first report, José Figueroa had collected nearly $200, mostly in small donations of a few dollars, at his store. By the following day, nearly $400 had been collected. The last published reference to the fund, eleven days after the first report, notes that nearly $500 had been collected, and that groceryman José Figueroa had been "officially designated as treasurer of the hospital expense fund."[34] Through these bits and pieces spliced from various newspaper articles, one captures the sense of an angry, mobilized community.

Denunciation of the Aguirre beating also came from some quarters on the Anglo side of town. (This may have been the first sign of disagreement among Anglo Americans about the nature of race relations in San Angelo.) The local newspapers, the *Standard-Times* and the *Evening Standard*, took the lead in criticizing and investigating the police. A few days after the initial reporting, the *Evening Standard* editorialized that the incident was a "blot" on the image of San Angelo and that it was "more than passing strange" that the police chief and the sheriff had initially known nothing of the attack on Aguirre.[35] The San Angelo Ministerial Association, representing the major churches in the city, passed a strongly worded resolution deploring "this un-American and despicable act by a gang of Anglo American youths." The Goodfellow Post of the American Legion unanimously condemned the "gangsterism" and offered support in "bringing to justice the guilty persons." Several speakers mentioned the part that Latin Americans have played "in behalf of this country in wartime." One Legionnaire, a former paratrooper, related that "of a group of more than 30 Mexican soldiers at the front most of them had been wounded and they were still in there battling. They commanded his utmost respect."[36] The resolution condemned "the beating of an ex-soldier, a Latin American, who served his country honorably . . . as entirely un-American, as contrary to the principles for which this Latin-American swore to serve his country." The veterans then contributed $21 to the Aguirre hospital fund.

Such reaction and pressure from both Mexican and Anglo sides of town apparently surprised the local police, and they moved, somewhat belatedly, to curtail the activities of Anglo gangs. Chief of Police Lowe joined Sheriff J. F. Bryson in an ultimatum to the teenage gangs to "break it up."[37] Within a few days of the first *Standard-Times* article, eleven of the twelve boys, ages sixteen and older, had been identified and arrested. Initially all were charged with assault with intent to murder. All the boys, including the twelfth, who turned himself in a week later, posted bond or were released to their parents. Some of the boys were sons of prominent ranchers and attorneys. All twelve defendants were represented by the father of one of the boys, attorney William C. McDonald, Sr.[38]

The seven youths who were sixteen years of age were arraigned as juveniles before County Judge I. J. Curtsinger on September 19. Although Judge Curtsinger said he understood the Latin American "still is at the point of death," and that "his condition is doubtful even if he lives," he placed all seven on probation for five years and paroled them to their parents. At the sentencing, he took into account that none of them was involved in "the final close-up attack . . . although all were participants in some degree." He set a curfew hour of 10:30 p.m. and warned them to stay away from intoxicants. A violation of probation would land them in the Gatesville training school without further hearing. Finally, he admonished the youths to improve their school grades and to "have plenty of honest fun—for example, in different forms of athletics—but stay off the streets at night."[39]

There was, of course, a strong current of support in the Anglo community for the twelve boys. During the juvenile hearing, McDonald, the boys' attorney, suggested that the Aguirre incident was in retaliation for an earlier assault by Mexicans. He asked one of the boys if he "knew about George Beaty being beat up and put in the hospital by some Mexicans." The boy replied that he had known about it.[40] In a letter to the *Standard-Times*, George Beaty's mother accused the paper of "crucifying 12 little boys in order to gain a few votes against public officials whom it dislikes." Mrs. Beaty wanted to know why the *Standard-Times* had neglected to mention that her son had been beaten up last July by "a bunch of Mexicans" near the Mexican Grill.[41] Along these lines, City Manager Sam Lawhon expressed regret that "a Latin-American boy was injured," but he personally believed that "this is not a one-sided affair" and that some Latin Americans "have started their share of the fights."[42]

Perhaps this sentiment explains what happened with the five older boys—Leon Hunter, Jr., seventeen; Pat Carnes, seventeen; Bill McDonald, Jr., seventeen; Leland Brashers, seventeen; and E. A. Chapman, twenty—whose cases were brought up before the District Court grand jury on charges of assault with intent to murder. The grand jury no-billed four of the boys, and indicted only Leon Hunter of a reduced misdemeanor charge of aggravated assault. As a misdemeanor, Hunter's case was transferred from the District Court back to the jurisdiction of County Court Judge Curtsinger. There, as a result of a settlement agreement, Hunter pleaded guilty and received a fine of $125. Thus ended the legal proceedings in the Aguirre case, or, as the *Standard-Times* put it, "Finis Written in Attack Case."[43]

The Mexicano community was angered and embittered by the outcome. "The whole affair was just a farce, a whitewash job," Aurora García commented. "These boys were from some very prominent families."[44] The beating had left Aguirre near death. He had been unconscious for a month and had required brain surgery. The doctors were not hopeful about a recovery. But after the legal proceedings ended, the *San Angelo Standard-Times* ceased reporting on the Aguirre incident. The only record we have of further community reaction involving Ben Aguirre is that voiced through my uncle's story.

Benigno Aguirre, at sixty-nine years, looks healthy. He is a slender man, about 5 feet 9 inches tall, with silver-gray thinning hair. He greets us and immediately begins to talk about the beating. We have not yet sat down, nor have I turned on the tape recorder, before he describes the general situation, that whites would drive through the Mexican neighborhoods looking for Mexicans to harass and beat up. Mr. Aguirre is eager to tell his story.[45]

The mayor and most of the police force didn't like Mexicans—*para mí eran del* Klan [to me, they were from the Klan]. The police would escort the Anglo boys to the barrio as if this was a sport. The white boys admitted that the police had them doing this kind of stuff. The police would step in if the Mexicans tried to fight back. When they beat me up, the police were nearby—White and another cop whose name I can't remember were around there.

Aguirre relates that after the beating, the cops took the boys to a ranch to let things cool off.

Aguirre is still upset, fifty years later, at the newspaper reporting of the incident. He feels that the coverage had made him look like a gang member or troublemaker. They hadn't yelled or thrown things at the whites as reported in the newspapers. "The whites were in our part of town and they came looking to cause trouble. Who caused the assault should not be a question."[46] Aguirre continues: "There were fifteen guys. They left me for dead. They broke my skull. After the deputies took me to the hospital I blacked out, so I only know what the others told me and what came out in the papers. I was unconscious for thirty-two days. I revived on the twentieth day for a while."

I ask him about the metal plate in his head. Aguirre replies sharply, "The doctors didn't even put a plate in my head; they just pulled my skin over this hole in my skull." He adds, "I still feel pain."

Aguirre credits his salvation to Aurora Jáquez (Mrs. Aurora García): "If Aurora Jáquez had not caused a commotion at the hospital, the doctors would not have operated on me. If it weren't for Aurora, they would have left me for dead. Everything would have been silenced." I am struck by the reference to silence. Had Aurora not intervened, his death would have been recorded as the result of an attack by unknown assailants. The police would never have investigated. There would have been no incident. Everything would have been silenced.

Aguirre recounts that when he came out of the coma, he could not remember what had happened. His father initially told him that he had been operated on because of his appendix, but that didn't make sense since it was his head that was bandaged. His doctor would only say that he had been in an accident. His friends were afraid to tell him because they were concerned that his health would worsen with the truth. Finally, his dad gave him the newspaper clippings, and he read about his beating.

Aguirre brings out the newspaper clippings to show me. These yellowed clippings, many of them torn or incomplete, had been collected in two over-sized laminated pages. What stands out in the collage of clippings are the repeated references in the headlines to "attack case" or "Aguirre beating."

Aguirre still maintains, as his companions did fifty years ago, that there were fifteen boys. Aguirre notes that Hunter, who weighed two hundred pounds, was the one who got the blame. The other guys said they didn't take part in the beating. These were the sons of lawyers and ranchers; one was the son of a city commissioner, while another was the son of McDonald, the attorney who defended the boys. Hunter was the poorest of the group, and he was made the scapegoat. "Hunter was given a $125 fine! And the others were let go!" Aguirre is still upset.

My uncle points out, as if to remind Ben, that his beating aroused and unified the Mexicano community of San Angelo. "*La gente se juntó* [the people came together]," recalls my uncle, who was sixteen at the time. The people carried out a door-to-door campaign, raising funds for Aguirre's medical expenses: "When they began to ask for support in the barrio americano, the white people put signs on their doors that said, 'Ask Mexicans for help' and 'We don't help Mexicans.'"

Aguirre nods in agreement: "*Estaba carajo en esos días.* [It was terrible in those days.] Ray Garza knifed a white man while I was in the hospital, because of my situation. He stabbed him at school." Aguirre adds that some Mexicanos blamed him for their troubles at work, because of all the publicity. He pauses and then says, "A lot of people don't believe how bad it was then. We had to suffer a lot for things to be better now."

Ben and Lico agree that conditions improved after the assault. Ben continues: "Things changed after the incident. They took down the signs ["No Mexicans Allowed"] and let people into restaurants— not everywhere but in a lot of places. *Sabes qué, la gente se levantó bien duro* [you know what, the community rose up real strong]."

Aguirre himself became a charged symbol of the changes. Years after the incident, his presence would still upset some Anglos. Before he went on disability, Aguirre notes that he had trouble finding and keeping work. After two or three months, the Anglos "would find out it was me and then they would fire me." His horses were killed and his goats were stolen. I ask him if he had ever run into any of the twelve Anglos again. "Once when I was in town," Aguirre replies, "these two Anglos came by and pushed me. Then my friend went after them and they apologized." In sharp contrast, for the Mexican community Ben was the young man whom they had saved. I ask rhetorically, "Do people today remember?" Aguirre responds without hesitation, "There are still many who see me and ask about my health. For the people from here, they will never forget." "He is history," adds my uncle.

That there has been considerable change over the last fifty years is evident on the living-room mantel, where photos of Aguirre's three sons and their wives are prominently displayed. One of the wives is an Anglo blonde. Two of his sons, he tells me, are store managers in Dallas; the other became a cop and is now a narcotics agent. The narcotics agent is married to the blonde.

"What would you advise your children?" I ask Ben. He replies, "I would advise them to forget the past. I don't talk to them about it. We lived in a different system. They can become better."

"Do they all know the story?" I ask.

"Yes," Ben responds, "but I didn't want them to resent whites. San Angelo has changed a lot."

Aguirre does not want to stir malice or ill feelings with his story. But he is eager to correct the historical record. Oral histories circulate among family and friends, and Aguirre's extended circle is already familiar with the corrected version. This is for a different audience.

Benigno, perhaps in a sign that he is tiring, says, "I can't tell you much more; I was in the hospital a long time. You should talk to Aurora Jáquez. She called for the Texas Rangers." I know my history of this event is incomplete without the recollections of Aurora Jáquez, the articulate young organizer who directed much of the civil rights strategy of the Mexicano community. In a paradoxical sense, I realize, she and not Benigno Aguirre is the central person in the story of the "Aguirre beating."[47]

Aguirre is instead the living icon of an incident that exposed the ugly face of the old segregated order, an incident that local "old-timers"—Anglos and Mexicans—still remember well, even if few like to talk about it. I know that I have barely scratched the surface of an important chapter in the history of San Angelo. Yet somehow, as incomplete as the story remains, I feel a sense of closure. My uncle and I have found Ben Aguirre.

After two hours of conversation, we thank Mr. Aguirre for the visit and leave. By this time the humidity of a hot July afternoon has given way to lightning, thunder, and a heavy shower. "Is this tornado weather?" I ask Lico, half-jokingly. My uncle points in a northwesterly direction, toward the river, and recalls again that in 1952 or 1953 *"un tornado venía por el barrio mexicano, y parecía que era el fin del mundo. Pero al último momento hizo un* 'U-turn,' *brincó el río, y limpió todo el barrio gabacho* [a tornado was coming toward the Mexican neighborhood, and it looked as if this was the end of the world. But at the last minute it made a U-turn, jumped across the river, and cleared the entire Anglo neighborhood away]. The Anglos came and asked for help, and the Mexicanos put up signs, 'Remember Ben Aguirre. This was an act of God. Ask God for help.'"

A tornado sent by a vengeful God—is there a more perfect ending for this kind of Texas "folk story"? Again I am impressed by the tenacity of community memory implied by the story: eight years after the incident of waiting for some justice, a tornado provides divine retribution. Bitter memories sink deep roots in small towns. When I first heard the Ben Aguirre story, the memory was nearly fifty years old. Some of the details had become frayed over the years as the story was retold over and over. Contrary to my uncle's version of the incident, Aguirre had not been in uniform when he was nearly beaten to death. Nor did he have a metal plate in his head. Nonetheless, Lico's story, by highlighting the treatment of Mexican Americans, uniformed or not, unambiguously captured the truth of the incident.

And the avenging tornado? My uncle, it turns out, did not exaggerate in describing a catastrophic event. Extremely intense tornadic activity devastated parts of San Angelo and Waco on May 11, 1953. It also sparked "the first thoroughly documented investigation" of major cities following catastrophic disaster.[48] A team of social scientists, organized by the Hogg Foundation and the Sociology Department of the University of Texas, studied San Angelo and Waco for over a year, investigating "everything they could lay their hands on," from economics to emotions.[49] Thus, again, ample documentation surfaces to confirm critical elements of my uncle's narrative.

The San Angelo event unfolded as follows. In the early afternoon of May 11, 1953, two patrolmen of the Texas Department of Public Safety reported sighting a funnel over Sterling City, forty miles to the northwest of San Angelo. They followed the funnel down the valley of the North Concho River, with a forward speed of about ten to fifteen miles per hour. As the tornado approached the city, it changed direction, "cutting across the highway less than a block behind the patrol car." The officers turned around and followed the tornado into the Lake View area, where it lowered and "wrought such intense damage." The damage was concentrated in a trail of approximately two and a half miles through the Lake View neighborhood.[50]

The tornado obliterated Lake View. It claimed 11 lives, injured 66 people seriously, and left 1,700 homeless in the few minutes it took to sweep across Lake View. About 430 homes, or nearly 80 percent of the homes in the tornado area, were totally destroyed or rendered uninhabitable.[51] The emotional impact was also severe, resulting in "intense feelings of desolation, of depression, of loss, or of apathy."[52] Four out of ten families had members who experienced serious emotional disturbance, and eight out of ten families had members who had developed "undue fear of bad weather." Wayne Holtzman, research director for the Hogg Foundation, drew an analogy to war conditions, noting that "striking similarities are apparent between the traumatic neuroses in bombed cities in the Second World War and the emotional disturbances manifested by some victims of the tornadoes."[53]

But my uncle's story would suggest that another comparison, of the bitter "eye for an eye" sort, be drawn with the situation of the Mexican barrios of that time. There is no question that the crises of these two communities were set off by categorically distinct threats— storm clouds for one, teenage gangs for the other. Yet each underwent a similar experience of being under siege. It is difficult for me to read that fear had become "the constant companion of many people in Lake View"[54] and not think immediately of everyday life for Mexicans in San Angelo during the war years. It is difficult not to think of

Ben Aguirre in reading about the terror and the resulting fear experienced by one Lake View woman: "I was terrified. I was like a trapped animal that didn't know what way to run. . . . I just—when those storms come up, I just—just feel like for sure this may be the end. That it could be a cloud that could swoop down before you could get to protection. They are murderous things. There's—there's a fear you can't conquer."[55] Storm clouds and teenage gangs are threats of very different character, but the persistent anxiety and fear of Lake View residents must have been familiar emotions in the San Angelo barrios before the Aguirre beating. The Aguirre incident, my uncle's narrative suggests, transformed fear into anger and defiance. What else could the tornado in his story represent?

A good number of Angeleños on both sides of the Concho River thought that the 1953 tornado represented God's will. The social scientists from the University of Texas, wanting to understand the meanings that the victims had attributed to this disaster, asked Lake View families, "Why do you think this storm hit Lake View?" Almost half had no explanation. But of those who offered reasons, "the greatest number, by far, were couched in religious terms—the storm was God's will, His punishment for sins committed, or some other motive attributed to Him. The belief in a divinity actively interested in, and interfering with, terrestrial affairs is evident."[56] For many Lake View victims, the tornado was general punishment for a sinful life. For many in the Mexicano community, the tornado that made a "U-turn" was "an act of God" meant to redress long-outstanding grievances.

The team of social scientists, in San Angelo for a year, did not perceive the symbolic importance of the Lake View tornado in the context of local San Angelo society. They failed to see any signs of racial tension because the Lake View neighborhood was strictly a "whites only" area; the Mexican barrios that had been miraculously spared were on the other side of the Concho River. They thus missed some of the most important signs of stress and conflict, signs that literally and figuratively said "Remember Ben Aguirre."

It is still raining when we drive to a covered icehouse for some beer. As we drink and talk about the rather long day, I comment on the irony that the Aguirre incident took place at the end of World War II.

"Ben was beaten on the same day that Japan formally surrendered," I note.[57] The war overseas had ended. Thinking of the much-publicized meetings of former Japanese and American soldiers taking place today, I ask Lico if he thinks that something similar could happen between Mexicans and Anglos who had fought each other back then.

"Do you think that some of those twelve *gabachos* who assaulted Ben fifty years ago would be willing to shake hands with Ben and exchange good wishes?"

"I think so," replies Lico. "Are you going to organize it?"

I laugh nervously and take another swallow of beer. Outside the rain has let up.

The trip to find Ben Aguirre took place on July 15, 1995. Nine months later, on April 27, 1996, Ben G. Aguirre passed away.

Notes

1. I want to thank Patricia Martínez, Veronica Martínez, Emilio Zamora, Jaime Mejía, and Arnoldo De León for their assistance and comments on earlier drafts.

2. David Montejano, *Anglos and Mexicans in the Making of Texas, 1836–1986* (Austin: University of Texas Press, 1987).

3. For instances of Mexican Americans being refused service because they were not accepted as white or Caucasian, see Alonso Perales, *Are We Good Neighbors?* (San Antonio: Artes Gráficas, 1948), 139–212.

4. See Montejano, *Anglos and Mexicans*, 268, 272–273. The reaction of the workers must have been similar to that of a truck driver who was taking seasonal workers to West Texas in October 1947. After being denied service at a café, the truck driver had appealed to the city marshal, noting that he had fought and been wounded in the war. The marshal said he could do nothing but he, too, was sorry because they were having difficulty obtaining Mexican labor. The truck driver responded that, as far as he was concerned, the marshal and the café's proprietor "could both start picking the cotton and we would be glad to remain away from his community." See Perales, *Are We Good Neighbors?*, 141–142.

5. As important, during the war and immediately afterward, there was a significant migration of Texas Mexicans from the rural areas to the cities, where veterans' benefits and federal jobs could be secured. My family was part of that migration. My father, a World War II veteran, moved the family from Del Rio to San Antonio in 1950 and began work at the Post Office while attending college on the G.I. Bill. My uncle Lico, a Korean veteran, would follow a few years later, lured by work at Kelly Air Force Base.

6. *Texas: A Guide to the Lone Star State* (New York: Hastings House, 1940), hereafter referred to as *Texas*. This travel guide was one of the first compendiums of its type about Texas, with several printings after 1940.

7. Perales, *Are We Good Neighbors?*

8. Perales testified on behalf of Senate Bill S101, which would have established a permanent Fair Employment Practice Commission. Perales was Chairman, Committee of One Hundred, and Director General, League of Loyal Americans, San Antonio, Texas. See ibid., 114–133.

9. Ibid., 130–131.

10. Ibid., 121, 123, 139–213, esp. 156.

11. *Texas*, 604.

12. Ibid.

13. Ibid., 610.

14. Perales, *Are We Good Neighbors?* 222.

15. *Texas*, 610.

16. Ibid., 611.

17. Ibid., 612.

18. Ibid.

19. Ibid., 475.

20. For a well-documented history, see Arnoldo De León, *San Angeleños: Mexican Americans in San Angelo, Texas* (San Angelo: Fort Concho Museum Press, 1985).

21. See Montejano, *Anglos and Mexicans*, 192; Perales, *Are We Good Neighbors?* 290.

22. *Texas*, 475.

23. Ibid., 474.

24. De León, *San Angeleños*, 51–54, 58.

25. "Writer Says Latin Americans in This City Discrimination Victims," *San Angelo Standard-Times*, July 27, 1945, 2.

26. See Perales, *Are We Good Neighbors?* 170, 179, 202, 209.

27. See discussion in De León, *San Angeleños*, 70–71.

28. *San Angelo Standard-Times*, July–October 1945; also De León, *San Angeleños*, 72–73.

29. "Ex-Soldier Still Unconscious Week after Assault; None of Assailants Apprehended," *San Angelo Standard-Times*, September 9, 1945, 1, 22; "Latin War Vet Beaten by Gang," *San Angelo Evening Standard*, September 9, 1945, 1.

30. "Seven Boys Put on Probation by County Judge," *San Angelo Standard-Times*, September 20, 1945, 1, 16.

31. "Ex-Soldier Still Unconscious," *San Angelo Standard-Times*, September 9, 1945.

32. "11 Youth Identified in Aguirre Attack," *San Angelo Standard-Times*, September 11, 1945, 1, 2.

33. "11 Youth Identified," *San Angelo Standard-Times*, September 11, 1945; "Four Post Bond on Assault Case against Aguirre," *San Angelo Standard-Times*, September 12, 1945, 1, 13; "Ministers Deplore Aguirre Attack; Two Suspects Held," *San Angelo Evening Standard*, September 10, 1945, 1. As an indication of the racial climate of the time, a "Latin-American youth" was charged with carrying a deadly weapon and taken to the Gatesville School for Boys. The county probation officer said that the sixteen-year-old carried a long knife on his person and had intimidated children of the San Angelo Junior High School. The boy declared that he wasn't looking for trouble but was ready to accommodate any "white boy" who wanted it. "16-Year-Old Boy to Gatesville Today," *San Angelo Standard-Times*, October 11, 1945, 1.

34. Calculating from the reported listings, the average contribution was about $2.50. This would suggest that close to two hundred people contributed to the Aguirre hospital fund. See "11 Youth Identified," *San Angelo Standard-Times*, September 11, 1945; "Four Post Bond," *San Angelo Standard-Times*, September 12, 1945; "Seven Boys Put on Probation by County Judge," *San Angelo Standard-Times*, September 20, 1945, 1, 16.

35. The editorial added:

This isn't the first time that these gangster tactics have been adopted by San Angelo hoodlums. In fact, there is reason to believe that yet a fourth Latin-American was injured by another group of "white boys," or the same group, in another part of South Angelo at about the same hour of the night of Sept. 1. There were several previous cases, which weren't so well-reported.

See "It Happens in San Angelo," *San Angelo Evening Standard*, September 10, 1945, 4.

36. "11 Youth Identified," *San Angelo Standard-Times*, September 11, 1945; "Resolution by Legion Assails Aguirre Attack," *San Angelo Standard-Times*, September 11, 1945, 2.

37. "Ex-Soldier Still Unconscious," *San Angelo Standard-Times*, September 9, 1945.

38. "7 Juveniles to be Arraigned in Aguirre Attack," *San Angelo Standard-Times*, September 13, 1; "12th Youth Charged in Aguirre Beating Posts Bond Friday," *San Angelo Standard-Times*, September 15, 22.

39. "Seven Boys Put on Probation," *San Angelo Standard-Times*, September 20, 1945, 1, 16.

40. Ibid.

41. The *Standard-Times* interviewed George Beaty and uncovered a pattern similar to that of the Aguirre case: Anglo boys cruising through the Mexican neighborhood until "provoked" by Mexican boys. The difference in this instance was that "maybe three carloads" of Latin American youth showed up unexpectedly, outnumbering Beaty and his companions. "Standard Is Charged with Skipping Attack on Beaty," *San Angelo Standard-Times*, September 21, 1945.

42. "Aguirre Rallies; Five Make Bail in Assault Case," *San Angelo Evening Standard*, September 12, 1945, 1, 13.

43. "Finis Written in Attack Case; Hunter Fined," *San Angelo Evening Standard*, circa October–November 1945. Ben Aguirre's collection of newspaper articles had no dates, and I have not been able to locate this particular article.

44. Letter from Aurora García to Arnoldo De León, May 2, 1984.

45. Interview with Benigno Aguirre, July 15, 1995. Mr. Aguirre spoke mainly in Spanish. The English translations are mine.

46. Aguirre was also upset with the description of the incident given by Arnoldo De León in his history of San Angelo. See De León, *San Angeleños*, 72–73.

47. Aurora García (Jáquez) moved with her husband to Dallas in 1946. In a 1984 letter to Arnoldo De León, Mrs. García recalled:

During my involvement in the years 1945–46 I was just 23 years old and I was lacking in maturity, in the know-how of what channels one must go through to try to get things done. I was unhappy to see the deplorable conditions under which we lived in our barrio, but the main motivating force that really made me decide to do something was anger and sadness at the atrocious crime committed against one of my race. Fortunately, I think that after the war conditions turned for the better. Our ex-soldier population and their families had learned to be more tolerant to the different cultures, to realize that we can and must co-exist.

Letter from Aurora García to Arnoldo De León, May 2, 1984.

48. The findings were published in Harry Estill Moore, *Tornadoes over Texas: A Study of Waco and San Angelo in Disaster* (Austin: University of Texas Press, 1958).

49. Ibid., vii.

50. Ibid., 27.

51. Ibid., 25, 90, 91, 92.

52. Ibid., 265.

53. According to Holtzman, the research director for the Hogg Foundation,

Of all the natural calamities confronting man, the tornado is most like the man-made disaster of bombing civilian populations. The lack of forewarning, the complete helplessness of a community when disaster strikes and the wake of desolation and destruction which follow, the sudden, explosive fury of winds, and the brief duration of onslaught so characteristic of a tornado are also characteristic of bombing in war.

Ibid., viii–ix.

54. Ibid., 256.

55. Ibid., 257.

56. Almost half (47 percent) ventured no explanation. Of those who answered, 16 percent divided their responses between "atom bombs," "fatalistic acceptance," and "in pathway of storms," another 16 percent said it was due to "natural causes," and 21 percent said that it was the "Lord's will or punishment." Ibid., 219–220.

57. There was no apparent connection between Japan's surrender and the adventure of the "white boys" on the weekend of September 12. The Mexican community, of course, was well aware of the irony of fighting for democracy abroad and at home.

CHAPTER 3

On the West Side

A Portrait of Lanier High School during World War II

JULIO NOBOA

The Second World War's effect on American schooling was felt throughout urban public schools in a variety of ways. Myriad responses from educational leaders, the federal government, and local districts exerted influences on a wide range of educational aspects, from the curriculum itself to extracurricular activities. These included specialized courses or changes in content as well as patriotic assemblies and drives to collect scrap materials for the war effort.

Not long after the official declaration of war on December 8, 1941, the Office of Education established a Wartime Commission to promote war-related activities at all educational levels. Leading educators and national organizations joined in, exhorting public schools to promote democratic values and freedoms.[1]

School administrators responded to the war in various ways, according to the district's own local conditions and attitudes. New programs were created and existing ones were expanded; some districts emphasized math and science, while others stressed more immediate practical skills such as food preparation, clothing design, conservation, or nutrition.

There was also an increased interest in providing vocational education, and, to a lesser extent, social studies and foreign languages. New courses were added, such as aeronautics, and war-related content permeated all subject areas. This was especially evident in the larger urban school districts. Children in New York City, for example, were learning how to spell words like *torpedo* and *bombardier*.[2]

On the predominantly Mexican American West Side of San Antonio, Sidney Lanier High School was profoundly transformed. During the war years, Lanier transcended social constraints, including low expectations of its student body, and fostered a patriotism that would lead to 550 of its young men serving in the military, scrap-metal drives that collected 123,000 pounds, a vigorous ROTC program, and a deep pride in its contributions.

This essay provides a general portrait of Lanier during the World War II years. It places Lanier within the low-income barrio of West San Antonio, considering in particular one of its most important landmarks, the first successful housing project. It also examines how the school's curriculum responded to the climate and socioeconomic conditions of the school's community during that time. Lanier High School, predominantly Mexican American, offers a particularly interesting vantage point, as it illustrates how World War II's effect was not limited to the schooling of these young Mexican American students. They also made significant contributions to the war effort, both in manpower and in terms of their home-front support.

Covering the years from about 1941 through 1945, the components of this historical portrait were drawn from several sources: school records, literature about the topic, and oral history interviews with men and women who were Lanier students during the World War II era. Areas considered were clubs and extracurricular activities as well as routines, norms, and other practices and policies that created the overall school climate. This chapter also explores how vocational education came to be viewed as a natural fit for Lanier High School students. Information on the Lanier High School curriculum was also compared to that of two other high schools in the San Antonio Independent School District. Examined together, these themes will also provide a context for understanding how the curriculum fits into Lanier's cultural climate and socioeconomic status.

The West Side of San Antonio has been a traditional Mexican barrio and home to many recent arrivals from Mexico for many decades. Near Lanier High School is the historically preserved and currently flourishing Guadalupe Theater and Center. Also nearby is the first and oldest public housing community in the nation, the Alazan/Apache Courts, built during the New Deal era of President Roosevelt.

The impact of the Depression on students and their families was painfully felt before and during the World War II years on the West Side.

Rita Gomez explained how Depression-era conditions forced her to drop out of Lanier in the ninth grade to work and help feed her family:

> I was the oldest in the family . . . [there was an] economic war to feed one's family . . . there were no school lunches provided . . . those years were a struggle . . . I was fourteen when I left school, [so] didn't graduate, but later received my G.E.D.[3]

However, Gomez also recalled that the "war brought things and money" to the barrio. She and the other interviewees agreed that, despite the poverty and deprivation, there was a strong sense of community among the residents of the West Side:

> One great thing about the neighborhood is that there were faces you knew. . . . You could talk to your neighbor. . . . We didn't have privacy fences. . . . You knew the people on the block.[4]

The local Catholic church, Our Lady of Guadalupe, and in particular the head priest there during that era, Father Carmelo Tranchese, played a major role in establishing a sense of community among the residents. Again, Gomez:

> I recall as a child, I would go barefoot down the street to a *cantina* [bar], *botica* [pharmacy], *tiendita* [small store] and look inside and always see the Lady of Guadalupe with lights. . . . [It represented] the spirit the church brought to this community. . . . Father Tranchese gave life to the community, he livened it up, gave it hope.[5]

Father Tranchese was remembered very fondly by the interviewees with a mixture of admiration and nostalgia for his contributions and achievements on behalf of his parishioners. Pablo Martinez recalls that "Father Tranchese spoke and wrote in six languages and played the flute."[6]

Rendon de Rosales described the elaborate parade Tranchese would organize for December 12, the feast day of the Virgin of Guadalupe. And on a more regular basis, "On Sunday morning, he would have one mass strictly for children, [and even] hired a music instructor for the kids. He was here for twenty years and passed away in New Orleans."[7]

But before his departure, the priest left behind perhaps his greatest historical legacy: it was through his advocacy and personal sacrifice that the first public housing in the United States was built on the West Side of San Antonio. Erected during the Roosevelt administration, the Alazan/Apache Courts owed their very existence to Father Tranchese's tenacity and skill.[8]

There were numerous legal, political, and economic obstacles that arose to block the building of this first public housing project in our nation; even the U.S. Supreme Court had intervened at one time to declare such projects unconstitutional. When all seemed lost, Father Tranchese picked up his pen and wrote what a *Saturday Evening Post* article calls "the magic letter" that began with the words "My dear Mrs. Roosevelt . . ."

The letter was ultimately effective in securing the housing project.

Several interviewees said living at the Alazan/Apache Courts significantly improved their living conditions. Hernandez told us her family was

> on the list to live in the courts. [We had been] used to living in shacks. . . . [The courts] were brand new. . . . Living in the projects to us were the best conditions we ever had. . . . We had individual rooms, running water . . . [definitely] a step up.[9]

Rendon de Rosales also recalled that

> the courts were a beautiful area, [with] flowers and fruit

trees. . . . [We] took a lot of pride. . . . All six kids worked in the yard on Saturdays.[10]

Before the war, Eleanor Roosevelt had visited the West Side.

Martinez confessed that at first, "I had no idea she was the wife of the president." But he was convinced that when it came to the building of the Alazan/Apache Courts, "Father Tranchese as a personal friend of Eleanor Roosevelt definitely was an influence."[11]

Later, the priest sent a letter of thanks and a poem to the president himself. According to Maury Maverick, who had served as mayor of San Antonio, tears welled up in President Roosevelt's eyes as he read the letter and poem, and later he remarked to Maverick: "To think of the things I try to do for people . . . things they seldom appreciate and often hate me for. Yet this little priest makes me know what gratitude really is."[12]

From a broader perspective, beyond the Guadalupe church, and the Alazan/Apache Courts, the city of San Antonio provided a socioeconomic and cultural context which affected deeply the character and development of the West Side during this historical era. San Antonio was a central place for the fusion of Texan, Mexican, and Southwestern cultures. It was also recognized as an industrial and urban center.[13]

Yet despite the belief among San Antonio's Anglo city leaders that the Mexican West Side had to be fully integrated in order to push the city toward modernization, life in the "Latin Quarter" of San Antonio remained much the same throughout the Depression. Some viewed the West Side as "one of the most extensive slum areas anywhere in the world."[14]

Garcia describes conditions that existed on the West Side, where the majority of San Antonio Mexicans were living by 1930:

The Latin Quarter . . . was characterized by poverty, dilapidated housing, and almost no sanitary facilities. Within this slum area . . . there was a cycle of sickness, unemployment, poor living conditions, poor diet, poor education, and poor health. On the whole, the Mexicans were handicapped by menial jobs, burdened by myths and superstitions, weakened by malnutrition, and confronted with a daily struggle for survival in crowded, run-down housing and unsanitary conditions.[15]

In addition to clergy, elected officials, and other influential personalities, there were several generations of educators who also helped ameliorate the poverty of the West Side and the hopeless despair that often accompanied it. These administrators attempted a response to the difficulties plaguing the West Side through the resources of the public educational system. The following section will examine some of the structural and institutional transformations which occurred in the San Antonio Independent School District, which eventually gave rise to Lanier Senior High School.

It was in 1923 that the superintendent of the San Antonio Independent School District (SAISD), Jeremiah Rhodes, decided to provide young adolescents a school and curricula specific to their age group. Thus SAISD established the first junior high school system in the nation. The eight schools were all named after American authors: Emerson, Harris, Hawthorne, Irving, Lanier, Page, Poe, and Twain.[16]

Sidney Lanier Junior High had the further distinction of being the first vocational junior high school of its kind in the nation. In keeping with the educational philosophy of the day, and in response to the peculiar conditions of low-income Mexican American students, the school's two main objectives were to teach English proficiency and provide students with preparation in a trade or skill. Along with preparing them for earning a livelihood, there were also attempts to inculcate in students a strong sense of civic responsibility.

By 1929 Lanier had become a six-year combined junior/senior high school and its program was expanded to include the minimal requirements for college entrance. The number of Lanier graduates who went on to successful careers in the skilled trades, business, and community service grew, and gradually more also went on to college and into the professions.[17]

Being part of a Mexican American community which has for generations maintained its ethnic and cultural character, Lanier High School shared many of the issues and problems confronting Mexican American schools and students throughout the Southwest. The more salient of these difficulties will be outlined in the following section.

From the turn of the century and into the late 1930s American education enjoyed its "Progressive Era," during which a new educational philosophy flourished. This new concept advocated a more "child-centered" curriculum and instruction. Best articulated by John Dewey, the progressivist position rejected the rigid curriculum uniformity, passive learning, and reliance on rote memorization that characterized public education then. Learning, in their view, should foster social, cultural, and intellectual meaning for the students.

Progressivism, however, was developing at a time when such practices as testing, tracking, Americanization, bureaucratization, and vocational education were becoming entrenched as permanent features of the American public education system. Researchers have concluded that despite its lofty goals, the progressive movement was more a statement of faith than an applied reality since it lacked grassroots support. Issues of race and ethnicity were barely considered by progressivists. They also avoided any systemic critiques of the inequalities within the economic order, let alone of the role American schools played in perpetuating these.[18]

Nevertheless, progressivism sought to construct an improved society, which included providing help to poor immigrants and ensuring that schools assimilated them into the American way of life. Americanization efforts were common in most urban public schools, especially in response to the massive wave of new immigrants coming from Southern and Eastern Europe. Mexican Americans were also schooled with Americanization in mind; but there were other conditions and responses that distinguished their Americanization process, as well as their education, from that provided to European immigrants.

The process of Americanizing Mexican American students was affected by special conditions, including the segregation of Mexican American students and the emphasis placed on vocational education. The influence of these and other aspects, combined with negative Anglo attitudes toward the Mexican American culture and community, created formidable obstacles to providing adequate, let alone equal, educational opportunities for Mexican American students.

Throughout the Southwest and in San Antonio, most Mexican American students were segregated into separate schools or classrooms. Unlike that of African American students, however, segregation was not based solely on race, but also on even more complex factors of ethnicity, culture, and language.

Several methods, reasons, and justifications were employed by school districts to establish and maintain segregation between Mexican American and Anglo students. Among the reasons given: American (Anglo) parents opposed sending their children to schools with Mexican children. Some even pressured school officials to gerrymander boundaries to prevent it.[19]

During the 1930s, the Texas Department of Education rationalized its support for segregating non-English-speaking children in the earlier grades by citing a need for specially trained teachers and specialized resources. Nevertheless, even Texas officials who supported segregation on pedagogical grounds also recognized that too many educators were isolating Mexican children in order to give them "a shorter school year, inferior buildings and equipment, and poorly paid teachers."[20]

Educators often pledged to integrate Mexican American children in their later grades after they became Americanized and learned sufficient English. But those pledges were not usually honored. Many English-speaking Mexican American students were still attending segregated schools in higher grades.[21] This was true not only in Texas, but also in other Southwestern regions, such as Southern California, where a significant number of schools had enrollments of between 90 and 100 percent Mexican American students.[22] Up to 85 percent of Mexican American children in the Southwest were attending either separate classrooms or entirely different schools by the 1930s.[23]

A further justification for segregation was based on negative assessments of the hygiene, temperament, morality, and virtues of the Mexican student, family, and community. One researcher claimed that Mexicans had different standards of morality, justice, honesty, and cleanliness from those of the average American family. He assumed that given the "Mexican temperament, the high percentage of juvenile arrests among Mexicans, and the nature of offenses committed, and their low moral standards, it would be advisable to segregate the Mexican and American children in the school."[24]

These negative attitudes toward Mexican Americans prevailed in the prewar years. In combination with the use of psychometric tests, which consistently demonstrated lower scores (thus, lower "intelligence") among Mexican students, these attitudes not only maintained a rationale for segregation but may also have determined the instructional process used to Americanize and educate Mexican students.

Gilbert G. Gonzalez affirms that Americanization was the prime objective in the education of Mexican children during the era of segregation. Schooling administrations and practices were reorganized by authorities to establish special programs and Americanization classes whenever the population of Mexican students increased to significant numbers.[25]

"The desired effect," Gonzalez writes, was not only the "political socialization and acculturation of the Mexican community," but also, "more than anything else, Americanization tended to preserve the political and economic subordination of the Mexican community."[26]

Underlying Americanization programs was the firm belief in the superiority of Anglo American culture to Mexican culture. Thus not only would cultural and linguistic differences be eliminated, but also an entire culture deemed undesirable, and ultimately un-American. Yet there was some significant variation among programs. Some programs, based on popular and academic literature, reinforced the negative stereotypes of Mexicans. Other programs took more of a patronizing than a negative approach and urged teachers to gain more knowledge about the characteristics of Mexican children to provide them with more effective instruction.

In larger districts with very large Mexican enrollment, such as those in Los Angeles and San Antonio, administrators organized courses for teachers so they could understand the objectives and learn the methods for the effective Americanization of Mexican students. Eventually some smaller districts started doing the same.[27]

At the core of pedagogical practice in responding to the special needs of Mexican children was the issue of language. Gonzalez states: "The essence of Americanization programs across the Southwest was language instruction. In fact, most of the literature on the education of Mexican children focused on language." A connection was made between the retention of Mexican culture and the use of Spanish as having a detrimental educational effect on bilingual children. Spanish use was considered a "bad habit" which together with

Mexican "customs . . . and attitudes retarded learning; therefore, assimilation could not be realized until Spanish was eliminated."[28]

Thus, schools developed an entire repertoire of ways to discourage or even forbid the speaking of Spanish by Mexican students. Policies varied: in some schools English was the official language of instruction and communication, but Spanish was permitted for translation or for the definition of words. Some teachers required students to ask for permission only in English if they wanted to leave the school grounds at noon.

The Mexican schools in Harlingen, Texas, instituted an English Club composed of students who had not spoken Spanish in the previous six weeks. Only club members could participate in picnics and other club activities held regularly. Those who had spoken Spanish were required to remain in the room and study. "Indeed, in the schooling atmosphere based upon the forcible elimination of one language by another, school authorities organized the system of rewards and punishments accordingly."[29]

As a curricular activity, Americanization was a formal practice until the late 1930s, close to the beginning of World War II. Yet even during the 1940s and beyond, the underlying message to most Mexican children and youth was that their language and culture were obstacles to success. Ironically, the coming of the Second World War and the Good Neighbor Policy would generate interest in learning Spanish and in things Latin American.

The United States government had already begun to prepare for war by, among other things, seeking closer unity with other countries, especially those of strategic geopolitical interest such as in Latin America. "The bombing of Pearl Harbor on December 7, 1941, left no doubts that America would now join the fight against dictatorship and totalitarianism. With America's entry into the Second World War, efforts to promote hemispheric defense measures and greater cultural and economic cooperation between the Americas were accelerated."[30]

The Office of the Coordinator for Inter-American Affairs was established by the federal government in 1940 to consolidate hemispheric cooperation, promote economic relations, encourage cultural exchanges, and inform citizens. Two central aspects of this "Good Neighbor Policy" campaign were to educate Latin Americans about

U.S. ideals, peoples, and democratic principles and to inform Americans about the languages, heritage, and history of Latin America.

But in contradiction to official policy, the home front was everything but neighborly. Guadalupe San Miguel contrasts this stated policy with the realities of interethnic relations on the home front:

> All institutions, including public schools, were to play an important part in disseminating this information and in developing the appropriate attitudes for understanding the peoples and cultures of Latin America. But from the start efforts to promote unity between the Americas were undermined by reports of widespread discrimination against Spanish-speaking people in the United States—of Mexicans refused service in public places, segregated in the schools, and denied their civil rights.[31]

The most violent expressions of this anti-Mexican sentiment occurred in California, where the Good Neighbor Policy was challenged in 1943 with the Zoot Suit Riots. During the disturbances, Anglo sailors beat Mexican zoot-suiters on Los Angeles streets, while law enforcement agencies looked the other way, or even arrested the zoot-suiters. The news media all but promoted the violence.[32]

Despite the problems in California, it was in Texas that the mistreatment of and discrimination against Mexicans, both citizens and noncitizens, were most intense. For example, an employee of the Mexican consulate in Austin was denied his son's baptism in a church because of his Mexican origin, while a municipal council ex-president was denied service in restaurants displaying signs reading "No Mexicans Allowed." The acts of discrimination became so intense that the Mexican government placed a ban on the importation of agricultural workers much needed by Texas farmers because of the wartime labor shortage.[33]

Finally on June 25, 1943, Texas governor Coke Stevenson issued an executive proclamation declaring that the "Good Neighbor Policy is the Public Policy of Texas." In part it stated that Texas was to give "full and equal accommodations, advantages, and privileges of all public places of business or amusement to Mexicans and other Latin Americans residing or visiting in the state."[34]

Public education was impacted in several ways by the Good Neighbor Policy. For the first time in Texas, there was official and systemic recognition and involvement of Mexican American teachers, educators, and scholars in the development of materials appropriate for students in their communities. Materials were collected in four bulletins developed for elementary, junior high, and high school teachers using the inter-American approach to understanding Spanish-speaking groups in the United States.[35]

Of the two guides developed for high schools, one was for English and social studies, providing facts on Mexico and other Latin American nations, suggesting projects, and recommending reading lists. The other provided suggestions on teaching Spanish at the high school level.

Among the educational influences and spillover effects of the new inter-American education movement was the convening of Southwestern conferences, sponsored by the Office of the Coordinator for Inter-American Affairs, where among other positive developments, there was a redefinition of the "Mexican problem" in the public schools. George I. Sanchez, H. T. Manuel, and other scholars and educators participated in these and other activities.

This new redefinition, especially as promoted by Sanchez, stipulated first of all that Spanish speakers were not a homogeneous but rather a diverse group in terms of rural versus urban, settled versus migratory, and living in barrios versus integrated neighborhoods. It was further established that general teaching principles should be applied to Spanish-speaking students as well. Educators proposed that, in addition to learning English, students should receive instruction in their native language. Some even argued that the need for Spanish-language instruction was greater for Spanish-speaking students, who could derive both affective and academic benefit from being truly bilingual.[36]

With the war's end came the demise of the inter-American education movement. Still, the contributions of Mexican American educators and scholars, together with those of Anglos, did have a positive impact and proved that viable options did exist to counter prevailing assumptions about how best to educate Mexican American students.

One of those assumptions had much to do with the perceived

potential or capacity of Mexican students for academic and occupational achievement. Vocational education was thought to be the best approach for making useful and employable American citizens of these disadvantaged students.

The debate about vocational education had begun early in the century. Eminent educators and leaders such as John Dewey and W. E. B. Du Bois got involved, often casting doubts on the value, efficacy, and democracy of vocational education for high school–aged youth. But there were larger, more powerful social and political forces at work that ensured the establishment of vocational education as a permanent fixture of many American high schools.

Educational historian Herbert M. Kliebard asserts:

> To be sure, the particular course that vocational education in fact followed was influenced by social conditions existing at the time that the drive was at its height. . . . [However,] vocational education did not emerge as a supremely successful curricular innovation because social changes made it so. It succeeded because certain ways of interpreting social change made the infusion of vocational education into the public school curriculum the most plausible and politically expedient, although not necessarily the most efficacious, response to those perceived changes.[37]

The evolution of the American high school from an elite, selective institution to one that opened doors of opportunity for immigrants and working-class students has been well documented by educational historians. In this context vocational education in high schools was seen by many as a win-win situation in which labor market needs were met and the previously disadvantaged could develop skills to at least survive, if not succeed, in that market.

However, in addition to making high schools more comprehensive and accessible to a wider diversity of students, vocational education also channeled students into predetermined educational tracks that simply reproduced the inequities of the class structure. A dual system of education developed which gave minority and working-class youth those skills required for lower levels of the labor market, while providing middle-class youth with a more academic, college-preparatory education.

Although a variety of measures or "specific tests" were created and used to sort students into vocational tracks, other sorting devices included not only teachers' judgments and students' behavior and grades, but also students' social and ethnic backgrounds.[38]

How the Above Factors Influenced Life and Learning at Lanier

Given the socioeconomic conditions and ethnic identity of the Lanier student population and their surrounding community, it is valid to assume that, to a greater or lesser extent, Lanier High School was affected by all of the factors and influences which relate to Mexican schools at the time of World War II.

In terms of segregation, in SAISD, as throughout most of the Southwest during this time period, Mexican American students were considered "white," as opposed to "colored"—that is, African American students, who, by law, attended separate schools. Notwithstanding their racial classification as "white," Mexican students in Lanier were attending an effectively segregated high school with an overwhelming predominance of their own ethnic group. Nevertheless SAISD contained not only a white Anglo high school, the very prestigious Jefferson High School, but also schools such as Brackenridge and Burbank, which had a mixed Anglo and Mexican population.

During the World War II years, there were six high schools altogether in SAISD, which varied in size, racial composition, and curricular emphasis. Just before the war, enrollment figures for the 1938–1939 school year showed that the two largest were Jefferson and Brackenridge, with 2,479 and 2,196 students respectively. Both schools had a college-prep orientation, with Jefferson being the elite, flagship school in the district. San Antonio Technical, which later became Fox Tech, was a vocational magnet school with 1,416 students that year.

The fully segregated "colored" high school, Wheatley, with 591 students, was vocationally oriented. Following next by size were Lanier, 318 students, with a strong vocational education program, and Burbank, 241, an ethnically mixed school with a significant proportion of Mexican students.[39]

In addition to the conditions of segregation and vocational emphasis, Lanier High School also was affected by lingering vestiges of the Americanization movement. Ex-senator Joe Bernal, a student at Lanier during World War II, recalled how there were monitors in the halls to ensure that nobody spoke Spanish, even outside of the classroom. As a good student, Bernal himself was also honored with the task of being a monitor for a time. He recognized later the irony of these policies, and decades later, as a state senator, championed the cause of bilingual education in Texas.[40]

Hernandez recalls that "we were not allowed to speak Spanish in the hallways; school monitors reported us."[41]

Nevertheless, Spanish was the vernacular language of the West Side, one of the West Side's distinguishing characteristics. According to Martinez, "Everyone spoke Spanish. Zarzamora Street was the dividing line; on the other side of Guadalupe [Street] there were Germans, Polish, and Belgians [who] never mingled."[42]

Despite widespread negative attitudes toward the use of Spanish (outside the Spanish-language classroom), and despite the misunderstanding, if not the outright denigration, of Mexican cultural values and traditions, the teachers and administrators at Lanier did attempt to integrate elements of Mexican culture and language into certain aspects of school life.

The extent to which this was influenced by the wartime inter-American education movement is difficult to ascertain; however, in apparent contradiction to its no-Spanish-in-the-halls policy, the Lanier High School yearbook was called *Los Recuerdos*, Spanish for "The Memories." The first Lanier "Senior Year Book" was published in 1939 with no special name, but by the subsequent year and throughout World War II and beyond, *Los Recuerdos* was the name that appeared on the nameplate of each yearbook. On the last page of each yearbook and set in small print at the lower right-hand corner was the statement, "This issue of *Los Recuerdos* was set and printed in the Lanier School Print Shop."[43]

Also published by the students at Lanier Print Shop was the school newspaper, *El Nopal* ("The Cactus"), which was first issued in the spring of 1924 and continued to grow in size and scope. By 1940 *El Nopal* was described thus in the yearbook:

Among the many different articles featured by *El Nopal*
today are campus news, school activities, contests for the students and above all its support of the school teams by urging
students to attend games. The main purpose for the publication of *El Nopal* is to bring about a closer relationship
between the school and the home.[44]

As I do not have available a copy of this paper for this time period, it
is unclear whether that "closer relationship" included printing some
stories or information in Spanish, the home language for many students and parents. Some parents were English-proficient readers, but
perhaps not a significant number.

Mexican and Latin American cultural influences were also evident
in other group activities and clubs. There was the singing group
called *Los Trovadores* ("The Troubadours"), which was originated
at the suggestion of the principal, R. H. Brewer, in 1935. Talented
boys able to play stringed instruments and sing were recruited. Ralph
Cardenas, a community musician, taught and rehearsed Mexican
folk songs with them. The group appeared at local civic clubs and
school activities and created a demand for this type of entertainment.
The *Trovadores* eventually generated enough interest that other such
groups were formed, culminating in a Mexican chorus of nearly one
hundred mixed voices.

The young women had a dancing group called *Las Mejicanitas* (a
diminutive term for "Mexican women"), organized by Rosa Cardenas in 1933. The group's purpose was to "present the colorful, typical and original folk dances of the Mexican people." They traveled
throughout south central Texas performing before civic clubs, school
festivals, and out-of-town conventions, representing Lanier.

Three of the four interviewees mentioned the *Trovadores* or the
Mejicanitas by name. Hernandez asserts that the *Mejicanitas* group
"[were] like today's *folklórico*. They danced at downtown fiestas . . .
[and] performed on stage in the school auditorium and community
functions."[45]

Of all the yearbooks from 1939 through 1946, one was especially
designed with a Mexican motif throughout. *Los Recuerdos* of 1942,
with Art Deco–inspired lettering and design, was filled with a series
of drawings by "Segovia," perhaps a student at Lanier. Images of

palm trees, cacti, burros, Southwestern landscapes, and characters with *sarapes* and huge sombreros decorated key and transitional pages of the yearbook. But beyond the visuals was this dedication, which expressed an unmistakable tone of hemispheric unity in a time of war:

> To youth—the youth of the Americas—we dedicate this volume of *Los Recuerdos*. From the icy borders of the Dominion of Canada on the north to the tip of Argentina on the south, we see the youth of today—courageous in heart, sturdy in body, undaunted in spirit—bearing the torch of liberty in a common interest against a common foe that threatens our democratic way of life.[46]

Beyond the opposing tendencies between Americanization and traditional Mexican influences, there was another, more urban, contemporary lifestyle choice. Those were the pachucos, who were not confined to the barrios of Los Angeles. With their own hybrid style of dress, lingo, and dance music, pachucos were a bicultural combination of hip, urban Americana with barrio culture.

Hernandez noted the difference in dress:

> [Most] girls dressed like ladies, skirts were below the knees, [they] wore socks all the time . . . [but] the pachucas dressed differently. Pachucas weren't bad people . . . pachucos used a jar of Vaseline in their hair.[47]

Martinez provided a more detailed description:

> Pachucos . . . their drapes (pants) were tapered at the bottom, long chain, pointed shoes, long coats and hats. . . . Pachucos talked a different way called *calo*, [and] danced on Saturday nights to Glenn Miller and other big band music.[48]

Notwithstanding these influences, the vast majority of the clubs, activities, and events at Lanier, such as sports, orchestra, band, chorus, glee club, Girl Scouts, and student council, were firmly grounded in the traditions of mainstream American culture.

All of these factors, inter-American education, segregation, and Americanization, combined with the special circumstances associated with World War II, created a cultural climate at Lanier Senior unique to that school. Yet at the core of this setting was the course work which Lanier students took, their reason for being there. The following section will look at the available information on just what kind of curriculum was provided to Lanier students during these years.

During, before, and after the Second World War years, every school in SAISD, including the high schools, submitted an annual report to the Texas State Department of Education. Titled the "Head Teacher or Principal's Term Report," it usually included information on teachers, including their positions, training, certification, experience, and tenure. The information on students included age and grade distribution as well as attendance and overall enrollment.

Senior high school consisted then of three grades, ninth through eleventh, with some school buildings, like Lanier, also housing a junior high school, which filed a separate report.

All the above information is available for several decades in the volumes at the district archives; however, specific information on the curriculum is limited. In fact, Term Reports for several years before, after, and during World War II contain no consistent information on curriculum at all—except for the Term Report for the school year 1938–1939.

Only the reports for this year, at least at the high school level, included a chart called "Special Distribution of Pupils as to Subjects of Instruction." Looking at this chart for three high schools, Lanier, Jefferson, and Brackenridge, the following information can be derived:

Students at all three high schools took English (three years), world history, American history, algebra (two years), plane geometry, bookkeeping, business arithmetic, biology, chemistry, Spanish (two years), home economics, and clothing.

More interesting to note are the courses students took at Jefferson and Brackenridge which were not offered at Lanier. These courses were Texas history, solid geometry, German, Latin, commercial geography, physiology, physics, and public safety. In addition, the more privileged students at Jefferson even had French available to them.

There were several courses, however, offered at Lanier and not at the other two schools: agriculture, for one, although another high school, Burbank, had an extensive agricultural program, including an eighty-acre farm. Two other courses were offered at Lanier and not at the other two schools—art and public speaking.[49]

The curricular variations in some ways seem justified: art was certainly a natural for Lanier students, whose cultural traditions from Mexico had a strong folk-art component, as well as a history of great painters and muralists of the century. The emphasis on public speaking might have been motivated by the objective of increasing the English proficiency of Lanier students, whose bilingual backgrounds might have been viewed as an obstacle to speaking English well.

Perhaps more significantly, Lanier students did not have access to the higher-level math and science courses, such as solid geometry, physics, and physiology, which could prepare them for college work as well as careers in the rapidly expanding and emerging technologies of this era.

However, the shop courses for Lanier boys prepared them as skilled tradesmen, if not as engineers or scientists. Even the 1938–1939 Term Report evidently does not give us a complete picture of the scope of vocational courses offered at Lanier during the years just before the war.

Nevertheless, some issues of *Los Recuerdos* during these years did document the wide variety of shop classes available, mainly to boys. Among them were the vocational arts and crafts shop, which specialized in the making of jewelry and leather goods. There were shops or classes as well in auto mechanics, body and fender repair, and landscape gardening, as well as an auto paint and trim shop. In addition to a well-equipped print shop, which trained boys for jobs in the publication industry, there was a mill shop, also well equipped, which "prepared future mill workers, cabinet makers and furniture repairmen." For the young women, there was a course in vocational dressmaking that prepared them for that trade.[50]

Although not a complete overview of the curriculum during these years, the above information does confirm that significant curricular differences did exist among high schools in SAISD. Clearly, Lanier's curriculum was more oriented toward preparing skilled tradesmen and -women for the working class. The very abundance of shops and the absence of advanced math and science courses was a marked characteristic of Lanier recognized even decades later by its former students.

All six interviewees commented on the courses offered at Lanier and recognized the limitations of the choices they were given. Gomez asserted, "School did not promote higher education . . . and assumed you were not going to college [nor] were college material. That is why my husband transferred to another school in his senior year." Later she explained, "My husband did not know [about college prep courses], he went to another school to try and get a scholarship . . . counselors did not tell you."[51]

Hernandez agreed. "We were not expected to go to college, teachers did not make any bones about it. They would say there are shop courses and directed the boys to those courses."[52]

World War II was the other great influence on this generation of Lanier students. The following section identifies the war's impact on Lanier.

Influences of World War II on Lanier High School

Judging from the wealth of information contained in *Los Recuerdos*, the impact of World War II was felt in every aspect of Lanier's life and learning. The 1941 yearbook made no mention that war had been declared that year.

The following year, however, *Los Recuerdos* documented a significant shift in attention to wartime matters. In terms of ROTC, there was now a "Crack Squad" armed with rifles as well as a "Drill Platoon" and an ROTC Band.[53] (In 1941, there were four companies of ROTC in the school, all boys, and a group of girls, also in uniform, who served as ROTC sponsors.)[54]

The 1943 yearbook had the following dedication: "To all former Lanier teachers and students in the armed forces of our country who are fighting to keep open the gateway to democracy and freedom."[55]

There was an "In Memoriam" page with the pictures and dates of death of three former Lanier students, each in uniform.[56]

The student council had a new committee, named after General Douglas MacArthur, which led Lanier's participation in the "Schools at War" program. In addition to the sale of war bonds and stamps, the MacArthur committee organized a drive which resulted in salvaging 123,000 pounds of scrap metal. Stamp windows were set up inside the school to facilitate their sale.[57] Lanier's first Victory Day was celebrated in 1943 with a new military organization for the young women, the Junior WAACs.[58]

Martinez remembers very well "the gas rationing and also saving dimes to buy stamps and war bonds. [We] would have big rallies and show you what your stamps and bonds bought. [There was] no bus transportation due to the gas rationing; football players rode in open trucks to games because of this." Later in the interview Martinez noted that "there were newspaper drives, rubber drives . . . the spirit it had, [with] the flag-raising ceremony to remind everyone about the war."[59]

"Gasoline and tires were rationed," recalls Rendon de Rosales. "We could not wear caps and gowns at graduation, and half the boys graduated in December due to going into the military."[60]

According to Edward Calderon, "some of our boys, even at seventeen, enlisted in the military, and we were proud of them."[61] Especially after Pearl Harbor, there was an obvious transformation of the school climate which compelled students to join or eagerly serve when called to duty. Calderon clearly recalls walking down Commerce Street near the Majestic Theater on a Sunday, with a school friend who later enlisted. Suddenly, they heard the news about Pearl Harbor on the radio.

> We just stopped . . . we were in shock. We were only fifteen, but it impacted on me personally, as if it had been in my own house. The next Monday morning at Lanier, everybody was transfixed by the horror. We were in mourning. But the older boys, the eighteen-year-olds, in their faces you could see the sadness, the anger, and the wanting to retaliate, it was a mindset. How dare they hurt our boys, our boys in the military? It was very telling on us, very emotional.[62]

There was no doubt in Calderon's mind as to why so many of his classmates were ready to fight, and even make the ultimate sacrifice.

They were angered by the sheer affront of the Pearl Harbor attack, like other Americans, but there was another element, something deeper that had to do with who they were.

> When a Mexican American goes to war, he goes to defend his country . . . [as a Mexican American] you would die for your country—*y siendo méjico-americanos*—which is odd. I was in awe, but then again, I could understand their feeling.[63]

Calderon remembers his own elation when, after graduating and turning eighteen, he got his draft notice to serve in the Navy. While many enlisted, like most other young men, he simply waited for the inevitable draft letter to arrive. His eagerness, however, was eventually turned into disappointment and even shame, when, because of a childhood eye injury, he was rejected for service.

Calderon protested forcefully, pointing out that another soldier, also with a missing eye, and who was moreover married, should stay instead. The officer was adamant, and a dejected Calderon was sent home.

> Well, I really felt bad, because now you were 4-F . . . the stigma of all that. I wasn't good enough . . . but they always let you know that you could serve your country in other ways.[64]

Some of these other ways of serving were an extension of what Calderon and his classmates had already been doing while at Lanier. He remembers the drives and the rationing of critical items and commodities. He bought his share of war bonds, but it wasn't quite the same as serving in battle, as did his cousins and classmates.

Notwithstanding what happened to Calderon after graduation, while he was at Lanier during the war years, many of his fellow students were also supporting the war effort through the electives they chose and the class projects they completed.

In the classes and shops, there were some innovative and interesting developments. Seventy-five boys in the mill shop were making model airplanes for Uncle Sam, including such important and interesting miniatures as the Hurricane, the Mosquito Bomber, and the Flying Fortress. These models were used in civilian defense classes where adults learned how to identify airplanes and distinguish between airborne friends and foes.[65]

An entirely new course in aviation science was added that year as well, providing students with an understanding of how aircraft had affected world affairs. Students also learned about the requirements and qualifications necessary to pursue careers in aeronautics.[66]

The yearbook also listed two pages of names, totaling approximately 250 young men, all Lanier graduates who were serving in the armed forces.[67] Two other pages showed a collage of pictures of Lanierites who were serving all over the globe.[68]

By 1944 the four ROTC companies had grown to six and the number of names of former students and teachers serving in the armed forces had more than doubled to over 550.[69] An aviation-oriented club was also started, called the Air Scouts.[70]

All this extraordinary activity nevertheless came to an end with the cessation of hostilities and the Allied victory.

The 1945 edition of *Los Recuerdos*, as one indicator, had very little that related to the war, with the exception of a memorial page honoring the war dead. By the following year, *Los Recuerdos* was already reflecting a campus life moving back to normalcy; the theme of that 1946 edition was simply "Everlasting Peace."[71]

A war memorial was erected in the front entrance of Lanier High School by the school's PTA in 1948. The "Honor Roll" of forty-four Spanish surnames etched in stone reads thus: "Dedicated to the memory of these former students of Sidney Lanier School who gave their lives in World War II for the peace and freedom of the world." On either side of this memorial is an extension, added many years later, with another thirty names of former students who had served and died in either the Korean or Vietnam wars or in Desert Storm. Also etched into the World War II memorial is this motto: "Ever protect the freedoms for which they fought."

Clearly, there are patriotic values expressed here, and the pride of a community that did its part to support America, even sacrificing the lives of community members, as needed, during times of war and conflict.

The memorial is consistent with the composite portrait of Lanier High School presented above. We may draw certain conclusions. For one thing, it is clear that the war afforded the students of Lanier a unique opportunity to demonstrate their love and loyalty to country. That was shown in the number of young men of Lanier who served in the military and students in ROTC-related activities, as well as other home-front activities.

It is also noted that although challenges abounded for most Mexican American schools at that time, there were still valuable opportunities at Lanier High School for achievement, advancement, and self-expression through academics, the arts, sports, clubs, and other extracurricular activities. Many of these opportunities for personal development also had strong linkages with traditional Mexican culture. Lanier students, in other words, were not deprived of platforms for personal achievement—and, like any other students, they took advantage of those opportunities.

In a related vein, the focus on vocational education did not prevent some Lanier students from going on to college, including Senator Bernal. There was a cadre of leadership developed over the years at Lanier High School which impacted the wider city and state in significant ways. In fact, one of the fascinating aspects of Lanier's history is how it reflects the political, cultural, and economic evolution of San Antonio's Mexican American community.

Later, in the 1960s and 1970s, when there was heightened awareness of civil rights issues, Lanier High School and the West Side community felt a surge of ethnic pride through the Chicano Movement.[72] Still today, they are impacted by the ideals and struggles championed by that movement.

Notes

1. Richard D. Cohen, "Schooling Uncle Sam's Children: Education in the USA, 1941–1945," in *Education and the Second World War: Studies in Schooling and Social Change*, ed. Roy Lowe (London: Falmer Press, 1992), 46–47.

2. Ibid., 48–49.

3. Rita Gomez, interview by the author, tape recording, San Antonio, Texas, May 30, 2001.

4. Ibid.

5. Ibid.

6. Pablo Martinez, interview by author, tape recording, San Antonio, Texas, May 30, 2001. Martinez graduated in 1946; his brother served in the Pacific during World War II.

7. Maria Isabel Rendon de Rosales, interview with author, tape recording, San

Antonio, Texas, May 30, 2001. Rendon de Rosales graduated from Lanier in 1945. Her husband served in the Pacific during World War II in the Army Air Force.

8. George Sessions Perry, "Rumpled Angel of the Slums," *Saturday Evening Post*, August 1948. In the article, Perry wondered, "how might he, an obscure little priest, gain the ear of the vast and harried Government of a mighty nation, one in which, politically, his little brood of poor immigrants amounted to less than a grain of sand?"

9. Olga Hernandez, interview with author, tape recording, San Antonio, Texas, May 30, 2001.

10. Rendon de Rosales interview.

11. Martinez interview.

12. Perry, "Rumpled Angel of the Slums," 43.

13. Richard A. Garcia, *Rise of the Mexican American Middle Class: San Antonio, 1929–1941* (College Station: Texas A&M University Press, 1991), 8.

14. Ibid., 38.

15. Ibid.

16. Paula Allen, "Historic District: Quiz about SAISD Tests Old-School Knowledge," *Images*, a supplement to the *San Antonio Express-News*, January 12, 1997, 12.

17. San Antonio Independent School District, "The Philosophy of Sidney Lanier High School," 1996.

18. Rubén Donato, *The Other Struggle for Equal Schools: Mexican Americans during the Civil Rights Era* (Albany: State University of New York Press, 1997), 11.

19. Annie Reynolds, *The Education of Mexican and Spanish-speaking Children in Five Southwestern States* (Washington, D.C.: U.S. Department of the Interior, GPO, 1933), 9.

20. Ibid.

21. Henry W. Cooke, "The Segregation of Mexican American Children in Southern California," *School and Society* 67 (1948): 417.

22. Charles Carpenter, "A Study of Segregation versus Non-Segregation of Mexican Children" (M.A. thesis, University of Southern California, 1935), 29.

23. Gilbert Gonzalez, "System of Public Education and Its Function within the Chicano Communities" (Ph.D. diss., University of California, Los Angeles, 1974).

24. Carpenter, "A Study of Segregation," 149 and 80.

25. Gilbert G. Gonzalez, *Chicano Education in the Era of Segregation* (Philadelphia: Associated University Presses, 1990), 30.

26. Ibid.

27. Ibid., 36 and 38.

28. Ibid., 41.

29. Ibid., 43.

30. Guadalupe San Miguel, Jr., *Let All of Them Take Heed: Mexican Americans and the Campaign for Educational Equality in Texas, 1910–1981* (Austin: University of Texas Press, 1987), 91.

31. Ibid.

32. Ibid., 92.

33. Cary McWilliams, *North from Mexico: The Spanish-Speaking People of the United States* (New York: Greenwood Press, 1968), 240–244; Pauline Kibbe, *Latin Americans in Texas* (Albuquerque: University of New Mexico Press, 1946), 252–254.

34. San Miguel, *Let All of Them Take Heed*, 93.

35. The Texas Education Agency collected and distributed these materials statewide.

36. San Miguel, *Let All of Them Take Heed*, 100–107.

37. Herbert M. Kliebard, *The Struggle for the American Curriculum: 1893–1958* (New York: Routledge, 1995), 131.

38. Donato, *The Other Struggle*, 19–21.

39. Department of Education, *Head Teacher or Principal's Term Report*, 1938–1939 (Austin: State of Texas, 1939).

40. Joseph Bernal, interviews with author, tape recordings, San Antonio, Texas, June 11, 1997, and September 24, 1997. Bernal also currently serves as a member of the Texas Board of Education.

41. Hernandez interview.

42. Martinez interview.

43. Lanier High School, *Los Recuerdos* (Yearbook) (San Antonio, Texas: Lanier School Print Shop, 1940, 1941, 1942, 1943, 1944, and 1945).

44. Lanier High School, *Los Recuerdos*, 1940.

45. Hernandez interview.

46. Lanier High School, *Los Recuerdos*, 1942. Page numbers were not used in these issues, except for 1941.

47. Hernandez interview.

48. Pablo Martinez interview.

49. Department of Education, *Head Teacher or Principal's Term Report*, 1938–39.

50. Lanier High School, *Los Recuerdos*, 1942.

51. Gomez interview.

52. Hernandez interview.

53. Lanier High School, *Los Recuerdos*, 1942.

54. Lanier High School, *Los Recuerdos*, 1941, 41–42.

55. Lanier High School, *Los Recuerdos*, 1943.

56. Ibid.

57. Lanier High School, *Los Recuerdos*, 1943.

58. Ibid.

59. Martinez interview.

60. Rendon de Rosales interview.

61. Edward Calderon, interview with author, tape recording, San Antonio, Texas, October 17, 2002.

62. Ibid.

63. Ibid.

64. Ibid.

65. Lanier High School, *Los Recuerdos*, 1941.

66. Ibid.

67. Lanier High School, *Los Recuerdos*, 1943.

68. Ibid.

69. Lanier High School, *Los Recuerdos*, 1944.

70. Ibid.

71. Lanier High School, *Los Recuerdos*, 1946.

72. See Doris Wright, "Lanier High Students Get Civic Leaders' Support," *San Antonio Express*, Thursday, April 11, 1968; Doris Wright, "Student Plea Gets Support," *San Antonio News*, Friday, April 12, 1968; and Exhibit No. 15, letter, San Antonio Independent School District, in Hearing before the U.S. Commission on Civil Rights, San Antonio, Texas, December 9–14, 1968.

CHAPTER 4

Lost Momentum

World War II and the Education of Hispanos in New Mexico

LYNNE MARIE GETZ

World War II had the ironic effect of moving Hispanic New Mexicans further into the mainstream than they had ever been before, while at the same time pushing them ever further into obscurity. On the one hand, Spanish-surnamed New Mexican soldiers took their place on the battlefield, fighting valiantly and suffering alongside their Anglo counterparts; the 200th Coast Artillery, made up of a sizable number of New Mexicans, became known for their heroism in the faraway Filipino province of Bataan.

In other war efforts, the U.S. government gratefully relied on New Mexican authorities on the Spanish language and culture to implement the Good Neighbor Policy for hemispheric allies. After the war, an appreciative nation bestowed G.I. Bill benefits on all veterans—including Hispanos—allowing thousands to acquire the education and buy the homes that would land them squarely within the middle class. Thus, the war accelerated the rate of assimilation by New Mexico's Spanish Americans. However, it simultaneously interrupted an educational movement designed to give them greater opportunities while preserving their unique Hispano identity.[1] In fact, some of the wartime programs, like the Good Neighbor Policy, put the Hispano culture in a new light: making Spanish a foreign language, rather than one inherently New Mexican. In that sense, the war unraveled the prewar efforts of champions of Hispano cultural preservation.

The unique educational campaign, begun before the war, would use the schools as vehicles for Hispano cultural preservation. But as New Mexico got caught up in the war mobilization effort in the early '40s, and as a Spanish American middle class rose in New Mexico in the '50s, that campaign came to a virtual halt. World War II, by disrupting careers, distracting attention from reform, luring outsiders to New Mexico, and opening new modern opportunities for Hispanos, changed the educational landscape of New Mexico. Some thirty years later, the work that was initiated in the '30s and dropped in the '40s would be largely forgotten; activists of the '60s would accuse schools of ignoring the very issues that had been cultivated earlier.

This essay explores in greater detail the reasons for the change in educational priorities in New Mexico during the war years and how that loss of momentum affected the postwar period.

The effort to preserve Hispano culture came about in the 1930s, as a number of New Mexican educators turned their attention to the needs of Hispano children, many of whom spoke little or no English and lived in rural areas. In a remarkable flurry of activity, educational leaders at the local, university, and state levels initiated programs to preserve traditional culture, to discover better methods of bilingual teaching, to train native Spanish-speaking teachers, to build new school buildings in rural districts, and to revise the state curriculum.

Hispanos themselves played active leadership roles in these developments. Furthermore, these efforts were undertaken in a positive spirit with a self-conscious recognition of Hispanos as a viable and cherished component of the larger community.

State education officials like George I. Sánchez, university professors like Loyd S. Tireman and James F. Zimmerman, and local teachers and superintendents, like Mary Watson, Jennie Gonzales, and Nina Otero-Warren, all explored methods in bilingual instruction during the 1930s. State superintendents of public instruction—especially Atanasio Montoya, Georgia Lusk, and H. R. Rodgers—endorsed such efforts, creating positions within the state bureaucracy for individuals such as Sánchez to pursue their work, and obtaining funds from the legislature.[2]

School people across New Mexico recognized that Spanish-speaking children needed special curricular adaptations, features not offered in the typical American school program. In 1930, a coalition of university professors, state officials, and local citizens worked together to establish the San José Training School in Albuquerque, under the direction of Tireman, professor of education at the University of New Mexico from 1927 until his death in 1959.[3] Hoping to discover the teaching methods that best suited the needs of Hispano children, San José offered several innovative programs, including bilingual instruction, an intensive reading program, a pre–first grade, and a traditional arts and crafts program.

San José also trained teachers who would work in the rural areas where so many Hispanos lived. The state later institutionalized several features of the San José teacher-training program, including the use of model schools and rural supervisors. The emphasis in much of this work was to encourage native Spanish-speaking teachers to acquire formal training in bilingual methods and to remain in their villages and hometowns to teach Spanish-speaking children.[4] Tireman also worked to build community-based schools such as the experimental program at Nambé. Under principal Mary Watson, the Nambé Community School adapted the curriculum to the needs of the community. Following the San José model, the teachers implemented a program of bilingual instruction in the early grades.[5]

The impact of these programs began to be seen as teachers trained at San José or Nambé acquired teaching positions around the state. In 1932, Jennie Gonzales, who had trained at San José, became the teacher at Cedro, an isolated community in the Cibola National Forest east of Albuquerque, where she introduced bilingual instruction.[6] Gonzales's success at Cedro was recognized by her appointment three years later to the position of state rural-school supervisor. Gonzales's appointment, by State Superintendent of Public Instruction H. R. Rodgers, gave her an opportunity to reach teachers across the state with the ideas she had learned at San José.[7] Other school districts started their own bilingual programs independent of state direction. In 1938, Taos County superintendent Lionides Pacheco and Rural Supervisor Ruth Miller-Martinez initiated a bilingual instruction program in the Taos schools that was endorsed by the Taos County Teachers' Association. The teachers themselves resolved that all teachers working with Spanish-speaking children ought to have passed oral and written examinations in both English and Spanish before being allowed to hold a teaching job.[8]

In 1941 the state legislature created the Spanish Research Fund for the purpose of exploring the best method of teaching Spanish in the schools of New Mexico. Antonio Rebolledo of Highlands University, the project director, approached his task "with a view to improving the teaching of this language, today the key for national defense and for continental economic and social cooperation."[9] Rebolledo planned to prepare teaching materials "for both the English and Spanish-speaking student groups," making it clear that he believed different objectives existed for teaching Spanish to each group.[10] In teaching Spanish to English speakers, who needed to be able to communicate with Spanish speakers, the goal was to impart the ability to understand and speak simple conversational Spanish.

For native Spanish speakers, however, Rebolledo thought other factors had to be considered. Most of these children, he reasoned, would not go to high school and would not need to write in Spanish. What they did need was the ability to read, in any language, so they could complement their education after leaving school. Therefore he argued:

> Reading for meaning and vocabulary building should then, be the main objectives in teaching Spanish to Spanish-speaking children.
>
> In order to give different instruction to the two language groups, the ideal situation is to have them segregated. And there is nothing wrong in segregation for instructional purpose.[11]

Other educators readily accepted Rebolledo's assumption that separate classes and teaching materials offered the best approach for teaching Spanish to the two groups. Summer workshops held at the University of New Mexico in 1942 to prepare teachers of Spanish for the elementary grades reinforced this approach. Two sessions were offered, "one for teachers of Spanish to English-speaking children, and one for teachers of Spanish to Spanish-speaking children."[12]

On the face of it, perhaps it made sense to teach Spanish-speaking and English-speaking children separately in Spanish. After all, native Spanish speakers were leagues ahead of their English-speaking peers in vocabulary, pronunciation, and grammar. Certainly the Spanish-speaking children were ready to learn at a more advanced level. But this segregation was not undertaken to teach advanced Spanish to Spanish-speaking children. It was to be done because educators like Rebolledo assumed that Spanish-speaking children would not go to high school and would not learn to read well in English. Therefore giving them some reading ability in Spanish might help them to educate themselves after they dropped out of school. So the goal of fostering better relations between Americans and Latin Americans applied only to the English-speaking children, who needed conversational Spanish to talk to Spanish speakers, whether at home or abroad.

Rebolledo's program demonstrates New Mexican educators' good intentions, but low expectations. Many of the curricular reforms attempted in New Mexico were based on the premise that the Spanish American children by and large had a predictable future of living in their ancestral villages, performing the same jobs on the land that their fathers and mothers had done. The vocational arts and crafts programs of the New Deal era, continued in limited scope during the war, certainly aimed to provide students with traditional skills, rather than skills and knowledge needed to participate successfully in an atomic-age economy.

The Nambé Community School, for instance, aimed to prepare Hispanos to live in their own self-sustaining communities, living on the land. Later, in light of the opportunities posed by the atomic age, that training would seem naive and paternalistic. Educators could not have foreseen that the future of New Mexico would change radically from its past.

These and other limited perspectives might have been corrected over time had the same attention been given to Hispano education after the war as before. But the 1930s innovations regarding the education of New Mexico's Hispanos gradually died away, and the New Mexico school system increasingly came to reflect the same curricular patterns as mainstream schools across the country.

In the short term, immediately before and during the war, educators were being exhorted to inculcate the values of democracy. U.S. Commissioner of Education John W. Studebaker urged the nation's schools to prepare students for a "war-torn world," even before the attack on Pearl Harbor. Studebaker exhorted schools to instill in students an appreciation of their democratic heritage and an understanding of "the nature and menace of totalitarian doctrines."[13]

After the United States entered the war, other features of a war curriculum emerged. The New Mexico State Board of Education recommended that schools make "adjustments in the curriculum necessary to meet the war needs of the nation," with special emphasis on mathematics, science, English, and industrial training. Schools were told that "courses of study must be changed and those not essential to the war effort dropped."[14] In extracurricular activities, students practiced marching and drilling, rolled bandages for the Red Cross, and learned airplane engine mechanics in shop class.[15]

Even programs that brought special recognition to New Mexico because of its unique cultural composition drew important educators away from the state and distracted attention away from educational innovations for Hispano schoolchildren. The implementation of the Good Neighbor Policy, intended by the Roosevelt administration to foster friendly relations between the nations of the Americas, involved many New Mexican educators and schools. The U.S. Office of Education sought out New Mexico educators, including Tireman and Otero-Warren, because of their experience in multicultural and bilingual instruction.

Nina Otero-Warren, former Santa Fe County school superintendent and one of the state's leading proponents of bicultural education, participated in a program to teach Spanish to servicemen who would be stationed in Latin American countries. In 1941 she went to Puerto Rico as a special consultant to set up a program to train teachers in bilingual and multicultural methods.[16] In the meantime, back in New Mexico, such programs lapsed as the teacher shortage mounted and Anglos flooded the state.

Other efforts to implement the Good Neighbor Policy had a strange effect on bilingual and multicultural teaching in the New Mexican schools. Whereas before the war educators had addressed methods for teaching Spanish-speaking children in Spanish while simultaneously teaching them English, during and after the war the emphasis shifted to teaching Spanish as a *foreign* language. Whereas before the war educators had tried to encourage local schools to incorporate local culture into the curriculum, during and after the war students began to study Latin American cultures as *foreign* cultures that existed outside of New Mexico.[17] Under the auspices of implementing the Good Neighbor Policy, the curriculum underwent a subtle but highly significant shift. No longer was diversity at home to be studied and celebrated, but diversity was redefined to mean us—those residing within the United States—and them—those living in Latin America; Latin Americans became "the other."

The long-term change in emphasis in New Mexico could be attributed to several other causes. One important factor was the change in the state's demographics, with Hispanos going from a majority to a minority of the population, due to both in-migration of non-Hispanos and out-migration of Hispanos. With the loss of Hispanos, there was a severe teacher shortage, with many of the new teachers out-of-staters who may not have fully understood the Hispano culture. New Mexico's economy was also transformed from an agricultural economy to one including more technology, making some of the "back to the land" emphases of the educational reform school obsolete. And, finally, there was the loss of the leading advocates of the emphasis on Hispano culture, men and women who moved physically for other jobs, or who took on other, demanding, responsibilities.

As to the demographics, before the war, the Hispano people composed half the population of the state; after World War II, they became a minority in their own homeland, and their proportion of the state's population steadily declined afterward. By 1950 Hispanos made up only 36 percent of the population, and by 1960 that number had fallen to 28.3 percent.[18] The influx of newcomers, arriving in the state to work in the wartime defense industries or to reap the benefits of New Mexico's dry climate and natural environment, diluted the traditional political power of Hispanos and marginalized their historic issues. It is tempting to explain postwar educational changes simply by pointing to the influx of Anglos into the state and the concomitant dilution of the Hispano voice as a result. It could be argued that newcomers to New Mexico likely wanted to re-create schools that were similar, if not identical, to schools in the places they had left behind.

During the war, there was also an exodus of Hispanos who left the state to enter the armed services or to work in defense industries on the Pacific Coast. It has been estimated that one-third of Hispano men under the age of twenty-five left New Mexico during the war. Hispanos also moved in great numbers to cities within New Mexico during the war, leading to the depopulation of the traditional rural villages where so many Hispanos originated.[19]

Spanish-speaking New Mexicans had traditionally enjoyed significant political power in the state before the war, especially in comparison to Hispanics in other Southwestern states. Hispanos forged a potent voting bloc, with their population concentrated in north-central counties and along the Rio Grande, which bisects the state. From 1850, when New Mexico became a territory, to the writing of the state constitution in 1910, through the implementation of the New Deal in the 1930s, this political power enabled Hispanos to influence developments.[20] Throughout New Mexican history, Hispanos had not hesitated to engage in acts of collective protest against incidents of blatant racism and defamation.[21] Following the war, New Mexico politics continued to reflect this pattern, even as the proportion of Hispanos in the population dropped.

Political scientist F. Chris Garcia has suggested that New Mexican politics can be explained by a "continual and constant effort to maintain harmonious relationships between at least the three major cultural groups in the state—the Hispanics, the Indians, and the Anglos." In order to avoid conflict, all the interests in the state became accustomed to compromise and accommodation. While this pattern succeeded in muting controversy, it also resulted in a highly decentralized and fragmented governmental structure.[22]

Hispanos maintained their political influence after the war, but they found they had many more Anglo neighbors. The newcomers, drawn by new federal activities, oil and mineral development, and New Mexico's natural environment, changed the demographic landscape of their new home. Perhaps the most vivid example of the changes wrought by the war was the transformation of Los Alamos from a sleepy mountain village into a bustling city supporting a federal atomic laboratory.[23] Other federal installations and military bases located near Albuquerque, Alamogordo, Las Cruces, Clovis, and Roswell helped to swell the populations of these cities. Immediately after World War II, the cold war spurred the growth of even more federal plants, such as Sandia Laboratories, established outside of Albuquerque in 1947. Improved technology in oil, gas, and mineral extraction led to the growth of cities such as Hobbs, Lovington, Farmington, Artesia, Carlsbad, and, perhaps most dramatically,

Grants, which ballooned from a population of 841 in 1940 to 10,274 in 1960, largely as a result of the uranium boom.[24] Hispanos benefited from these increased economic activities, but they also now faced greater competition in the struggle for state funds and attention to issues.

The significant economic and demographic shifts that began during the war and continued through the next few decades transformed New Mexico. As the state's defense and technology industries developed, a new cohort of highly educated scientists, technical people, and military personnel moved into the state for the first time. Educators had assumed that they were training New Mexican children for jobs in agriculture and trades, not atomic science or technology. Without the educational background to perform highly skilled technical work, Hispanos were often relegated to service and labor jobs. It was apparent, in the postwar years, that in terms of preparing Hispanos for scientific, engineering, or technical careers, even the best-intentioned educators had failed the Hispano community.

Besides a change in demographics and the change from an agriculture-based economy to one based on defense and technology, the wartime emergency resulted in a vast reshuffling of careers of New Mexico's Hispano educational advocates. That reshuffling dramatically affected the continuity of programs begun in the late 1930s. By the mid-1950s the highly visible and energetic efforts made to address the educational situation for Hispanos in the years before the war had disappeared for lack of leadership and interest.

Not only were the schools encouraged to focus on a war curriculum; almost immediately they were deprived of the personnel needed to do so. Even before the war broke out, teachers throughout New Mexico began leaving the schools to enter the military or to take better-paying jobs. Native Spanish-speaking teachers, mainly women, had been the backbone of the school systems in the Hispano-dominated counties in the 1920s and '30s. Many of these teachers and many potential teachers succumbed to the lure of better jobs in the war economy.

As the war went on, the attrition rate increased. The *New Mexico School Review*, the official periodical of the New Mexico Teachers Association, reported that many teachers were leaving for jobs in "fields better compensated than teaching."[25] The teacher shortage threatened to undermine the efforts of state officials who had been trying to improve teacher certification standards. In early 1941 the State Board of Education put into effect a requirement of a minimum of two years of professional training for teachers, a reform that educators had worked for years to achieve.[26] By the end of the war the state was forced to issue emergency certificates for teachers who did not have the standard qualifications, thus reversing the upward trend toward better teacher preparation.[27]

The severe teacher shortage led to intense recruiting outside the state during and immediately after the war, resulting in a huge increase in teachers trained in states with no Hispano populations. The editors of the *New Mexico School Review* announced that "of 4,999 teachers, principals, and supervisors employed in the New Mexico elementary and secondary schools during 1947–1948, 964 were new to their positions." Of these new teachers, only 254 had taught in other New Mexico schools the previous year, and "710 were teaching in the state for the first time."[28] This influx of outsiders not only diluted the percentage of Hispano teachers, but also introduced hundreds of teachers who had no awareness of the language, culture, or needs of New Mexico's Spanish Americans and who had been trained in the curriculum and pedagogy of mainstream America.

And while New Mexico was importing teachers with little awareness of Hispano culture, the state was also exporting its expertise in handling Spanish-speaking students, important leaders who had shown a genuine interest in the education of the Spanish American population. One of those was Loyd Tireman, who became involved in promoting Pan-Americanism, a way of shoring up support for the United States among Latin American countries, during the war. Tireman left New Mexico in intervals to work for the U.S. Office of Education both within the United States and throughout Latin America. Tireman visited schools across the country to instruct teachers on methods for introducing Pan-American topics into their courses of study. He also traveled throughout South America, learning about school systems and dispensing advice on multicultural education. After the war his vigor for the issues of bilingual and bicultural education that had occupied his attention during the 1930s seemed diminished. For the duration of the war and the immediate postwar years he continued to work outside of the state as a consultant on two continents. From 1950 until his death in 1959, poor health prevented him from taking an active role in state educational matters.[29]

The war effectively marked the end of Tireman's personal contributions in the interest of Hispanos. His influence continued to be felt, of course, through the work of his students and his ideas. Unfortunately, the numbers of individuals who had worked with Tireman dwindled with the war, and his ideas failed to be implemented on a large scale.

Jennie Gonzales, who had become the co-director of the curriculum division of the State Department of Education, left New Mexico in 1941 to join her husband in Texas, where he had a federal job. Other teachers whose work had focused on teaching young Hispanos left for the service. Frank Angel, one of the teachers at the Nambé Community School, left to join the Army.[30] The loss of these native New Mexican teachers left few voices to argue against the imposition of a standardized curriculum throughout the state's schools.

Losses of vital personnel also occurred that had nothing to do with the war. Dr. James F. Zimmerman, president of the University of New Mexico, died unexpectedly in 1942. Zimmerman had been a powerful and influential voice on behalf of Hispano education. It was he who had first appealed to the Rockefeller Foundation–supported General Education Board to fund a variety of endeavors aimed at improving education for New Mexico's Spanish-speaking people.[31] Both the San José Training School and the Nambé Community School received GEB support. Zimmerman understood the importance of encouraging bright young Hispanos to become educated and enter the professions.

The loss of George Sánchez may well have been the greatest blow to the prospects of New Mexico's schoolchildren. Zimmerman had noticed Sánchez, who was a student at UNM in the late 1920s. Zimmerman had persuaded the General Education Board to give Sánchez a fellowship for graduate study at the University of Texas in 1930 and helped Sánchez navigate the tumultuous minefield of New Mexico politics through the 1930s.[32]

Sánchez often defended the interests of Hispanos, as when he challenged the status quo of school fund distribution in the state in 1935. From his office as Director of the Division of Information and Statistics in the State Department of Education, he took on powerful political forces within the state to champion a more equitable formula for distribution of state educational money. When his political enemies persuaded the legislature not to continue to fund his position in the Department of Education, Sánchez resigned.[33] Sánchez was indeed a "prophet without honor," as he has been called, for he had pinpointed many of the most serious obstacles placed in the way of equal educational opportunity for Hispanos.[34] Early in his career he had exposed the cultural biases of intelligence testing and supported Tireman's experiments with bilingual instruction.[35] Along with the League of United Latin American Citizens (LULAC), Sánchez exposed the political corruption and cronyism of the state educational system and acted as a watchdog in uncovering misappropriation of state funds.[36] Although Zimmerman had secured him a faculty position at UNM, Sánchez finally chose to leave New Mexico in 1940 for Texas, where he became a forceful voice for educational reform.[37]

The combined circumstances of the war brought tragic results for many Hispano schoolchildren. The great promise of the reformers' work of the 1930s failed to materialize in the wake of shifting careers, teacher shortages, and changing economic circumstances. During the chaotic years of the war, school attendance dwindled and dropout rates soared. Out of a total school-age population of 142,741, some 38,781 children did not attend school on a regular basis during the year 1944–1945.[38] The El Porvenir Superintendents' Study Conference found that 69 percent of elementary school pupils in New Mexico quit school between the first and eighth grade. Of those, 45 percent dropped out before completing the fourth grade. Only 15 percent of New Mexico's schoolchildren reached the twelfth grade. The superintendents blamed these shocking results on a number of causes, including the lack of money to retain qualified teachers, to lower the teacher-pupil ratios, to offer remedial work for slow children, or to move beyond the traditional curriculum.[39]

Some educational leaders understood the consequences of losing the momentum of the prewar years. W. E. Kerr, president of the New Mexico Education Association in 1947, pointed out the costs of overloading teachers in the elementary grades: "I estimate that we are spending this year approximately $2,000,000 reteaching children who should have been adequately taught in preceding years." Students were failing grades because the teacher-pupil ratio was so high, he argued.

"This is especially true in the primary grades involving bilingual children. No teacher should be permitted to teach more than 20 beginners, more especially bilingual groups," Kerr said. "If the retardation problem is to be overcome, it must be done in the primary grades."

Contributing to this was a shortage of qualified teachers to teach bilingual groups in the primary grades. Kerr reminded teachers that Mary Watson, who had worked with Tireman at San José and Nambé, had developed a course of study for teaching bilingual children, but "a course of study does not implement itself. This can only be done through teacher training in its use and by proper supervision."[40] The solution lay within reach, but beyond realization.

Ironically, Mary Watson's course of study for teaching bilingual children did become part of a new Curriculum Guide for the Elementary Schools of New Mexico issued in 1950. And Watson herself served in the capacity of Director of Elementary Education in the State Department of Education, a position she earned after many years of working with New Mexico's leading educational reformers. A native of Logan, New Mexico, Watson became involved with the New Mexico Curriculum Revision project at the University of New Mexico in 1936.[41] This project, jointly sponsored by UNM and the State Department of Education, and funded by the GEB, was an attempt to improve the curricula of the state's rural schools. Loyd Tireman, who served as director, hoped to apply the ideas generated by the San José Training School and to explore innovative ideas from teachers all over the state. The Curriculum Revision Committee considered, but ultimately rejected, proposals for bilingual instruction.[42] It is not entirely clear why bilingual instruction was not included in the final revised state curriculum, although correspondence between Tireman and GEB officials suggests a political squabble between the university people and State Superintendent of Public Instruction Grace Corrigan.[43] The office of state superintendent, an elected position, had always been politicized, a situation that educators such as Tireman and George Sánchez found deplorable and frustrating.

After years of study and negotiation, and certainly some delay as a result of the war, the State Department of Education finally issued its revised Curriculum Guide for the Elementary Schools of New Mexico in 1950. Mary Watson chaired the committee that wrote the section on "Teaching the Non–English Speaking Child." Many suggestions reflected the sympathetic and positive approach to Hispano children and culture that so many educators had embraced in the 1930s. The guide encouraged teachers to make the child "feel at home in his new surroundings," and to impress upon him "the contributions in culture which his ancestors have made to our American way of life."[44] In teaching the child to read, the guide adopted the highly successful method of vocabulary building developed at the San José Training School, in which the child mastered a speaking vocabulary of five hundred to eight hundred basic words before beginning the formidable challenge of learning to read.[45]

Yet the guide's authors rejected bilingual instruction outright. They instructed teachers to:

> Use the "direct method" in teaching English to non–English speaking children. In this method no translation is used, and only in emergencies should the native language be used. Set up situations that require English. If the child feels that he can make his wants known without using English, there is no incentive for learning it.[46]

Furthermore, children with no English skills were placed in a pre–first grade class and held there until they learned English.[47] This led to a de facto system of segregation of Spanish-speaking children, and held many children behind classmates of the same age, thus earning them the label "retarded" simply because their native language was Spanish. Both problems contributed to alienation as the child grew older, leading to higher dropout rates for Hispano children.

The 1950 Curriculum Guide also reveals the degree to which New Mexican schoolteachers were being encouraged to impose a standard American curriculum rather than find ways to adapt the curriculum to the special circumstances of New Mexican history and culture. Despite statements asking teachers to impress children with the Hispano contributions to America, the course of study highlighted very few such contributions. A few Spanish games and *canciones* (songs) were recommended for use, but these constituted a small minority of the games and songs suggested in the guide.[48] No Hispanic holidays were mentioned, while activities for Halloween, Thanksgiving, Lincoln's Birthday, Valentine's Day, and Easter were all stressed.[49] Among the ten pages of verses, stories, and books recommended for use in classrooms, only biographies of Kit Carson and Pecos Bill reflected New Mexican history, and no Spanish-surnamed authors appeared. Teachers could choose from a veritable canon of Anglo-American literary culture, including Hans Christian Andersen, the Brothers Grimm, Robert Louis Stevenson, Rudyard Kipling, Eugene Field, Edna St. Vincent Millay, Robert Burns, Vachel Lindsay, Emily Dickinson, Aesop, Lewis Carroll, and others. Children could read about Humpty-Dumpty, Winnie-the-Pooh, Aladdin and the Wonderful Lamp, Pinocchio, the Swiss Family Robinson, Daniel Boone, Paul Bunyan, and Uncle Remus. They were exposed to Abraham Lincoln and Robert E. Lee, Beethoven and Bach, and Mike Mulligan and his steam shovel. They could revel in *Old Norse Fairy Tales*, *Hiawatha's Childhood*, *Little Black Sambo*, and *Tales of the Punjab*.[50] But the closest any recommendation came to anything Hispanic was a little book titled *Manuela's Birthday* by Bannon, described as a story of

> Manuela, a little Mexican girl, [who] wanted a blue-eyed doll with light golden hair as all her dolls were dark-complexioned. And on her fifth birthday her wish comes true.[51]

Eight years later, UNM sociology professor Horacio Ulibarri was asked to author a report for a UNM College of Education study project titled "The Adjustment of Indian and Non-Indian Children in the Public Schools of New Mexico." Ulibarri contributed a synoptic analysis of Spanish American culture as he saw it in the late '50s, from a long perspective as scholar and resident of New Mexico.[52]

Ulibarri noted that the Spanish American people had increasingly embraced Anglo culture in the late '40s and '50s. They were, he said, "enthusiastic about the future and only now, after over a hundred years of cultural subjugation, are the Spanish beginning to enjoy and appreciate American democracy."[53] He attributed the change to the war:

When World War II began and the country demanded the services of the Spanish American, he willingly went. The 200th Coast Artillery, which was in the Bataan Death March, was composed mostly of New Mexico Guardsmen or enlistees. The veterans coming back home had seen a new world. They had associated with the Anglo, and had fought side by side with him. They became friends and developed a common language of mutual respect. When he came back, Uncle Sam offered him a college education and he took advantage of it. His brothers and fathers had been to the West Coast working in shipyards. They, too, had seen a new world and had decided to better their environment. Thus the transition, the great flux in which the Spanish American finds himself today, gathered great momentum in 1945.[54]

Yet Ulibarri also asserted that lack of equal educational opportunity still constrained Spanish American youth. He lamented that the successful ideas generated by Loyd Tireman and others had not been accepted by schools dealing with Spanish American children.

"Why the methods advocated by Tireman and his associates were not adopted in the state is a moot question that has never been satisfactorily answered," Ulibarri wrote. "The schools continued, and still persist in using, the methods developed for Middle West and Eastern schools."[55]

In the following decades, young Hispano activists, calling themselves Chicanos, reiterated these questions. In the 1960s and 1970s the Chicano movement listed the lack of equal educational opportunities as one of its most important issues. Students at the University of New Mexico formed an organization called the United Mexican American Students (UMAS) in 1968 to work for the creation of a Mexican American studies program and the hiring of more Chicano professors at UNM. In 1970 the university inaugurated its Chicano Studies Program.[56] New Mexican activists joined Hispanics from across the Southwest in advocating bilingual education as a means of improving educational achievement for Spanish-speaking children. Mexican Americans welcomed the Bilingual Education Act passed by Congress in 1968, and New Mexicans moved quickly to implement it, establishing ten experimental programs by 1970.[57] In 1972 the

New Mexico State Board of Education endorsed a bill before the New Mexico legislature titled the Bilingual-Multicultural Education Act, which passed the following year. The Department of Education immediately called for proposals for bilingual multicultural education projects, stressing the need for programs "designed to improve the language capabilities of culturally and linguistically different students in grades K–3."[58]

Ironically, the educators of the 1970s were exploring the same issues that had preoccupied the educators of the 1930s.

What happened to the reform momentum of the 1930s? Why had the ideas of reformers in that decade been forgotten? What is clear is that educators in New Mexico embraced a standardized American curriculum more thoroughly in the postwar era than at any time previously in New Mexican history.[59] Perhaps this was due to the increased proportion of Anglos in the population. Anglo parents and teachers would likely have wanted curricular patterns similar to those they had known in their former places of residence. But given the continued pattern of accommodation of ethnic interests in New Mexico politics, it is unlikely that the schools would have succumbed entirely to Anglo pressure for a standardized curriculum had Hispanos themselves not wanted it as well. The tremendous change wrought by World War II may have convinced many Hispanos of the necessity of greater assimilation for themselves and their children. Now aware of new opportunities in science, technology, and business, Hispano parents might have thought the time had come to demand an education that prepared their children to enter these fields alongside their Anglo counterparts. And in doing so, they might have been prepared to sacrifice certain aspects of their own cultural heritage. In doing so, they could not have foreseen that their children would feel deprived of exposure to that heritage and demand to restore it.

World War II disrupted careers of educators, siphoned attention away from reform, encouraged the movement of outsiders to New Mexico, and opened new opportunities for Hispanos, thus changing the educational prospects for the Hispanos of New Mexico. Many Hispanos prospered after the war because of expanding economic opportunities, but they did so often at the expense of their cultural heritage and language. Although Hispanos benefited in many ways from World War II, there is no doubt that the war broke the continuity of reform efforts that had the potential to create a truly remarkable specialized curriculum for Spanish Americans in New Mexico. Fortunately, the quest for such a curriculum began anew in the 1960s, bringing New Mexicans full circle back to an appreciation of their unique and vital heritage.

Notes

The author gratefully acknowledges the assistance of Dr. Linda L. M. Bennett, Dean of the College of Arts and Sciences, and Dr. Judith Domer, Dean of the Graduate School of Appalachian State University, for providing funds for travel to the Conference on Latinos and Latinas and World War II in Austin, Texas, May 26–27, 2000.

1. A measure of Spanish-speaking New Mexicans' changing self-identity is the almost universal acceptance of the term *Spanish American* in the years after the war. Whereas the term *Hispano* had been widely used in the territorial and early statehood period, its use began to diminish in the 1930s. By the 1950s the term had all but disappeared in favor of *Spanish American* to indicate Spanish-speaking persons of the northern part of the state, or *Mexican American* for more recent immigrants from Mexico who predominated in the south. In this essay I will use the terms *Hispano* and *Spanish American* where appropriate. The term *Anglo* will be used for all non-Hispanic whites, conforming with popular usage in the Southwest.

2. *Report of the State Superintendent of Public Instruction for the Twelfth Biennium Period Beginning July 1, 1932 and Ending June 30, 1934* (Las Vegas: Optic Publishing Co., 1934), 22; "Mrs. Gonzales Appointed State Rural School Supervisor," *New Mexico School Review* 14 (January 1935): 15; W. W. Brierly to Georgia Lusk, State Superintendent, April 24, 1931, and Georgia Lusk, John Milne, and J. F. Zimmerman to General Education Board, March 6, 1931, in NM 1, Box 100, Folder 900, Ser. 1, General Education Board Papers, Rockefeller Archives Center, Pocantico Hills, New York (hereafter GEB).

3. David L. Bachelor, *Educational Reform in New Mexico: Tireman, San José, and Nambé* (Albuquerque: University of New Mexico Press, 1991), 12.

4. L. S. Tireman to James F. Zimmerman, January 28, 1931, Departments—Education File, Box 1, University Secretary Record Group, Special Collections, Zimmerman Library, University of New Mexico, Albuquerque; Marie M. Hughes, "The County Extension Program of the San José Project" (1933), in 1033.1, Box 599, folder 6361, Ser. 1.4, GEB.

5. L. S. Tireman and Mary Watson, *A Community School in a Spanish-Speaking Village* (Albuquerque: University of New Mexico Press, 1948), 53–57, 163–164.

6. Jennie Gonzales, "What I Hope to Accomplish: Address Given at the Rural Section of the New Mexico Educational Association," November 2, 1932, pp. 2, 5, in 1033.1, Box 599, Folder 6361, Series 1.4, GEB.

7. "Mrs. Gonzales Appointed State Rural School Supervisor," 15.

8. *Taos Review,* September 29, 1938, and March 2, 1939.

9. Antonio Rebolledo, "Spanish in the Public Schools of New Mexico," *New Mexico School Review* XXI (November 1941): 6.

10. "Spanish Research Program Progresses," *New Mexico School Review* XXI (May 1942): 10.

11. Antonio Rebolledo, "Shall Language Groups Be Segregated for Teaching Spanish," *New Mexico School Review* XXII (December 1942): 3–4.

12. "Summer Session Workshops," *New Mexico School Review* XXI (April 1942): 2.

13. "From the Office of the State Superintendent," *New Mexico School Review* XXI (September 1941): 8.

14. "New Mexico Schools Launch War Program," *New Mexico School Review* XXII (October 1942): 4.

15. Henry A. Gonzales, "Trade and Industrial Education in New Mexico," *New Mexico School Review* XXIV (January 1945): 4.

16. Nina Otero-Warren, "My Work on the Island: An Account of the WPA Adult Education and Public School Projects in Puerto Rico," manuscript in Folder 54, A. M. Bergere Papers, NMSRCA.

17. Maureen Johnson, "Global Foundations," *New Mexico School Review* XXII (January 1943): 2–3.

18. Warren A. Beck, *New Mexico: A History of Four Centuries* (Norman: University of Oklahoma Press, 1962), 283; and "Population Characteristics of Selected Ethnic Groups in the Five Southwestern States, 1960 Census of Population: Supplementary Report PC (S1) 55" (U.S. Department of Commerce, Bureau of the Census, 1968), 1.

19. Gerald D. Nash, "New Mexico since 1940: An Overview," in *Contemporary New Mexico, 1940–1990*, ed. Richard W. Etulain (Albuquerque: University of New Mexico Press, 1991), 6–7.

20. E. B. Fincher, "Spanish-Americans as a Political Factor in New Mexico, 1912–1950" (Ph.D. diss., New York University, 1950; reprint ed., New York: Arno Press, 1974), 163–167; and Carolyn Zeleny, "Relations between the Spanish-Americans and Anglo-Americans in New Mexico: A Study of Conflict and Accommodation in a Dual-Ethnic Situation" (Ph.D. diss., Yale University, 1944; reprint ed., New York: Arno Press, 1974), 275; and Beck, *New Mexico*, 311–313.

21. Phillip B. Gonzales, "*La Junta de Indignación*: The Hispano Repertoire of Collective Protest in New Mexico, 1884–1933," *Western Historical Quarterly* 31 (Summer 2000): 162–164.

22. F. Chris Garcia, "To Get Along or to Go Along? Pluralistic Accommodation versus Progress in New Mexico Politics and Government," in Etulain, ed., *Contemporary New Mexico*, 29.

23. Lillian Hoddeson, Paul W. Henriksen, Roger A. Meade, and Catherine Westfall, *Critical Assembly: A Technical History of Los Alamos during the Oppenheimer Years, 1943–1945* (Cambridge, England: Cambridge University Press, 1993), 97–110.

24. Beck, *New Mexico*, 289–294; and Nash, "New Mexico since 1940," 6–12.

25. "Teacher Supply and Demand," *New Mexico School Review* XXI (October 1941): 20.

26. Mary Jo Scott, "Are Teachers Preparing for the Wrong Positions?" *New Mexico School Review* XXII (September 1942): 19.

27. "Teacher Supply and Demand."

28. "Teachers from Everywhere," *New Mexico School Review* XXVIII (September 1948): 14.

29. "Dr. Tireman Goes to Government Post," *New Mexico School Review* XXII (October 1942): 26; and Bachelor, *Educational Reform*, 102.

30. Bachelor, *Educational Reform*, 147.

31. Jackson Davis and Leo M. Favrot, Memo of January 23–25, 1930, visit to New Mexico, in 1033.1, Box 598, Folder 6357, Ser. 1.4, GEB.

32. James F. Zimmerman to Leo M. Favrot, February 11, 1930, in 1033.1, School of Education, 1929–1930, Box 598, Folder 6357, Ser. 1.4, GEB.

33. Tom Wiley, *Public School Education in New Mexico* (Albuquerque: University of New Mexico Press, 1965), 43–46; and George I. Sánchez to Leo M. Favrot, March 20, 1935, in NM I, Box 100, Folder 901, Ser. I, GEB.

34. Michael Welsh, "A Prophet without Honor: George I. Sánchez and Bilingualism in New Mexico," *New Mexico Historical Review* 69 (January 1994): 29–32.

35. George I. Sánchez, "Bilingualism and Mental Measures: A Word of Caution," *Journal of Applied Psychology* 17 (1934): 765–766, 770; *Albuquerque Tribune*, December 12, 1938; and *Santa Fe New Mexican*, December 22, 1938.

36. *Santa Fe New Mexican*, February 20, 1935.

37. Guadalupe San Miguel, Jr., *Let All of Them Take Heed: Mexican Americans and the Campaign for Educational Equality in Texas, 1910–1981* (Austin: University of Texas Press, 1987), 95–98. For more on Sánchez's career in Texas see James Nelson Mowry, "A Study of the Educational Thought and Action of George I. Sánchez" (Ph.D. diss., University of Texas at Austin, 1977), and Gladys R. Leff, "George I. Sánchez: Don Quixote of the Southwest" (Ph.D. diss., North Texas State University, 1976).

38. "Where Are Our Children?" *New Mexico School Review* XXV (October 1945): 20.

39. "The Five Year Program for the Public Schools of New Mexico," *New Mexico School Review* XXIV (September 1939): 14.

40. W. E. Kerr, "Unfinished Business," *New Mexico School Review* XXVI (January 1947): 8–9.

41. Bachelor, *Educational Reform*, 60.

42. Ruth Miller Martinez, "Taos County Rural Schools, 1938–39: Suggestions to Teacher No. 4—Supplementing Suggestions No. 3," pamphlet in Nina Otero-Warren Papers, Bergere Family Papers #43, NMSRCA; and *Taos Review*, March 2, 1939.

43. Tireman also hinted that Corrigan failed to offer adequate support for the Nambé Community School. "FMR, Interview with Prof. L. S. Tireman," July 25, 1940, 1033.1, Box 599, Folder 6359, GEB; and Jackson Davis, "Nambé Demonstration School," Field Report, September 3, 1940, in 1033.1, Box 599, Folder 6359, Ser. 1.4, GEB.

44. "Curriculum Guide for the Elementary Schools of New Mexico," Bulletin No. 11, State of New Mexico, Department of Education, 1950, p. 83, in Curriculum Guides and Manuals for Elementary Schools, 1906–1950, File 2, Box 50, State Department of Education Papers, NMSRCA.

45. Ibid., 83.

46. Ibid., 83–84.

47. Ibid., 85.

48. Ibid., 147.

49. Ibid., 152.

50. Ibid., 71–81.

51. Ibid., 80.

52. Horacio Ulibarri, "The Effect of Cultural Difference in the Education of Spanish Americans," prepared for the University of New Mexico Research Study, "The Adjustment of Indian and Non-Indian Children in the Public Schools of New Mexico," College of Education, University of New Mexico, 1958, pp. 50–51, unpublished manuscript in Dorothy Woodward Collection, NMSRCA.

53. Ibid., 4.

54. Ibid.

55. Ibid., 50–51.

56. Nancie L. González, *The Spanish-Americans of New Mexico: A Heritage of Pride* (Albuquerque: University of New Mexico Press, 1969), 189–190.

57. San Miguel, *Let All of Them Take Heed*, 192–193; and Thomas R. Lopez, Jr., *Prospects for the Spanish American Culture of New Mexico* (San Francisco: R and E Research Associates, 1974), 123 and 138–139.

58. "New Mexico State Board of Education Statement of Policy: Bilingual-Multicultural Education," 1972; and "Guidelines for Submitting Bilingual-Multicultural Education Proposals," 1973, in Topics on Bilingual-Bicultural Education, File 10, Box 56, State Department of Education Papers, NMSRCA.

59. For a discussion of education in New Mexico prior to World War II, see Lynne Marie Getz, *Schools of Their Own: The Education of Hispanos in New Mexico, 1850–1940* (Albuquerque: University of New Mexico Press, 1997).

CHAPTER 5

The Mexican American Dream and World War II

A View from the Midwest

DIONICIO VALDÉS

Recent scholarship considers World War II a watershed in consolidating an era in Chicano history—the Mexican American generation.[1] It suggests that the U.S. entry into the war in 1941 stimulated a new wave of migration and population growth, afforded better times and more stable employment, and accelerated an attitudinal shift among people of this generation in associating with the United States instead of Mexico. In challenging an earlier literature[2] it also suggests that the war assisted in the consolidation of a middle class activist leadership that cultivated a distinct identity—Mexican American. While the argument has many broadly compelling features, a close reading of the history of Mexicans in the Midwest raises questions regarding the watershed role attributed to the war in causing these changes, the scale of improvement in conditions, and attitudinal changes that involved accepting a "Mexican American" identity.

In this article I will focus on the Mexican community on the Lower West Side of St. Paul, Minnesota. The case files from the International Institute, a nongovernmental social service agency engaged in the Americanization of immigrants and their children, permit an examination simultaneously from the top down (the perspectives of institutional agents of Americanization) and the bottom up (the actions of Mexican clients). The records include observations and reports from local agencies involved in institutional Americanization, including social welfare and school officials, priests, and settlement-house workers, as well as families of clients. They permit a detailed probe into aspects of family life for brief periods between the late 1920s and the late 1940s.

A close reading of the files, as well as other literature, offers a picture that is not consistent with the rosy prospects for Mexican Americans often suggested elsewhere. While living conditions for some families did improve, the economic boom did not extend to everyone. The departure of young adult males to the battlefront, meaning the loss of the major breadwinner, often meant hard times for those who remained. Furthermore, the intrusive and often arrogant actions of agents of institutional Americanization afforded little inducement for behavioral change by Mexican families long accustomed to life in the United States.

The small cadre of International Institute social workers viewed their own successes and failures in light of their primary responsibility of Americanization. They offered classes in the community; engaged in casework in their offices and the homes of their clients; and in conjunction with the Neighborhood House, a settlement house modeled after Jane Addams's Hull-House in Chicago, conducted detailed surveys of the Mexican community of St. Paul in 1936 and 1945 in which they contacted every Mexican family in the city.[3] The caseworkers of the International Institute regarded themselves as enlightened liberal advocates, and as a group viewed the Americanization of Mexicans in a more positive and sympathetic manner than county social welfare workers or school officials with whom they often worked.[4]

This study will first examine the early history of the St. Paul community in light of the importance of 1941 as a watershed, then consider agents' views on the Americanization of Mexicans, patterns of employment, institutional Americanization, and identity change among Mexicans in the Midwest.

The rapid growth of the St. Paul colonia was related initially to Minnesota's sugar-beet industry, which turned to Mexicans as field laborers in large numbers shortly before World War I. It continued to seek different groups of agricultural workers from Mexico and Texas throughout the twentieth century as its operations expanded.[5] From their initial arrival in the state, many sugar-beet workers spent the "dead time" of winter in St. Paul and other nearby cities, although most could not find work until the spring. The St. Paul Mexican community grew rapidly in the 1920s, and despite a modest repatriation campaign in 1932, its expansion accelerated throughout the 1930s. The census of 1920 reported fewer than one hundred Mexicans in St. Paul, concentrated overwhelmingly on the Lower West Side. The population of the colonia approached five hundred by 1930, reached at least two thousand by 1940, and exceeded three thousand in 1946.[6] World War II did not represent a demographic watershed for Mexicans in the city.

The colonia's population growth in the early 1930s was a direct result of the Great Depression, when a regional migration pattern unfolded. Local authorities in the rural Midwest started discouraging sugar-beet workers from remaining on local farms and in camps and small towns during the winters. Concerned about welfare costs, they urged workers to depart, and many moved to larger cities, including the West Side of St. Paul, only to return to the beet fields in the spring.

National political factors contributed directly to a second and even larger wave of migration evident by the mid-1930s. New Deal legislation, including the Wagner Act of 1935, stimulated labor organizing, and in several sugar-beet-producing sections of the region, both the American Federation of Labor (AFL) and the Congress of Industrial Organizations (CIO) engaged in campaigns to unionize workers. To thwart the organizing campaigns, employers turned to a new source of workers from south and south-central Texas. Their actions displaced thousands of Mexican immigrants and their children who had often worked for years in the fields, and many headed directly for St. Paul and other nearby cities. In addition, thousands of the *Tejano* newcomers to the beet fields settled in nearby small towns and larger cities. Prior to World War II, they were already clustered in dozens of communities throughout the region. In several Midwestern states, including Minnesota, the migration originating in Texas in the mid-1930s, rather than a somewhat distinct wave stimulated by the war, was the largest single source of migration of Mexican-origin peoples during the generation. Even in states where the renewal of large-scale migration from Mexico was linked to World War II, particularly Illinois and Indiana, workers in the migration wave that began in Texas during the 1930s and accelerated afterward made a significant demographic contribution.

In the long-running public debate about whether Mexicans could and should assimilate and Americanize, St. Paul's social workers were vigorous participants. Social welfare workers from agencies providing relief for unemployed workers tended to be the least accepting, while those from the International Institute and the settlement houses were more favorable. Yet the latter were often hesitant, as a 1935 International Institute report asserted, "If we feel that there is a 'Mexican Problem,' it has only two solutions, first to proceed with all the wisdom we have to assimilate the Mexicans already resident here and, second, to discourage any more from coming (if we can)."[7] In general, sympathizers and opponents reached a political compromise, supporting able-bodied and "Americanizing" Mexicans not likely to become a public charge and discouraging others from remaining. Filling their functions as intermediaries between clients and school officials or welfare agents, caseworkers from the International Institute saw themselves as a vanguard in the Americanization and defense of Mexicans.

The International Institute considered Americanization a top priority, whether dealing directly with citizenship, public welfare, education, or employment. The agents worked closely with individual families and with local officials responsible for the social welfare and schooling of their clients; reports and statements from different agencies and their clients appear in many case files. The reports often portrayed an intimate side of family life and uncovered caseworkers' concerns about physical conditions in the home, cleanliness, and the intellectual capacities of their clients.[8] Despite the limitations of these and similar reports by caseworkers and church and school officials, in conjunction with related documents they offer particularly valuable insights into the lives of Mexican families.[9]

Most parents of the first generation were born between the mid-1880s and the 1910s, overwhelmingly in Mexico, and many families had a long history of migration prior to arriving in St. Paul. A smaller but still significant number of individuals and families migrated directly from the Mexican interior or the border to St. Paul and elsewhere in the Midwest. The birthplaces of children were often determined by the father's work history. In one particular family with eleven children, the eldest child was born in Jalisco; the next two in Amarillo, Texas; the next in Newton, Kansas; the next two in Elmore, Minnesota; the next two in Mankato, Minnesota; and the last three in St. Paul.[10] The parents could find only occasional work on the railroads and in agriculture, and other odd jobs.

A married couple from Nuevo León crossed the Texas-Mexico border at Laredo with two small children in 1921. They resided for seven years in Texas, where the father was employed in various short-term jobs as a laborer in agriculture, for a power company, in construction, and as a hotel dishwasher and coal miner. In 1928 they were recruited in Texas to work for the American Beet Sugar Company near Cambria, Minnesota, before they established permanent residence in St. Paul in 1934. Three additional children were born in Minnesota. The family continued to obtain most of its earnings from employment in the sugar-beet industry, augmented by income from other short-term jobs until 1942, when the father finally obtained a permanent job at the Cudahy Packing Plant at the Union Stockyards in South St. Paul. This case does indicate that the wartime economic boom afforded some people the stability of employment they had long sought after working in the United States for many years in seasonal, unstable, dead-end jobs.[11]

Social workers participated in the contemporary debate in dominant society over whether Mexicans were capable of being assimilated, which they understood explicitly as "Americanization," and for which Americanization programs had been created initially for immigrants from Europe. While social workers disagreed on some aspects of Americanization, their own records indicate that they agreed that "assimilable" meant "not liable to become a public charge." They kept detailed records on their Mexican clients, basing their assessments of assimilability on material factors including whether people could support themselves, how they maintained their homes, and their capacity for adjustment to the United States.

The International Institute, often in cooperation with the Neighborhood House, offered practical English-language instruction for parents seeking citizenship, and classes in homemaking and domestic training for women based on "modern" technology. In their capacity in St. Paul of offering English-language classes, caseworkers in the 1920s first went after the men, not the women.[12] However, as the number of women in the community increased, the social workers quickly turned their attention to them as well. In 1936, when the adult sex ratio of Mexican St. Paul was fifty-four males to forty-six females, 62 percent of the students enrolled in the English language classes for Mexicans offered by the International Institute were adult males.[13] But the caseworkers were most interested in families even when they offered classes for men or women, and following demographic trends they increasingly made special appeals to children, who usually were born in the United States and reared in St. Paul, and thus would seem to be less in need of learning about the American way of life. The classes varied widely in size, hour of offering (typically during the day for women and in the evening for men), and setting (usually at the Neighborhood House but occasionally in individuals' homes). While the instruction focused on practical subjects, it ultimately aimed at preparing immigrants to pass an examination granting them United States citizenship, the ultimate goal of Americanization projects.

Social caseworkers considered work critical to Americanization, and recorded work experiences in detail, offering data relevant to the importance of the outbreak of World War II on their clients' work histories. This section first examines how families were affected by Mexican men joining the military; next, attention will be turned to Midwestern workers on the domestic front.

World War II had a profound impact on the employment of Midwestern Mexicans. Paralleling trends elsewhere, Mexican men in the region participated in the armed forces at extremely high rates. Oral histories, social work records, and other documents record numerous instances in which all physically able brothers of age entered the military, and all of their sisters were married to men in the service.[14] The widely documented case of Hero Street, heart of the small railroad community of Silvis, Illinois, is not an exception, but rather a reflection of regional and national trends.[15]

Young soldiers of Mexican origin from St. Paul who entered the military recall that World War II disrupted their lives. They shared a common experience of separation from the familiar, new acquaintances, and constant change. Sent to different theaters of war, they faced the horrors of battle heroically, but most shared the opinion that heroes were made, not born.[16]

Several factors might explain the high rates of military participation. Some observers have emphasized cultural factors, including machismo. But economic and demographic arguments are more compelling: Mexicans were concentrated in the age cohort susceptible to the draft, seldom were eligible for deferments based on employment, and lacked connections on draft boards.

Another factor was that military service represented a monthly paycheck: outside the military, Mexican men's employment options were restricted by discrimination and lack of formal training. Many individuals joined the military because they were unable to find employment outside agriculture, despite the economic boom.[17] Employment in the military during the war also offered the families an expectation of financial security through monthly allotments and an understanding that social caseworkers would ensure that family members would receive insurance and other social service needs.

Another possible explanation for the high rate of military service among Mexican Americans during World War II—a higher degree of loyalty toward the United States—would suggest that Mexicans were more Americanized than any other nationality group. Agents of Americanization—school officials, settlement house staff, and welfare caseworkers—would have considered themselves successful by inducing strongly pro–United States attitudes among young men and persuading them to enlist in the military. Those authorities' success in this regard would have been particularly noteworthy as the Mexicans' immigrant fathers a generation earlier often stated that if it came to war between the two countries, they would choose Mexico over the United States.[18] Throughout the 1930s and 1940s, however, the agents of institutional Americanization in the Midwest viewed Mexicans as the most alien group in the region, and considered assimilation a future expectation rather than an accomplished fact, despite the military record.

Participation in the U.S. military enhanced the identification of Mexicans with the United States, and among noncitizen men and women who entered the Armed Forces there were simplified procedures for naturalization. A not unusual Midwestern soldier was born in Etucuaro, Michoacán, in 1910. He arrived in St. Paul in 1929, and later obtained employment at the Armour meatpacking plant. Inducted into the Army in 1942, he remained in the service for three years, fighting in England and France. During his tour of duty in 1943 he became a citizen by naturalization. On return to St. Paul he regained his job at Armour, with veteran's benefits.[19]

Contrary to expectations, families commonly experienced downward mobility when husbands, fathers, and sons entered the military. Their incomes could not be replaced, and in particular many wives with young children suffered, some of them fortunate if they could return to the homes of their parents. Older parents dependent on adult children for support were also likely to endure privations. In a family in which two boys were adopted by an aunt and uncle when their own mother died, the aunt asserted they were "treated as though they were my own child providing food, shelter and clothing which our means permitted."[20] When the elder boy entered his teens, he "used to help in the beet fields although we never overworked him." In fact, "it might be said that for four or five years his earnings in the summer about covered his keep during the winter when he also lived with us." The aunt emphasized that he was "always a part of my family even when we went out to work in the beet fields until he entered the Army."

The aunt and uncle were in their mid-fifties when the United States entered the war, and as their conditions worsened when the nephew entered the military, they became dependent on welfare. When he was killed in action in Italy in 1944, the adoptive parents were granted a pension.

Many Mexican-born parents were also negatively affected by Americanization in the 1930s and 1940s because federal, state, and local governments increasingly pressured employers to hire only U.S. citizens. One St. Paul father who had worked many years in the sugar-beet fields before obtaining a job at the Griffin Wheel factory lost his position in 1938 due to the imposition of citizenship requirements for continued employment. International Institute classes helped him acquire citizenship in 1940 with the explicit aim of regaining his job. When he was drafted in 1944, his wife suddenly had to care for a widowed mother and four children under age five. With the husband gone, the Red Cross sent coal for heating and promised to provide for current grocery bills until the monthly allotment check arrived. But the caseworker observed that she and the children were in desperate need of clothes and overshoes, while the bed linens "had become threadbare."[21] Her infant child had fallen ill from a severe state of malnutrition and had to be taken to a local clinic.

On the domestic front, World War II has been considered by many as a watershed in creating new jobs and reinvigorating communities by luring Mexican workers. In the Midwest, large-scale migration to the region had begun in the middle years of the Great Depression, when labor contractors began hauling thousands of workers to beet-growing sections by truck from south and central Texas.[22] By 1940, as the U.S. entry into the war approached, large-scale migration from Mexico began again, augmenting the movement of workers into the Midwest.

Employment in Midwestern agriculture was already expanding before the war, as employers attracted thousands of Mexican workers into new sectors, including the fruit belts near Lake Michigan and Lake Erie that produced cherries, apples, strawberries, peaches, nectarines, pears, and blueberries. In the late 1930s and 1940s, additional thousands of people were lured to employment in fields and canneries to produce pickling cucumbers, onions, carrots, asparagus, corn, peas, tomatoes, and other crops.

The expansion of employment in urban manufacturing predated the declaration of war, stimulated by the Lend-Lease Program of 1939. Midwestern factories were recruiting from afar and luring tens of thousands of workers from many locations by 1940. The most important sector of production involved shops and factories connected with the steel and automobile industries, responsible for producing goods under defense contracts, and they attracted thousands of workers from Texas and the Mexican interior. Employment in this occupational sector was more stable, wages were higher, and conditions were superior to those of earlier decades—largely the result of workers' own successful unionization drives in the 1930s. Although Mexicans remained overwhelmingly in unskilled tasks, with only a small amount semiskilled or higher, it was a significant change. They became a stable segment of the region's urban industrial workforce, and among Mexican workers in the Midwest, they most closely approximated the wartime American Dream of upward occupational mobility and a stable life.

The entry of thousands of young Mexican men into the armed services helped push Mexican women into the wage labor force—whether or not they were eager to enter. As many others have documented, women handled their jobs admirably, working in steel, autos, packing plants, and other industries that earlier had been deemed men's work.[23] But most were still relegated to tasks long designated as Mexican women's work—either with their families in the fields or in household tasks.

In response to limited occupational opportunities for young Mexican women in St. Paul, International Institute caseworkers adopted a plan. It was "based on the experience of some committee members that the young women would make good domestic servants—the one occupation not over crowded—and has plans to train a small group of girls for this work as an experiment."[24] Through its Mexican Girls Household Training Course, the International Institute hoped to offer young women immediate wage-paying jobs while preparing them for long-term employment that the social workers considered befitting of Mexican women. The social workers could thus feel good about helping to train *Mexicanas* while the trainees cared for the committee members' homes.[25]

As in the case of men, overt job discrimination restricted the upward mobility of thousands of young women, among them one of five children of Mexican-born parents. This young woman moved with her family to Minnesota to work in the beet fields, the principal source of income for several years after the father left erratic railroad employment in Kansas in 1934. Her files indicate that she was a very good student at Harding High School in St. Paul, but dropped out in 1938, according to one caseworker, "because there was always so much work to be done at home and she never had a place in which to study."[26] The young woman stated emphatically that "her parents did not want her to leave school" and that she wanted to continue. But the social worker shared a widespread stereotype among school officials and social workers that Mexican parents did not care about their children's education. For example, one caseworker observed that a St. Paul school principal stated that some Mexican children made definite progress in terms of better nutrition, better personal hygiene and a better attitude toward life . . . [for] those whom she would grade poor and worse because of their indifference, slovenliness and irregular attendance. . . . The fault lay with the mothers, she said. Unlike the mothers of other immigrant groups, they do not seem to appreciate the value of schooling for their children. Ignorant themselves, they care little whether their children learn anything either. There is a complete lack of cooperation on the part of these families and an inability or unwillingness to improve their conditions. For this group she saw hope only in some form of supervised living in a public housing project.[27]

The young woman wanted to attend Mechanic Arts High School, "where Spanish was offered," and where more Mexican youth were enrolled. School officials at first did not admit her, asserting that "there were too many requests," until the outside intercession of another International Institute caseworker.

She had excellent grades, and on graduation wanted to attend a business college, but the costs were prohibitive. She spent the summer following graduation working in the beet fields to save money, but was ruled ineligible for employment with the National Youth Administration (NYA) in the fall because her family was not on relief and her father was employed, although only part-time. She managed to enroll in a less expensive course with the YWCA, after which she passed the Minnesota State Employment test with a high score. Nevertheless, a caseworker reported, despite her schooling, "it was impossible for her to get office work" because she lacked experience. Yet even the caseworker acknowledged that other recent graduates of European background had the same schooling, had to pass the same test, similarly lacked experience, and obtained employment. Her case suggests that the absence of Mexican women in office work at this time occurred because Minnesota employers considered such employment out of bounds for them, a discriminatory behavior that caseworkers reinforced.

Despite the young woman's excellent record as a student and her desire to be a secretary, she returned to the beet and onion fields in 1940 and 1941. Systematic discrimination restricted young Midwestern women of Mexican descent from secretarial jobs that were more readily available for a small but important segment of female Mexican workers in some locations in the Southwest.

In sum, as a result of changes in the late 1930s and the war years, more Midwestern Mexicans found steady employment than ever before, but a much larger number were relegated to unsteady and seasonal work characteristic of earlier years. Men experienced practically no movement into skilled industrial employment, the trades, the professions, or even service industries. Mexican women did not become schoolteachers, typists, or secretaries, and rarely could find employment as sales clerks or waitresses. Even young women with experience in Texas were barred from such employment.[28] Midwestern Mexican women were discouraged from enrolling in training courses, and the few who did enroll and graduate from study programs found it almost impossible to find employment in those job sectors. Mexican women and men in the Midwest faced sharper limits on the dream of upward occupational mobility, which had a critical influence on their institutional Americanization.

Officials from settlement houses, the International Institute, social welfare agencies, and the public schools were responsible for converting aliens into Americans. Although the various entities sought a common goal of assimilation for Mexicans, their efforts often clashed because they disagreed on the attributes of a good American, or even if Mexicans (whether born in the United States or Mexico) had the potential to assimilate.

The agents had different understandings of the meaning of Americanization when they applied it to parents and children. For the former, it typically meant learning English, adopting a set of prescribed behaviors, learning modern ways of living, staying off welfare, and becoming citizens. For children born and schooled in the United States, language and citizenship rarely concerned officials, who were interested in behavior, particularly not rocking the boat and attending enough school to become self-supporting in adulthood.

In fact, children often helped parents negotiate hurdles toward Americanization. A father born in 1891 came to the United States in 1924 and settled in Minnesota in 1925, learning English very slowly. When he appeared in court in 1940, he was advised to continue his language study because he "could not carry on a conversation in

English with the judge; he depended upon his daughter to interpret for him."[29] While some caseworkers noted with pleasure how children assisted in the Americanization of their parents, including another daughter who took her father regularly to naturalization class, others were wary of the power children acquired over their parents because of their facility in English.[30]

The caseworkers' contacts with mothers included a particular interest in the domestic realm. They offered courses on housekeeping to teach immigrant women how to maintain their homes, and they conducted inspections of houses during their frequent visits. They commonly expressed an obsessive concern about germs and neatness, justifying their actions based on concerns about the spread of contagious diseases. Their view of Americanization, based on middle-class values and current modernization theory, left Mexico and Mexicans far behind. A typical visit began with commentary on the upkeep of a home, "which was very untidy."[31] Frequently caseworkers' observations on housekeeping were interspersed with other physical indicators of assimilation. Their assessments were laden with contradictions, as a caseworker met a "large, pleasant woman (not too clean) who spoke excellent English . . . at the door."[32] In a few instances including the following 1943 visit, caseworkers reported positive first impressions: "The home was not in a bad condition compared to some of the other homes we had called on before. . . . The man is pleasant and talks very good English."[33] In another visit in 1943, the caseworker was unexpectedly impressed: "The house, although very old, was very clean and tidy. The old steps outside were freshly scrubbed. Worker was surprised of [sic] the cleanliness of the home, as most of our clients' houses on that street are not clean."[34] A visit to a rented house in 1940 offered contradictory assessments, as the dwelling was "in a very bad state and needs repair," papering, and painting, yet the children were described as "healthy looking and very quiet and nice."[35] In a 1949 visit the International Institute worker reported, "The house was the nicest in the block. It was very neat and clean and seemed in good repair," yet the wife "spoke very halting English so most of the conversation was carried on through her son."[36] A tidy house might even offset other negative indicators, as one caseworker reported a dwelling in which the "floors were scrubbed snow white," yet recent IQ tests for the children ranged in the 60s and 70s.[37] These individual reports suggest that housekeeping habits had little relationship to other indicators of assimilation, yet the caseworkers were persistent.

Social workers frequently referred to "second generation problems" among Mexican young people.[38] One report noted,

> With few exceptions, Mexicans are not found in any of the youth organizations of the city. They are as yet too unassimilated and under-privileged to normally find a place in the youth agencies which are functions of the American community. Many children have complained that they are not welcome in the playgrounds except West of the [Mississippi] river[39]

where most Mexicans lived. While acknowledging the profound impact of prejudice and discrimination in hindering assimilation, the social workers focused primarily on altering the behavior of Mexican youth and their families.

When dealing with children, social workers operated closely with the most important agent of Americanization for youth, the public school system. While caseworkers and school officials commonly assumed that parents were not concerned about education, the latter frequently stated that they left the beet fields for the city in order to send their children to school regularly. An International Institute report at the end of World War II observed that Mexican children in St. Paul "attended school for brief periods only and then in special ungraded classes where they learned very little."[40] Despite the improved economic opportunities afforded by the wartime boom, a very large number of Mexican school-aged children in the city were not attending school. Officials recognized, but did not seek systematic ways to overcome, the negative impact of poverty and segregation on school attendance and performance, and engaged in disparate treatment toward Mexicans by failing to enforce mandatory school attendance laws. The agents of assimilation frequently attributed poor school achievement to parents. Yet a 1943 report of a family whose mother was working in the onion fields observed that a son in high school "won a medal as the best student in the school," and suggested that the family members "are proud and do not like to receive charity."[41]

Poverty kept many children away from school, as in a 1945 case when a junior high school boy "had to stay home for a few days while his only pair of shoes was being mended. He had to pay out $5 for books which was an added hardship."[42] His thirteen-year-old sister was described as "thin and anemic" yet "attends school regularly and likes it, but in her case too, the problem of clothes is precarious." While she expressed an "eagerness to learn the piano," the caseworkers considered her desire impossible to realize due to the lack of financial resources.

The policies of hostile school administrators and welfare agents often pushed youth out of school. In a 1943 case, a seventeen-year-old boy with good grades had to accompany his family to the beet fields and was forced to miss examinations. The caseworker reported: "The principal did not allow him to make this up so he quit."[43] Yet if family members had refused employment in the beet fields, they would have been removed from the county welfare rolls in the winter. Such contradictory policies confined many Mexican families to the reserve labor army and restricted prospects of future upward social mobility for children, key to understanding the American Dream.

Furthermore, sympathetic agents had little success in stemming overt racial discrimination. In one case a young girl entering kindergarten at Lincoln Elementary in St. Paul during the last year of the war was, according to her mother, "happy about going" to school.[44] But the mother told the social worker that her daughter "was being tormented by one of her blond classmates, who pulled her hair, spat on her, and called her 'nigger.'" Intervening on behalf of the mother, the International Institute caseworker called the school principal, who promised to speak to the teacher, as both had been unresponsive to the mother's complaints about harassment until then. Hostility and discrimination were not as intense on the Lower West Side as in the Lincoln school area, a largely Italian section, and the caseworker observed that neither mother nor children had any friends, for European Americans in the neighborhood refused to associate with Mexicans. Furthermore, systematic housing discrimination made it difficult for families to find dwellings beyond the Lower West Side. In a 1945 case a family was frustrated after looking in various neighborhoods with the help of a caseworker, who reported that "the landlords of the majority of the places which would have been all right for the family would not accept Mexicans."[45]

Mexican clients often resisted efforts by social workers and teachers to conform to their demands and assimilate according to their ideals. Social workers considered one bright young Mexican woman, reportedly a good student at South St. Paul High school, to be a problem. Through a newspaper advertisement she found employment cleaning and washing clothes for a family for a salary of $3 per week, plus room and board. Family members left early in the morning and returned late at night, permitting her to continue school, but she was unsupervised. Furthermore, the social worker reported, the house belonged to "a Negro family who own a cheap saloon . . . [that] had a bad reputation," and she was a close friend of the daughter of the employer.[46] The school principal stated that she was "accepted by all the students on an equal basis," but contradictorily noted that she "was aware of being a Mexican and that the boys at school did not date her." As there were no other Mexican students at the school, she "was unhappy and quit." She wanted to transfer to Mechanic Arts High School, where there were more Mexican students and she could take Spanish classes. After consultation with her former elementary school principal the caseworker helped her change schools. But the unsupervised girl did not attend classes regularly, and the caseworker advised her to return to South St. Paul High or find a job elsewhere to "find work in a home where she could be supervised by her employer so in that way become an efficient maid." The caseworker wanted her "with a woman who could supervise her at all times . . . as she was too free to run around" and "no one knew what she did in her spare time." The caseworker considered problems of supervision common in homes where parents were not citizens while children were "adjusted to the American way of life." Threatening court proceedings to have her sent to a correctional home, the caseworker convinced her to return home to live and return to South St. Paul High. As she neared graduation in 1943, she was informed that "housework was the only thing available for her unless" she had additional schooling, and she was encouraged to enroll in a three-month course offered by the NYA to train as a waitress. The pressure succeeded, and in the spring of 1944, the caseworker reported that the young woman had found employment as a waitress at the Union Station. The caseworker appeared relieved that the young Mexican woman "gave up the Negro family for whom she was working." She had been assimilated into a European American, suburban environment and gained a job not commonly achieved by young Mexican women.

Caseworkers steered young people into employment they deemed appropriate for Mexicans, men into unskilled jobs, women into sewing and domestic work, and all Mexicans into farm work. One bright *Mexicana* who dropped out of school in 1943 "hates housework and does not want that type of work," but had poor eyesight and therefore could not get a job sewing.[47] Yet the social worker seemed more concerned about her attitude, namely that "she did not appreciate" the used clothes that social workers provided her, and that she criticized school officials for their treatment of her younger brothers and sisters. Unwilling to comment on whether her criticisms were accurate, they considered her willingness to stand up as out of line. Rather than focusing on finding her employment, their top priority was to get her involved in a group or another outlet where she would be useful "and at the same time distract her entire attention on the family."

Many families were reluctant to accept "assistance," knowing that it came at a price. One such family included parents born in rural San Luís Potosí and Guanajuato. The father had served in the armed services during World War I, and had worked at various jobs in Minnesota for many years. He was hospitalized with tuberculosis in 1941, and instead of turning to charity the mother and children went to work in nearby onion fields, although they had to request clothing from the County Welfare Board (CWB). They had never received charity when the father worked, and the "children didn't like to receive clothing from the CWB because the children feel very conscious about wearing the same kind and pattern of clothing that CWB distributes to all its clients. . . . They are proud and do not like to receive charity."[48] When the mother was working in the onion fields, a son cared for his younger siblings. The CWB offered to pay their gas and electricity bills, and they accepted, unaware that the Board expected repayment. They asserted that had they known, "they would have used kerosene," which cost less.

Many Mexicans were wary of IQ tests whose scores were used to determine whether they could perform certain jobs or enter programs of study, and could also be used to take children away from parents on the grounds of mental incompetence. IQ tests had been popularized during World War I, yet by the 1930s and 1940s there was little systematic study of their biased outcomes stemming from failure to consider language facility, cultural factors, or even incompetent examiners and poor examination conditions. Reporting on one test imposed on a Mexican family against its will, a caseworker noted that the "smaller children were frightened and it was difficult to get results, but [the] unofficial report was that they seemed to be 'borderline cases'" (of mental incompetence). The caseworker rhetorically wondered if "fright, lack of proper living conditions and unaccustomedness of children to new and unusual conditions would not make some difference in their response to tests."[49]

In another instance, a social worker dealing with an "uncooperative" father sought to administer tests to justify separating him from his children. In an earlier exam he scored a 59 (indicating "moron"), although "he did not complete the test because he objected so much to doing so."[50] His refusal to complete the test would have rendered its results invalid. But agents were able to administer tests to other family members when he left home to work in the beet fields. The caseworker asserted that on return "he particularly resented the mental tests which he felt were forced on the family during his absence." A more sympathetic caseworker who considered him to be "at least of average intelligence" questioned the test results. She observed that "he had done very well in his English classes at the International Institute, and it seemed that he perhaps would not have done as well if his IQ were really below normal to the extent the mental examination revealed."

Unwilling clients often challenged the impositions of social workers, including a 1941 case involving a seventeen-year-old Texas-born girl who complained about their intrusiveness. She, her U.S.-born siblings, and her Mexican-born parents moved to St. Paul in 1934, and they struggled through the Depression years, with occasional public assistance. In a 1940 report a caseworker observed that the "family had been threatened to be returned to Mexico" by a social worker from the Bureau of Public Welfare.[51] The young woman resented the threat, both because she was a citizen and because the family had not been on welfare for more than two years. The caseworker also noted that they were too proud to request clothing or shoes, despite their desperate need. In seeking employment for her, the women of the Mexican Committee of the International Institute (all European American) promised to "check with friends about her and probably would be able to employ her evenings to take care of their small children." The European American social workers were willing to hire Mexican girls and women to work as their maids, housekeepers, and childcare attendants, which they considered appropriate occupational expectations.

On other occasions youth and young adults expressed resentment about the intrusiveness of social workers, agencies, and school personnel. When a caseworker visited a family in 1943, the seventeen-year-old daughter tried to get the social worker to leave by asserting that her mother was "very busy. From their last experience with their boy . . . worker thought perhaps they are suspicious of any strange person that comes to the door."[52] In another instance, a young Mexican woman challenged authority more directly. The social worker described the young woman as "intelligent and well groomed, but carrying with her a defiant attitude." She was also unusually successful occupationally, being a "demonstrator and saleswoman . . . and seems inordinately proud of the fact. But the [Case] W[orker] found out later that she distrusts the social workers and any others outside the Mexican group, characterizing as hypocritical and morbid curiosity any interest they may show for their welfare."[53]

In a more direct confrontation, in 1942 a seventeen-year-old girl wrote a letter to the principal of Lincoln Elementary School in response to complaints about the attendance of her younger brothers and sisters. According to the school social worker, she informed the principal "in a nasty way that the children would come to school when they could."[54] The girl was defending her siblings, who lacked clothes and shoes to attend classes. She also "stated that the school nurse had it in for them and that she would never come to the house as the former nurse [had done]." The girl considered the new nurse unfriendly and unsympathetic. In retaliation for her behavior, the school social worker "promised to get a behavior report on her" from her school principal, who to her dismay reported "no complaints whatsoever," and that she was a good average student. Meanwhile International Institute caseworkers "felt that [her] impertinence and attitude was causing a great deal of trouble, and [were concerned about] her influence on the other children and her mother." Yet the report failed to address the lack of clothing that prompted her actions, instead focusing on the defiance of authority, behavior not expected of Mexican girls.

While Mexicans individually challenged the visions and actions of many agents of Americanization, social structural factors tended to inhibit their success at articulating a systematic, organized opposition. In the Midwest during World War II, they were not themselves welfare workers or public school teachers. Even the most liberal and pro-Mexican of the institutions of socialization in St. Paul, the International Institute and the settlement houses, did not have a single Mexican board member. Mexicans were solely their clients, students, and, when they considered themselves filled with largesse, their own domestic servants, cooks, and housekeepers. In this regard, some settings in Southwestern states where one might encounter occasional schoolteachers or social workers were modestly different.

In documents dealing with Midwestern Mexicans during the war years, the term *Mexican American* almost never appeared. It was used infrequently in the late 1940s, and even in the 1950s and 1960s it was not very common, except among a handful of academics and bureaucrats. The widely accepted identifier among English speakers, including Mexicans when they spoke English, continued to be *Mexican*.

Two major considerations help account for the continued use of the term *Mexican* in the Midwest, both stemming from the regional social formation. The first was that ethnicity as expressed by national origins was very important. The majority European American population was divided by ethnicity, so the Irish, Germans, French, Italians, Lithuanians, Poles, Russians, Swedes, Albanians, and Mexicans were among those who were identified and who identified themselves with the nation of their ancestral homeland. The Midwest was unlike Texas in particular, where the Anglo-American population had engaged in a war with Mexico and had long used the term *Mexican* in a particularly denigrating manner, causing many people to distance themselves from identifying as Mexican. There was less shame in identifying as Mexican in the Midwest.

A second important factor was the occupations available to the Mexican population regionally. In the Southwest, the agents of Americanization first sought to socialize Mexicans of the middle class to identify as Americans beginning in the 1920s, and increasingly in the 1930s and 1940s. But in the Midwest, a similar critical mass of middle-class Mexicans did not appear and did not become conscious of itself as a group by the end of World War II. The region historically did not have a Mexican landowning group that preceded European Americans, and a large number of Mexican immigrants of middle-class origins repatriated from the Midwest during the Great Depression. Mexicans came to the Midwest to work, even during World War II, and there were fewer opportunities for social mobility beyond unskilled labor.

Statewide, it wasn't until late 1941 that the first Mexican person born or reared in Minnesota enrolled in college, a girl who went to Duluth State Teacher's College (later University of Minnesota–Duluth). On graduation from high school and in the summers immediately afterward, she continued to accompany her family in the commute to the onion fields. As a high school student she had hoped to attend college to study Spanish, and explicitly expressed no desire to attend a teachers college, as she was not interested in teaching. But social workers of the International Institute "felt that it would not harm" her to "prepare herself either for social work or teaching," occupations that were acceptable for European American women.[55] The social workers even assisted her in enrolling in college at Duluth. An International Institute caseworker considered her an important role model, writing that "she is a grand girl, and has contributions to make necessary to the assimilations [*sic*] of Mexicans in the United States." She apparently adjusted quickly, and in a letter from college during her first year she wrote that "everyone is friendly," although she was disappointed that the college did not offer any courses in Spanish. Her own effort to resist one aspect of Americanization was also evident, as she added: "I am having a little trouble having people pronounce my name." She was the only Mexican to attend a college or a university in the state, which had an estimated five thousand permanent Mexican residents at the time, plus an additional nine thousand to ten thousand seasonal workers who came each year for agricultural employment.[56]

She enjoyed college and got good grades, but like other young Mexican women during the war boom, she was confined to Mexican jobs. She was employed during the school year as a domestic worker cleaning houses, and in the summer she joined her family in the fields. During her second year in college she dropped out to marry, ending, or at least postponing, the realization of a European American Dream for a Mexican in Minnesota.

Her case also is significant because the same International Institute report identified her as "the first native-born Mexican-American" from Minnesota to attend college. It was the first time I encountered the use of the term in that state in a written document. The lack of young women attending colleges and universities in the Midwest contrasted with the Southwest, where a few Mexicans had been able to attend college or enroll in technical or secretarial courses and teacher education programs. The combination of educational and occupational barriers for Mexicans in Minnesota and other Midwestern states further helps explain why they did not articulate an identity as Mexican Americans or form organizations they referred to as Mexican American at the time.

While World War II was a very important moment in the history of Mexican Americans, the case of St. Paul in particular, and the Midwest in general, conforms only in part to generalizations posited by the scholars of the Mexican American generation in the Southwest. As elsewhere, Mexicans' enlistment and induction as soldiers took place at extremely high rates, employment expanded as a result of the wartime boom, and women entered the workforce outside agriculture in larger numbers than before.

With Mexico as an important ally, World War II was significant in silencing extremists in the Americanization debate who considered deportation the ultimate solution. Many welfare workers had continued to threaten Mexicans and their children born in the United States even after deportation from the region subsided after 1933. During the war only contract braceros were systematically returned to Mexico. Threats to resident Mexicans subsided, only to be renewed after the war ended, along with actual deportations.

Demographically, World War II was not a watershed in the history of the Mexican community in St. Paul or the Midwest. The Mexican community of St. Paul actually countered trends in most of the Southwest and Midwest, as it grew very rapidly throughout the Great Depression, despite repatriation. In the early 1930s, a regional migration of agricultural workers from rural settings augmented the city's Mexican population. By the mid-1930s, sugar-beet companies initiated a much larger migration that reversed the population decline in many parts of the Midwest when they began recruiting *Tejanos* systematically. Every year thousands of workers who came for seasonal agricultural employment settled permanently in Minnesota and elsewhere in the region. The 1930s movement from Texas marks the demographic watershed, which World War II intensified and extended to the major cities of the region.

World War II did not profoundly alter the occupational profile of all Mexicans, particularly those in the Midwest, and its immediate impact on upward mobility among families, a key aspect of the American Dream, was inconsistent. Among families in which men joined the armed services, separation and the loss of income from the principal breadwinners commonly resulted in economic difficulties and suffering, even when women were able to find employment.

A cohort of workers—primarily men employed in the region's steel mills and automobile factories—experienced noticeable improvement in their working lives, gaining higher earnings and more stable employment. Their own efforts in unionization struggles during the 1930s, rather than the war itself, propelled this change. Yet even the unionized factory workers found very limited opportunities for upward occupational advancement.[57]

Mexican and non-Mexican women did encounter a broader range of jobs directly as a result of the war, as in other parts of the country, but most were quickly pushed out once the hostilities subsided.[58] In the Midwest, Mexican women rarely found work in the service industries and were excluded from the professions. The restricted opportunities for upward mobility into the middle class among Mexican men and women during and after the war largely accounts for the minuscule presence of a self-conscious Mexican American leadership comparable to that of the Southwest to serve as intermediaries with agents and institutions of Americanization.

Limited occupational advancement and ongoing segregation in large part explain why the agents of Americanization in St. Paul portrayed Mexicans in practically the same way in 1935 as in 1946, as the most alien of the foreign groups in the Midwest, with a potential for assimilation that was as yet unfulfilled.

Notes

1. Mario T. García, "Americans All: The Mexican-American Generation and the Politics of Wartime Los Angeles, 1941–1945," *Social Science Quarterly* 65 (June 1984): 278–289; Mario T. García, *Mexican Americans: Leadership, Ideology, and Identity, 1930–1960* (New Haven, Conn.: Yale University Press, 1984); Richard A. García, *Rise of the Mexican-American Middle Class: San Antonio, 1929–1941* (College Station: Texas A&M University Press, 1991).

2. See, e.g., Manuel P. Servín, "The Post–World War II Mexican-Americans, 1925–65: A Non-Achieving Minority." In Manuel Servín, ed., *Mexican Americans: An Awakened Minority*, 2nd ed. (Beverly Hills, Calif.: Glencoe Press, 1974), 160–174.

3. International Institute and Neighborhood House, "Mexican Survey" (St. Paul, 1935), Immigration History Research Center, International Institute Papers, Box 13, folder 200 (hereafter cited as International Institute, 1935); International Institute and Neighborhood House, St. Paul, "The Mexican Nationality Community in St. Paul" (St. Paul, 1936), Immigration History Research Center, International Institute papers, Box 13, folder 200 (hereafter cited as International Institute, 1936); International Institute and Neighborhood House, "A Study of the Mexican Community in St. Paul" (St. Paul, 1946), International Institute Papers, Box 13, folder 201 (hereafter cited as International Institute, 1946).

4. Alice Sickels, "The International Institute in the Field of Folk Arts," paper presented at the National Conference of International Institutes, Grand Rapids, Michigan, May 25, 1940, Minnesota Historical Society pamphlet.

5. The sugar-beet industry in Minnesota expanded erratically but continuously for most of the twentieth century, and by the 1980s Minnesota became the leading sugar-beet-producing state in the nation. Throughout its history it attracted thousands of workers of Mexican birth and descent to work in the fields. On the relationship between the sugar-beet industry and the formation of St. Paul's Mexican colonia, see especially Dionicio Valdés, *Barrios Norteños: St. Paul and Midwestern Mexican Communities in the Twentieth Century* (Austin: University of Texas Press, 2000), 48ff. For a more detailed history of the Midwestern sugar-beet industry and beet workers, see also Dionicio Valdés, *Al Norte: Agricultural Workers in the Great Lakes Region, 1917–1970* (Austin: University of Texas Press, 1991).

6. Louisa Lambert, "Tank Town: Mexicans in Minnesota," *Hamline Piper* 15 (May 1934): 24–31; International Institute, 1946, 2; and Valdés, *Barrios*, 112.

7. International Institute, 1935, 2–3.

8. These issues will be discussed in greater detail in later sections. Individual identities will not be revealed in deference to relatives, as per agreement with the Immigration History Research Center, University of Minnesota.

9. Historical studies examining the interactions of social agencies and public officials with Mexicans include Sarah Deutsch, *No Separate Refuge: Culture, Class, and Gender on an Anglo-Hispanic Frontier in the American Southwest, 1880–1940* (New York: Oxford University Press, 1987); Ruth Hutchinson Crocker, "Gary Mexicans

and 'Christian Americanization,'" in James B. Lane and Edward J. Escobar, eds., *Forging a Community: The Latino Experience in Northwest Indiana, 1919–1975* (Chicago: Cattails Press, 1987), 115–134; Vicki L. Ruiz, "Dead Ends or Gold Mines? Using Missionary Records in Mexican-American Women's History," *Frontiers* 12, no. 1 (1992): 33–56; and George J. Sánchez, "Go after the Women: Americanization and the Mexican Immigrant Woman, 1915–1929," in Ellen Carol DuBois and Vicki L. Ruiz, eds., *Unequal Sisters: A Multicultural Reader in U.S. Women's History* (New York: Routledge, 1990), 250–263.

10. International Institute of Minnesota Papers, Immigration History Research Center (hereafter cited as II), Box 24, folder 706.

11. II, Box 25, folder 1295.

12. This pattern conflicts with that reported by Sánchez in "Go after the Women."

13. International Institute, 1936, 13, 16.

14. II, Box 25, folder 1281; II, Box 30, folder 744.

15. Bill Vogrin, "Hero Street: Mexican-Americans Cut a Path to Patriotism," *Chicago Tribune*, March 14, 1988; Monty Brower, "A Proud Street Mourns Its Fallen Sons," *Time* 123 (May 28, 1984): 76.

16. Interviews with Manuel Aguirre, Augustine Martínez, and George Vásquez, all videotaped recording, by Angela Macías, St. Paul, Minnesota, August 11 and 12, 2002, U.S. Latino and Latina WWII Oral History Project, University of Texas at Austin School of Journalism.

17. II, Box 27, folder 1206, a case in which a young man joined the military precisely because employment options were blocked outside of agricultural labor.

18. George T. Edson, "Mexicans in Toledo, Ohio," Paul Taylor Papers, Bancroft Library, University of California, Berkeley, 1926.

19. II, Box 33, folder 1414.

20. II, Box 34, folder 1277.

21. II, Box 29, folder 1271.

22. II, Box 24, folder 706.

23. "Women in Steel: They Are Handling the Tough Jobs in Heavy Industry," *Life* 15 (August 9, 1943): 75–81; Richard Santillán, "Rosita the Riveter: Midwest Mexican American Women during World War II, 1941–1945," *Perspectives in Mexican American Studies* 2 (1989): 115–147.

24. International Institute, 1936, 3.

25. II, Box 31, folder 713.

26. II, Box 30, folder 744.

27. International Institute, 1946, 7.

28. David E. and Mrs. David E. Henley, *Minnesota and Her Migratory Workers: Land of Promises—Partially Fulfilled* (Minneapolis: Minnesota Council of Churches and Home Missions Council, 1950), 25.

29. II, Box 34, folder 926.

30. See e.g., II, Box 30, folder 1271.

31. II, Box 27, folder 1206.

32. II, Box 27, folder 1580.

33. II, Box 34, folder 1259.

34. II, Box 32, folder 896.

35. II, Box 24, folder 880.

36. II, Box 30, folder 1763.

37. II, Box 24, folder 706.
38. II, Box 30, folder 744.
39. International Institute, 1936, 21.
40. International Institute, 1946, 6.
41. II, Box 28, folder 1244.
42. II, Box 30, folder 1006.
43. II, Box 30, folder 744.
44. II, Box 30, folder 1006.
45. Ibid.
46. II, Box 24, folder 1173.
47. II, Box 30, folder 1006.
48. II, Box 28, folder 1244.
49. II, Box 30, folder 1006.
50. II, Box 24, folder 706.
51. II, Box 34, folder 926.
52. II, Box 32, folder 896.
53. II, Box 29, folder 1271.
54. II, Box 30, folder 1006.
55. II, Box 30, folder 744.

56. Resident Mexican population of early 1940s; estimates based on "5,000 Take Part in Mexican Fiesta," *St. Paul Pioneer Press*, September 17, 1943, which conforms to a 1940 estimate by the Minnesota Governor's Interracial Commission, *The Mexican in Minnesota* (St. Paul: Governor's Interracial Commission, 1948), 10. The latter report also stated that 4,000 Mexican Nationals were imported annually between 1944 and 1946 to work in agriculture. In 1945 the Migrant Ministry estimated that 4,500 Spanish-speaking workers (Mexicans from Texas) migrated to the state annually for agricultural employment; in Home Missions Council of North America, "Statistical Material on Migrants, Projects and Costs, Midwestern Area (1945)," Presbyterian Historical Society, Home Mission Council Papers, Box 41, folder Midwest 1940s.

57. Jorge Hernández-Fujigaki, "Mexican Steelworkers and the United Steelworkers of America in the Midwest: The Inland Steel Experience (1936–1976)," Ph.D. diss., University of Chicago, 1991, 89–92.

58. See, e.g., International Institute, 1946, 4; Mexican Governor's Interracial Commission, *The Mexican in Minnesota*, 23.

CHAPTER 6

Zoot Violence on the Home Front

Race, Riots, and Youth Culture during World War II

LUIS ALVAREZ

On the evening of June 7, 1943, in Los Angeles, Vicente Morales carefully dressed in one of his tailor-made zoot suits for a night on the town. With his broad-rimmed hat, baggy pants tapered closely at the ankle, oversized coat, and gold watch chain hanging from the pocket, the young Mexican American teenager planned to dance the night away with his girlfriend to the jazzy sounds of the Lionel Hampton Band at the Orpheum Theater. Midway through the show, however, Morales was accosted by a group of white American sailors who, without provocation, began shoving him and screaming obscenity-laced insults. Before long, Morales found himself surrounded by as many as eight sailors outside of the theater. As they beat him, Morales passed out, only to awaken with a broken rib and nose, black-and-blue all over. After being covered by his girlfriend with her coat because his attackers stripped him of his own clothes, Morales was handcuffed, arrested, and transported by police wagon to city jail by the Los Angeles Police Department (LAPD) on charges of disturbing the peace.[1]

The story of Morales is appalling for its reckless brutality and injustice, yet is a familiar one for those knowledgeable of Mexican American history in Los Angeles during World War II. The unleashing of physical violence against Mexican American youth during the so-called Zoot Suit Riots has been well documented by Chicana/o historians.[2] However, less has been said about the diversity of those who experienced zoot violence and the fact that it extended beyond Los Angeles. This essay examines how zoot violence pitted not only white sailors and soldiers against Mexican American males, but also involved young Mexican American women and African American youth. The Zoot Suit Riots, in other words, were neither a singular ethnic nor a strictly male phenomenon. Moreover, while Los Angeles was home to the most massive assaults and serves as the primary case study, violence against zoot-suiters also occurred in New York, Philadelphia, Detroit, and elsewhere during the first week of June 1943.[3]

This essay argues that while violence against zoot-suiters was encouraged by wartime nativism that called for a culturally homogeneous home front, it was also, at least in part, a response to the construction of unique race and gender identities by youth of color. Zoot-suiters, by performing subversive masculinities and racially mixed social activities, for example, challenged dominant notions of wartime manhood and womanhood, as well as the prevalence of de facto segregation. The beatings, humiliation, and incarceration of zoot-suiters were thus a figurative and literal slap in the faces of youth of color by white America for infringing on social taboos.[4]

Zoot violence further illustrates how the politics of youth, in addition to more traditional political arenas like labor organizing and middle-class Americanization programs, raised critical questions about what and who was considered a legitimate part of American society during World War II.[5] From Los Angeles to New York City, zoot-suit culture became a violent stage in which black and brown youth, local police, regional politicians, the armed forces, and the media fought over nothing less than who was included in and who was excluded from the wartime polity.[6] The rioting against zooters exposed the limits of inclusion in wartime America by revealing that there were multiple American identities entitled to their place in the nation's cultural landscape.

On the heels of violence against zoot-suiters in Los Angeles, seemingly sporadic acts of violence targeting African Americans and ethnic Mexicans, many of them youth wearing zoot suits, spread to almost every metropolis in the United States.[7] The agitators of violence did not discriminate between zooters based on race, gender, or region. Nor did they distinguish between those zoot-suiters who were critical of wartime expectations to fight overseas and others who voluntarily joined the service to demonstrate their patriotism. This essay, consequently, contends that the message delivered by anti–zoot-suiters was that zoot-suiters did not meet the criteria for first-class membership in American society.

With a broader interpretation of the racial, gender, and regional aspects of zoot violence, moreover, we are less likely to view zoot-suiters as mere victims. As much as violence against zoot-suiters was a resounding statement of intolerance by the mainstream United States, it is also evidence of the struggle by many working-class youth of color for control over their own identity, adulthood, and dignity. As we listen to former zoot-suiters through oral histories and reread wartime propaganda and the written records of local authorities, the social struggles encountered by youth of color emerge as one way to enrich our understanding of the American home front during World War II. Ultimately, the youth who practiced the exaggerated styles of the zoot showed that cultural difference was not easily dismissed in an era of wartime consensus and conservatism.

With an eye toward acknowledging the complex state of race relations in World War II America, part one of this essay outlines the contours of zoot-suit culture in the early war years, paying close attention to how the multilayered meaning of style and the occupation of public space by zooters challenged notions of American identity as fundamentally white. This brief survey of zoot culture underscores that the state of race relations in 1940s America was as much about relationships among black and brown youth as it was about those among white and minority communities. The second section examines more closely the episodes of violence targeting zoot-suiters during the first week of June in 1943, focusing primarily on Los Angeles but also outlining the national explosion of violence against zooters, including physical assaults by white servicemen and cultural attacks by the mainstream media. This outline of physical, cultural, and structural devastation against zooters highlights violence as one generative source of social relations, debates over American identity, and battles over community boundaries.[8] The third section concludes by briefly speculating on how such a revised interpretation of zoot violence illuminates the importance of charting the intersections between racialized communities in Chicana/o and African American history.

Beginning in the late 1930s and into the mid-1940s, an increasingly diverse group of youth was active in zoot-suit culture.[9] From a young Malcolm X in New York to second-generation Mexican American women in Los Angeles, the sharing of flamboyant zoot style across boundaries of race, region, and gender was one response by youth of color to wartime shifts in the economy and shifting perceptions of American identity. Living conditions were hard for many African American and ethnic Mexican youth during the war years. On the one hand, there was greater upward mobility and prosperity for minorities and women as a result of access to defense industry jobs. However, there was also, on the other hand, wartime propaganda that promoted cultural sameness, respect and fear for white authority, and very real discrimination in employment, housing, social services, and education.[10] Ultimately, the meaning of the zoot is best gauged not only by analyzing the suit of clothes itself, but also by understanding how black and brown youth produced novel social relationships and rich centers of urban culture to create fresh meanings of gender, race, and nation as they lived in wartime America.[11] Regardless of their motivations for practicing zoot style, which ranged from a desire to be "cool" to escaping the alienation of wartime, the activities of zoot-suiters suggest that there was more than one "American identity."

The zoot was perhaps most notable among young males of color. With "the pants that hug the ankle and [are] low at the knee, the coat that comes nicely below the fingertips, and the double-thick-soled shoes,"[12] black and brown youth across the country used their own bodies to fashion their own unique style. Recalling his one and only zoot suit, a former zooter from Los Angeles described the typical West Coast version of the drapes.

> Yeah, everything was brown. And the coat came down to here [motioning to his knees], right down to here. And the silver chain from the pocket, and the wide like a pancake hat, with a real wide brim. If you were short, you would look like a thumbtack! And we used to dress up like that to go to the

dances. All of us, all wearing the same thing. With the big chain, we'd twirl the chain.[13]

After being measured for his first zoot suit on the East Coast, a young Malcolm X similarly recalls with a sense of dignity walking out of the store and immediately taking photographs of himself.

I took three of those twenty-five-cent sepia-toned, while-you-wait pictures of myself, posed the way "hipsters" wearing their zoots would "cool it"—hat dangled, knees drawn close together, feet wide apart, both index fingers jabbed toward the floor. The long coat and swinging chain and the Punjab pants were much more dramatic if you stood that way.[14]

Juxtaposed to the all-white, tight-fitting, starched uniforms worn by young American sailors, one of the most celebrated images of wartime manhood, the zoot style of Malcolm X and his ethnic Mexican counterparts was a drastically different masculine performance.[15] The white color of the naval uniform, in fact, serves as a metaphor for the whiteness of sailors' masculinity, a gender identity that excluded even the many black and brown youth who faced discrimination in the course of their military duty. While many black and brown males, including many zooters, actively participated in the war effort as servicemen or by supporting home-front patriotism, the popularity of the zoot was a stark reminder that there were deep ethnic and racial fissures in the United States. The zoot suit's exaggerated pants, hat brim, coattails, and sometimes flashy colors, not to mention its generous use of fabric, were all deemed excessive in an era of wartime shortages and detrimental to popular campaigns to conserve resources. The "duckbill" or "conk" haircuts worn by young ethnic Mexican and African American men and their "Spanglish" or "jive" dialects further marked them as acting outside the boundaries of proper male behavior. Some contemporary observers also marked male zooters as overly feminine for their constant attention to dress, hairstyle, and appearance, further marking them as a gendered other.[16] Characterized as pleasure-seekers obsessed with leisure, zooters were quickly deemed an illegitimate drain on domestic tranquility when contrasted to hardworking, responsible, and devoted sailors and soldiers. By proffering an alternative American manhood—nonwhite, rebellious, and wildly extravagant—zoot-suiters were considered a threat to much-needed social stability on the home front.

Zoot masculinity, sometimes at the expense of young women of color, also operated as a vehicle for young black and brown men to claim dignity and pride in a society that dehumanized and denigrated their existence.[17] It is likely, for example, that zooters in Los Angeles were suspicious of servicemen who visited the historically black Central Avenue area or East Los Angeles seeking the companionship of African American or ethnic Mexican women. Rumor had it that men in uniform were attracted to such areas of the city in search of young women of color who were easily seduced.[18] This practice undoubtedly agitated the already simmering tension between minority civilian youth and servicemen, as fights over young women broke out. While zooters articulated their own style of manhood, white servicemen regarded zoot style and dress as a challenge to their own training and masculinity.

Of course, young women were more than sexual objects in the gaze of young white, black, or brown men.[19] One contemporary observed that "the girls, too, the 'pachucas' had their version of drapes. This included very short dresses; very long bobby socks, and an elaborate hairdo with a high pompadour."[20] With their skirts or draped slacks, oxford shoes, and heavy use of mascara and lipstick, pachucas, or *slick chicks* as they were often labeled, constructed their own sense of style. Many young women even wore the dark-colored fingertip-length coats favored by male zooters to match their black fishnet stockings. One former pachuca, Maria, remembers when at age fifteen she and her friends in Los Angeles would "wear zoot suits too, with the skirts short and the jackets long. We'd wear socks up to here [motioning to her thighs]. We'd buy them at the Men's Department. Men's socks. I even had a friend who used to put glue on her leg so her socks wouldn't fall down!"[21] The pachuca style, a common practice for young women from working-class barrios, combined the use of men's and women's clothing to form a unique cultural style that provided validation for many young ethnic Mexicans.

Maria described this process by saying:

I felt good dressing like that. I think it's because . . . you felt like people were kind of looking down on you. You didn't feel like you belonged. But it didn't bother me, but I know a lot of people it did. They wanted to belong to a certain group, so we formed our own little group. And the girls I went to high school with, we liked it. I don't know why, and my sister felt the same way.[22]

Even at only fifteen or sixteen years old, claims Maria, women zooters "loved" the zoot-suit culture because "we knew from day one what we were [Mexican]."[23] For many young women, practicing zoot style was one way to both explore and affirm their own sense of ethnic and gender identity.

For young women, however, there was also an anticipated performance of masculinity encouraged by wartime images of "Rosie the Riveter" as a dedicated factory worker dressed in heavy-duty work clothes and helping to produce war materials, or of women becoming heads of households left behind by men who had gone to fight overseas. These dominant tropes of female behavior clashed with the style and experiences of streetwise pachucas who, like their male counterparts, transgressed the boundaries of expected gender roles. Pachucas employed their own bodies as the vehicle for a style that simultaneously extended the limits of womanhood and crafted their own version of wartime masculinity.

Throughout the prewar and early war years, African American and ethnic Mexican zoot-suiters across the country modeled their fashionable identities in community parks, on street corners, and at local business establishments, an occupation of public space that invoked concern from much of white America. The exposure of the zoot, along with its extensive social networks and leisure-based activities, only intensified views of the style and its practitioners as a detriment to the war effort. The creativity of zooters was interpreted not as a response to discrimination and poor life conditions, but as a desire to avoid work, responsibility, and their expected place among the proletariat. The "congested terrain" of public space, which also included movie theaters, public playgrounds, and nightclubs, emerged as the most contested arena for zooters and the anti-minority American establishment.[24] In a time of increasing hostility toward black and brown communities, these public spaces were home to the social experimentation of zooters and, eventually, the violent crackdown against them.

Zoot-suiters of all colors in Los Angeles, for example, frequented the African American center of town along Central Avenue to pick up the latest clothing fashions or listen to touring jazz performers like Duke Ellington and Dizzy Gillespie. Pete, a former zoot-suiter who grew up in the Echo Park neighborhood of Los Angeles, recalls how the clubs, eateries, and shops in the area attracted zooters.

> Yeah, I used to go down there to listen to the jam sessions. Louie Armstrong and Duke Ellington and all those guys. All those world known musicians used to go there near 4th and Central. They called it the Chicken Basket. That was the name of a nightclub where they had all the jam sessions. . . . Man, was that the place to be.[25]

When asked about the racially diverse makeup of the many social gatherings she attended in early 1940s Los Angeles as a young woman zooter, Maria recalls how

> everybody from all over L.A. would come to the big dances at the Diana Ballroom or other places near Central to hear the big bands. Mexicans, blacks, Filipinos, and even the white kids. I remember the black guys always looked so sharp and were the best dancers. We used to love to dance with them.[26]

A similar sharing of dance floors, bars, and public settings between black and white patrons occurred in other zoot cultural centers around the country. In Harlem, in particular, hotspots like the Savoy Ballroom catered to a multiracial clientele who socialized with each other, formed friendships, and established dating patterns with one another. Recalling his zoot-suit days, Malcolm X described a night of dancing in his autobiography.

> Once I got myself warmed and loosened up, I was snatching partners from among the hundreds of unattached, freelancing girls along the sidelines—almost every one of them could

really dance—and I just about went wild! Hamp's band wailing, I was whirling girls so fast their skirts were snapping. Black girls, brownskins, high yellows, even a couple of the White girls there. Boosting them over my hips, my shoulders, into the air. Though I wasn't quite sixteen then, I was tall and rawboned and looked like twenty-one; I was also pretty strong for my age. Circling, tap-dancing, I was underneath them when they landed doing the "flapping eagle," the "kangaroo," and the "split."[27]

Such activity was shunned to the extent that city authorities identified desegregated behavior as a moral threat to the home front. The Savoy Ballroom in New York, one of the world's most famous jitterbug and zoot dance halls, was even closed down by city police for its breaking of public taboos against "race mixing."[28]

The occupation of public space by zoot-suiters, albeit only temporary for any given night at a club or several hours at a movie theater, was consistent enough to elicit distaste from many whites. Zoot-suiters, perhaps unintentionally, collectively established a visible and intense network of cross-racial social activity that contested the status quo segregated sensibilities of wartime America. Moreover, as increasing numbers of white youth became enthralled with zoot and jazz cultures, race mixing threatened white privilege because it incorporated white, black, and brown youth together on relatively equal footing. Indeed, it was one thing for African American and ethnic Mexican youth to fraternize with one another, but it became a much bigger problem for many Americans when white youth were also part of the overt cultural and social miscegenation of the jitterbug or lindy hop. The melding of whiteness with the racialized categories of black and Mexican, even if only on the dance floor, challenged popular conceptions of a universal and superior white identity.[29]

For zoot women, especially in the face of popular wartime discourse that targeted them as a drain on the moral character of the home front for carrying venereal disease and infecting servicemen, their occupation of public space discarded the submissive roles they were assigned by parents, middle-class Mexican Americans, and even their zoot boyfriends.[30] While the discourse of public health was employed to marginalize young women of color as dangerous and diseased, the youth themselves made a different use of their public presence.[31] The frequenting of dances, parties, and concerts by women zooters contested their confinement to the private sphere, though such activity took on different meanings depending on whom they associated with.[32] Going to the movies with their parents, for example, was very different than going with a boyfriend or a group of girlfriends. Mixed-gender dates pushed the boundaries of acceptable behavior for young women by allowing them to interact with the opposite sex in a wide range of social networks usually unavailable at home.[33] Same-sex social relationships prevalent among zoot women who frequented public places together on a regular basis may have further disrupted domestic gender norms by fostering a homoeroticism of female-female interaction viewed as unhealthy and alien.

The activities of zoot-suiters are not only a window to view wartime race and gender composition, but also functioned as an intricate cultural infrastructure. Zoot culture, in other words, is not simply a "text" to be read, but also the everyday context and social relationships that helped define life for thousands of youth. In addition to the nightclubs and clothing shops, we might think of home sewing machines where some zoots were made, or the malt shops and pool halls where youth gathered, as new kinds of cultural institutions that sustained minority youth livelihood during the war.[34] While certainly not all African American and ethnic Mexican youth participated fully, nor even fleetingly, in zoot culture, it did play an important part in the lives of many young people. Though not a formal method of political organizing or even always a conscious decision to critique American racism, zoot culture was one strategy for black and brown to claim space for themselves, create an extensive network of social practices, and thrive amid alienating wartime conditions.[35]

For zooters, perhaps the most immediate front on which they negotiated power and formed social relationships was with one another.[36] While most shared an affinity for similar fashions, jazz music, and youthful creativity, zooters were by no means a homogeneous group. Because the zoot captivated the imagination of ethnic Mexican, African American, Asian American, and white youth, zooters had conflicting familial, cultural, and social backgrounds. Such diversity was even reflected in the subtle efforts to craft a specific style through the particular cut or color of the suit. African American youth on the East Coast, for example, often preferred bright colors and flat-soled shoes, while ethnic Mexicans on the West Coast favored dark browns and blacks with double- or triple-soled shoes.[37] At the same time as they were dealing with their own fissures and contradictions—including patriarchal claims to authority by male zooters over female zooters, which were evident everywhere from the dance floor to ownership of the zoot style—zoot-suiters also clashed with youth not involved in the style, who often saw them as wearing "clown suits" or belonging to a "lower class."[38]

Both male and female zooters formed neighborhood groups that, while labeled by local authorities and journalists as gangs, also functioned as support networks. In Los Angeles, for example, ethnic Mexican male cliques like the 38th Street and Alpine Street gangs were accompanied by groups of young women. One contemporary recalls that of the pachucas,

> the best looking ones that dressed nice were the girls from [the] Maravilla [barrio in East L.A.]. The Black Widows! They all died their hair black. Some of them had natural little streaks. They were pretty. I used to look at them at the dances, we all used to go to the dances, and they used to come in their little groups from different areas from all over.[39]

Competition between these groups for supremacy of barrio turf, boyfriend-girlfriend relationships, and ownership of zoot style resulted in fistfights and brawls among both men and women zooters.[40]

Zoot-suiters also engaged the rest of ethnic Mexican and African American communities. Just as the general public found zoot behavior to be unacceptable, so too did the working-class parents of many zooters and the growing minority middle class. Many older African Americans or ethnic Mexicans viewed zoot-suiters as violent thugs damaging larger efforts for communal upward mobility and inclusion in American society. Zoot-suiters' extension of community boundaries to include other racialized populations and their unwillingness to always enthusiastically pursue cultural assimilation underscored the generational conflict. As young people, zooters shared similar life experiences, including an abundance of free time, less familial responsibility, and the freedom to experiment socially, that allowed them to remake long-standing social traditions in their communities.[41] One Southern California zooter, Tony, even remembers refusing to wear his zoot suit at home for fear of disrespecting his mother.[42] Servicemen of color had mixed reactions to the zoot: some respected zooters for their courage to be culturally different, and others viewed the suits as a sign of youthful rowdiness.[43] Ironically, of course, it was sometimes difficult to differentiate between zooter and servicemen points of view, since many youth were both.

Of course, as became increasingly clear with the advent of zoot violence, the zoot also served as the context in which black and brown youth engaged the armed services, police, media, and local politicians. To the Anglo-dominated American state and general public, the racial pluralism of zoot culture and its bold statements of gender difference destabilized accepted social hierarchies in the United States. By the summer of 1943, in fact, the zoot suit was a national icon for wartime juvenile delinquency and was seen as a major threat against domestic unity.[44] Consequently, zoot culture soon became the target for violence in urban areas across the United States.

As racial tension over the zoot increased around the country, Los Angeles in particular evolved into a virtual tinderbox. Leading up to the Zoot Suit Riots, a number of skirmishes between white servicemen and zooters propelled the area's black newspaper, the *California Eagle*, to charge that "powerful interests in Los Angeles are desperately attempting to provoke a mass race clash in the city through piling grievance after grievance upon the Negro and Mexican community, on the one hand, and through smearing Mexicans and Negroes as 'zoot suit killers' on the other." The local chapter of the National Association for the Advancement of Colored People (NAACP) even held a meeting the day before the outbreak of the riots that drew over 1,500 citizens to discuss ways to avoid the impending violence.[45]

On the night of Thursday, June 3, 1943, however, fears of rioting were realized when eleven white sailors walking along Main Street in East Los Angeles alleged they were jumped and beaten by a gang of at least thirty-five zoot-suiters. In this predominantly ethnic Mexican neighborhood, the street lined with "ramshackle" houses and a large brewery on one side and a series of bars, small factories, and boarded-up storefronts on the other, the group of Anglo servicemen suffered only a few minor injuries. However, officers of the LAPD responding to the call, many of them off-duty at the time, dubbed themselves the Vengeance Squad and arrived at the scene seeking to cleanse Main Street of what they viewed as the loathsome influence of pachuco gangs.[46]

The next day, following the lead of the LAPD's Vengeance Squad, more than two hundred members of the U.S. Navy hired a caravan of at least twenty taxicabs and set out for East Los Angeles. When sailors in the lead car spotted a young ethnic Mexican in a zoot suit, a signal was sent to the rest of the procession and the boy was beaten within minutes.[47] Violence against ethnic Mexicans and African Americans, many wearing zoot suits and others not, continued for the next four days and nights. Anglo soldiers and marines soon joined sailors to cordon off sections of city blocks, raid places of business, and form posses in attempts to purge L.A.'s streets of zoot-suiters. Throughout the next week, it was not uncommon for zooters to be beaten, stripped of their clothes, and left humiliated in front of gathering crowds of onlookers. Carey McWilliams, a longtime activist on behalf of Mexican rights in California, later recalled, "They'd [sailors] barge into the downtown theaters, and drag them [zoot-suiters] out of the theaters, and work them over, and all that sort of thing. And the zoot suit costume was an incitation to these mobs that were roaming the city. They went on for about a week before it quieted down."[48]

Pete, who was involved in confrontations with sailors, soldiers, and marines throughout the early 1940s, remembered clearly

> when we were fighting with the sailors and soldiers in downtown. They were running in the theaters and grabbing any Chicano. But first they used to check you over to see if you had drapes on and it got to the point where they couldn't find too many of those guys anymore. They were hanging around the neighborhoods, in case we came their way. So, anybody that's Mexican they dragged their ass out there and take your pants off in the middle of Broadway.[49]

Lupe, an ethnic Mexican woman who was in her mid-teens at the time, similarly recalled that white servicemen "beat up on any Mexican, whether they were young kids or older kids. . . . I remember it because I saw it. To the degree that younger people [ethnic Mexicans and African Americans] in the streets were hiding behind houses" so as not to be seen by sailors looking for them.[50] Lupe further remembers feeling

> sorry for those poor guys [zooters]. I think now, if I would have had sons and grandsons at that time and they beat up my kids like that, I'd have been right in there with them. But they'd have to beat me up with them. I wouldn't be fighting with sticks and candles either; I'd be out there with shovels and rakes and whatever I could get my hands on.[51]

Still another observer of the Los Angeles Zoot Suit Riots remembers how the sailors "picked on the weak" by singling out zooters who were walking on their own and were badly outnumbered, sometimes by as much as fifteen or more to one.[52]

Everyone wearing the flashy zoot garb was a target of the wild mobs of Anglo servicemen and civilians, including ethnic Mexicans, African Americans, Filipinos, and even some Anglo youth.[53] After the first days of rioting in Los Angeles, for example, the NAACP released several reports from its branch office noting that several African American youth wearing zoot suits were attacked in the downtown area, with at least four suffering serious injuries.[54] Eighteen years old at the time of the Riots, Maria recalled that after the second or third day of violence, any minority youth became fair game for the rioting servicemen, regardless of the degree of their zoot style. "They [sailors] got the boys in our neighborhood," she remembers, "and they weren't even the real heavy duty pachucos. They were moderate and they got beat up!"[55]

There are also reports of several Anglo zooters coming under attack from servicemen.[56] *Time* magazine reported in its June 21 edition, for example, the beating of a seventeen-year-old Russian boy, Pete Nogikoss, by sailors who saw him talking with two ethnic Mexican zooters on a street corner. Sailors and soldiers armed with sticks and weighted ropes commandeered long caravans of cabs and private cars in their search for zooters of all colors, leaving many beaten and stripped of their clothes only to be arrested by police for vagrancy and disturbing the peace. Summing up the riots, *Time* chimed that "California's zoot-suit war was a shameful example of what happens to wartime emotions without wartime discipline."[57] One zooter put it more bluntly, saying "They [sailors] had it against the zoot-suiters real bad in those days. They had it against them real real bad. If they caught you by yourself wearing a zoot suit, they'd kill you, them bastards."[58]

Young women were also active participants in the violent events plaguing Los Angeles in early June. The initial clashes between zooters and sailors are at least partly attributable to competition over young ethnic Mexican women, who were often seen as hypersexualized, but because they were also active participants in the zoot culture, young women of color were also attacked.[59] Though they were not targeted to the degree of their male counterparts, young women did endure physical harassment. One young ethnic Mexican girl, who was thirteen years old at the time, remembers, "My best friend was attacked by some white sailors. They asked her if she had been in Tijuana the week before with them. Four of them grabbed her. I was the only one she told."[60]

Though the areas near Broadway and Main Street were the major areas of violence, young ethnic Mexicans and African Americans also found themselves under scrutiny far from the city streets of East Los Angeles. The Santa Monica lifeguards, for example, went on alert the week of the riots after receiving warning of an ethnic Mexican zoot-suit gang on the prowl looking to cause trouble at the beach. After leading a search up and down the beach amid sunbathers and swimmers, the chief of the Santa Monica Lifeguards was left puzzled as to the whereabouts and identity of the zooters. Unable to find any zoot-suiters or "how to tell a zoot-suiter when he isn't wearing his zoot suit," the chief later remarked, "some of them had long hair, which curled up at the back like a drake's tail, but their bathing togs weren't any different from those of others, so we were unable to tell just how many, if any, were gang members."[61]

Wartime xenophobia certainly played a key role in igniting the riots. After all, as 1940s Los Angeles resident and prominent community organizer Alice McGrath later remarked, "It was as though the frustration of not being able to go over and kill Japs, or whatever it was that they [the Navy] were building them [sailors] up to, they could go beat up on kids with zoot suits."[62] As the Zoot Suit Riots intensified throughout the first weeks of June, however, it became clear that servicemen were also attacking zooters for their alternative visions of race and gender in the United States. Zoot-suiters threatened standard views of how youth should act and what they should wear, and were persecuted as subversive to the war effort and popular attitudes that minorities were politically passive. As historians Shane and Graham White argue, "This new youth culture—vibrant, autonomous, and not segregated—was of concern to the authorities."[63]

Such concern was evident, for example, in the hundreds of complaints filed with naval authorities by white sailors charging zoot-suiters with physical and verbal assault. Fears of black and brown zooters interacting with white Angelenos, particularly women, were a major concern for servicemen involved in the riots. One sailor, for example, complained to his superiors that his wife was accosted by two zooters cruising by in a car as she walked along Chavez Ravine in Los Angeles after visiting her husband at the nearby military base. Allegedly, the zooters pulled up close to her, asked her to get in the car, and propositioned her.[64] Another report filed by white naval personnel on June 10 noted that several sailors were sitting with their girlfriends and mothers on the terrace at the Armory in Los Angeles when a group of "up to twenty" zooters drove by in a black Plymouth coupe and shouted, "Fuck you, you bastards."[65] Still other reports filed by white sailors included two zooters charged with molesting sailors' girlfriends outside a drugstore; two zooters in a car asking the wife of a sailor, "What the fuck's the matter with you; are you too good to go with us?"; zooters harassing the wife and children of a sailor near their home in Los Angeles; and the pregnant wife of a white sailor being pushed down to the ground by zooters yelling "Eah, Navy!"[66] This last incident, in particular, illustrates how zooters were deemed a volatile threat to the reproductive capacity of the United States, so crucial during wartime.

The sheer volume of reports by white servicemen against zooters who were allegedly violating the servicemen's girlfriends, sisters, and mothers through physical or verbal assault illustrates the perceived danger zooters posed to the segregated social sensibilities of wartime America. Indeed, it is possible, perhaps even likely, that many of the complaints made by sailors and soldiers were fabrications, or at least exaggerations, based on fears of miscegenation and the belief that minorities should not socialize beyond their own ethnic boundaries. While it is certainly possible that some black and brown zooters did harass white women in Los Angeles without provocation, it is also likely that white sailors harassed women of color, although those incidents were not reported to police or military officials. If it was black and brown zooters who were constantly abusing white women, as naval records suggest, they were guilty not only of infringing upon the most sacred ground of American sailors, their relationships with women, but also of threatening the racial hierarchy of the United States through casual sex with white women.

Zooters did not submit meekly to the beatings or accusations without a fight: they actively defended themselves and retaliated physically and verbally. In doing so, zooters claimed their own sense of belonging in the country. Recalling one incident the week of the riots, Pete vividly illustrates the conflict with servicemen.

> It was bad enough that we seen a bunch of White cats and we said "what the hell's going on." So they go to this restaurant and somebody comes out and says, "Hey you guys are Mexicans, you guys better go." Why? "They come looking for you, they're looking for Mexicans." I says "Oh yeah. Well let 'em come. Come on." So as they're coming out, boom bang boom, you know. There was only about seven or eight of them, you know. There was four of us, but we kicked some good ass, you know. And they left. All that started. That was on a Monday or Tuesday evening. Come Friday, man, 500 guys coming through there.[67]

Following the initial battles of the riots, some zooters even began organizing trips in pickup trucks to Southern California military bases as far away as San Diego in hopes of rumbling with servicemen.

> The guys from [the] Alpine [street gang]. They would get in their trucks and drive them through the neighborhoods, in their trucks, you know. And go down to San Diego to kick some ass over there. I says, "What are you guys crazy? We got the bases there and got about a thousand guys. You guys

gonna go to war and start your own war?" And they went. I never asked them what happened or what, but I heard a lot of them got their asses kicked. Driving down the freeways in those trucks. You guys are crazy.[68]

The energy to strike back against white servicemen was at least in part a response to the hypocrisy of domestic racial violence occurring simultaneously with the massive effort to defeat fascism overseas. One former zoot-suiter remembered the Los Angeles riots in this context. "It lasted only for the summertime," he said,

and after that it was all over. But those guys [sailors] made a lot of people unhappy with their driving the Mexicans out. Even a lot of the white people were saying, "I thought the war was over there with the Japanese and you got Americans as prisoners over here, you know. Who's next?" "If they got all the Mexicans in jail, are we next?" the white people are saying. "Who's going to fight the war?" So they started getting all the soldiers and the servicemen to cut out that bullshit, you know. Then, after that all happened, I got drafted.[69]

Although zooters were usually construed as antiwar, unpatriotic, and even pro-Axis, they were being drafted into or voluntarily joining the Navy and Army with regularity, serving their country with great vigor. Later, some of them used their service to broaden the movement for civil rights in the United States.

One irony is that there were consistent rumors in the years leading up to the riots that Hitler was actively recruiting Los Angeles–area zoot-suiters as fifth-column agents.[70] In fact, throughout the week of the rioting in Los Angeles, the mainstream press instigated physical violence, supported the actions of city police and servicemen, and launched culturally violent propaganda against minority communities.[71] Building on months of sensational criminalization of ethnic Mexican and African American youth as zoot-suiting punks, the mainstream press clearly supported the actions of the Anglo sailors and further vilified zoot-suiters as deserving of every punch, kick, and injury they received. The *Herald Express*, for example, headlined "Sailor Task Force Hits LA Zooters" and justified the riots in defense of the morality, patriotism, and safety of wartime Los Angeles.[72] Championing the efforts of the servicemen rioters, the *Times*'s front-page headline news story reported that "those gamin dandies, the zoot suiters, having learned a great moral lesson from servicemen, mostly sailors, who took over their instruction three days ago, are staying home nights."[73]

The mainstream Los Angeles press continued to vilify zooters, in particular, and ethnic Mexican and African American communities more generally. Among the journalistic strategies employed was an unequal emphasis on servicemen injured in the violence, fanning hysteria over the criminal elements of black and brown youth, and juxtaposing photos of vicious-looking zooters brandishing knives and other weapons next to innocent-looking or beaten servicemen.[74] While the national press was more inclined to spread blame for the riots to all parties involved, the major newspapers in Washington, D.C., Chicago, and Atlanta, for example, all followed their Los Angeles counterparts in labeling zooters as gangsters threatening the stability and production of one of the country's most important war industry sites. During the week of the riots, headlines across the country included "Zoot-Suiters Again on Prowl as Navy Holds Back Sailors,"[75] "Los Angeles' Zoot War Called 'Near Anarchy,'"[76] "Punish Guilty in Zoot Fights, Probe Urges,"[77] and "Zoot Suit War Grows; Army and Navy Act."[78] The onslaught of the press against youth of color prompted one young African American to question reporters on Central Avenue in Los Angeles. "You gonna take pictures of us so you can put them in them damn Hearst papers and call us gangsters again?" he asked. "You won't take no pictures here and make us look like murderers to White people—too much damn prejudice, that's what!"[79]

The press also deliberately and viciously attacked young ethnic Mexican women. The *Times* took a particular interest in reporting alleged attacks by ethnic Mexican girls on white women. Headlines during the week of the riots included "Brass Knuckles Found on Woman Zoot Suiter" and "Zoot Girls Use Knife in Attack as War Eases." In the first case, a twenty-two-year-old ethnic Mexican woman was arrested for disturbing the peace and carrying a concealed weapon after questioning how police treated a group of zoot-suiters outside her home in East Los Angeles. Amelia Venegas, who claimed to have a husband serving in the Navy, saw no reason why zoot-suiters could not walk the streets like any other resident. For Venegas, however, challenging the public condemning of zooters led to her arrest and incriminating picture on the front page of the *Los Angeles Times*.[80] In the second case, a white woman claimed she was attacked by three "slick chicks" when the girls jumped her at the entrance to the Third Street tunnel in Los Angeles and sat on her chest, kicked her, and slashed her face with a razor.[81] As were their male counterparts, women zooters were portrayed in the press as ruthless killers eroding wartime morality through violence, prostitution, and the spread of venereal disease.[82] One former zooter remembers the ways in which the mainstream Los Angeles press described the popular hairdos of young women zooters.

> They made it out like we had knives in our hair and all that. That was comical, actually, to hear about things like that. Every girl was going from one guy to another, you know, for sexual favors. The papers made us out to be real tramps. They said [Mexican] girls met a boy and that was it. They were like married already! That's a lie! And I know it not just for me, but my girlfriends. We laughed when we talked about it. Hey, did you do what they said you did. Heck no, you know. Girls talked just like anyone else. They made up lies. Us carrying knives and things in our hair. You just can't believe the stories they put out.[83]

Similar stories racializing juvenile delinquency and portraying zoot women as un-American ran in most Los Angeles–area newspapers throughout the coverage of the Zoot Suit Riots. The mainstream press served to encourage servicemen's violence, implicate zooters as criminals draining the war effort, and incite public opinion against zooters.[84]

While the mainstream Los Angeles press was relentless in its barrage of attacks against zooters, it was not to be outdone by city and county officials. In addition to the physical and cultural violence against youth of color, the Los Angeles Zoot Suit Riots exposed deep-seated structural violence that helped limit their life chances.[85] The LAPD, the Navy's shore patrol, and the offices of local authorities reinforced the assaults on zooters through an intense propaganda that further marginalized and alienated them. Law enforcement and political agencies throughout the city participated in the estrangement of zoot-suiters either by joining the rioting or by publicly characterizing zooters as ruthless villains disrupting the war effort.

The LAPD and the Navy's shore patrol did little to discourage the rioting. In fact, they were complicit in the violence against minority youth. Several reports exist of city police and naval authorities not only refusing to stop Anglo sailors from beating zooters, but congratulating the assailants for a job well done or even participating in the physical and verbal abuse of zooters.[86] Police were seen joking and laughing while mobs of sailors beat ethnic Mexican and African American youths in zoot suits.[87] Witnesses also noted police cars and motorcycle officers of the highway patrol accompanying and escorting taxis full of sailors looking for zooters through East Los Angeles streets.[88] One Los Angeles resident at the time, also a former zoot-suiter, remembered how "instead of arresting the sailors, they [the LAPD] helped kick them [ethnic Mexican and African American zooters] around! The cops were even leading them [sailors] to the areas they could find them [zooters]."[89] Another simply states that the police "allowed them [sailors] to do it."[90]

Such a relationship with the police left African American and ethnic Mexican communities in a no-win situation. Lupe, a former pachuca, remembers the tenuous relationship between city police and communities of color.

Who could you complain to? When the police themselves were beating you up and kicking you around! Who are you going to complain to? They'd deny it. I seen kids taken out of a theater for throwing popcorn in the show, which every kid does at sometime or another. They took 'em out of the show and took them to the police station and then later on that night they dropped them off all bloody. This was in East L.A. at one theater. They dropped the kid off all beat up. You think the parents are gonna complain? There are ways of thinking that the police are always right, that they were just there for our good. The kids knew they weren't. They were there for their own good.[91]

After more than four full days of violence in Los Angeles during the first week of June, naval authorities finally announced the city as a restricted area for enlisted men in an effort to limit the clashes between servicemen and zoot-suiters. In its official statement announcing the ban, the Navy described sailors as defending themselves against the "rowdy element" of the city streets.[92] The Army soon followed suit by declaring the Main Street area of downtown out of bounds to its enlisted personnel.[93] Despite the bans, mob violence continued for another two nights.

City officials, led by Mayor Fletcher Bowron, expressed support for the police and armed forces by legitimizing police and military authority, discounting racial discrimination as a factor in the uprising, and claiming the disturbances were caused by the activities of local gangs.[94] In a letter to Los Angeles Police Chief C. B. Horrall shortly after the riots, Bowron commended the LAPD for emphasizing the "acts and conduct, not citizenship, color, or location in city or parentage of persons" who were being arrested.[95] In fact, the mayor said, there was "no substantial anti-Mexican feeling and that all those involved have been treated alike, regardless or race, color or creed."[96] Still, however, the mayor claimed the riots were initiated by youthful gangs of Mexicans who had been subjected to a "lack of restraint and discipline"[97] or by ethnic Mexican girls who caused fights between sailors and zoot-suiters as each group of young men sought their companionship.[98] In a public statement the week of the riots, Bowron claimed that

> there are too many citizens in this community, some of them good intentioned and a few whose intentions I question, who raise a hue and cry of racial discrimination or prejudice against a minority group every time the Los Angeles police make arrests of members of gangs or groups working in unison. They all look alike to us, regardless of color and the length of their coats.[99]

The Los Angeles County Board of Supervisors, similarly, immediately downplayed the racial tension and seriousness of the riots by stating, "Some of this lawlessness was little more than college hazing carried on on a large scale, yet some of it inevitably produced retaliation and did serious bodily harm."[100]

Despite the efforts of local officials to smooth over the explosive racial nature of the riots, not all legislative action was so subtle. The Los Angeles City Council, for example, considered a proposal making it a jailable offense to wear "zoot suits" within city limits. Supporters of the proposal argued police had lost control of the riot situation, that zoot-suit "hoodlums" now had the cops "buffaloed," and that it was up to the city government to limit any further disturbances.[101] Though the proposal was not officially passed, it helped set the tone for police protocol in arresting zooters, represented the public's distaste for zooters, and facilitated further anti-zoot action by other government legislative bodies. In the first action of its kind, for example, the U.S. Department of Justice outlawed the manufacturing and selling of zoot suits on the grounds that the material used was unlawfully cut and in violation of orders to conserve fabric by the War Production Board.[102] Even at the most local of city institutions governing youth behavior, the zoot generated distrust and hatred. During the first week of June, just as the riots were about to erupt, the principal of Dorsey High School in Los Angeles addressed a school-wide assembly by stating, "I don't want any of that low zoot suit stuff from the Eastside on this campus."[103] Ultimately, city, state, and federal governments' unofficial sanctioning of physical violence against minority youth only reflected structural inequities in employment, housing, and formal political representation for ethnic Mexican and African American communities during the war.

Though the violence directed at black and brown youth in Los Angeles stemmed in part from local conflicts, including the sharing of public space by servicemen and zooters and the economic constraints of wartime Southern California, violence simultaneously erupted elsewhere in the United States. On June 9, just down the coast in San Diego, at least two separate mobs of nearly three hundred Anglo servicemen scoured the streets for zooters. Though zooters escaped the wrath of the mobs without serious injury, the San Diego chief of police warned that anyone seen in zoot-suit apparel would be questioned and given "shakedowns" to determine if they were concealing weapons or if they were vagrants.[104]

Violence aimed at zooters soon spread across the country and foreshadowed race riots in Beaumont, Texas, Detroit, and Harlem later in the summer of 1943. On June 9, police in Baltimore placed extra squads on duty to watch for African American zoot-suit gangs.

The heightened alert came one day after at least three black zoot-wearing youth were arrested, fined, and jailed for charges ranging from disorderly conduct to carrying concealed weapons.[105] Two days later in Detroit, sporadic fights broke out between Anglo youth and African American zoot-suiters. Police dispersed several groups from each side of the conflict after brawls left at least one seriously injured. As in Los Angeles, Detroit zooters were labeled as violent thugs carrying knives, clubs, and tire irons, while Anglo rioters were lauded as innocent high school students battling the unsavory elements of the city.[106] Just the next day, four African American boys wearing zoot suits were attacked and badly beaten on a Philadelphia street corner by a group of at least twenty-five Anglo boys. While the assailants escaped the scene, the zooters were arrested by police "for their own protection" on charges of disturbing the peace.[107]

In the end, violence against the zoot cannot be understood as strictly a Los Angeles local or even western regional phenomenon. Zoot violence, rather, was an American experience. As zooters claimed public space across the nation—on street corners and in dancehalls, movie theaters, and bars—many Americans responded violently to the expression of radically different notions of manhood, womanhood, and interracial relations by black, brown, and white youth.

Previous interpretations of zoot violence view it as a singular ethnic, largely male, and strictly Western phenomenon. Prevailing arguments assert that Los Angeles–area servicemen symbolically annihilated the masculinity of ethnic Mexican zoot-suiters and that the Zoot Suit Riots were a watershed moment in the politicization of the Los Angeles ethnic Mexican middle class.[108] Although these arguments account for the devastating effects of physical violence and the important gains made by middle-class politicization in response to the riots, they do not consider the racial, gender, or geographic complexity of zoot violence. Moreover, narratives of zoot violence from the perspective of the American state or the minority middle class often obscure the views of zoot-suiters themselves, making it difficult to see the violence as anything but blind expressions of wartime xenophobia. However, it is also critical to examine how the working-class minority youth themselves produced unique race and gender identities that, wittingly or not, provoked the violence.

The angry response to zoot culture by white America illustrates how violence was one mechanism to draw the boundaries of American community and identity. The violence against zoot-suiters that plagued much of the United States during the summer of 1943 was a very public ground zero for a diverse group of Americans to negotiate the race and gender contradictions of wartime nationhood. The struggle of zoot violence, consequently, cannot be fully explained by using models of race and gender relations that emphasize a single minority community's relationship to the Anglo-dominated American State. Understanding zoot violence as a multiracial, transregional, and gendered experience locates a vibrant cultural politics of the zoot in the activities of working-class youth of color. The politics of zoot violence alerts us to the challenges by zooters to popular conceptions of wartime race, nation, and gender as fundamentally white.

Zoot-suiters deserve recognition for creating an awareness and a record that there was racial and ethnic difference, even at a time when cultural differences were being stifled. The riots foreshadowed more stringent battles for equality in the 1950s and 1960s. Perhaps, as African American writer and activist Ralph Ellison noted in 1943, "the zoot suit conceals profound political meaning; perhaps the symmetry frenzy of the lindy hop conceals clues to great potential power."[109]

Rather than dismiss youth of color and their cultural creativity as easily managed or displaced, the zoot historically roots black and brown youth culture in violent social struggle. Zoot violence was exacerbated by wartime race and class tensions that exposed the failure of city, state, and federal authorities to address the needs of urban communities of color. Ultimately, however, the violent zoot summer of 1943 was not a series of disconnected xenophobic reactions against a hapless group of black and brown youth, but a deeply layered struggle over identity and belonging in wartime America.

Notes

1. Vicente Morales, interview by Sandy Mercado, May 1972, transcript, 9–10. Mexican American Collection, Chicano/Chicana Experience, Binder #25, Department of Special Collections, California State University, Long Beach.

2. See, for example, Mauricio Mazón, *The Zoot-Suit Riots: The Psychology of Symbolic Annihilation* (Austin: University of Texas Press, 1984); Edward J. Escobar, *Race, Police, and the Making of a Political Identity: Mexican Americans and the Los*

Angeles Police Department, 1900–1945 (Berkeley: University of California Press, 1999); Eduardo Pagán, "Sleepy Lagoon: The Politics of Youth and Race in Wartime Los Angeles, 1940–1945," Ph.D. diss., Princeton University, 1996; Patricia Rae Adler, "The 1943 Zoot-Suit Riots: Brief Episode in a Long Conflict," in Manuel P. Servín, ed., *The Mexican-Americans: An Awakened Minority* (Beverly Hills, Calif.: Glencoe Press, 1970), 142–158.

3. In this essay I use the terms *zoot-suiter* and *zooter* to refer as a whole to the diverse group of youth who participated in zoot culture, including ethnic Mexican, African American, and white youth. During the height of zoot culture in the early 1940s, these terms, like the more ethnically and racially specific terms *pachuco* and *pachuca* for ethnic Mexican youth and *hep cat* for African American youth, came to have negative connotations in popular discourse. My use of *zoot-suiter* and *zooter* does not intend to invoke such negativity nor ignore the differences and conflict between zoot-suiters, but rather serves to highlight the shared social and cultural experiences among them. For more on the terms *pachuco* and *pachuca* see, from example, Arturo Madrid-Barela, "In Search of the Authentic Pachuco: An Interpretive Essay," *Aztlán* 4, no. 1 (Spring 1973): 31–60; Catherine S. Ramirez, "Crimes of Fashion: The Pachuca and Chicana Style Politics," *Meridians: Feminisms, Race, Transnationalism* 2, no. 2 (2002): 1–35; Rosa Linda Fregoso, "Homegirls, Cholas, and Pachucas in Cinema: Taking Over the Public Sphere," *California History* 74, no. 3 (1995): 316–327. For more on the term *hep cat* see, for example, Robin D. G. Kelley, *Race Rebels: Culture, Politics, and the Black Working Class* (New York: Free Press, 1994); Bruce Tyler, "Black Jive and White Repression," *Journal of Ethnic Studies* 16, no. 4 (Winter 1989): 31–66.

4. Of course, whiteness itself is a complex racial identity fractured by class, ethnicity, and gender that merits further consideration in future research of zoot violence. For more on specific constructions of whiteness see, for example, Neil Foley, *The White Scourge: Mexicans, Blacks, and Poor Whites in Texas Cotton Culture* (Berkeley: University of California Press, 1997). Foley argues that "whiteness also came increasingly to mean a particular kind of white person. Not all whites, in other words, were equally white," 5.

5. Following anthropologist Steven Gregory, I understand politics to include "the production and exercise of social relationships and the cultural construction of social meanings that [both] support and undermine those relationships." Thus politics does not necessarily include any particular set of institutions or actions, but describes a field of variable social practices. See Steven Gregory, *Black Corona: Race and the Politics of Place in an Urban Community* (Princeton: Princeton University Press, 1998), 13. See also Kelley, *Race Rebels*, 8–10.

6. Following cultural critic Lisa Lowe, this notion of inclusion/exclusion does not rest on legal definitions of national citizenship, but a more flexible cultural citizenship. According to Lowe, "Although the law is perhaps the discourse that most literally governs citizenship, U.S. national culture—the collectively forged images, histories, and narratives that place, displace, and replace individuals in relation to the national polity—powerfully shapes who the citizenry is, where they dwell, what they remember, and what they forget." Lisa Lowe, *Immigrant Acts: On Asian American Cultural Politics* (Durham: Duke University Press, 1996), 2.

7. In this essay I use the term *ethnic Mexican* to refer to all persons of Mexican origin, regardless of citizenship. The term does not mean to suggest that ethnic Mexicans were not a racialized group during World War II. For more on the term *ethnic*

Mexican, see David Gutiérrez, *Walls and Mirrors: Mexican Americans, Mexican Immigrants, and the Politics of Ethnicity* (Berkeley: University of California Press, 1995), 218.

8. Anthropologist Steven Gregory explains community "not as a static, place-based social collective but a power-laden field of social relations whose meanings, structures, and frontiers are continually produced, contested, and reworked in relation to a complex range of sociopolitical attachments and antagonisms." Gregory, *Black Corona*, 11.

9. Most scholars agree the zoot originated in African American jazz culture during the 1930s and developed unique regional styles after touring jazz performers facilitated its growth in popularity. On the origins of the zoot see Stuart Cosgrove, "The Zoot-Suit and Style Warfare," *History Workshop Journal* 18 (Autumn 1984): 77–91; Beatrice Griffith, *American Me: Fierce and Tender Stories of the Mexican-Americans of the Southwest* (New York: Pennant Books, 1954); Luis Plascencia, "Low Riding in the Southwest: Cultural Symbols in the Mexican Community," in Mario T. García and Francisco Lomeli, eds., *History, Culture, and Society: Chicano Studies in the 1980s* (Ypsilanti, Mich.: Bilingual Press, 1983), 141–176; Steve Chibnall, "Whistle and Zoot: The Changing Meaning of a Suit of Clothes," *History Workshop Journal* 20 (Autumn 1985): 56–81.

10. Luis Alvarez, "The Power of the Zoot: Race, Community, and Resistance in American Youth Culture, 1940–1945," Ph.D. diss., University of Texas at Austin, 2001, 33–75.

11. On how youth cultures negotiate and engage the power of the state and dominant national cultures, see Dick Hebdige, *Subculture: The Meaning of Style* (New York: Routledge, 1977), 1–19.

12. "The Wearing of the 'Drape' Is No Sign of Delinquency," *Daily World*, May 21, 1945, found in Alice McGrath Collection, University of California at Los Angeles, Department of Special Collections, Collection 1290, Box 5, Folder 4.

13. Tony, interview by author, tape recording, San Diego, California, February 25, 1994. Several of the individuals interviewed during research for this essay requested anonymity so as not to have any embarrassing, illegal, or personal experiences publicly disclosed. Out of respect for these requests, all of the participants in interviews conducted by the author are cited with pseudonyms.

14. Malcolm X, *The Autobiography of Malcolm X* (New York: Ballantine Books, 1964), 52.

15. Masculinity, as literary and cultural critic Judith Halberstam argues, not only isn't the sole property of male bodies, but "heroic" or white middle-class male masculinity is inscribed with power and privilege only when juxtaposed to alternative racialized and female masculinities. Anthropologist Alejandro Lugo similarly argues that questions of the masculine and feminine should not be addressed through biological or societal assumptions, but through analyses of power, historical context, and gender, particularly how men and women negotiate their cultural subjectivities. See Judith Halberstam, *Female Masculinity* (Durham: Duke University Press, 1998); Alejandro Lugo, "Destabilizing the Masculine, Refocusing 'Gender': Men and the Aura of Authority in Michelle Z. Rosaldo's Work," in Alejandro Lugo and Bill Maurer, eds., *Gender Matters: Rereading Michelle Z. Rosaldo* (Ann Arbor: University of Michigan Press, 2000), 54–89.

16. Ralph S. Banay, "A Psychiatrist Looks at the Zoot Suit," *Probation* 22, no. 3 (1944): 81–85. See also Catherine S. Ramirez, "Crimes of Fashion: The Pachuca and

Chicana Style Politics," *Meridians: Feminism, Race, and Transnationalism* 2, no. 2 (2002): 10–11.

17. On dignity as a category of analysis see John Holloway, "Dignity's Revolt," in John Holloway and Eloina Pelaez, eds., *Zapatista! Reinventing Revolution in Mexico* (London: Pluto Press, 1998), 159–198; John Holloway, *Change the World without Taking Power: The Meaning of Revolution Today* (London: Pluto Press, 2002). According to Holloway, as a struggle against its own denial, dignity is the struggle for hope and humanity against poor life chances and a politics of refusal to accept humiliation, to endure dehumanization, and to conform. For Holloway, dignity is also very much a class concept that links people based not on their subordination to capital, but on their insubordination to domination. Thus, the class nature of dignity is primarily a relation of struggle shared by groups who experience an antagonism between their own creativity (work in the broadest sense) and their own dehumanization by capital or the nation-state. Following Holloway's lead, this essay suggests that zoot-suiters experienced a series of social antagonisms during World War II based on their class, race, and gender positions.

18. Alice McGrath Oral History, *The Education of Alice McGrath*, interviewed by Michael Balter, Tape IV, side two, January 20, 1985, UCLA Special Collections, 300/269, 153–154.

19. Though this essay primarily examines the role of young ethnic Mexican women in zoot culture, several interviewees involved in the research for this project alluded to the role of young African American women in zoot culture. Their role, however, has been largely ignored in the archival and press records of the era, inviting the critique that in studies of race and gender, black women are often forgotten. On ethnic Mexican women zooters, see Cosgrove, "The Zoot-Suit and Style Warfare," 77–91; Griffith, *American Me*; Ramirez, "Crimes of Fashion."

20. "The Wearing of the 'Drape' Is No Sign of Delinquency."

21. Maria, interview by author, tape recording, Los Angeles, January 13, 2000.

22. Ibid.

23. Ibid.

24. Kelley, *Race Rebels*, 75.

25. Pete, interview by author, tape recording, Los Angeles, February 14, 2000.

26. Maria, interview by author, tape recording, Los Angeles, January 13, 2000.

27. Malcolm X, *Autobiography*, 58–59.

28. On the closing of the Savoy Ballroom see "Mixed Dancing Closed Savoy Ballroom," *Amsterdam News*, May 1, 1943, 1; "What's Behind Savoy Closing: Is It Police Move to Bar Whites from Harlem?" *People's Voice*, May 1, 1943, 1; Bruce Tyler, "Black Jive and White Repression," *Journal of Ethnic Studies* 16, no. 4 (Winter 1989): 31–66.

29. George Lipsitz argues that white privilege is part and parcel of "an identity created and continued with all-too-real consequences for the distribution of wealth, prestige, and opportunity." See George Lipsitz, *The Possessive Investment in Whiteness: How White People Profit from Identity Politics* (Philadelphia: Temple University Press, 1998), vii.

30. See, for example, Letter to Dr. Thomas Parran, Surgeon General, United States Public Health Service, Washington, D.C., from Fletcher Bowron, Mayor of Los Angeles, October 13, 1943, Fletcher Bowron Collection, 1934–1970, Box 1, Huntington Library and Art Gallery; Letter to John Anson Ford, Los Angeles County Supervisor, from Josephine Fierro de Bright, General Secretary, National Congress of the Spanish

Speaking Peoples of the USA, September 1, 1939, John Anson Ford Collection, Box 75, Folder 5, Huntington Library and Art Gallery.

31. For elaboration on how the discourse of public health is used to mark racialized communities as dangerous, infectious, and different in another historical context, see Nayan Shah, *Contagious Divides: Epidemics and Race in San Francisco's Chinatown* (Berkeley: University of California Press, 2001), 105–110.

32. Rosa Linda Fregoso, "Homegirls, Cholas, and Pachucas in Cinema: Taking Over the Public Sphere," *California History* 74, no. 3 (1995): 316–327.

33. For elaboration of mixed-gender dating in another historical context, that of young immigrant women in New York at the beginning of the twentieth century, see Nan Enstad, *Ladies of Labor, Girls of Adventure: Working Women, Popular Culture, and Labor Politics at the Turn of the Century* (New York: Columbia University Press, 1999), 179.

34. John Clarke, "Style," in Stuart Hall and Tony Jefferson, eds., *Resistance through Rituals: Youth Subcultures in Post-War Britain* (London: Routledge, 1993), 187.

35. Michel Foucault, *Power/Knowledge: Selected Interviews and Other Writings, 1972–1977* (New York: Pantheon Books, 1980); Hubert L. Dreyfus and Paul Rabinow, *Michel Foucault: Beyond Structuralism and Hermeneutics* (Chicago: University of Chicago Press, 1982). Foucault illuminates power not as some essential political attribute or economic resource, but rather as a series of social relationships that occur

> between every point of a social body, between a man and a woman, between the members of a family, between a master and his pupil, between every one who knows and every one who does not, there exist relations of power which are not purely and simply a projection of the sovereign's great power over the individual; they are rather the concrete, changing soil in which the sovereign's power is grounded, the conditions which make it possible for it to function [187].

Dreyfus and Rabinow interpret Foucault to suggest that "power plays a directly productive role; it comes from below; it is multi-directional, operating from the top down and also from the bottom up," 185.

36. Jorge Gonzalez, "The Willingness to Weave: Cultural Analysis, Cultural Fronts and Networks for the Future," *Media Development* 44, no. 1 (1997): 30–36. Gonzalez suggests that a "cultural fronts" perspective "allows us to observe symbolic forms and social practices which, over time though multiple operations (economic, political and especially cultural in nature), have become obvious, common and shared between socially different agents" (32). Cultural fronts further make "visible the multiple symbolic skirmishes unleashed between combatants with unequal power and resources: it is these that enable us to create and recreate the shared sense of what is 'necessary' to live, of what is 'worthy' in life, and of 'who we are' in the world. There, where we find shared meanings between socially differentiated agents, lies a historical process of multiple symbolic struggles, that upon being made visible through a methodologically complex strategy, shows us what makes up the social relationship that we call hegemony and how it has been negotiated (certainly in unequal circumstances)" (32).

37. Pete, interview by author, tape recording, Los Angeles, February 14, 2000; Tony, interview by author, tape recording, San Diego, California, February 25, 1994;

Perry, interview by author, tape recording, San Diego, California, December 20, 2001.

38. Interview with Rose Echeverria Mulligan in "Rosie the Riveter: Women and the World War II Work Experience," Volume 27, p. 55, Department of Special Collections, California State University, Long Beach; interview with Maria Salazar McSweyn in "Rosie the Riveter: Women and the World War II Work Experience," Volume 25, p. 67, Department of Special Collections, California State University, Long Beach.

39. Maria, interview by author, tape recording, Los Angeles, February 14, 2000.

40. Ibid.; Pete, interview by author, tape recording, Los Angeles, February 14, 2000.

41. On youth as a category of analysis see, for example, Tracey Skelton and Gill Valentine, eds., *Cool Places: Geographies of Youth Cultures* (London: Routledge, 1998), 2–6; Dick Hebdige, "Posing . . . Threats, Striking . . . Poses: Youth, Surveillance, and Display," in Ken Gelder and Sarah Thornton, eds., *The Subcultures Reader* (London: Routledge, 1997), 398–400.

42. Tony, interview by author, tape recording, San Diego, California, February 25, 1994.

43. On the response of Latino servicemen to zoot culture see, for example, *Narratives: Stories of U.S. Latinos and Latinas and World War II*, vol. 1, no. 1 (Austin: U.S. Latino and Latina WWII Oral History Project, 1999).

44. On the racialization of juvenile delinquency see Escobar, *Race, Police, and the Making of a Political Identity*; Eduardo Pagán, "Sleepy Lagoon: The Politics of Youth and Race in Wartime Los Angeles, 1940–1945" (Ph.D. diss., Princeton University, 1996); Luis Alvarez, "The Power of the Zoot: Race, Community, and Resistance in American Youth Culture," Ph.D. diss., University of Texas at Austin, 2001.

45. "Mass Meet Charges Attempt to 'Goad Riot,'" *California Eagle*, May 27, 1943. The *California Eagle* was the major African American–operated newspaper in the Los Angeles area, owned and edited by Charlotta Bass, a longtime community activist. For more on Charlotta Bass and the history of the *California Eagle*, see Charlotta Bass, *Forty Years* (Los Angeles: Charlotta Bass, 1960); the Charlotta A. Bass Collection, 1874–1968; and the archives of the *California Eagle*, all housed at the Southern California Library for Social Studies and Research in Los Angeles. Prior to the initial confrontations of the Zoot Suit Riots in June of 1943, there was a long history of violent skirmishes between zooters and servicemen in Los Angeles. For numerous examples of such violence see Records of Shore Establishments and Naval Districts, 181, Eleventh Naval District, Records of the Commandant's Office, General Correspondence, 1924–1955, Folder P8-5 (Zoot Suit Gang) 1943 [3/4], Box 296, National Archives and Records Administration, Pacific Region (Laguna Niguel). Years of tense zooter-servicemen relations are corroborated by Tony, interview by author, tape recording, San Diego, California, February 25, 1994, and Pete, interview by author, tape recording, Los Angeles, California, February 14, 2000. Specifically, in the week before the Zoot Suit Riots, servicemen clashed violently with zooters in Venice near Los Angeles, helping to intensify relations between the two groups. On the rioting in Venice see Eduardo Pagán, "Sleepy Lagoon: The Politics of Youth and Race in Wartime Los Angeles, 1940–1945," Ph.D. diss., Princeton University, 1996, 238–239; Solomon James Jones, *The Government Riots of Los Angeles, June 1943* (San Francisco: R and E Research Associates, 1973).

46. On the initial sequence of events during the riots see Carey McWilliams Per-

sonal Notebook, entry titled "The Riots," Carey McWilliams Papers, University of California at Los Angeles, Department of Special Collections, Collection 1243, Box 27, Folder "McWilliams, Carey—as author"; "We Have Just Begun to Fight," no date, the Sleepy Lagoon Defense Committee Archive, Department of Special Collections, University of California, Los Angeles, Collection 107, Microfilm Reel 1 of 8, Box 1, "News Releases," Folder 1, "mimeographed copies"; Carey McWilliams, *North from Mexico: The Spanish-Speaking People of the United States* (New York: Greenwood Press, 1968), 244–245; Escobar, *Race, Police, and the Making of a Political Identity*, 234–236.

47. Carey McWilliams Personal Notebook, entry titled "The Riots." Carey McWilliams Papers, University of California at Los Angeles, Department of Special Collections, Collection 1243, Box 27, Folder "McWilliams, Carey—as author."

48. "Honorable in All Things," Carey McWilliams Oral History, interviewed by Joel Gardner, July 13, 1978, Department of Special Collections, University of California, Los Angeles, Collection 300/195, 163–164.

49. Pete, interview by author, tape recording, Los Angeles, February 14, 2000.

50. Lupe, interview by author, tape recording, Los Angeles, February 14, 2000.

51. Ibid.

52. Maria, interview by author, tape recording, Los Angeles, January 13, 2000.

53. Alice McGrath Oral History, "The Education of Alice McGrath," interviewed by Michael Balter, University of California at Los Angeles, Department of Special Collections, Collection 300/269, 161–162; "Report and Recommendations of Citizens Committee" appointed by California Governor Earl Warren, June 12, 1943, Manuel Ruiz Papers, 1931–1986. Stanford University, Department of Special Collections, Collection M0295, Box 4, Folder 1, "California Committee on Youth in Wartime, 1943–1944."

54. Letter to Walter White from Thomas L. Griffith, Jr., June 9, 1943, Papers of the NAACP, University of Texas at Austin, Part 15, Segregation and Responses, 1940–1955, Series A.

55. Maria, interviewed by author, tape recording, Los Angeles, January 13, 2000.

56. Letter to Elmer Davis, Office of War Information, June 11, 1943, Papers of the NAACP, University of Texas at Austin, Part 15, Segregation and Responses, 1940–1955, Series A; *Time*, June 21, 1943, 18.

57. *Time*, June 21, 1943, 18.

58. Tony, interview by author, tape recording, San Diego, California, February 25, 1994. Even though no deaths were reported as a direct result of the riots, the physical health of zooters was severely threatened.

59. On the alleged hypersexuality of ethnic Mexican women as a spark to the riots see, for example, Statement on Behalf of the Los Angeles County Board of Supervisors, presented by John Anson Ford, June 8, 1943, John Anson Ford Collection, Huntington Library and Art Gallery, Box 51, Folder 4; Griffith, *American Me*, 6. Griffith, for example, describes young female zooters as "little tornadoes of sexual stimuli, swishing and flowering down the streets" who were "attractive to all males." On examples of female zooters coming under attack during the riots see "Zoot Suits and Service Stripes: Race Tension behind the Riots," *Newsweek*, June 21, 1943; "Zoot-Suiters Again on Prowl as Navy Holds Back Sailors," *Washington Post*, June 9, 1943, 1, 5; "Brass Knuckles Found on Woman Zoot Suiter," *Los Angeles Times*, June 10, 1943, A; "Clashes Few as Zoot War Dies Down," *Los Angeles Times*, June 11, 1943, 1.

60. Interview by Larry R. Solomon with Juana Alvarez, July 26, 1992, as quoted in Larry R. Solomon, *Roots of Justice: Stories of Organizing in Communities of Color* (Berkeley, Calif.: Chardon Press, 1998), 27.

61. "Lifeguards Can't Tell Zoot Suit Bathers," *Los Angeles Times*, June 7, 1943, 1.

62. Alice McGrath Oral History, *The Education of Alice McGrath*, interviewed by Michael Balter, Tape IV, side two, January 20, 1985, UCLA Special Collections, 300/269, 155. Both Alice McGrath and Carey McWilliams were active on the Sleepy Lagoon Defense Committee, organized to defend twenty-two ethnic Mexican youth arrested for the murder of fellow teenager Jose Diaz at a local East L.A. swimming hole in 1942. Despite overwhelming evidence supporting their innocence, after a prejudiced trial in which the defendants were not permitted to consult with their attorneys, change clothes, or cut their hair, nineteen of the boys were convicted, including three on first-degree murder charges. Those found guilty spent up to three years in San Quentin Prison before their release in 1945, due in no small part to the efforts of the Sleepy Lagoon Defense Committee to overturn their convictions. Sleepy Lagoon is perhaps the best-known case to have contributed to the antiminority youth climate in Los Angeles leading up to the Zoot Suit Riots. For more on Sleepy Lagoon see, for example, Guy Endore, *The Sleepy Lagoon Case, with a Foreword by Orson Welles*, prepared by the Citizens' Committee for the Defense of Mexican American Youth, Los Angeles, California, 1942, Bert Corona Papers, Stanford University, Department of Special Collections, Box 28, Folder 25; Eduardo Pagán, "Sleepy Lagoon: The Politics of Youth and Race in Wartime Los Angeles, 1940–1945," Ph.D. diss., Princeton University, 1996.

63. Shane White and Graham White, *Stylin': African American Expressive Culture from Its Beginnings to the Zoot Suit* (Ithaca: Cornell University Press, 1998), 260.

64. Report on Attack on Naval Personnel by "Zoot-Suiters," June 10, 1943. Records of Shore Establishments and Naval Districts, 181, Eleventh Naval District, Records of the Commandant's Office, General Correspondence, 1924–1955, Folder P8-5 (Zoot Suit Gang) 1943 [3/4], Box 296, National Archives and Records Administration, Pacific Region (Laguna Niguel). According to the complaint filed by the sailor, the zooters cursed his wife by yelling, "How about a fuck?"

65. Ibid.

66. Ibid.

67. Pete, interview by author, tape recording, Los Angeles, February 14, 2000.

68. Ibid.

69. Ibid.

70. On debates over zoot culture's affiliation with fascist Germany, see Thomas Sanchez, *Zoot-Suit Murders* (New York: Vintage Books, 1991). In his novel, Sanchez draws on the contemporary debates over zoot–fifth column affiliation that are also evident in the archived correspondence of Carey McWilliams, Alice McGrath, and the Sleepy Lagoon Defense Committee. Despite no small amount of literature and press reporting on such a relationship, the links between zoot-suiting and fascism are unsubstantiated and most likely another discursive attempt to discredit the zoot culture as an "un-American" phenomenon.

71. Cultural violence includes the symbolic sphere of society—including ideology, religion, language, and art—that can be used to legitimize physical violence, economic exploitation, or political marginalization. See Johan Galtung, "Cultural Violence," in Manfred B. Steger and Nancy S. Lind, eds., *Violence and Its Alternatives:*

An Interdisciplinary Reader (New York: St. Martin's Press, 1999), 39–53.

72. Carey McWilliams Personal Notebook, entry titled "The Riots." Carey McWilliams Papers, University of California at Los Angeles, Department of Special Collections, Collection 1243, Box 27, Folder "McWilliams, Carey—as author"; *Los Angeles Herald Examiner*, June 5, 1943, 1.

73. "Zoot Suiters Learn Lesson with Servicemen," *Los Angeles Times*, June 7, 1943, 1.

74. See, for example, "Riot Alarm Sent Out in Zoot War," *Los Angeles Times*, June 8, 1943, 1; "City, Navy Clamp Lid on Zoot-Suit Warfare," *Los Angeles Times*, June 10, 1943, 1; "Zoot Suit War Runs Course as Riots Subside," *Los Angeles Times*, June 12, 1943, A; "Punishment of All Urged to Break up Zoot Suit War," *Los Angeles Times*, June 13, 1943, 1A; "Southland Zoot Riots Reported Stamped Out," *Los Angeles Times*, June 14, 1943, A. See also *Los Angeles Herald Examiner*, June 8–11, 1943; *Los Angeles Daily News*, June 8–11, 1943.

75. *Washington Post*, June 9, 1943, 1.

76. *Washington Post*, June 11, 1943, 1.

77. *Atlanta Constitution*, June 13, 1943, 13A.

78. *Chicago Daily Tribune*, June 9, 1943, 1.

79. "Press Blamed for Spread of Zoot Suit Riot," *PM*, date unknown, Carey McWilliams Papers, University of California at Los Angeles, Department of Special Collections, Collection 1243, Box 5, Folder 4.

80. "Brass Knuckles Found on Woman Zoot Suiter," *Los Angeles Times*, June 10, 1943, 1.

81. "Zoot Girls Use Knife in Attack as War Eases," *Los Angeles Times*, June 11, 1943, 1.

82. See, for example, ibid.; "Black Widow Girls Beat, Slash Woman; Police Tighten Controls," *Washington Post*, June 11, 1943, 1.

83. Lupe, interview by author, tape recording, Los Angeles, February 14, 2000.

84. The role of the mainstream press in the Zoot Suit Riots was different from that of the ethnic and leftist press. Though the Spanish-language newspaper *La Opinion* was slow to support and defend zooters, the African American–run *California Eagle* and the leftist *PM* consistently condemned the city police, armed forces, and general public for their role in the riots. Other African American publications around the country, including the *Amsterdam News*, the *Pittsburgh Courier*, and the *People's Voice*, also expressed outrage at zoot violence to varying degrees.

85. For more on structural violence see, for example, Galtung, "Cultural Violence," 39–53.

86. Letter to Robert W. Kenny, California Attorney General, and Bishop Joseph T. McGucken, Chairman, Governor's Special Committee on Los Angeles Emergency, from the Los Angeles Committee for American Unity, Provisional Chairman, Harry Braverman, and Provisional Executive Committee, including Carey McWilliams, Al Waxman, Carlotta Bass, Eduardo Quevedo, Ben Margolis, and Manuel Avila, Manuel Ruiz Papers, 1931–1986, Stanford University, Department of Special Collections, Collection M0295, Box 16, Folder 5, "Sleepy Lagoon Murder Case, Zoot Suit Riots, 1943–44"; Carey McWilliams Oral History, "Honorable in All Things," interviewed by Joel Gardner, University of California at Los Angeles, Department of Special Collections, Collection 300/195, 163–164.

87. Letter to Martin Popper of the National Lawyers Guild, from Carey McWilliams, June 9, 1943, Carey McWilliams Papers, University of California at Los

Angeles, Department of Special Collections, Collection 1243, Box 31, Folder "Race Riots—Los Angeles."

88. Minutes of the Citizens' Committee for Latin-American Youth, June 7, 1943, Manuel Ruiz Papers, 1931–1986, Stanford University, Department of Special Collections, Collection M0295, Box 4, Folder 6, "Citizens Committee for Latin-American Youth, 1942–1944."

89. Lupe, interview by author, tape recording, Los Angeles, February 14, 2000.

90. Maria, interview by author, tape recording, Los Angeles, January 13, 2000.

91. Lupe, interview by author, tape recording, Los Angeles, February 14, 2000.

92. For more on the debate and eventual decision by the Navy to restrict leave, see Records of Shore Establishments and Naval Districts, 181, Eleventh Naval District, Records of the Commandant's Office, General Correspondence, 1924–1955, Folder P8-5 (Zoot Suit Gang) 1943 [1/4], Box 296, National Archives and Records Administration, Pacific Region (Laguna Niguel); "Tension High in Zoot War after Navy Ban," *Los Angeles Times*, June 9, 1943, A; "City, Navy Clamp Lid on Zoot-Suit Warfare," *Los Angeles Times*, June 10, 1943, 1.

93. "Zoot-Suiters Again on Prowl as Navy Holds Back Sailors," *Washington Post*, June 9, 1943, 1.

94. See, for example, letter to Elmer Davis, Office of War Information, from Mayor Fletcher Bowron, May 18, 1943, Fletcher Bowron Collection, 1934–1970, Huntington Library and Art Gallery, Box 1, Folder, "Extra Copies of Letters, 1943, Jan.–June"; Letter to State Department, Washington, D.C., from Mayor Fletcher Bowron, August 3, 1943, Fletcher Bowron Collection, 1934–1970, Huntington Library and Art Gallery, Box 1, Folder, "Extra Copies of Letters, 1943, Jan.–June."

95. Letter to C. B. Horrall, Chief of Los Angeles Police Department, from Fletcher Bowron, July 19, 1943, Fletcher Bowron Collection, Box 1, Folder, "Extra Copies of Letters, 1943, Jan.–June."

96. Letter to State Department, Washington, D.C., Phillip W. Bonsal, Chief, Division of American Republics, from Fletcher Bowron, August 3, 1943, Fletcher Bowron Collection, Box 1, Folder, "Extra Copies of Letters, 1943, Jan.–June."

97. Ibid.

98. Ibid.

99. Statement by Mayor Fletcher Bowron, June 9, 1943, Fletcher Bowron Collection, 1934–1970, Huntington Library and Art Gallery, Box 34, Folder, "Statements to the Press, 1942–1944."

100. John Anson Ford, answer to *Hoy* magazine editorial of June 26, 1943, dated July 1943, John Anson Ford Collection, Huntington Library and Art Gallery, Box 51, Folder 4.

101. "Ban on Freak Zoot Suits Studied by Councilmen," *Los Angeles Times*, June 10, 1943, A. For more on the actions of the city council see Alice McGrath Oral History, "The Education of Alice McGrath," interviewed by Michael Balter, University of California at Los Angeles, Department of Special Collections, Collection 300/269, 159–160.

102. "WPB Enters Zoot Suit Turmoil," *Atlanta Constitution*, June 12, 1943, 8.

103. "Dorsey High Principal Wants No 'Zoot Suits,'" *California Eagle*, June 3, 1943.

104. "Zooters Escape San Diego Mob," *Los Angeles Times*, June 10, 1943, A.

105. "Baltimore Acts to Break up Zoot Suit Gang," *Chicago Daily Tribune*, June 10, 1943, 9.

106. "Army, Navy Promise to Halt Zoot Riots," *Washington Post*, June 12, 1943, 3.

107. "Four Zoot-Suiters Beaten," *Washington Post*, June 12, 1943, 12; "Four Men Wearing Zoot Suits Attacked," *Los Angeles Times*, June 13, 1943, A.

108. Mazón, *The Zoot Suit Riots*; Escobar, *Race, Police, and the Making of a Political Identity*.

109. *Negro Digest* 1, no. 4 (Winter–Spring 1943): 301, as quoted in Kelley, *Race Rebels*, 161.

CHAPTER 7

What a Difference a War Makes!

MARIA EVA FLORES

"When the war started, I became a white man."
Aniceto Nuñez

In 1940, Tony Benavides knew everyone in his world in the West Texas town of Fort Stockton. Every household and every person in every household were as familiar to him as his own. But after only three years, everything had changed. The United States and the world had changed. And so had Benavides. Antonio S. "Tony" Benavides struck out from Fort Stockton, Texas, to join the United States Army, in search of work and, perhaps, some adventure; he found combat in North Africa, Sicily, Belgium, France, and Germany. And then, after thirty-three months in Europe, a lone Mexicano in the 66th Armored Division, he returned to Fort Stockton to encounter numerous changes in his neighborhood and community.

Benavides's experience was not singular. The war in Europe and the Pacific affected small American towns, like Fort Stockton, in large and small ways. The war brought change, slowly but inexorably, for those who left to fight and for those who stayed home. The discrimination that had been tolerated by Mexican Americans in pre–World War II Texas was no longer to be accepted. The war had made Mexican American men and women feel entitled to equal treatment. The Mexican American community would never be the same—and neither would Fort Stockton.

Institutions that were traditional hardline bastions of a segregated community softened in the face of undeniable patriotism. In particular the local Fort Stockton newspaper had, before the war, denied Mexican Americans general news coverage as average citizens. During the war, however, the Fort Stockton newspaper couldn't carry enough news about Mexican American soldiers' achievements in and out of combat.

Fort Stockton, Texas, like many other Texas communities, lived by the principle that Mexicans, a conquered people after the U.S.-Mexican war, were to act as laborers and servants. The town began as St. Gall in 1858, as a result of the Treaty of Guadalupe Hidalgo. Mexicanos, like all pioneers in the vast West Texas desert, faced a daunting task in subduing the harsh land in order to provide food and shelter for their families. In addition, Mexicanos faced racial antagonism. Journals of military personnel stationed there demonstrate the pattern established early on.

Carlysle Graham Raht, a railroad man writing in 1919, provides a telling version of early times in Fort Stockton.

> The community life in Fort Stockton differed little from that in other settlements. At the army post, three or four companies of troops were constantly stationed. This blending of army and civilian life produced a kaleidoscopic picture. The pioneers and their families, the West Pointers, their wives, and daughters, presented a contrast which was heightened by the sprinkling of Indians, army scouts, cowboys, and Mexicans.[1]

Raht's writing indicates the position of the Mexican community vis-à-vis the military and the civilian Euro-American community. In Raht's account, the Mexicans are few and provide a "contrast" to the Euro-Americans. While the survival of the fort and the community depended to a large degree on mutual acceptance, an anti-Mexican attitude found early expression in the writings of military personnel. Writing in 1875, two visiting surgeons describe the residents of the area: "The inhabitants of the vicinity are chiefly Mexicans, a cross between the Spaniard and Indian, which seems to have deteriorated both races."[2]

In spite of such attitudes, the Army officers, at least, managed to socialize with the leading residents, including Mexican families. Lieutenant John Bigelow, whose journals provide the basis for a biography published in 1998, indicates that at least one of the Garza daughters mingled in the company of the post's officers. On August 18, 1878, Bigelow writes that at a ball given for a captain traveling from Fort McKavett, twenty-two miles southwest of Menard, Texas, to Fort Davis, "Miss Candelaria Garza was considered the belle of the ball. Her mother is pure Spanish and her father a Mexican."[3] Bigelow made the stereotypical distinction between the "pure" Spaniard and the Mexican, implying the Spaniard's superiority.

Life at the post in Fort Stockton did not hold much to occupy an officer's time outside the routine daily duties and the occasional Indian raid. Whenever an officer visited the post, a social gathering took place, and Bigelow noted the event and the attitudes of officers and wives.

> There was the usual variety of dress and physiognomy. Mrs. Sweet remarked, in regard to a couple of Mexican girls, that some of the ladies did not at all like to have these ranch girls brought to the hops. I replied that, if we know nothing against them and they are introduced by an officer, that ought to be sufficient. She said, "Yes, it ought to be," in a tone to imply that it was not.[4]

To take up some of his free time, Bigelow chose to study Spanish, and after discontinuing his lessons with an officer's wife, he studied with "Señor Lujan, a local tailor." Bigelow's characterization of his tutor makes the distinction, again, between Spaniard and Mexican: "He [Lujan] talks good Mexican, not the best Spanish." Curiously, Bigelow, a neophyte at the language, makes an assessment of what constitutes "good" Spanish.

The last part of the nineteenth century saw the migration of southerners into Texas. Neil Foley's *The White Scourge* describes the movement of southern whites and the racial attitudes they cultivated in central Texas. Similarly, in West Texas, white southerners moved into the area in smaller numbers, with no less conviction of white superiority. In 1875, the civil community of St. Gall became Fort

Stockton, and Division Street, which had marked the boundary between Fort Stockton and St. Gall, began to serve as the dividing line separating the Mexican community from the American community, the Catholics from the Protestants, the poor from the rich.

Fort Stockton, from 1875 to World War II, was clearly home to two separate communities, one Mexican, one American. The designation had nothing to do with citizenship or place of birth. Rather, as Foley points out, racial identity provided an important parameter in the socioeconomic relations in central Texas.[5] Like the southerners in the Texas Blacklands, West Texas southern immigrants set up the parameters of movement for those they considered nonwhite. In Fort Stockton, Mexicans fit the bill. Division characterized almost every facet of life in Fort Stockton prior to World War II; employment opportunities were limited to low-skilled labor on ranches and farms for men and domestic work for women. Mexicanos could enter only the west and north parts of town to work; they worshiped in a segregated church and attended a segregated school. Most Mexican children attended the Mexican school to the sixth grade; a few managed eighth grade.

Until 1942, those Mexican students who wished to attend high school continued to attend classes in the same building with limited subjects. Spurred to action by the LULAC Council, the State Department of Education investigated the school offerings for Mexican Americans and advised the school board to make necessary changes. On August 12, 1942, the school board authorized the superintendent of schools to withdraw the high school subjects from Butz School, the Mexican school.[6] With the withdrawal of the high school subjects, the road was opened for Mexican American students to integrate Fort Stockton High School in the fall semester of 1942. Integration of middle schools occurred in 1954, and almost twenty years later, in 1974, new elementary schools were built and total integration became a reality for the Fort Stockton School District.

Like many Mexicanos before and after him, Tony Benavides had a limited educational background, and his prospects in a small, isolated, and racially segregated community were dim and dismal—until the war. On a warm spring day, Manuel "Mel" Nuñez approached Benavides and said, "Let's join up." After a brief hesitation, Benavides agreed and they caught a ride to the nearest recruiting office, about ninety miles northeast in Big Spring, Texas. They were both twenty years old and needed parental or guardian signatures before they could be accepted.

Benavides wrote a quick note home and Nuñez remembers, "I had no mother, and I was not going to ask my stepmother," but he could get an older sister to sign for him and she lived in Colorado City, not far from Big Spring. They took the bus to Colorado City and by 4:00 a.m. they had found the farm where Tecla and her husband worked. Without much money and nothing to do except wait for Tony's letter from his father, they signed on to pick cotton for the week. Completing the week's work, they returned to Big Spring, where they were sent to El Paso and Fort Bliss. Sent in different directions, Benavides and Nuñez met again only when they returned to Fort Stockton after their discharge.[7]

Both Nuñez and Benavides had served in the Civilian Conservation Corps (CCC) before the war and had experience working in a military-style setting. Nuñez had worked with stonemasons at Balmorhea State Park, just forty miles from his hometown.[8] Army experience shared some similarities with CCC experience, especially for Nuñez. He recalls that in the CCC, he had expressed his sense of dignity and human rights by organizing a "protection" club for Mexicanos. Often Mexican American young men would get into fights with Anglo youth, and Nuñez and others would come to their defense. Nuñez and his companions had decided "not to take any of the crap."[9] He recalls that in one rock-throwing fight after lights out, the doctor in the camp came out with a white flag to stop the fight. The CCC experience proved useful during basic training and throughout his Army experience. He handled his first opposition with his brains instead of his fists. After the swearing-in ceremony at Fort Bliss in El Paso, Texas, a colonel ("he kinda reminded me of the school principal of the Mexican school [in Fort Stockton]") reviewed his file. The colonel recommended Nuñez be assigned to transportation, but Nuñez insisted he wanted field artillery. The colonel shot back a challenge: "Okay, but you have to be good at math."

"He gave me one hundred problems, fractions. And I did them, then he gave me one hundred more. I passed."[10] Good with his fists, Nuñez boxed and played every sport he could manage. As a boxer, he received enough attention that an Anglo opponent advised him that regardless of his achievement, "the highest rank a Mexican could get is a corporal. I told him 'I'm not bucking for anything. I box because I like it and I can whip your butt once a day and twice on Sunday; my parents are American. They were born in Texas and I was born in Texas and I am an American—more, maybe—because I am older than you!'"[11]

His fists and his wits earned him sergeant's stripes and he took charge of recruits stateside for the entire war.

For many white American servicemen from outside of the Southwest, World War II would be the first time they had encountered Mexicanos.[12] On occasion, those whites didn't know how to categorize Mexican Americans. In many of the enlistment papers of Mexican Americans, in the box reserved for "race," many times "white" was used as the classification.

"Cheto" Nuñez, Manuel Nuñez's younger brother, recalls that a particularly difficult instructor challenged his identity. "'Are you Spanish or Mexican?' he asked. I told him, 'I was Mexican, but when the war started I became a white man.' He said again, 'Mexican?' 'No, I was not born in Mexico; I was born in Fort Stockton, but they called me Mexican. And when the war started, I became a white man.'"[13]

The only Mexican American in his outfit, Benavides noted that his combat experience confirmed for him that he was, indeed, an American. Joe Urias found the Army experience "a change; you had three meals a day, you were always doing something, playing ball. It wasn't that bad at all. I enjoyed the Army."[14]

Carlos Granado, another veteran from Fort Stockton, shared Urias's enthusiasm for military life; in addition Granado recalled the erstwhile taboos of speaking with, dancing with, and dating a young "American" woman. While stationed at Camp McCoy in Wisconsin, Granado and other soldiers were taken into St. Paul, Minnesota, to enjoy a parade. At the meal after the parade he met Helen Anderson, who danced with him then and many times after that; she even invited him to dinner at her home. "It seemed strange to me, to be dating an American girl; here [Fort Stockton] we couldn't do that."[15]

Benavides, Nuñez, Urias, his little brother "Cheto," and Granado were five of an estimated "375,000 to 500,000 Mexican Americans who served in the armed forces."[16] They were among the 750,000 Texans who served in World War II (including 12,000 women)[17] and among more than two hundred Mexican American young men from Fort Stockton who entered the military, leaving rural West Texas to explore the United States and the world.

Writing immediately after the war, Pauline Kibbe, executive director of the Texas Good Neighbor Commission, which sought better relations with Mexico, asserted that "the Spanish names appearing in the casualty lists of any South or Southwest Texas paper consistently numbered from one-third to as much as three-fourths of the total. Proportionately, Latin American families in Texas have contributed more to the Armed Forces than have Anglo American families, for they have more sons to give."[18]

The Pablo Gonzales family illustrates the point. In an article in the local newspaper, the story of the four Gonzales brothers is told:

Pablo Gonzales of Fort Stockton is the father of four sons in active service with the United States Army. The four brothers, whose mother died when they were small lads, have been reared to a great extent by their maiden aunt, Carrie Gonzales, who has worked as a maid for Mrs. S. S. Harris for 20 years, in addition to looking after her nephews, of whom she is naturally very proud.

The four brothers, all privates are in varied branches of service, and all, thus far have been sent westward for duty.

Nicolas V. Gonzales is a member of an anti-aircraft unit of the Coast Artillery in Hawaii.

Natividad V. Gonzales, is a member of a field artillery unit in training at Camp Roberts, Calif.

Abran V. Gonzales is stationed at Tucson, Ariz. as a member of bomb squadron unit [*sic*].

Reyes V. Gonzales, the last son to enter service, is at the Fort Bliss Reception Center awaiting assignment to a training unit.[19]

Later, two more Gonzales boys would join, making it a total of six sons. Many other families in Fort Stockton sent two and three sons to war. The families saw them off at the bus station on the first leg of a very long journey. The emotional send-off prompted the local priest to comment.

The priest dared to say, "I don't know why they are crying." And one of the women informed him, "Because we gave birth to them; you never had any children." And that put him in his place.[20]

The socioeconomic structures and dynamics of the small West Texas community had limited their intellectual development by segregating them into an inequitable school system, and the local newspaper had denied them recognition of their special talents and abilities. Their new status as soldiers brought home the news of achievement in and out of combat.

The local newspaper serves as an important indicator of local mechanisms employed to exclude segments of the population. When the United States declared war on Japan and joined the Allied Forces against Hitler in Europe, the local newspaper, the *Fort Stockton Pioneer*, printed accounts and names of its citizens who participated in the war effort. Since its founding in 1908 the newspaper had confined the Mexican population to certain spheres; that is, news items generally identified them as "Mexicans" and pertained to only a few areas of life, including crime, baseball games, and deaths of prominent members of the Mexican American community.

Once West Texans enlisted or were drafted and the government sent news about local men (and one female) to the *Fort Stockton Pioneer*, the policy changed. Neither editorial nor feature explicated the policy, but change was apparent. The term *Mexican* was no longer used to identify the soldiers or their families. Breaking all precedents, the newspaper included photographs of all the men who died during the war. At least one week after the initial announcement was printed, a photograph appeared, often with a recap of the deceased's experience and the identities of parents and other relatives.

However, even the death of Mexican American men in battle did not change the racial attitudes in their hometown. On V-E Day, the mayor of the city experienced a lapse of memory about one segment of the community.

Formal observance of VE Day in Fort Stockton was appropriately solemn, as citizens reflected on the price that victory over one enemy has cost the community and contemplated the toll likely to be exacted by further conflict against Japan.

Mayor Moses paid tribute to Fort Stockton men who have given their lives in battle.[21]

The newspaper did not note that Moses said there were four Ft. Stockton men who had died in battle; however, those present at Moses' speech heard the mention of the four—which left out the eight Mexican Americans who had died in the war. The LULAC Council #62 took exception. On May 20, 1945, the mayor received a letter from the Office of the Secretary General of LULAC in El Paso.

Honorable G. C. Moses
Mayor, Fort Stockton, Texas

Sir:
A letter from one of the members of LULAC, in your City came to this office today. This LULAC member requested that the contents of his letter be given some publicity, not only within the organization, but wherever it may bring to light the conditions under which some of the Citizens of Fort Stockton are now living.

A celebration was held on V-E Day in Ft. Stockton, after a parade, an assembly was held in one of the schools, the Mayor, Honorable G. C. Moses made the principal speech of the occasion, very appropriately he mentioned the fact that four Ft. Stockton boys had made the supreme sacrifice for our Country, after his speech, he was reminded that there were eight other Ft. Stockton boys, who had also given their lives for our country. The Mayor made an apology for not remembering the fact that these other American boys of Spanish Speaking Extraction had also given their all for our Country.[22]

The Mexican American community found it impossible to accept Moses' poor memory as an excuse. He had served as principal of the Mexican school throughout the 1930s, and during his tenure as mayor he managed the movie theater that segregated Mexicanos in the balcony. To Lulacers familiar with his history, Moses' oversight seemed less than innocent. It was the lack of justice which Pauline Kibbe's 1946 work on the social conditions in Texas addressed.[23]

For young men who had been born in Fort Stockton and had never traveled beyond the Pecos County line, the war provided a vantage point to a different world. The hometown newspaper told of brushes with celebrities: "Joey Gonzalez wrote home of having seen the Jack Benny Show."[24] "Eddie Gonzalez meets Joe Louis."[25] And overseas assignments gave the young men glimpses of world figures and historic sites:

> T-5 Joey Gonzalez who has been in Italy since last September with the Fifth Army, has written that he has reached Rome with the outfit and has seen Pope Pius [XII].
> Natividad Gonzales writes a note of appreciation for his copies of The Pioneer and incloses [sic] a descriptive pamphlet about the Sanctuary of Pompeii which he visited on a short trip.[26]

What must have the experience been like for two sons of the desert to stand on the deck of a U.S. ship in the North Pacific and see the Bering Strait?[27]

> Louis B. Urias, won desirable publicity, as well as establishing a new record for physical stamina when he performed 85 push ups in an athletic contest at the Naval Training Station at San Diego. The previous record for the station was 84, established more than a year ago. Navy physical training developed Urias's stamina to the extent that he was able to perform 30 more push ups on the final test than when he arrived at the station. The pushup is a standard exercise given military personnel in calisthenics.[28]

> PFC Joey Gonzalez writes of his win over Joe Montierro in the Boston Garden, in his first boxing match of 1943.[29]

> J. G. Fuentes from Fort Stockton has had his picture in a West coast paper showing him demonstrating Judo tactics.

He appeared at the Presidio YMCA at a Judo exhibition and downed his man very rapidly.[30]

The men and the one woman also received a significant number of armed services medals and decorations testifying to the caliber of service and patriotism they displayed.

PFC Jesus Ramirez, son of Manuel Ramirez, awarded the Good Conduct ribbon for exceptionally efficient and capable performance of duties. He is also authorized to wear his Aleutian islands campaign star on his Asiatic-Pacific Theatre ribbon.[31]

Conrado Armendarez, son of Simon Armendarez, has won the right to wear Wings and Boots of the United States Army Paratroops. He has completed four weeks of jump training during which time he made five jumps, the last a tactical jump at night involving a combat problem in landing. He also has two years of overseas service to his credit.[32]

Alberto V. Gonzales has been awarded the Silver Star for gallantry during actions in Germany. He is in the 5th Army Division; he is the youngest son of 5 brothers, sons of Pablo Gonzales, in the service.[33]

PFC Melquiedes S. Villalba has received the award of the Purple Heart for wound [*sic*] received in action on June 14th on the coast of France and is now recuperating at a hospital in England. He is the son of Mr. and Mrs. Atilano G. Villalba and has been serving with the engineers unit for three years, he is 25 years old. He received a leg wound.[34]

Official commendation by the Chief of Naval Personnel has been given to Johnnie Robles Casas, seaman first class USNR of Fort Stockton, Texas, for outstanding bravery and skill while a member of the Armed Guard unit aboard an American Liberty Ship during a recent mission to Malta.[35]

Besides traveling the globe, Mexican American men and one woman also traveled several psychological worlds away from the limitations of West Texas. But they strained to recognize similarities between West Texas and their new locales. In one V-mail letter from North Africa, T-Sgt. Tony Benavides writes, "Have been here in Africa for quite some time. Some of this country looks like West Texas, which makes me a little homesick when I see it. But instead of seeing a big herd of cattle and sheep, you see herds of camels. Wish I could tell you some more but spare time here is very precious."[36]

Only one Mexican American woman from Fort Stockton served in the armed services during World War II. Anita Pineda, the daughter of T. A. Pineda, decided to join the Army because "she was the head of the household and this way she could help the family out."[37] Anita, like some of the men in Fort Stockton, found herself the oldest daughter of a single parent and felt the responsibility of assisting the family. With few job opportunities in the small town and a limited educational background, she saw the Army as a viable alternative. "She was a nurse; learned in the service."[38] On September 29, 1944, the *Fort Stockton Pioneer* printed the brief notice, "Pvt. Anita Pineda, awarded Good Conduct medal, Camp White Oregon, daughter of T. A. Pineda." The newspaper printed a second item about her on August 3, 1945.

> Cpl. Pineda, Fort Stockton WAC who was assigned to the United Nations Conference for International Order, San Francisco, was awarded two certificates, one from the International Secretariat and the other from the Army-Navy Coordination Group when the historic conference closed.[39]

Perhaps a small but significant part of the war experience for Mexican Americans from Fort Stockton and similar small segregated communities in the Southwest was the chance encounter with Anglo men and women from their hometown. The war put Mexican American and Anglo soldiers on an equal footing, making possible friendships among equals, unlikely, if not impossible, in peacetime in their hometown. "Tiodoro Moreno and W. R. McKay have met at their new station in Camp Breckenridge, Ky."[40] Outside of Fort Stockton, the men could acknowledge their meeting.

Also, outside of Fort Stockton, Carlos Granado found out he could dance and visit in the home of "Americans." While Benavides, Mel and Cheto Nuñez, Urias, and Granado served as Americans in Europe, the United States, and the Pacific, their families, friends, and relatives continued to be treated as second-class citizens and kept "in their place." Mexican Americans continued to be refused service in restaurants throughout the West Texas area, required to attend racially segregated schools, and banned from tax-supported public sites. If, at the onset of the Depression, Mexicanos "knew their place," they also recognized the inherent injustice of that place in the American system. While the community at large seemed to be willing to remain in "their place," individuals raged against the injustices and sought to redress them.

The Fort Stockton Mexican American community shared the outrage with Mexicanos throughout Texas and the Southwest. In central and south Texas, where the larger population of Mexicanos resided, Mexican Americans had been fighting discrimination for several decades. As early as 1911, the Idars of Laredo had convened mutual aid societies in the Primer Congreso Mexicanista to address lynchings and other cultural issues; by the late 1920s, leaders of various organizations, including the Order of the Sons of America, the Knights of America, and Loyal Mexican American Citizens of Brownsville, met in Corpus Christi, Texas, and "from that meeting of February 17, 1929, evolved the modern League of United Latin American Citizens (LULAC)."[41]

Seven years after LULAC organized in Corpus Christi, Texas, Fort Stockton Mexicanos established their own Council #62. The profile of the organizers and leaders resembled the profile of the state LULAC organizers.[42] While they had no professionals among them, they did constitute the rising middle class of the small West Texas community. Sotero Piña, a World War I veteran, and M. R. González, Raymond Barrón, and Sixto Terrazas comprised the charter members, each of them an independent businessman. After working for many years in a feed and grain store, Piña opened a small grocery store, Piña and Piña, on Second Street, two blocks west of Main Street. M. R. González, having closed his small grocery store on Nelson and First at the outbreak of the Depression, hauled dirt for WPA projects. Raymond Barrón and Sixto Terrazas owned a market and a grocery store, respectively, on Nelson Street. It is important to note the location of these enterprises in 1936. Prior to 1955, Mexican Americans did not own or run establishments on Main Street. "We were restricted to that area, Nelson, First, Second, Callaghan; that was the barrio."[43]

Convinced of their rights as American citizens and committed to retaining their Mexican cultural ways, they sought equity. While the organizers and leaders of LULAC fit into the "upwardly mobile sector" which Márquez describes, rank-and-file Lulacers in the rural area of Fort Stockton did not conform well to that characterization. The membership of Council #62 included working-class members such as Cosme Ureta and Nuñez Villalba; some businessmen, like Don Pancho Urias, never joined the organization.

Fort Stockton Lulacers adopted the aims and purposes of the national LULAC Code, "equal rights under the Constitution of the United States and an equal opportunity,"[44] and to "use all the legal means at our command to the end that all citizens in our country may enjoy equal rights, the equal protection of the laws of the land and equal opportunities and privileges."[45]

The push for full access to the educational, political, and economic systems of the United Sates meant that Fort Stockton Lulacers fought for access to the movie theater and the swimming pool. The swimming pool provided Fort Stockton with some distinction. Built on the natural springs which provided irrigation to the farm area north of town, the pool, with its beauty and bounty of water, attracted both residents and tourists. "Pecos County is far fame [sic] for its natural waters. Comanche Springs in Fort Stockton flows 60 million gallons per day."[46] In their appeal for WPA funds, County Judge C. E. Casebier wrote Senator Tom Connaly in 1936:

> Comanche Springs draws large crowds of people from all our surrounding towns who enjoy these bathing facilities without any cost to them; consequently Pecos County, through its fine park and swimming pool, renders a service not only to its own people, but to all the surrounding counties who are less fortunately situated in regard to water supply. This swimming pool and park is also quite a drawing card for tourists that travel the highways through Pecos County.[47]

The swimming pool and the park built and named in honor of James Rooney saw marked improvements with WPA funding.

IMPROVEMENT OF SWIMMING POOL IS SOUGHT

LIONS CLUB SEEKS ACTION FROM COUNTY

HOPE GET BATH HOUSE READY BY OPENING OF NEXT SEASON

Improvement for the swimming pool at the county park and the building of a permanent bath house by the time the bathing season opens this year is [*sic*] to be urged upon the county officials, according to the discussion at the Lions Club Wednesday noon.[48]

On November 11, 1935, the Pecos County Commissioner's Court approved a resolution

> authorizing the County Judge to file an application to the United States of America through the Federal Emergency Administration of Public Works for a grant to aid in financing the construction of a Bath House for [the] General Public, one for Mexicans exclusively and a Community House for Mexicans and designating David Castle Co of Abilene, Tx to furnish such information as the Government requests.[49]

Both places were understood to be off-limits to Fort Stockton's Mexican community in the 1930s. Perhaps because of the improvements to the bathhouse and swimming pool with WPA funds and the organization of LULAC Council #62, Mexican American citizens presented the county judge with a petition in 1939:

> We, the undersigned—American citizens and tax payers—do hereby file this as a protest for denying the use of the County parks to the Latin American citizens of Fort Stockton, and hereby urge you to give due consideration as you have always done in the past. We consider you our friend and fairminded

enough to ignore a minority that is always working against our interest and against our purpose of bettering our social, moral and economic conditions.[50]

Apparently, the signers received no response. C. E. Casebier, to whom the petition was addressed in 1938, continued as head of county government, while his brother, John Casebier, headed Water Improvement District #1. In 1939, they had appealed to the "fair mind" of the county judge and naively depended on his friendship.

In their original application to the WPA, the county had proposed building a separate bathhouse for the Mexicans. But by 1943, the improvements to the swimming pool and the bathhouse had been completed, but the Mexican bathhouse had not materialized; Mexicanos continued to be excluded. So, on July 6, 1943, when young Jesse Garcia, a U.S. soldier, attempted to enjoy the waters of the famed Comanche Springs, the reality of life in West Texas was forcibly brought into focus.

The local LULAC Council #62 outlined the incident in a letter to M. C. González, attorney and national LULAC leader.

On the 6th of July Cpl Jesse Garcia in his uniform went to swim in the public swimming pool and the care taker of the swimming pool chased him away on the ground that he was a Mexican. He resented it, and told the care taker that if he was good enough to fight along side of the American boys, he would also be good enough to swim with them.

After some argument the boy went home, and on July the 7th some of us went to the swimming pool to protest such arbitrary use of power; there was [sic] a few words exchanged with the Americans and the local authorities. After that things came to a pitch, and had [it] not been for the good office of some of our friends [there] may [have] occurred a race riot.

On the 7th of July a resolution was passed by the Pecos County Water Board a resolution to oust from the swimming pool all the Latin Americans. We Tax payers have helped the fixing and the building of said swimming pool, and now we are robbed of every right because we are Mexicans.

As to the swimming pool proposition, we would like to know if there is any law depriving us of our rights, and if the Government will approve such resolutions, after encouraging the GOOD WILL RELATION amongst the different races.

We are all doing the best we can for the good of the country, but the action of the Americans in Fort Stockton puts a demper [*sic*] on it all, when we think that our boys are in Guadalcanal, Africa, etc. to protect not our friends, but our enemies.[51]

The day after the incident, July 7, 1943, the directors of the Water Improvement District #1, which owned the rights to the water, made the ban explicit. In a resolution submitted to the county commissioners, the directors delineated the use of the bathhouse and the waters of the Comanche Springs.

That the property set out in said lease contract above referred to is owned by said district, and partly by Pecos County, and being a stone bath house near the waters of Comanche Chief [*sic*] and Government Springs, and the water from said springs and water that may flow into the swimming pool from said springs, and all of said property now being in use for bathing purposes be used soely [*sic*] by the Angleo-American [*sic*] people, and that no person or persons of the Latin-American race shall be permitted to use said property for swimming, bathing, drinking or for any other purpose.[52]

In 1948, the pool was opened to Mexican Americans.

The preceding detailed account provides a fairly succinct picture of the social structure of the small West Texas community and the Mexican Americans' growing understanding of their rights and the means to secure them.

Although the Mexican Americans seemed to be butting their heads against a veritable brick wall of collusion and "arbitrary use of power," they had gained enough political savvy to move outside the perimeters of the small community, as well as to speak collectively, rather than as individuals. In touch with the state's own attempts to establish "good neighbors" relations with Mexico and Latin American governments, Lulacers Piña and González challenged it to practice being good neighbors at home. The appeal to patriotism notwithstanding, Fort Stockton "Latin Americans" did not break down the formidable rigid social structure in 1943; but there had been some progress.

Among the survivors returning to Fort Stockton, Juan "Johnny" Garza could have served as the model for Pauline Kibbe's American hero. Garza, descendent of pioneer founder of Fort Stockton, Félix Garza, returned to his hometown minus an arm and a leg and his eyesight.[53]

> Juan Garza, son of Mr. and Mrs. Marcos Garza on the Rachal ranch is recovering from serious wounds received in Germany on February 13th. He has been evacuated from base hospitals in France to a California hospital. The extent of his injuries was learned this week when his wife, Mrs. Angelina Garza, received a letter from his brother, Tom, stationed at Camp Roberts, California, written following a visit to him. He suffered the loss of his right hand and foot and his sight. His left leg was broken in the encounter. He was with Gen. Simpson's Ninth Army in Germany.[54]

At the conclusion of Pauline Kibbe's account, a returning Mexican American is unable to reconcile the betrayal felt after suffering serious wounds in war and coming home to face discriminatory treatment. He asks, "What is wrong with Texas?"[55] The men and women who lived in West Texas could have provided numerous examples to illustrate what was wrong with Texas at the end of World War II.

As men and women began to return from war, the local newspaper sent out a questionnaire asking for their postwar plans. While the response was low—there were 42 responses out of 323 questionnaires—78 percent indicated that they planned to "come back to Pecos County after the war is over."[56]

Upon returning home, Tony Benavides found himself without a ration card and unable to buy a pair of shoes. When he obtained the card and bought some civilian clothes, he looked for a job. He worked for several months with the Texas State Highway Department on Texas roads. Following that, he got a job driving for Alamo Freight, transporting goods for local businesses for delivery around the state. He retired from Alamo Freight after twenty-nine years. Benavides did not take advantage of the G.I. Bill because he had not finished school and had to work.

Like Benavides, Joe Urias did not use the G.I. Bill; he found a job clerking in a small department store that provided $3.00 or $4.00 a week. Selling clothes in a larger department store on Fort Stockton's Main Street provided Urias with an opportunity to move out of Fort Stockton. "But if I leave Fort Stockton, I'll die!" Joe thought. Joe discovered not only that he didn't die, but also that he was an excellent salesman. "I broke all the records as the highest seller. I got different awards for that. Instead of waiting four or five years to become a manager, they gave me a store in Santa Fe in less than three years."[57]

For Manuel Nuñez, though, the G.I. Bill was the means of escaping the confines of the small town. When Nuñez left Fort Stockton to join the Army, he was only twenty years old and could not find a job to help his brothers and sisters. When he returned, things were no different, but he now had enough experience and knowledge to know that there was a way out. He took his G.I. Bill benefits and moved, with his wife, to San Antonio, Texas. There he enrolled in Fox Tech and learned to be an electrician. Hoping to make his life in the big city, he stayed in San Antonio looking for jobs. None was forthcoming; finally, concern for his brothers and sisters, as well as a lack of adequate jobs in the city, drove him back to Fort Stockton.[58] His training in electrical services proved adequate for moving to the good life, and his Army experience developed his leadership qualities.

> After I returned to Fort Stockton, I got a job with Mr. Lance and one day listening to the radio I heard Walter Winchell, the commentator. He said, "Do something now for all the veterans." I thought we should go to church and say thanks and pray for those who didn't make it. Henry Scott, and I, and Cipriano got together with quite a few guys, Sotero Piña, from World War I, and we formed the Veterans' Club; I was elected president. Henry and I talked to Fr. Franchi for a spe-

cial Mass; we put on our uniforms and went from the
LULAC hall to church, over twenty of us. They had the
American Legion, but I didn't know anything about it.[59]

While the men had changed, their hometown held on to its pattern of racialization. Nuñez's brother, Aniceto, "Cheto," describes the membership of the Veterans' Club as "all Mexicans," and is uncertain about the exclusion from the American Legion or the VFW. "There was an American Legion and a VFW, but I don't know if they didn't invite us."[60] The Veterans' Club proved to be the foundation for the establishment of the G.I. Forum.

In 1952, our club chaplain Johnny "Whito" Urias moved to
Corpus Christi where he met Dr. Hector P. García, the
founder and organizer of the American G.I. Forum. Dr. García wrote me and asked if we would be interested in joining
the Forum, he recalled.[61]

The younger Nuñez acknowledges that anti-Mexican attitudes prevailed in Fort Stockton long after the war. In the late 1950s and early 1960s, he worked at a service center which provided a variety of repair services, and while the owner/manager was a good employer, he often would indicate to his Anglo American customers, "I'll send two Mexicans to do that."

"They knew our names, but they would say 'Mexicans.'"[62] Mauricio Herrera concurs and adds, "Change was very slow; la raza, here began to get agitated, you know the swimming pool."[63]

World War II ended in 1945 and the servicemen returned home. For Mexicanos from Fort Stockton, the world had grown larger. They had served in the armed services as Americans; many had been wounded; some had not returned at all. Life in Fort Stockton had changed very little. They resumed their lives, looking for employment to raise growing children, chasing the American dream, seeking the good life. For them, the war against racial discrimination still held many battles to fight before they could declare victory. Small victories finally came—the desegregation of the swimming pool in 1948, for example, and the gradual desegregation of the schools, which became desegregated at all grade levels in 1974. The World War II generation's children and grandchildren continued to carry out the legacy of challenge and resistance to discriminatory treatment, as well as to assimilation.

Toño "Tony" Benavides's service in World War II continues to be honored; in 1998, he received the Jubilee of Liberty Medal from the French Government. In appreciation for the freedom they now enjoy, the French presented the medal to veterans that participated in D-Day.[64] In the community he became a leading member of St. Joseph's Church, entrusted with the preparation of the church's annual festival dinner for over twenty-five years.

Manuel Nuñez continues as a leader in the American G.I. Forum; the community honored his leadership and service by naming a county park after him.

In 1940, when "Mel" Nuñez and Tony Benavides got on the bus to Big Spring, Texas, they had no idea how far that journey would take them. They survived the battlefields of Europe and the Philippines and came home to continue the struggle against racial discrimination. For them, the war had made a difference. The hometown newspaper ceased to use racial labels; the schools, the movie theater, and the swimming pool were integrated. They had fought as U.S. soldiers and could no longer accept second-class citizenship.

Citizenship, higher education, and participation in electoral politics count as some of the many benefits gained by the post–World War II Mexican Americans in Fort Stockton, Texas. Tony Benavides, Manuel Nuñez, Joe Urias, Aniceto Nuñez, and Carlos Granado are now retired;[65] their children and grandchildren attended an integrated high school and earned college degrees, and, perhaps, gained some knowledge and understanding of the distance their fathers traveled and their mothers' persistence and endurance on the road to the good life.

Notes

Aniceto R. Nuñez, interview by the author, tape recording, Fort Stockton, Texas, March 10, 2000.

1. Carlysle Graham Raht, *The Romance of Davis Mountains and Big Bend Country: A History* (Odessa, Tex.: Rathbooks Company, Texana Edition, 1962), 175–176.

2. U.S. Army, Surgeon's General Report, Fort Stockton, Texas, quoted in Marcos E. Kinevan, *Frontier Cavalry Man, Lieutenant John Bigelow with the Buffalo*

Soldiers in Texas (El Paso: Texas Western Press, 1998), 108.

3. Ibid., 130.

4. Ibid., 163.

5. Neil Foley, *The White Scourge: Mexicans, Blacks, and Poor Whites in Texas Cotton Culture* (Berkeley: University of California Press, 1997), 41.

6. Minutes, Fort Stockton Independent School District, August 12, 1942.

7. Antonio S. Benavidez, interview by the author, tape recording, Fort Stockton, Texas, February 26, 2000. Manuel R. Nuñez, interview by the author, tape recording, Fort Stockton, Texas, January 24, 1999.

8. Manuel R. Nuñez interview.

9. Ibid.

10. Ibid.

11. Ibid.

12. Raúl Morin, *Among the Valiant: Mexican-Americans in WWII and Korea* (Alhambra, Calif.: Borden Publishing Company, 1963), 100.

13. Aniceto R. Nuñez interview.

14. Joe Urias, interview by the author, tape recording, Fort Stockton, Texas, March 11, 2000.

15. Carlos Granado, interview by the author, tape recording, Fort Stockton, Texas, March 16, 2000. "*Nos llevaron a un* 'parade,' a St. Paul, Minn., *Nos llevaron a comer, una muchacha que conocí, se llamaba* Helen Anderson. *Se me hizo raro que uno anduviera con Americanas, aquí no podíamos. Una vez me dijo,* 'Come to my house.'"

16. "Rodriguez, Cleto L." The Handbook of Texas Online. <*http://www.tsha.utexas.edu/handbook/online/articles/view/RR/frobv.html*>.

17. Robert A. Calvert and Arnoldo De León, *The History of Texas* (Arlington Heights, Ill.: Harlan Davidson, 1990), 326.

18. Pauline Kibbe, *Latin Americans in Texas* (Albuquerque: University of New Mexico Press, 1946), 223.

19. "Four Sons of Pablo Gonzales Serving in Army of United States in Varied Branches of Service," *Fort Stockton Pioneer*, November 4, 1942.

20. Mauricio Herrera, interview by the author, Fort Stockton, Texas, March 10, 2000. "*El padre, se le ocurrió decir, 'no sé por qué lloran.' 'Porque los tuvimos,' le dijeron, 'usted nunca tuvo hijos.' Ya se compuso el padre.*"

21. "V-E Day Observed Quietly in Fort Stockton," *Fort Stockton Pioneer*, May 11, 1945.

22. Modesto A. Gomez to G. C. Moses, May 20, 1945, El Paso, Texas. Copy of letter in M. R. González Papers, private collection, Fort Stockton, Texas.

23. Kibbe, *Latin Americans in Texas*, 3. She wrote:

He was a little thin, this boy who joined the group in the room behind the grocery store; and he moved rather slowly like one who has recently spent long, weary weeks in a hospital bed. He still wore the uniform of the United States Army, and on his chest were displayed five ribbons, including the Purple Heart, and the coveted blue and silver badge of the combat infantryman.

He was an American hero, and his face and neck offered mute testimony of the sacrifice he had made for his country. The shrapnel that caught him in Germany had shattered his left cheekbone, drawing up his mouth in a set grimace. He was blind in his left eye, deaf in his left ear, and was just regaining the power of speech. He had been unable to utter a sound for forty days after the shrapnel hit him. Around his neck ran a long, angry welt, like a saber cut.

He was an American hero but his name was Arturo Músquiz, and his home was a little town in West Texas.

24. "Our Men and Women in Uniform," *Fort Stockton Pioneer*, December 11, 1942.

25. "Our Men and Women in Uniform," *Fort Stockton Pioneer*, September 11, 1943.

26. "Our Men and Women in Uniform," *Fort Stockton Pioneer*, April 28, 1944.

27. "Our Men and Women in Uniform," *Fort Stockton Pioneer*, October 1, 1943.

28. "Our Men and Women in Uniform," *Fort Stockton Pioneer*, August 18, 1944.

29. "Our Boys with the Colors," *Fort Stockton Pioneer*, January 1, 1943.

30. "Our Boys with the Colors," *Fort Stockton Pioneer*, June 4, 1943.

31. "Our Men and Women in Uniform," *Fort Stockton Pioneer*, January 7, 1944.

32. "Our Men and Women in Uniform," *Fort Stockton Pioneer*, October 13, 1944.

33. "Our Men and Women in Uniform," *Fort Stockton Pioneer*, February 9, 1944.

34. "Our Men and Women in Uniform," *Fort Stockton Pioneer*, September 15, 1944.

35. "Johnnie Casas, S1-C Takes Part in Exciting Defensive Battle against German Planes Attaching Ship," *Fort Stockton Pioneer*, October 8, 1943.

36. "Our Men and Women in Uniform," *Fort Stockton Pioneer*, May 21, 1943.

37. Joe Urias interview. Joe Urias was married to Anita Pineda; she died of cancer in Fort Stockton.

38. Ibid.

39. "Our Men and Women in Uniform," *Fort Stockton Pioneer*, August 3, 1945.

40. "Our Men and Women in Uniform," *Fort Stockton Pioneer*, July 7, 1944.

41. Félix Almaráz, *Knight without Armor: Carlos Eduardo Castañeda, 1896–1958* (College Station: Texas A&M University Press, 1999), 67.

42. Benjamin Márquez, *LULAC: The Evolution of a Mexican American Political Organization* (Austin: University of Texas Press, 1993), and Mario T. García, *Mexican Americans: Leadership, Ideology, and Identity, 1930–1960* (New Haven, Conn.: Yale University Press, 1989).

43. Pete Terrazas, interview by author, tape recording, Fort Stockton, Texas, July 8, 1999. Sixto Terrazas was Pete's uncle.

44. Márquez, *LULAC*, 19.

45. *Aims and Purposes of the League of United Latin American Citizens* (n.p., n.d.).

46. *Narrative Annual Report, 1935*, Mrs. Mary Sue Gespell, County Home Demonstration Agent of Pecos County, 1935. County Judge Records, Pecos County Record Center, Fort Stockton, Texas.

47. Letter from County Judge C. E. Casebier to Hon. Tom Connaly, U.S. Senator, January 21, 1936, Fort Stockton, Texas. County Judge Records. Pecos County Record Center. Fort Stockton, Texas.

48. "Improvement of Bathhouse Sought," *Fort Stockton Pioneer*, January 12, 1932.

49. Minutes of Pecos County Commissioner's Court, Book 7, 67. Pecos County Clerk's Office, Pecos County Courthouse Annex, Fort Stockton, Texas.

50. Petition addressed to County Judge C. E. Casebier, August 10, 1939, Fort Stockton, Texas. The signers include M. R. González, Sixto Terrazas, Raymond Barron, S. L. González, J. M. Cordero, F. B. Casas, Juan Garza, G. R. Terrazas, J. S. Cano, Isaac Barron, Joe M. Urquidi, M. S. Benavides, Frank Ureta, Rosa Scott, M. L. Peña, Rafael G. González, Manuel Peña, Nieves Garza, Frank Barron, B. L. González, and Tomás Chavez. County Judge Records. Pecos County Record Center, Fort Stockton, Texas.

51. Excerpts from letter to Mr. M. C. González, Austin, Texas, July 25, 1943, from Sotero Piña and M. R. González, Fort Stockton, Texas. George Piña Papers. Private Collection, Fort Stockton, Texas.

52. Copy of Resolution in George Piña's Papers. Private Collection, Fort Stockton, Texas.

53. Garza's widow donated his photo albums, newspaper clippings, and medals to the Annie Riggs Museum. On March 9, 2000, the author sought to peruse the material, but museum personnel could not find it.

54. "Our Men and Women in Uniform," *Fort Stockton Pioneer*, March 30, 1945.

55. Kibbe, *Latin Americans in Texas*, 6.

56. "Service Men Make Replies to C. of C. Questionnaire on Present Post-War Plans," *Fort Stockton Pioneer*, January 19, 1945.

57. Joe Urias interview.

58. Manuel R. Nuñez interview.

59. Ibid.

60. Aniceto R. Nuñez interview. "*Puro mexicanos, sí había un* American Legion *y* VFW, *pero* I don't know if they didn't invite us."

61. Glen Larum, "Pearl Harbor Day Observance Here In '48 Led to G.I. Forum Chapter," *Fort Stockton Pioneer*, December 7, 1986. The writer, Larum, who is also the newspaper's editor, quotes Manuel R. Nuñez December 7, 1986.

62. Aniceto R. Nuñez interview.

63. Mauricio Herrera, interview. "*Cambio aquí. Fue muy despacio, pero aquí la raza se alborotó, el* swimming pool . . ."

64. Tony Benavides, e-mail communication to the author, June 12, 2000.

65. Since the interviews were conducted and this article written, Joe Urias and Carlos Granado have passed away.

CHAPTER 8

Framing Racism

Newspaper Coverage of the Three Rivers Incident

MAGGIE RIVAS-RODRIGUEZ

In mid-January 1949, Dr. Hector P. Garcia, the leader of the then-fledgling American G.I. Forum, shot off seventeen telegrams protesting a South Texas funeral chapel's denial of facilities for a Mexican American soldier killed three years earlier in the Philippines and buried there. The family had chosen to exhume the remains and rebury them in the South Texas town of Three Rivers.[1]

One of those telegrams was to then–U.S. Senator Lyndon B. Johnson asking for "immediate investigation of the un-American action" by the funeral home owner in Three Rivers, Texas, to prevent the family of Felix Longoria from using the chapel. Garcia's telegrams, and Johnson's subsequent arrangement for Longoria's burial at Arlington National Cemetery, would ignite a firestorm of accusations and protestations and, for one of the first times, if not *the* first time, make Mexican American civil rights a national news story.

For Texans, inured to the injustice that marked the treatment of Mexican Americans, it would be the first time that a light was to shine on the matter. Scholar Patrick J. Carroll notes that the "slight" the Longoria family suffered was actually part of everyday life for South Texas Mexican Americans:

> These glaring but mundane disparities in Mexican American and Anglo educational, working and living conditions existing in South Texas after World War II might never have

become a pressing concern had Dr. Garcia not had the presence of mind to make a narrower affront [the Longoria incident] an issue of national honor.[2]

The negative press treatment outside of Texas caught many by surprise. In the end, it wasn't so much the case itself as the accompanying publicity that wounded the civic leaders of Three Rivers. This essay considers the press's treatment of the Felix Longoria case, and how, in particular, the story and the persons involved were characterized.[3] It is helpful to consider that the most protective treatment of the Anglo-dominated town of Three Rivers, and its civic leaders, was possible only in the Texas of the late 1940s, an era when Mexican Americans faced segregation in many Texas towns, particularly the more rural ones.

Nearly thirty years later, Garcia would describe the Three Rivers incident as a "turning point for many things."

It was a turning point for the American G.I. Forum; it was a turning point for Lyndon Johnson—I think it pushed Johnson into national prominence; it was a turning point for the thinking of some Anglo Texans. It was a catalyst for the cause of Mexican-American civil rights.[4]

For the American G.I. Forum, the case represented instant national recognition. The Felix Longoria case would bring widespread acclaim—as well as, in other quarters, notoriety—to both the organization and its lead organizer, Dr. Hector P. Garcia. The forum had been organized only the previous year to advocate for Hispanic interests. At its first meeting at a high school gymnasium, it attracted more than seven hundred men.[5] Its goals included helping disabled veterans, encouraging the Spanish-speaking community to become civically engaged, and promoting the "basic principles of democracy, the religious and political freedoms of the individual, and equal social and economic opportunities for all citizens."[6] As part of its efforts, the American G.I. Forum protested to the state's Good Neighbor Commission incidents of racial discrimination.[7] In fact, letters to the commission at the State Archives show that Garcia was a frequent letter writer, protesting various instances of unfair treatment of Mexican Americans.

The incident afforded Lyndon Baines Johnson a chance to make his mark on the national stage. Johnson had been elected Texas junior senator in 1948, beating out former Texas governor Coke Stevenson in the Democratic primary, which was marked by accusations of voter fraud on LBJ's side.[8] The Three Rivers incident would put Johnson in the national spotlight, as well as bring him respect among progressives and Mexican Americans, who were beginning to garner political clout in his state; he would, however, incur the animosity of an Old Guard of institutions and individuals who had benefited from a system that left Mexican Americans virtually powerless. Years later, John Connally, then one of Johnson's aides, would admit that no one was prepared for the "furor" that surrounded the Longoria incident and that Johnson, sensing the political damage he could suffer, soon after sought to keep it at arm's length.[9]

Although there would later be disagreement about the reasons for the refusal to allow use of the funeral chapel, the basic facts were not disputed: Beatrice Longoria, widow of Felix Longoria, was told by Rice Funeral Home owner/manager Tom Kennedy that he would handle the actual burial, in the town's Mexican cemetery, but that the funeral chapel would not be used for services because the town's whites would object. Mrs. Longoria returned to her home in Corpus Christi, about one hour away, and discussed Kennedy's remarks with her sister, Sara Moreno. Upon hearing of Mr. Kennedy's remarks, Ms. Moreno, active with a girls' club sponsored by the G.I. Forum, contacted Dr. Garcia by telephone. Dr. Garcia then spoke to the widow. Garcia agreed to look into the matter on her behalf.

According to a deposition by Garcia, Kennedy reiterated to him in a telephone conversation that, as Three Rivers was a small town, and his was the only funeral home there, "I have to do what the white people want. The white people don't like it." Garcia reminded Kennedy that the deceased had died in service to his country. And Kennedy replied:

No that doesn't make any difference. You know how the Latin people get drunk and lay around all the time. The last time the Latin Americans used the home they had fights and got drunk and raised lots of noise and it didn't look so good. I—we have not let them use it and we don't intend to let them start now . . . I don't dislike the Mexican people but I have to run my business so I can't do that. You understand the whites here won't like it.[10]

Garcia called the *Corpus Christi Caller* and spoke to a reporter there about the incident. The *Corpus Christi Caller*, a major daily about an hour from Three Rivers, interviewed funeral director Kennedy and confirmed Garcia's account of the exchange between him and Kennedy.[11]

That story was printed in the *Caller*,[12] as well as carried by the Associated Press throughout the country. In the firestorm of news stories and commentary printed or broadcast throughout the country, Longoria and his family were frequently depicted as loyal Americans—Longoria an American who died in service to his country. Three Rivers was portrayed as racist for denying the war hero and his family a decent burial service. An editorial printed in the *Detroit Free Press*, for instance, said that Longoria, "an American of Mexican extraction," is not "entitled to the privileges of United States citizenship in life—or in death." The editorial said the

> patriots of Three Rivers, Tex. . . . have advanced the cause of civil liberties in the United States beyond all the efforts put forth in their behalf to date. . . . When the half-citizens of this land are finally granted full admission to American citizenship, they can thank the Three Rivers, of which, unfortunately, there are many in the South—and the North.[13]

Two Spanish-language newspapers owned by Ignacio Lozano, one in San Antonio and the other in Los Angeles, carried the wire stories on their front pages—*La Opinión* bannering a headline at the top of the front page, above the newspaper's nameplate.[14] Neither newspaper assigned its own reporter to the story, but instead carried wire-service stories. And the *New York Times* ran a front-page story headlined: "GI of Mexican Origin, Denied Rites in Texas, to be Buried in Arlington."[15]

The publicity stung. Letters shot back and forth among Johnson's office, veterans' groups, the G.I. Forum, the Good Neighbor Commission, and private citizens throughout the country.[16] A tersely worded telegram from the Three Rivers Chamber of Commerce to

Johnson was accusatory: "We deplore your (itchy trigger finger) decision and action without first investigating the Longoria case. We feel that you have done South Texas a great injustice."[17]

Johnson responded: "I regret that you deplore my prompt action in arranging the burial of an American soldier from Three Rivers, Texas, in the Arlington National Cemetery."[18]

The Chamber backpedaled the following day with another telegram to Johnson:

> Our complaint referred only to your hasty action without first investigating true fact from reliable sources stop We believe burial place of this American soldier Felix Longoria should be reconsidered and buried in Three Rivers his home we do not believe the stigma of this publicity should be enforced on the city of Three Rivers on the County of Live Oak or on the state of Texas due to the mistake of Mr. Kennedy.[19]

And Johnson, not one to leave the matter to rest, responded on January 17, with a final telegram: "[M]y action was not hasty. I did investigate the facts before replying. No action of mine has enforced any stigma on anyone. I merely did my duty as I know it by replying to wire asking my assistance."[20]

In Texas, where natives understood that discrimination against Mexicans and Mexican Americans was part of the state's social fabric, there was suddenly a defensive posturing by civic leaders.

Later, after the story had made national headlines throughout the country, and after Senator Johnson had arranged for the soldier's remains to be interred at Arlington National Cemetery, funeral director Kennedy amended his explanation, saying that the practice of allowing Latin Americans to use the chapel was "discouraged" but not forbidden. Kennedy also told the *Corpus Christi Caller* that he would make the chapel available "if necessary."[21]

In subsequent stories, Kennedy further added to his explanation of why he "discouraged" the use of the chapel: he had heard of "some conflict between" the soldier's widow and his parents, and he didn't want the chapel to be the scene of any trouble.[22]

Fallout from the incident prompted Three Rivers state representative J. F. Gray, sensitive to his constituents, to call for a legislative inquiry into the matter, as well as into the Good Neighbor Commission, which had attempted to intervene and seek Longoria's burial back home, or at least in Texas. In a three-day session in Three Rivers, from March 8–11, nineteen witnesses were called, and 372 pages of transcript and other records were compiled in the investigation.[23]

The committee's majority report favored Kennedy's interpretation of the events, allowing into testimony allegations of problems between Mrs. Longoria and her in-laws, saying that Kennedy had "used some very unfortunate expressions; upon reflection he explained and apologized for same."[24] The committee concluded that "there was no discrimination on the part of the undertaker at Three Rivers, Texas, relative to the proposed burial of the body of Felix Longoria."[25]

Frank Oltorf, in his minority report, reviewed the facts of the case and noted that the case received "widespread publicity due to Mr. T. W. Kennedy's statements" to the *Corpus Christi Caller*'s reporter, George Groh, Dr. Hector P. Garcia, and Thomas Southerland, the executive secretary of the Good Neighbor Commission.

Oltorf, in a conciliatory gesture, offered within his minority report that

> Mr. Kennedy admitted saying that "The Whites might object" and later publicly apologized to the widow and her sister for having made such remarks. There is no evidence that his words reflected the views of the citizens of Three Rivers. After publicity had been given the event, in the Corpus Christi paper, Mr. Kennedy and representative citizens of Three Rivers offered every honor and facility for the re-interment of the body. . . . The statements of Mr. George Groh, a disinterested reporter are indisputable and undeniable. I cannot look into the heart of Mr. Kennedy to ascertain his oral words which appear to me discriminatory.[26]

Years later, when he recalled the incident, Oltorf said the reasons for Kennedy's refusal of the funeral chapel were fairly clear-cut:

We went down, and I guess it was one of the most remarkable experiences in my life. This could only happen in Texas at that time; it couldn't now. They questioned this widow, and people, and everybody they could, all the Mexicans they could. And they tried to make it appear that the only reason they wouldn't bury him in the cemetery[27] was that the widow had been having friends while he was overseas, and they were afraid of some sort of fight between the family at the graveyard. This was so ridiculous. They had no testimony to prove it, nothing.

Finally they had the young undertaker on the stand. He was a decent person; he'd been caught in this; he'd done it. And I asked him, I said, "Now tell me just why did you refuse to dig the grave and bury him there?" and he said, "Well, some of the citizens talked to me, and they said the white people might object." Well, there were just the exact words. I said, "This is what caused you not to do this?" And he said, "Why yes." So, I mean it was there, so spelled out that should have ended.[28]

At the time, shortly after the end of World War II, discrimination against Mexican Americans was widespread and particularly unsavory in Texas. For those who deplored the situation, it was frustrating that it continued unabated, even after the war in which many Mexican Americans had fought. One of the first books to document the postwar challenges was by Attorney Alonso S. Perales, a World War I veteran from Alice, Texas, who compiled testimonials, newspaper accounts, congressional testimony, and letters, presenting them in book form at the height of the turmoil in the Southwest, in 1948.[29]

One deposition was from a man named Malcolm Ross, who said that as a young man working in the mines in Bisbee, Arizona, his "daily rate as a novice mucker topped that of skilled Mexican miners who had worked in the dangerous trade for years."[30]

The wife of a returning World War II soldier, Oralia Garza Rios, reported that she had contacted two home builders about subdivisions being built specifically for veterans and was told that because of "social restrictions," the homes could only be sold to "whites."[31]

And Perales chronicled the longstanding complaints of those who stood up for Mexican Americans' rights, without significant progress.[32]

It is unclear how many Mexican Americans were involved in the civic life of Three Rivers in 1949. But a small booklet prepared fourteen years later in celebration of the community's fiftieth anniversary provides some indication of the social order. The sixty-five-page booklet includes names and some photographs of the town's leaders, six Live Oak County judges,[33] the Rotary Club (twenty-five men and one woman, the "pianist and sweetheart"),[34] and the thirty-two-member Celebration Board (which organized the occasion).[35] Not a single Spanish surname is included among those civic leaders and participants.

The social role of Mexican Americans within the community is noted:

> Agriculture today bows in respect and gratitude to the man with the axe and grubbing hoe, for without him and his family, Three Rivers would still be brushland. True, modern machinery now moves a giant swath across the countryside. Yet who is driving these machines? Usually it is the son of the pioneering man with the axe.
>
> Families who helped clear the townsite and have stayed on to become permanent residents include the Lupe Longorias, Marcos Moreno, Guillermo Martinez, Manuel Munoz and Lucas Diaz.
>
> Others who came in the late 20s and are still contributing citizens of our town are the George Flores, Joe Mendez, Lupe Chaverra, Felix Ortiz, Pablo Cruz, Manuel Mosqueda and their many neighbors.[36]

The page featured a photograph of an unidentified man cutting brush in the bright sun, his face obscured in the shadows of his cowboy hat's broad brim.

Newspaper accounts of the incident reveal much about how the state of Texas wrestled with the national exposure of the state's festering race problem. And it wasn't only the newspapers seeking to uphold the social order that wished to keep the matter quiet. "The stigma of this publicity" about the incident would hurt the city, the county of Live Oak, and the entire state, the Chamber of Commerce wrote to Johnson.[37] And even the Good Neighbor Commission worried about the fallout from the negative publicity, asking Garcia to intercede so that the matter could be resolved in a way that would bring harmony rather than bring further shame on the community.[38]

In reviewing reports published in South/Central Texas newspapers[39]—the *Three Rivers News*, the *Corpus Christi Caller* and *Caller-Times*,[40] the *Austin American*,[41] and the *San Antonio Express*[42]—three basic frames emerge:

1. Blissful coexistence. In this representation, Anglos and Mexican Americans blissfully coexisted in the small community and the event had been blown out of proportion; the community and its Anglo leaders were maligned unfairly.
2. The fallen hero. Stories that followed this frame characterized Longoria as the fallen hero and the Three Rivers funeral home as "un-American" for practicing ethnic discrimination; thus the funeral home director and the power structure of the small town were the "other," while Longoria, a fallen American soldier who made the supreme sacrifice, was adopted as part of the American family.
3. Opportunists exploiting a misunderstanding. In this frame, "outsiders" like Garcia and Johnson were using the incident to build their own reputations at the expense of creating ill will in the region, and indeed, nationally, against Texas.

No newspaper took the matter more personally than the weekly *Three Rivers News*.[43] The small community of Three Rivers, population 1,337, published front-page editorials and reprints of letters from those involved, as well as a news story that maintained that the community had been supportive of Mexican Americans and had even raised money for a Hispanic schoolboy who had been paralyzed in a football game. All the articles attempted to underscore the injustice of the accusations against the community and the respectful coexistence of Anglos and Mexican Americans.[44] On that same day, it also published on its front page a three-paragraph letter from Mrs. Longoria to Kennedy, in which she acknowledged his letter and thanked him for his offer to use the funeral chapel, but "I feel it is still too late. . . . I bear no grudge and still think greatly of all the people of Three Rivers."[45] The January 20 edition also carried a front-page letter to Johnson, questioning whether he was "representing all of the people in this matter." The letter decried the notoriety that had been visited on the little town after the story became a national news item: "Wires and letters began coming in—not to Mr. Kenedy [sic] who had made the mistake—but to the Chamber of Commerce, citizens of Three Rivers, the Mayor and others blaming not Mr. Kennedy, but all citizens of Three Rivers, Live Oak County and the State of Texas."

Had it not been for Johnson's intervention, Felix Longoria's remains would be buried in his hometown, "where all men are treated fair and equal."[46]

One story attributing information to Lupe Longoria, the father of Felix Longoria, was fabricated, according to Carolina Longoria, daughter of Lupe Longoria. Ms. Longoria said in a deposition that March that Three Rivers civic leaders attempted to coerce her father into signing a letter that would have put his daughter-in-law in a bad light:

> My father was driven from home down to the bank by [Chamber of Commerce president] Mr. Ramsay [sic] and several other men, where they asked him to sign a letter which said he wanted Felix buried in Three Rivers. He didn't sign the letter, they brought the letter to the house when they took Daddy home. . . .
>
> . . . They told us that if Daddy didn't sign the letters they would not be printed. . . .
>
> . . . Daddy didn't sign the letters then or any time, because we tore them up, after we had studied them. A few days, later, though the letter was printed in the Three Rivers papers with my father's name on it.
>
> Also, statements were printed saying that my father opposed the collection of money to pay for the family's trip up there [to Washington, D.C.]. That is not so. He went to Dr. Garcia and offered to help get the money. If my father had opposed the trip, we wouldn't have taken the money and none of us would have come here.
>
> The men in Three Rivers—Mr. Ramsay, Mr. Kennedy, Mr.

Montgomery, and several others—kept trying to get him (my father) to say things and do things all during the time the stories were in the papers. Daddy got sick and on Dr. Garcia's instructions I made the men go away whenever they came to the house. It all got so bad finally, though, that Alberto had to take Daddy away to Laredo to get some rest.[47]

The *San Antonio Express* likewise took the side of the city's leaders. A story published in the days after the incident noted:

Latin-American children . . . go to school with Anglo-American youngsters after they learn the English language in the first grades. . . . They sit any place in the theater, eat anywhere in the city including the school cafeteria, go to some of the churches, work side by side in refinery, farm and ranch. . . .

A Three Rivers football player, Juan Diaz, received $1,000 for Christmas last year when he was hospitalized due to an injury. He has been in the constant care of his Anglo-American friends. . . . Recently the P.T.A. in the Latin-American section of town held a Christmas party which school board members and their wives, the superintendent, and other Anglo-Americans attended.

In fact, the people here feel so alike that both groups find it hard to understand why all Three Rivers boys who were heroes of the battlefields are not buried in Arlington National Cemetery.[48]

In another story, two days before, Kennedy is identified as a "partially disabled veteran of World War II," and is quoted as saying he only discouraged "use of the chapel because it possibly could not hold the crowd who would attend the funeral and because it is the custom of the Latin-Americans to hold their funeral ceremonies from the Catholic Church there." The article also says that Mrs. Longoria said it was her parents, not she, who had complained to Garcia.[49]

The *Three Rivers News* interpretation of events is consistent with a sense of community journalism common among smaller community news operations. One example of how a "community newspaper" approaches its relationship to the larger community was William Allen White's *Emporia Gazette* (Kansas). Writing about White, Sally Foreman Griffith notes that a newspaper publisher is a businessman and as such must uphold business interests, as well as the social order of the community. But, Griffith writes, "community" does not include those with dissident views. Minorities, in particular, were excluded from the pages of the *Gazette*.[50]

The *Austin American* likewise took the side of the town of Three Rivers. In its first story about the issue, it carried a United Press story that quoted the president of the Three Rivers Chamber of Commerce and the funeral director. A one-paragraph insert, in parentheses, which indicated that the newspaper added the paragraph to a United Press story, quotes Garcia as saying that Corpus Christi citizens had raised $300 to fly the widow to the funeral services in Arlington, Va. The story also used the frame of the outsiders exploiting the occasion to make headlines.

S. F. Ramsey, banker and Chamber of Commerce president, said he was angry with Senator Johnson: "It is our feeling that he capitalized on this to further his own standing with the Latin American population."[51]

The following month, State Rep. J. F. Gray, of Three Rivers, obtained a $1,000 budget to appoint a five-man investigating team to examine the incident, as well as the Good Neighbor Commission. Gray, who showed up at a news conference called by Good Neighbor Commission chair Bob Smith, a Houston oilman, said the commission was "used only as a sounding board and a magnifying glass of such little domestic incidents."

Smith countered: "Do you mean the Longoria case was a little domestic incident?"

"It was until you people, U.S. Senator Lyndon B. Johnson, and the press got through with it," Gray said.[52]

Later, in the *San Antonio Express* coverage of the investigation into the incident, one of the points brought up is that the "investigation [of the Good Neighbor Commission into the funeral director's decision] stemmed from a request from Dr. Hector P. Garcia of Corpus Christi, president of the American G.I. Forum there. . . . Dr. Garcia is 'quite a requester' of such investigations."[53]

The frame of "outside agitators" is used frequently in news framing of social movements. In viewing how Los Angeles newspapers portrayed blacks after the riots of 1965, Johnson, Sears, and McConahay found that the mayor of Los Angeles dismissed charges of police brutality by attributing the complaints to "Communists, dupes, and demagogues."[54] Similarly, in 1971, leaders of the National Organization for Women "condemned the infiltration of the feminist movement by socialist groups."[55]

Thus, it is not an uncommon practice to attribute a problem to "outsiders" trying to capitalize on an isolated incident for their own selfish gain. And in the Three Rivers incident, both LBJ and Garcia were, at various times, accused of being those outsiders.

Certainly in at least the *Corpus Christi Caller*, the Three Rivers incident followed more contemporary patterns of news coverage of racial minorities. Although mainstream news operations generally share a desire to uphold a social order, there is also a reformist element involved.[56] U.S. journalists tend to seek to uphold the values of democracy.[57] Considering coverage of racial issues in the 1960s through the mid-1970s, Gans wrote, the news reflected a white male social order, "although it sides with blacks and women who try to enter it and succeed. Nevertheless, its conception of both racial integration and sexual equality is basically assimilatory; the news prefers women and blacks who move into the existing social order to separatists who want to alter it."[58]

Thus, it could be said that although the Three Rivers story represented a change in the social order in the state of Texas, it was also essentially a story about democracy.

Among the four South Texas papers examined, the Corpus Christi paper stood alone in its insistence on interviewing sources on both sides of the issue and holding Kennedy accountable for his statements.

The *New York Times* carried a staff-originated story, immediately after the incident, which included comment only from Johnson and Garcia. The gist of the *Times* page-1 story was that arrangements had been made at Arlington National Cemetery after Kennedy had denied use of the funeral home to the Longoria family.[59] However, in a United Press wire story carried immediately below the staff-written story, T. W. Kennedy denied the allegation that he had refused to handle the reburial. Kennedy said: "There was no question whatever of discrimination involved."[60]

Contemporary practice would have folded Kennedy's comments into the staff story and would have given Kennedy's denial greater prominence.

Interestingly about the two Spanish-language newspapers' handling of the Longoria incident, the boldest aspects of their coverage were the paper's headlines, set in very large type; the stories themselves, however, were relatively mild wire-service stories. In particular, *La Opinión* carried a six-paragraph page-1 story from the United Press, which gave greater weight to Kennedy's denial of the charges as well as the Three Rivers Chamber of Commerce's criticism of Johnson. The story included no comment from Garcia, Johnson, or the Longoria family.

An Associated Press story that ran on page 1 of *La Prensa* in San Antonio was more sympathetic to Johnson, the Longoria family, and the G.I. forum. In fact, *La Prensa* carried three AP stories about the incident on January 13, two on page 1, one with a Washington dateline, another with an Austin dateline, and the third with a Corpus Christi dateline. The Washington-datelined story described the controversy; the Austin story carried a response from the Good Neighbor Commission; and the Corpus Christi story described an event on January 12 in which eight hundred people met to hear Dr. Garcia read the telegram from Johnson and heard from Beatrice Longoria that she had decided to accept Johnson's offer to arrange her husband's burial at Arlington National Cemetery. Those stories made no attempt to vilify any of the parties involved; the lead story quoted Three Rivers mayor J. K. Montgomery as saying that the incident had been a "mistake" and offering either his house or the American Legion hall as a location for the wake.[61]

How the Three Rivers incident was framed and presented in news stories reveals a great deal about postwar Texas.[62] There were three competing social frameworks evident in news stories about the incident, as well as those about the public hearings that following spring: one was that of a fallen American hero suffering discrimination even after death, which characterized the coverage in newspapers outside of Texas. Another is of opportunists (Johnson and Garcia) seeking to gain political currency from a "misunderstanding." And a third is of the small Texas town maligned by the national press and by both Johnson and Garcia.

The depiction of Mexican Americans, as well as of those who would defend Mexican Americans, becomes a telling detail about a social order in transition. Lyndon B. Johnson, in letters to both his supporters and his detractors on the issue, stood fast in recognizing Felix Longoria not as a member of an ethnic minority, nor as belonging to a minority that had been subjected to historic discrimination, but simply as an American soldier who had given up his life for his country.[63]

Years later, in a monograph about the American G.I. forum, Allsup describes the publicity surrounding the Three Rivers incident thus:

> The national media coverage of the incident demonstrated to many otherwise unconvinced or unknowing persons that being a Mexican was a different experience than being an Anglo American. . . . For the leaders of Three Rivers, a "Latin American" did not merit the same respect as "white people."[64]

After the national exposure, newspapers in South Texas were compelled to report on the incident, which was striking only in its ordinariness. Suddenly, the open contempt which many Anglos held for Mexican Americans became a source of shame for South Texas. In writing about and manipulating representations to make acceptable a commonplace practice, newspapers in South/Central Texas were forced to see an everyday practice as outsiders saw it. The coverage and the barrage of public opinion against the funeral home would have reverberations that would herald a new day in Mexican American civil rights. The type of discrimination that Alfonso Perales and others had called attention to had now become the stuff of national headlines. Problems would—and do—remain for Mexican Americans in Texas; however, the petty discrimination that would deny a family use of a funeral chapel for a soldier killed in defense of his country would no longer be tolerated.

Notes

1. Si Dunn, "The Legacy of Pvt. Longoria," *Scene*, the *Dallas Morning News* Sunday magazine, April 6, 1975, 8. Dunn writes that "two of Garcia's 17 telegrams went to radio news commentators Drew Pearson and Walter Winchell. Winchell reportedly went on the air the following night with these words: 'Mr. and Mrs. North American and all the ships at sea, this story is on the front page of every newspaper in the United States and that's where it should be!'"

2. Patrick J. Carroll, *Felix Longoria's Wake: Bereavement, Racism, and the Rise of Mexican American Activism* (Austin: University of Texas Press, 2003), 53.

3. This essay uses the concept of "framing"—that is, a method used to make sense of the social world.

4. Dunn, "The Legacy of Pvt. Longoria," 9.

5. Henry A. J. Ramos, *The American G.I. Forum* (Houston: Arte Público Press, 1998), 4.

6. Ibid., 5–6.

7. Nellie Ward Kingrea, *History of the First Ten Years of the Texas Good Neighbor Commission and Discussion of Its Major Problems* (Fort Worth: Texas Christian University Press, 1954), 9–36. Texas Governor Coke Stevenson in 1943 created the Good Neighbor Commission in an effort to ameliorate the concerns of the Mexican government, which had decided in 1942 to stop sending Mexican laborers to Texas as legally imported braceros because of "the number of cases of extreme, intolerable racial discrimination" (32). The state legislature passed a resolution proclaiming "good neighborliness as the policy of the state" and asked Texans to end discrimination against Caucasians, i.e., Mexicans (34). Governor Stevenson secured $17,000 in operating funds from the federal Office of the Coordinator for Inter-American Affairs (OCIAA), the bureau that was responsible for promoting the Good Neighbor Policy in Latin America. Although the Good Neighbor Commission had no enforcement powers, it did take complaints of racial discrimination and wrote letters inquiring about those reports. Minutes of the commission indicate that although the idea of passing legislation to outlaw discrimination was considered, it was tabled. The commission's legal consultant, R. W. Fairchild, said that he feared proposing such legislation would cause more harm than good. "The feeling against the Negro race in Texas is more heated and stronger than it has been in a generation, solely because of repeated attempts to enforce, by passage of laws, certain adjustments between the white and Negro races," Fairchild said (47).

8. Julie Leininger Pycior, *LBJ and Mexican Americans: The Paradox of Power* (Austin: University of Texas Press, 1997), 64–67.

9. Robert Caro, "The Compassion of Lyndon Johnson," *New Yorker*, April 1, 2002, 70–72.

10. Carl Allsup, *The American G.I. Forum: Origins and Evolution* (Austin: Center for Mexican American Studies, 1982), 41.

11. *Corpus Christi Caller-Times*, January 11, 1949, 1. In the article, which did not carry a byline, Kennedy was quoted as saying: "We just never did make a practice of letting them use the chapel . . . and we don't want to start now." The writer also paraphrased Kennedy: "Most of them, he added, don't want the chapel service."

12. "Funeral Home Action Draws Forum Protest," *Corpus Christi Caller*, January 11, 1949. The *Corpus Christi Caller* was the morning paper; the *Corpus Christi Times* was the afternoon paper; on Sunday, the papers published a joint *Corpus*

Christi Caller-Times, according to N. W. *Ayers and Son's Directory of Newspapers and Periodicals* (Philadelphia: N. W. Ayer and Son, 1949). Today, there is only the daily *Corpus Christi Caller-Times*.

13. "A Hero's Return," *Detroit Free Press*, undated clipping from the Hector P. Garcia Papers, Special Collections Archives, Texas A&M University at Corpus Christi, Bell Library.

14. *La Opinión*'s banner head: "Se Negaron a Dar Sepultura a un Heroe Mexicano" ("They Refuse to Bury a Mexican Hero"), January 14, 1949, 1; and *La Prensa*'s headline: "Los Restos del Heroe Felix Longoria Llegaran a San Francisco el Dia de Hoy; Elocuentes Palabras del Senador Johnson contra el Prejuicio" ("The Remains of the Hero Felix Longoria Arrive in San Francisco Today; the Eloquent Words of Senator Johnson against Prejudice"), January 12, 1949, 1.

15. *New York Times*, January 13, 1949, 1.

16. One hand-written letter, for instance, from Louis V. Opsinger, on letterhead from the Glorious Fruit Cake Company in La Salle, Illinois, to Garcia, sent condolences to the Longoria family and expressed anger at the funeral director. Pre-Presidential Confidential File, Box 2, Felix Longoria Folder, LBJ Library, Austin, Texas. Another, from Mr. and Mrs. Roy Navarro, city unknown, included a $5 money order to help the Longoria family make the trip to Arlington. The Navarros said they also had a brother who was killed in the war, but who was given a proper burial. "I hope the Longoria family will feel the same." Garcia Papers, Special Collections Archives, Texas A&M University at Corpus Christi, Bell Library.

17. Telegram, Three Rivers Chamber of Commerce to LBJ, 1/15/49, Pre-Presidential Confidential File, Box 2, Felix Longoria Folder, LBJ Library.

18. Telegram, LBJ to Three Rivers Chamber of Commerce, 1/15/49, Pre-Presidential Confidential File, Box 2, Felix Longoria Folder, LBJ Library.

19. Telegram, Three Rivers Chamber of Commerce to LBJ, 1/16/49, Pre-Presidential Confidential File, Box 2, Felix Longoria Folder, LBJ Library.

20. Telegram, LBJ to Three Rivers Chamber of Commerce, 1/17/49, Pre-Presidential Confidential File, Box 2, Felix Longoria Folder, LBJ Library.

21. George Groh, "Arlington Burial for Three Rivers Veteran Planned," *Corpus Christi Caller*, January 12, 1949, 1. LBJ's response to Garcia was in the form of a telegram: "I deeply regret to learn that the prejudices of some individuals extend beyond this life. I have made arrangements to have Felix Longoria buried with full military honors in Arlington National Cemetery where the honored war dead rest." The news story notes there were also apologies from Governor Beauford Jester, Representative John E. Lyle, Attorney General Price Daniel, and Three Rivers Mayor J. K. Montgomery. Montgomery said the incident was "a mistake" and said the Longoria family could use his own home for the funeral services.

22. *Corpus Christi Caller-Times*, January 14, 1949, 1. This story was from the "Caller Times News Service."

23. *Journal of the House of Representatives of the Regular Session of the Fifty-first Legislature* (Austin: A. C. Baldwin and Sons, 1949), 1420.

24. Ibid., 1423.

25. Ibid.

26. Ibid., 1424.

27. In truth, the issue was using the funeral chapel; it was a foregone conclusion that the soldier's remains would be buried in the Mexican cemetery. Oltorf's lapse in memory may be attributed either to the fact that the interview was conducted twenty-

two years after the hearing, or to the fact that in many later news stories and other articles, the problem is inaccurately described as Kennedy's refusal to "bury" Longoria's body, rather than Kennedy's refusal to allow the Longoria family to use the funeral chapel.

28. Transcript, Frank Oltorf oral history interview, 8/3/71, 18–21, LBJ Library.

29. Alonso S. Perales, *Are We Good Neighbors?* (San Antonio, Tex.: Artes Gráficas, 1948).

30. Malcolm Ross, "Our Personal Relations with Mexicans," in ibid., 64–66.

31. Oralia Garza Rios, deposition, 6/12/47, in ibid., 146.

32. Roman Catholic Archbishop Robert E. Lucy is painted by Malcolm Ross (in ibid., 68) as a champion of the Mexican worker—who "daily persuades the meek that they will inherit heaven just as easily on ten cents an hour more." Ross is described as the former chairman of the Fair Employment Practices Committee (FEPC) and previously director of information of the National Labor Relations Board.

33. *Three Rivers, Texas: Golden Age of Progress Celebration, History and Program July 5–6, 1963,* Archives Division, Texas State Library, 5.

34. Ibid., 65.

35. Ibid., 7.

36. Ibid., 20.

37. Telegram, Three Rivers Chambers of Commerce to Lyndon B. Johnson, 1/16/49, Box 2, Pre-Presidential Confidential File, Longoria Folder, LBJ Library.

38. Letter, R. E. "Bob" Smith to Dr. Hector P. Garcia, 1/17/49, Box 2, Pre-Presidential Confidential File, Longoria Folder, LBJ Library. Smith was the chairman of the Good Neighbor Commission. Smith wrote: "I am not condoning anybody and I regret it as much as anyone could regret anything of this sort; but bear the thought in mind that Texas and all Texans and the children of Texans now living will feel the effect of the criticism, and we all know that none of them had anything to do with it." Smith was urging Garcia to intercede in the affair and ask Longoria's widow to bring her husband's body back for reburial in Three Rivers, "or at least in Texas . . . back to Texas where it should be." Smith worried that "the reputation of Texas will be at stake in history's recording of our handling of this delicate matter."

39. It must be noted that there were several other newspapers across the state that covered the story; some included editorials sympathetic to the Longoria family. Archives at both the LBJ Library and Texas A&M University's Hector P. Garcia holdings include several clippings from newspapers across the state.

40. *N. W. Ayers and Son's Directory of Newspapers and Periodicals,* 945. The *Caller* was a daily morning paper, except for Sundays, with a circulation of 35,573; the *Times* was the afternoon paper, except for Sundays, with a circulation of 27,169. The *Caller-Times* was the Sunday paper, with a circulation of 42,790.

41. Ibid., 938. The *American* was a daily morning paper, except for Sundays, with a circulation of 25,977; the *Statesman* was the afternoon paper, except for Sundays, with a circulation of 19,738. The *American-Statesman* was the Sunday paper, with a circulation of 42,258.

42. Ibid. The *Express* was the daily morning paper, with a circulation of 71,974, and 124,271 on Sunday; the *News* was published evenings, except Sunday, with a circulation of 78,595.

43. Ibid., 978. No circulation figures are provided. The directory notes that Three Rivers is seventy-two miles southeast of San Antonio and is known for its glass fac-

tory, a creamery, refining, and a tile plant. The *Three Rivers News* was established in 1891.

44. "Three Rivers Replies" and "Live Oak County Report," *Three Rivers News*, January 20, 1949, 1.

45. "Letter from Mrs. Longoria," *Three Rivers News*, January 20, 1949, 1.

46. Cecil Cunningham and Della Goebel, editors, *Three Rivers News*, January 20, 1949, 1. Hector P. Garcia Papers, Special Collections and Archives, Texas A&M University at Corpus Christi, Bell Library.

47. Carolina Longoria deposition, 3/7/49, Discrimination Files, Good Neighbor Commission, Live Oak County, Longoria Case, Box 41, Texas State Archives.

48. Mrs. A. E. Adlof, "Three Rivers Dislikes All Its Publicity," *San Antonio Express*, January 14, 1949, 10.

49. "Latin-American Funeral Rites 'Not Refused,'" *San Antonio Express*, January 12, 1949, 5.

50. Sally Foreman Griffith, *Home Town News: William Allen White and the Emporia Gazette* (New York: Oxford University Press, 1989), 175–176. "Scandalous or humorous stories reinforced the 'otherness' of outsiders or marginal members of the community. . . . Much of the unequal treatment of black Emporians was caused by the difficulty that even well-meaning white Americans like White had in envisioning racial minorities as full-fledged members of the community."

51. "Three Rivers Up in Arms on Funeral Issue," *Austin American*, January 14, 1949, 8.

52. Fred Williams, "Good Neighbor Panel Seeks 'Full' Probe," *Austin American*, February 19, 1949, 1.

53. Bill Reddell, "Longoria Incident Aired in Probe," *San Antonio Express*, March 11, 1949, V3.

54. Paula B. Johnson, David O. Sears, and John B. McConahay, "Black Invisibility, the Press, and the Los Angeles Riots," *American Journal of Sociology* 76, no. 4 (January 1971): 714.

55. Monica B. Morris, "The Public Definition of a Social Movement: Women's Liberation," *Sociology and Social Research* 57, no. 4 (July 1973): 540. Morris took her information from a story that appeared in the *Los Angeles Times* on September 7, 1971.

56. Herbert J. Gans, *Deciding What's News: A Study of CBS Evening News, NBC Nightly News, Newsweek and Time* (New York: Vintage Books, 1980), 45. Gans writes that racial integration was one of the values of news operations in the civil rights movement. "Activists who strive for the realization of democratic norms are often described in the news as extremists or militants, but the activists supporting racial integration were never so labeled, much to the dismay of southern television stations affiliated with the networks."

57. Ibid., 43–44. Those values include participation in the democratic processes and are viewed as expressions of the public interest.

58. Ibid., 61. For more on how movements are covered by the news media, see Francesca M. Cancian and Bonnie L. Ross, "Mass Media and the Women's Movement: 1900–1977," *Journal of Applied Behavioral Science* 17, no. 1 (1981); Pamela J. Shoemaker, "Media Treatment of Deviant Political Groups," *Journalism Quarterly* 61 (Spring 1984); Harvey Molotch, "Media and Movements," in *The Dynamics of Social Movements: Resource Mobilization, Social Control and Tactics*, ed. Mayer N.

Zald and John D. McCarthy (Cambridge, Mass.: Winthrop Publishers, 1979); Monica B. Morris, "The Public Definition of a Social Movement: Women's Liberation," *Sociology and Social Research* 57, no. 4 (July 1973).

59. *New York Times*, January 13, 1949, 1 and 11.

60. *New York Times*, January 13, 1949, 11.

61. *La Prensa*, January 13, 1949, 1.

62. Carroll, *Felix Longoria's Wake*, 10–13.

63. Telegram, Lyndon B. Johnson to Three Rivers Chamber of Commerce, 1/15/49, Box 2, Pre-Presidential Confidential File, Longoria Folder, LBJ Library.

64. Allsup, *The American G.I. Forum*, 49.

CHAPTER 9

Mexico's Wartime Intervention on Behalf of Mexicans in the United States

A Turning of Tables

EMILIO ZAMORA

The restaurant owner in the West Texas town of Pecos who refused to serve Eugenio Prado in 1945 probably thought that his behavior was of little consequence; turning away Mexicans was common practice in the state.[1]

This time, however, the spurned Mexican was a senator from Mexico, a respected medical doctor, and president of the Mexican Congress. The restaurant owner, once apprised of his customer's position and status, may have thought that Prado would register a complaint with the State Department to embarrass him or, at worst, pressure him to integrate his establishment. Even in the face of such troubling prospects he could nevertheless expect to defend himself by claiming that his business would fail if he did not conform to the segregationist tendencies of his Anglo clientele. His Anglo neighbors may have found his defense laudable. But World War II had elevated such seemingly local incidents to the arena of larger causes.[2]

At other times, it may have been a serious, yet routine, matter for the Mexican government to ask the State Department and other government agencies to intervene. Now, Mexican officials demonstrated greater assertiveness and were even uncompromising, especially when the discriminatory acts targeted Mexican dignitaries such as Prado.[3] They were bold with their use of the wartime language of good neighborliness, generously punctuated with references to Mexico's position as the principal U.S. ally in the Americas. More important, Mexican officials often called on the United States to challenge discrimination on the home front.

The United States responded to Mexico's demands by expanding its Good Neighbor Policy, a foreign policy, into its home-front world of ethnic relations. One of the most important consequences was an interagency campaign to address the issue of discrimination against the "Spanish-speaking," a general term used in government circles with Mexicans in mind, often without consideration to their place of birth or citizenship.[4] The Office of the Coordinator for Inter-American Affairs (OCIAA), the bureau that was responsible for promoting the Good Neighbor Policy in Latin America, coordinated the campaign. Although Mexico's influence explains much of this change, President Franklin Roosevelt was also responding to domestic pressures. These included a concern in the State Department that Mexicans were subject to Axis influence by virtue of their grievances against discrimination. Other government officials felt that they had a moral responsibility to apply wartime principles of equality and justice on the home front. Adding to these influences was the fear in some government agencies, such as the Office of the Coordinator for Inter-American Affairs (OCIAA), that continuing discrimination and the emerging minority cause on behalf of Mexicans could aggravate social tensions and undermine the war effort.[5]

This essay neither provides a comprehensive analysis of the remarkable and largely unprecedented U.S. action nor suggests that the official campaign against discrimination was singularly responsible for the social gains that Mexicans made during the economic recovery of the war.

Rather, it outlines how Mexico influenced the United States to make discrimination a central issue in wartime relations and the manner in which such a diplomatic concern joined with domestic issues in the decision by the OCIAA to apply the Good Neighbor Policy at home. More specifically, this essay illustrates the process by which the United States translated good neighborliness in the Americas into a domestic agenda on behalf of Mexicans by examining how the agency responsible for investigating employment discrimination, the Fair Employment Practice Committee (FEPC), responded to the OCIAA-headed campaign.[6]

Latin American countries had entertained the idea of building hemispheric unity and understanding since at least the time of their independence movements in the early 1800s. They periodically undertook unifying initiatives, especially during the late 1800s and early 1900s, against the interventionist threat that the United States posed in the region. Paradoxically, it was the United States that led the effort beginning in the late 1930s with its Good Neighbor Policy, a plan of action that, according to Roosevelt, sought inter-American unity and new relations befitting neighbors that respected each other. Roosevelt announced the policy during his first inauguration as a call for worldwide unity against the Axis powers. Soon thereafter, he gave it hemispheric meaning as a rallying cry for inter-Americanism, a system of wartime cooperation and reciprocity in the Americas.[7]

Mexico welcomed the opportunity to be a major partner in building inter-Americanism by entering into cooperative agreements with the United States and encouraging other Latin American countries to follow suit. Mexico's leaders believed that the war offered a rare opportunity to improve future relations and place Latin America on a more equal economic footing with the United States. The hope for friendlier ties and the modernization of Latin American economies, however, did not materialize during the postwar period. The United States, according to historians Josefina Zoraida Vázquez and Lorenzo Meyer, thought less of its wartime promises of cooperation and more about encouraging Latin America to conform to a cold-war policy intended to avert the influence of the Soviet Union in the Americas.[8]

However momentary the hope of improved relations, President Manuel Ávila Camacho and his foreign affairs secretary, Ezequiel Padilla, avidly promoted the inter-American system. Ávila Camacho, for instance, distanced himself from his predecessor's distrust of the United States soon after his inauguration on December 1, 1940. While President Lázaro Cárdenas had refused to take sides in the war, Ávila Camacho and Padilla embraced the Allied cause and Roosevelt's political and commercial leadership in Latin America. Ávila Camacho also settled the oil crisis inherited from Cárdenas by signing "El Acuerdo del Buen Vecino," whereby Mexico paid the claims of U.S. oil companies in favorable terms and the United States extended loan credits to stabilize the peso.[9]

Such cooperative ventures did not mean, however, that Mexico's political leadership or its press quickly or fully embraced the idea of new wartime relations. Critics of Ávila Camacho, for instance, reminded him that the United States had treated Mexico poorly. They occasionally expressed concerns of possible U.S. default or betrayal even as diplomats drew up the terms of wartime cooperation.[10] Such apprehensions dissipated, however, when Japanese forces attacked Pearl Harbor and Mexico responded even more favorably to the U.S. appeals for unity. Mexico broke relations with Japan on December 8 and, soon thereafter, with Germany and Italy as well. Mexico also assumed greater leadership in support of hemispheric unity alongside the United States. Padilla, for instance, on his way to the January 1942 Conference of Foreign Ministers of the American Republics at Rio de Janeiro, endorsed the U.S. recommendation that Latin American governments sever relations with the Axis powers. He expressed the official commitment to continental hemispheric unity by evoking a central principle of the Monroe Doctrine: "An American nation had been brutally set upon. One of the twenty-one flags of the continent of brotherhood had been treacherously assailed."[11] The idea of continental defense acquired added importance after Mexico claimed that German submarines had sunk two of its oil tankers, the *Potrero del Llano* on May 13 and the *Faja de Oro* on May 22, 1942. By the end of the month Mexico had declared war on Germany.

At this time, the neighboring countries officially became wartime allies and began to more actively negotiate agreements of military, economic, and political cooperation.[12]

As cooperation began in earnest, however, Mexican negotiators raised the issue of discrimination as an obstacle to inter-American unity. A case in point is the Bracero Program, a labor importation program that supplied U.S. agriculturalists and railroad companies with hundreds of thousands of Mexican workers during the war. Discrimination was a central issue during the initial consultations, between February and August 1942, as well as during subsequent annual negotiations to extend the program. Mexican negotiators may have made their most important claims during February and March when State Department and OCIAA officials began to report widespread concern in Latin America, particularly in Mexico, over the problem of discrimination.[13]

Negotiations over the Bracero Program produced immediate

results. Soon after the meetings began, the U.S. Embassy sent a report to the State Department and the OCIAA's Coordination Committee in Mexico with a "Suggested Method of Improving the Situation."[14] The report called on government agencies to treat discrimination as an impediment to cooperation with Mexico. Although it is difficult to determine how the message from Mexico changed policy, it probably contributed to the increased governmental activity that Will Alexander, the head of the Minority Groups Branch of the Office of Production Management (OPM), reported during the latter part of February 1942:

> The matter of an overall program for the government in dealing with the problems of Spanish-Americans is under discussion here [Washington, D.C.], between the various agencies in the government that now have some responsibility in this general field.[15]

Soon thereafter, however, U.S. and Mexican officials expressed second thoughts about the negotiations because they feared that the imported workers would face discrimination and that the predictable publicity by Mexican newspapers would harm relations. Immediately after Mexico declared war on the Axis powers, however, the negotiations continued. A more receptive Mexico may have made the difference. U.S. farm and railroad interests had also increased their pressure for imported labor with claims of labor shortages.[16]

When Mexican negotiators of the Office of Foreign Affairs and the Department of Labor and Social Provisions came back to the bargaining table in June 1942, they once again strengthened their hand by raising old grievances. They claimed that the United States had not helped Mexico receive the tens of thousands of destitute repatriates left jobless by the Depression. Because of this, they proposed a program of labor guarantees dictated by Mexican legislation that anticipated a possible repeat of the abuses of the 1930s. The United States consented to a number of them, including free return transportation costs, a minimum wage, individual contracts, and, most important, the continuing approval of the program by the Mexican government.[17]

One of the most important results of the bracero negotiations was that Mexico gained the right to intervene on behalf of braceros. This had significance far beyond the program. It strengthened Mexico's hand when it spoke for other nationals on U.S. soil as well as for U.S.-born Mexicans. Also, agricultural workers and other low-wage laborers in the United States could make their own justifiable claims for equal treatment if the labor guarantees extended to braceros exceeded the conditions under which they labored. In other words, the contractual guarantees represented the minimal conditions that the United States approved for all workers.

The meetings on the Bracero Program gave Mexican officials the first important opportunity to negotiate protections for Mexicans in the United States, but it was the earlier attack on Pearl Harbor that encouraged the United States to listen more attentively to the southern rumblings over discrimination. By December 1941, OCIAA officials were noting that the "isolation of the Spanish-speaking minority" was weakening the war effort and that the United States had to act. They offered three explanations for this newfound interest, including "repercussions in Latin America," meaning statements of protest by Latin American governments, especially Mexico, against the problems facing the Spanish-speaking communities in the United States. OCIAA officials also reported problems in the relations between the Spanish-speaking in the United States and the larger society, as well as an unfavorable image of Latin American nations as allies in the war effort. They added that a long history of discrimination and segregation had isolated the Spanish-speaking population and caused a "weakening of the war effort." This was an obvious reference to an often-expressed fear within government circles that "fifth columnists" and Axis shortwave broadcasts could encourage dissent among an aggrieved Mexican population on the home front. These problems, according to OCIAA representatives, required bringing "the Good Neighbor Policy into effective operation even within the United States."18

Roosevelt responded with an executive order in February that broadened the purview of the OCIAA into the domestic arena. By March 1942, the OCIAA's head, Nelson A. Rockefeller, was noting that his agency had been concerned about the problem of discrimination "for some time." Recent expressions of concern by Mexican and U.S. officials encouraged him to add that "we are now in the process of formulating plans whereby it may be alleviated," an indication that the OCIAA was taking steps to implement a program that addressed discrimination against Mexicans.[19]

Rockefeller's plan resulted in the establishment of the Division of Inter-American Activities in the United States in March. This was the first time that a U.S. government agency had assumed responsibility over an interagency effort to promote a more positive view of Latin America as well as to encourage interethnic understanding. The United States extended its hand of good neighborliness in another way. In April 1942, the OCIAA established the Spanish and Portuguese Speaking Minorities Section within its Division of Inter-American Activities in the United States. The purpose of the section was to improve Mexican-Anglo understanding and to challenge prejudice and discrimination with public programs that offered social assistance, encouraged self-help actions, and propagandized the idea of wartime unity on the home front. The section included three employees and a temporary budget. It soon grew to more than five employees in Washington, an undetermined number of field representatives, and an improved appropriation that allowed it to fund local and regional projects.[20]

Once the United States committed itself to promoting the Good Neighbor Policy domestically, the Office of Facts and Figures, the OCIAA, and the FEPC conducted field studies to devise a program of action. Academic and government researchers had already been generating information on the social conditions of the community. On the surface it seemed as if Washington was not sufficiently informed to launch the campaign. The questions raised by the new researchers, however, did not simply seek to test prior findings of poverty, discrimination, and inequality. They also studied social conditions; but they did this primarily to explain how poverty, discrimination, and inequality undermined or weakened the war effort.[21]

Aside from confirming deplorable social conditions and widespread anti-Mexican attitudes, the researchers offered two basic findings. First, Axis shortwave radio messages broadcast in the Southwest capitalized on the attendant racial tensions and posed security risks for the United States. Related to this fifth-column threat was the possibility that increased Mexican civil rights activity would trigger an Anglo reaction and escalate tensions. Second, the continuing problem of discrimination, especially the publicity that it was drawing and the perceived inaction of U.S. authorities, undermined the wartime alliance with Latin America. It became obvious, as the OCIAA began to direct its intergovernmental activities, that the researchers' concerns over national security and hemispheric unity were a major driving force behind the decision to incorporate Mexicans in the war effort. The domestic issue of discrimination, in other words, obtained broader significance during the war. This can be illustrated with an examination of ethnic conflict in Los Angeles and the Good Neighbor Commission in Texas.

In Los Angeles, the potential for racial conflict between Mexicans and Anglos was brought into sharp focus in 1942 with the Sleepy Lagoon case. The trouble began in August 1942, soon after the establishment of the Bracero Program, when the *Los Angeles Times* began to report increased delinquency among Mexican youth. The police had arrested hundreds of young Mexicans as suspects in the murder of a person found near a swimming place called Sleepy Lagoon. Twenty-two of them were tried and twelve were convicted of murder. The courts exonerated the young men within two years, but not before the exaggerated reaction by the media had exposed an undercurrent of racism that troubled the Mexican community and, according to the security-conscience State Department and OCIAA, undermined the possibility for home-front unity.[22]

Walter Laves, the director of the Division of Inter-American Activities of the OCIAA, arrived in the city in October 1942 to moderate the conflict, soon after the court had convicted the Sleepy Lagoon defendants and the Los Angeles County Grand Jury had held open hearings to investigate claims that Mexican youth were prone to violence. Laves met with numerous journalists and local officials as well as persons who testified on behalf of the Mexican community before the grand jury. He and Alan Cranston, from the Minorities Section of the Office of War Information, urged everyone to exercise restraint because discrimination was encouraging resentment among Mexicans and complaints from Mexico. Laves also used the opportunity to promise that the government would intervene with a program of "rehabilitation" for the "submerged" Spanish-speaking population. Rehabilitating Mexicans mostly meant that the OCIAA would seek their social incorporation, largely through public information programs that acknowledged their wartime contributions. Upon returning to Washington, Laves made a successful bid for permanent funding for the Spanish and Portuguese Speaking Minorities Section.[23]

Laves's concern was that Los Angeles had revealed widespread anti-Mexican attitudes and thus underscored an underlying moral issue for the United States, that is, it was leading a war for democratic rights while many of its citizens were seconding Nazi proclamations against an "inferior" race. The OCIAA also feared that continued discrimination as well as Axis shortwave broadcasts on the subject would fuel Mexican resentment. The growing number of complaints submitted to the OCIAA in Los Angeles suggested that Mexicans were approximating such a level of discontent, which was also evident among African Americans in other urban areas throughout the United States. Although some observers inside and outside government believed that fifth columnists were behind the emerging discontent, it is more probable that the wartime pronouncements of democracy and justice and Mexico's expressions of concern encouraged the mounting outcry against discrimination.

Another concern was that Anglos would react further if they perceived that the OCIAA favored Mexicans. Aside from expressing a possible bias against the Spanish-speaking, this may explain why Laves opposed hiring someone with "Mexican or other Latin American blood" to head the Spanish and Portuguese Speaking Minorities Section.[24]

The section had remained dormant since its establishment in April 1942. Its staff typically encouraged local public and private groups to establish projects of "social rehabilitation." The Office of the Budget determined that the Office of War Information would assume the primary responsibility for leading a public information campaign of Mexican contributions to the war effort in order to discourage Anglo prejudice and facilitate social incorporation of the Mexican community. The troubles in Los Angeles changed everything. Los Angeles gave the agency the opportunity to make a stronger case for the volatility of Mexican-Anglo relations and the need to anticipate the possibility of wartime conflict in other places where Mexicans congregated.[25]

In directing Washington's attention to Los Angeles, the OCIAA proposed to address the issue of discrimination as a major cause of poverty and inequality. The Los Angeles case, however, also demonstrated that discrimination, if not properly managed, could seriously disrupt social relations and undermine the wartime effort at home and abroad. The OCIAA, in other words, maintained that the war had made discrimination an important political issue and that it was not enough to seek to alleviate living and working conditions. It was also necessary to improve understanding at home and in the hemisphere and to promote the idea of a responsive government. In other words, the need for a unified war effort at home and in the Americas ultimately justified a call for government action on behalf of Mexicans in the United States. This partly explains why the OCIAA broadened its work by encouraging and funding complementary efforts by regional organizations, such as the Texas Good Neighbor Commission (GNC). The GNC was an "inter-American" agency that Texas Governor Coke Stevenson established to investigate and settle complaints of discrimination as well as to improve the state's chances of securing braceros from Mexico.

The story of the GNC begins with Mexico's decision not to send braceros to Texas in 1942. The Mexican government may have decided to isolate Texas as a test case because of the high number of complaints that Mexican officials claimed to have been receiving from Texas since at least the early 1930s. The isolation of Texas led to even louder claims of a labor shortage among its farmers as they began to see the military draft and urban-based industries depleting their labor supply. Texas farmers made their renewed request for braceros during the spring of 1943, as the cotton crop neared maturity in the South Texas region.[26]

Before the 1943 cotton-picking season began, Mexico made a public pronouncement regarding discrimination against Mexicans in Texas. In a communiqué dated April 23, Luis L. Duplán, the Mexican consul, noted the official view that discrimination in Texas was a major impediment to hemispheric understanding and cooperation. Duplán, acting under standing instructions for consuls to bring complaints before Mexican and U.S. authorities, sent the report to numerous officials, including George I. Sánchez, then the head of the Texas-based Committee of Inter-American Relations.[27] Meanwhile, the Texas Farm Bureau hired a judge from Corpus Christi to remove Texas from Mexico's blacklist. The judge contacted William P. Blocker, U.S. Consul General in Ciudad Juarez, Chihuahua, and both men convinced Tom Sutherland, the field representative of the OCIAA in Texas, to urge the State Department to intervene on Texas's behalf. Meanwhile, the judge, Cullen Briggs, was consulting privately with Governor Stevenson, Congressmen Richard M. Kleberg, and the U.S. Embassy. During these private negotiations, Briggs and Ambassador George Messersmith offered Stevenson a plan to promote good neighborliness.[28]

Seeking to convince the Mexican government to lift the ban on Texas, Stevenson consequently set out to demonstrate his opposition to discrimination. All along, he consulted with Messersmith, who continued to urge him "to curb discrimination where it exists and to wipe it out altogether" so that Padilla would look favorably on Texas. At the insistence of the governor, the state legislature led the way with the passage of House Concurrent Resolution 105, otherwise known as the Caucasian Race Resolution. The 48th Legislature proclaimed good neighborliness as the policy of the state and asked its residents to end discrimination against Caucasians, that is, the Mexicans.[29]

Stevenson continued to follow Messersmith's advice when he issued a proclamation on June 25 urging the Anglo residents of Texas to be neighborly. Discrimination against Mexicans, announced the governor, now constituted a violation of the Good Neighbor Policy as noted in House Concurrent Resolution No. 105, "and though not punishable by criminal prosecution may be subject to civil action in the courts." At this time, the governor secured approximately $17,000 from the OCIAA for the operation of the GNC. Apparently convinced that such actions would help satisfy Mexico, Stevenson and Messersmith made public a letter, written jointly by them, to Mexican foreign secretary Padilla in which the governor made another appeal for braceros. Padilla responded publicly by applauding the effort, but rejecting the appeal. He promised to continue entertaining the request as long as state action demonstrated some change in race relations.[30]

Mexico decided to allow Texas farmers to recruit braceros beginning in 1947. During the war, however, it was obvious that Mexico used the case of Texas to keep the issue of discrimination alive. At the same time, Mexican civil rights leaders from Texas associated with the League of United Latin American Citizens (LULAC) agitated on behalf of Mexicans. Often acting in concert with Mexican consuls, they campaigned against discrimination in the schools, public establishments, and workplaces. They also maintained a steady critique against government agencies at the same time that they brought complaints to the GNC and the local FEPC offices. This, however, is a story that goes beyond the central point in this narrative. That is, the officially sanctioned campaign against discrimination in the United States drew its major impetus from Mexico's pressure and the OCIAA's concern with promoting understanding at home and abroad, notwithstanding the important domestic influences provided by Mexican American leaders.[31]

Soon after the Bracero Program was established and the problems at Los Angeles were temporarily settled, the OCIAA encouraged other agencies to address problems affecting the Mexican community. By the end of 1942, the OCIAA was hosting interagency meetings that included the FEPC. According to Laves, the OCIAA was to keep a "weather eye" open for trouble and act as if "riding herd on the rest of the federal bureaus." The FEPC, like other governmental agencies, thereafter acted more deliberately and effectively in providing to Mexicans the wartime opportunities offered to other workers since at least the beginning of the war. The manpower agency began establishing regional offices in the Southwest during the summer of 1943. This led to a substantial increase in the number of Mexican complaints of discrimination against wartime industries and in settlements that favored the complainants. The FEPC, as some historians have pointed out, may have failed to produce significant changes in the segregated workplaces of wartime industries. It also may have been late in coming to the aid of Mexican workers. However, the OCIAA campaign, born in the world of international diplomacy, made a difference, and some results were evident in the work of the FEPC.[32]

As previously noted, some government agencies had been directing their attention toward the Mexican community. This interest, however, remained limited until the OCIAA stepped in with its coordinated campaign. The War Manpower Commission (WMC) is a case in point. The agency had established the Minority Groups Branch within its Office of Production Management and set up a regional office of the FEPC, its subsidiary, in El Paso around July 1942. The opening of the office was a departure from the indifference that the FEPC demonstrated in October 1941, when its officials held the agency's first hearing on employment discrimination in Los Angeles. In that meeting, the FEPC officials focused most of their attention on the African American worker in the region. Soon thereafter, however, the FEPC, under instructions from the War Manpower Commission, set its mark on the Arizona–New Mexico–West Texas region with its El Paso office.[33]

The WMC established the El Paso office to ensure the effective utilization of labor in the region's copper industry. Aside from seeking to alleviate alleged labor shortages with training, transfers, and even Mexican immigrants, the WMC also sought to address the problem of discrimination as an impediment to the rational use of available labor as well as an obstacle to friendly relations with Mexico. Ernest G. Trimble, the FEPC field representative stationed in El Paso, investigated the hiring, wage, and upgrading practices of the mining companies and concluded that they discriminated against Mexicans and maintained racially segregated workplaces. His efforts to settle workers' complaints, however, failed because the FEPC did not have the necessary authority to force the companies to abide by the nation's nondiscrimination policy. In addition to the problem of recalcitrant employer representatives, who either denied discrimination or stalled compliance with FEPC directives, disagreements among the agency's officials on whether to seek plant-by-plant or industry-wide settlements undermined Trimble's work. The final setback occurred when the State Department blocked the FEPC's decision to hold an industry-wide hearing in El Paso scheduled for September 1942. State Department officials feared that the hearing would draw attention to discrimination and impair relations with Mexico. The FEPC closed its El Paso offices and practically ended its fight with the copper industry until the OCIAA prompted it to renew its efforts and the president's Executive Order 9346 of May 1943 made it possible for the agency to expand its operations into the Southwest.[34]

The FEPC's early efforts coincided with the initial flurry of government interest in the Mexican community that the OCIAA promoted during the first half of 1942. The OCIAA had been encouraging other agencies to promote good neighborliness and its representatives had successfully moderated the conflict at Los Angeles in the fall. The work of coordinating an interagency campaign began later, during November of the same year. In the meantime, and for the duration of the war, the OCIAA sponsored or encouraged educational and public information activities that promoted good neighborliness, primarily in Southwestern communities. This included financial and technical support—in the form of lists of speakers, suggestions for community activities, and networking ideas—for community self-help efforts, such as the Barelas Community Center in Albuquerque and the Taos County Project. The OCIAA also helped to initiate similar community projects in Chicago and the aforementioned one in Texas.[35] The OCIAA encouraged these organizations and projects to assist Mexicans with their everyday material needs and direct public educational campaigns among both Mexicans and Anglos in support of wartime unity and racial understanding.[36]

Laves called the first interagency meeting on November 13, 1942, to push for broad-based governmental action and to coordinate these activities for major effectiveness. The official purpose of the meeting was "to explore the possibilities of using the facilities of the various agencies in an effort to deal with the Spanish-speaking minority problem in general, and the Los Angeles situation in particular." The OCIAA officials that attended the meeting understood that they were to develop a program in cooperation with other offices represented at the meeting, most likely the War Manpower Commission, the Office of War Information, the Office of Civilian Defense, and the State Department.[37]

The OCIAA encouraged collaborating agencies to see their work on behalf of Mexicans as an important contribution to hemispheric unity. Examples regarding the OCIAA's coordination activities included the sharing of information and advice between the Department of Agriculture, the War Relocation Authority, and the Farm Security Administration on claims of discrimination made by braceros. OCIAA personnel also assisted other agencies with advice and support. In November, for instance, they attended a meeting with representatives from five governmental agencies to discuss a failed proposal by the War Manpower Commission and the U.S. Employment Service to recruit additional workers from Mexico for the Southwestern copper mining industry. The OCIAA representative noted that the idea of collaborating against discrimination had reached fruition when he pointed to the way in which some officials at the meeting challenged the WMC. According to David Saposs, the director of the OCIAA's Spanish and Portuguese Speaking Minorities Section, they were not satisfied with the WMC's apparent ineffective-ness in acknowledging and combating employment discrimination against Mexicans. The representatives of the Bureau of the Budget, the sponsors of the meeting, spoke for the participants as they report-edly expressed great concern

about the discrimination to which these Mexican miners might be subjected and the general effect it might have on the existing friendly relations between our country and Mexico, as well as our effort to strengthen and implement the good-neighbor policy.[38]

By the time the OCIAA had called the second interagency meeting on December 10, 1942, the Office of the Budget had approved its budget. This allowed the OCIAA to fund more "inter-American" activities and to advance its coordinating work further. The December 10 meeting included twenty-four participants representing four-teen government offices, a clear indication that the coordinated wartime program on the Spanish-speaking had grown and acquired added importance. Laves chaired the meeting and the participants agreed on an agenda that indicated new areas of emphasis for the "comprehensive program" that the OCIAA wished to coordinate. Representatives from the Office of War Information, for instance, reported on their public relations work in Los Angeles, while others from the California Farm Security Administration and the State Department informed the meeting on issues related to the Bracero Program. Laves also spoke about the OCIAA's renewed work on Spanish-speaking minorities. The OCIAA also gave major emphasis to employment discrimination against Mexicans in wartime indus-tries. This was evident in both symbolic and substantive terms as Lawrence Cramer, the Executive Secretary of the FEPC, and Alexander, the Chief of the Minority Groups in the OPM, joined the OCIAA-led campaign with their important contributions to the December meeting.[39]

Cramer announced what sounded like a determined plan of action. He reported that the FEPC had been investigating "the alleged discrimination of Mexican workers by six or seven industries in the Southwest," and that three of them had agreed to comply with the president's executive order. Cramer outlined his strategy: he would settle some "major cases" with the expectation that the attendant publicity would "bring the rest of the industries along." He ended on an optimistic note, stating that Spanish-speaking organizations had not complained "because they know that there is an agency that is actively concerned in this particular problem." Alexander was less effusive, preferring instead to report that the "worst situation in the country" was in Texas and that the "worst offenders" were the oil companies of the Gulf Coast. Alexander's comments foretold the initial offensive against employment discrimination of 1943, when the FEPC established its first regional office in Dallas and conducted its first major investigation of the oil refineries of the Texas coast.[40]

The reports by Cramer and Alexander demonstrate that the FEPC had decided to challenge discrimination and that this coincided with the launching of the OCIAA campaign in support of a broadened interpretation of the Good Neighbor Policy. By the summer of 1943, when the FEPC had established its Dallas office, the manpower agency was cooperating closely with the OCIAA, knowing that its work involved more than the efficient utilization of workers without regard to differences of race, religion, or national origin; it was also part of a broader campaign to promote the Good Neighbor Policy and build hemispheric unity.

The delayed attention that the FEPC gave Mexicans achieves special significance when cast within the diplomatic realm of the Second World War. The wartime attention that U.S. government agencies gave the Mexican community resulted from a special combination of foreign pressures and domestic concerns over the incorporation of a socially "isolated" group with ties to a cobelligerent and ally. An overriding factor was the intervention of the Mexican government. To state this differently, Mexicans appeared on the center stage of national minority and labor politics by way of an international, or more precisely hemispheric, body politic. Mexican government officials, facing criticism against agreements of cooperation with the North Americans, wished to demonstrate a measure of independence by testing the U.S. Good Neighbor Policy, especially its declared wartime aim of improving understanding and goodwill throughout the Americas. This challenge also suggested a hope in the administration of Ávila Camacho that wartime cooperation would improve relations between Mexico and the United States.

The U.S. government's continuing entry into the world of workers' and minority rights during the war had its advantages and disadvantages for the Mexican population in the United States. The promotion of the Good Neighbor Policy provided the justification for quick and, to some extent, effective attention to the problems of discrimination and inequality. Of special significance was the way the war emergency created by Pearl Harbor prompted governmental agencies to consolidate and advance their previously unfocused and ineffective efforts. This attention, however, was mostly dependent on the broader campaign to build hemispheric unity, especially Mexico's bargaining ability to encourage the United States to act on behalf of Mexicans. When the war ended, Mexico no longer pursued a forthright policy of advocacy for minority rights in the United States. This change may have reflected Mexico's loss of its favored status in the postwar period of cold-war politics. At any rate, the Mexican community was left to elaborate its cause for equality after the war largely without the help of the Mexican government.

The attention given to the Mexican community, however, was unprecedented and no doubt encouraged it to expect the U.S. government to assume a more active role in regulating social relations and combating racial discrimination, the war's much-discredited obstacle to equality. One can only conjecture on the extent to which a more active state, in combination with recovery and battlefront experiences, contributed to such rising expectations. Mexico's intervention nevertheless produced more observable results. Using its position as a key ally, Mexico influenced the United States to broaden the scope of its Good Neighbor Policy. This resulted in the increased attention that U.S. government agencies gave the Mexican community. Although the primary concern among some Mexican as well as

American officials was that Mexicans were being denied the opportunity to share equally in the wartime recovery, agencies such as the OCIAA often pursued a propagandistic strategy of changing public opinion rather than a more far-reaching one of correcting discriminatory behavior. Despite this inconsistency in the Good Neighbor Policy, some benefits occurred immediately, including the investigation and settlement of Mexican workers' complaints. A more significant result was that the plight of the Mexicans in the United States became an issue of hemispheric importance and the cause on their behalf obtained unmatched moral meaning during the war.

Notes

1. I use the term *Mexican* to designate both Mexican nationals and U.S.-born Mexicans, unless it is necessary and possible to identify their citizenship or place of birth.

2. Enrique Gonzalez Martinez, President of the Mexican Committee against Racism, to Alonso S. Perales, March 26, 1945, in Perales, *Are We Good Neighbors?* (San Antonio: Artes Gráficas, 1948), 177.

3. The final disposition of the Prado case is unknown. The State Department's protocol in such cases was to request the restaurant owner or other persons to end their discriminatory behavior because it impaired hemispheric unity. The archives of the Secretaría de Relaciones Exteriores (Foreign Affairs Office) contain a vast number of records, including complaints, consular reports, and diplomatic correspondence, that attest to the importance of discrimination in U.S.-Mexican relations. Complainants usually registered their protest with a local Mexican consular office. Consular staff would investigate the charges and forward their reports and recommendations to their superiors. The complaints were then communicated to U.S. governmental officials. See the following on the work of the Mexican consulates in the United States: Francisco E. Balderrama, *In Defense of La Raza: The Los Angeles Mexican Consulate and the Mexican Community, 1929–1936* (Tucson: University of Arizona Press, 1982); Juan Gómez-Quiñones, "Piedras Contra La Luna, México en Aztlán y Aztlán en México: Chicano-Mexican Relations and the Mexican Consulates, 1900–1920," In *Contemporary Mexico: Papers of the Fourth International Congress of Mexican History*, ed. James W. Wilkie, Michael C. Meyer, and Edna Monzón de Wilkie (Berkeley: University of California Press, 1976), and Archivo, Secretaría de Relaciónes Exteriores, México, D.F.

4. Luis G. Zorrilla, *Historia de las Relaciones entre México y Los Estados Unidos de America, 1800–1958*, Tomo II (México, D.F.: Editorial Porrua, S.A., 1966); Luis F. González-Souza, "La Política Exterior de México ante la Protección Internacional de los Derechos Humanos," *Foro Internacional* 18 (Julio–Septiembre 1977): 108–138; George J. Sanchez, *Becoming Mexican American: Ethnicity, Culture and Identity in Chicano Los Angeles, 1900–1945* (New York: Oxford University Press, 1993). Zorrilla makes the most compelling argument that the war gave Mexico the opportunity to challenge discrimination against Mexicans in the United States. González-Souza

reminds us that Mexico has a tradition of advocating human rights in international arenas. Sanchez includes the Mexican state in a recent history of Mexicans in the United States.

5. The following sources from the Records of the OCIAA provide this essay's basis for commentary on the history and operations of the agency: "Objective and Plan of Operation of Inter-American Activities in the United States," May 1, 1942; Office of the Coordinator of Inter-American Affairs, "Report, Division of Inter-American Activities in the United States, December 1941–1942," in U.S. Bureau of the Budget, Administrative Histories of World War II Civilian Agencies of the Federal Government, Research Publication of the Second World War History Program of the Bureau of the Budget, Microfilm 41 (New Haven, Conn.: Research Publications, 1974), 1–43. Other pertinent documents that were attached to this report included "Introduction to Appendix," 1–3, and "Draft of Memorandum to Be Attached to Annual Report Relating to Spanish-Speaking Minority Project," December 15, 1942, 1–7, Records of the Office of Inter-American Affairs, Record Group 229, National Archives and Records Administration, Washington, D.C. Hereafter cited as "Records of the OCIAA" in accordance with the agency's official name and its corresponding acronym that appears in the text of this essay.

6. Recent histories on Mexicans in the United States that inform this study include: Clete Daniel, *Chicano Workers and the Politics of Fairness: The FEPC in the Southwest, 1941–1945* (Austin: University of Texas Press, 1991); Mario T. García, "Americans All: The Mexican-American Generation and the Politics of Wartime Los Angeles, 1941–1945," *Social Science Quarterly* 65 (June 1984): 278–289; Lou Ella Jenkins, "The Fair Employment Practice Committee and Mexican-Americans in the Southwest," Ph.D. diss., Georgia State University, 1974; Gerald Nash, "Spanish-Speaking Americans in Wartime," Chapter Seven in Nash, *The American West Transformed: The Impact of the Second World War* (Bloomington: Indiana University Press, 1985), 107–127; Guadalupe San Miguel, Jr., *Let All of Them Take Heed: Mexican Americans and the Campaign for Educational Equality in Texas, 1910–1981* (Austin: University of Texas Press, 1987).

7. Sumner Welles, *The Time for Decision* (New York: Harper and Brothers, 1944), 192–193. See the following for a recent publication and a review of works on the U.S. Good Neighbor Policy: Fredrick B. Pike, *FDR's Good Neighbor Policy: Sixty Years of Gentle Chaos* (Austin: University of Texas Press, 1995); Richard V. Salisbury, "Good Neighbors? The United States and Latin America in the Twentieth Century," in Gerald K. Haines and Samuel J. Walker, eds., *American Foreign Relations: A Historiographical Review* (Westport, Conn.: Greenwood Press, 1981), 311–333.

8. Josefina Zoraida Vázquez and Lorenzo Meyer, *México Frente a Estados Unidos (Un Esayo Histórico, 1776–1988)*, 2nd ed. (México, D.F.: Fondo de Cultura Económica, 1992), 10–12.

9. Mexico and the United States came close to severing diplomatic relations when President Lázaro Cárdenas expropriated foreign-owned oil companies operating in Mexico and the United States took an aggressive posture in defense of U.S. oil companies. The Mexican Supreme Court had intervened in a national labor dispute by ordering the oil companies on March 1, 1938, to accept a plan arbitrated by a federal agency. When the oil companies refused to abide fully by the court order, President Cárdenas, on March 18, announced the expropriation. Clayton R. Koppes, "The Good Neighbor Policy and the Nationalization of Mexican Oil: A Reinterpretation,"

Journal of American History 69 (June 1982): 62–81; Zoraida Vázquez and Meyer, *México Frente a Estados Unidos*, 172–175.

10. Marquard Dozer, *Are We Good Neighbors? Three Decades of Inter-American Relations, 1930–1960* (Gainesville: University of Florida Press, 1959), 97. For an examination of the Mexican press's critique of discrimination against minorities in the United States, see Hensley C. Woodbridge, "Mexico and U.S. Racism: How Mexicans View Our Treatment of Minorities," *Commonweal*, June 22, 1945, 234–237.

11. Ezequiel Padilla, *Free Men of America* (Chicago: Ziff-Davis, 1943), 1; J. Lloyd Mecham, *A Survey of United States–Latin American Relations* (New York: Houghton Mifflin, 1965), 372–373.

12. Zoraida Vázquez and Meyer, *México Frente a Estados Unidos*, 185–187.

13. Carey McWilliams, *North from Mexico: The Spanish-Speaking People of the United States* (New York: Greenwood Press, 1968 [First Edition, 1948]), 269; "El Gral. Manuel Ávila Camacho, al Abrir el Congreso Sus Sesiones Ordinarias, El Primero de Septiembre de 1942," *Los Presidentes de México ante la Nación, Informes, Manifiestos y Documentos de 1821 a 1966*, 205; Zorrilla, *Historia de las Relaciones entre México y Los Estados Unidos*, 506–507.

14. Nelson Rockefeller, Director, OCIAA, to W. C. Longan, Executive Secretary, Coordination Committee for Mexico, March 7, 1942, Records of the OCIAA.

15. Will Alexander, Consultant on Minority Groups, WMC, to Isabel Leonard, Secretary, Foundation for the Advancement of the Spanish Speaking People, February 19, 1942, Records of the War Manpower Commission, Record Group 211, National Archives and Records Administration, Washington, D.C. Hereafter cited as "Records of the WMC."

16. Richard B. Craig, *The Bracero Program* (Austin: University of Texas Press, 1971), 40–42; Robert D. Tomasek, "The Political and Economic Implications of Mexican Labor in the United States under the Non Quota System, Contract Labor Program, and Wetback Movement," Ph.D. diss., University of Michigan, 1957, 50–52. The following discussion on the Bracero Program also draws on Wayne D. Rasmussen, *A History of the Emergency Farm Labor Supply Program, 1943–1947*, Agricultural Monograph no. 13, U.S. Department of Agriculture, Bureau of Economics (Washington, D.C.: U.S. Government Printing Office, 1954); Peter N. Kirstein, *Anglo over Bracero: A History of the Mexican Worker in the United States from Roosevelt to Nixon* (San Francisco: R and E Research Associates, 1977); Barbara A. Driscoll, *Me voy pa' Pensilvania por no andar en la vaganzia* (México, D.F.: Consejo Nacional para la Cultura y las Artes y Universidad Nacional Autónoma de México, 1996).

17. Zorrilla, *Historia de las Relaciones entre México y Los Estados Unidos*, 490–492. Consult the following book-length study on the repatriations of the 1930s: Abraham Hoffman, *Unwanted Mexican Americans in the Great Depression: Repatriation Pressures, 1929–1939* (Tucson: University of Arizona Press, 1974).

18. "Draft of Memorandum to Be Attached to Annual Report Relating to Spanish-Speaking Minority Project," December 15, 1942, 1.

19. Rockefeller to W. C. Longan, Executive Secretary, Coordination Committee for Mexico, March 7, 1942, Records of the OCIAA.

20. The section received approval from the State Department on May 15, with a temporary budget of $105,233 that was to keep the office operating until July 1. The Bureau of the Budget disallowed all appropriations in June on the grounds that such activities came under the jurisdiction of other offices. The bureau retracted the deci-

sion by the end of 1942 and made available the necessary appropriations. Walter H. C. Laves, Director of the Division of Latin-American Activities in the United States, to Arthur Jones, September 8, 1942, Records of the OCIAA; Program for Cooperation with Spanish-Speaking Minorities in the United States, "Progress Report of Resident Latin American Unit," July 1, 1942, Ernesto Galarza Papers, Department of Special Collections, Stanford University, Stanford, California.

21. Paul Horgan, "United States Latins in the Southwest, a Domestic Wartime Responsibility with Foreign Overtones," January 1942, Records of the OCIAA; David J. Saposs, "Report on Rapid Survey of Resident Latin American Problems and Recommended Program," April 3, 1942, *Records of the Committee on Fair Employment Practice*, Record Group 228, National Archives and Records Administration, Washington, D.C. (hereafter cited as "Records of the FEPC" in accordance with the agency's official name and its corresponding acronym that appears in the text of this essay); and Vincenso Petrullo, "Report on the Spanish-Speaking Peoples in the Southwest," Field Survey, March 14 to April 7, 1942, Records of the FEPC.

22. Sanchez, *Becoming Mexican American*, 264–267. Consult the following for more complete treatments of the ethnic tension in Los Angeles, the Sleepy Lagoon case, and the so-called Zoot Suit Riots of June 1943: McWilliams, *North from Mexico*, 228–258; Mauricio Mazón, *The Zoot-Suit Riots: The Psychology of Symbolic Annihilation* (Austin: University of Texas Press, 1984).

23. Laves to William G. McLean, Divisional Assistant, Division of American Republics, Department of States, November 7, 1942; Laves to Arthur Jones, September 8, 1942, Records of the OCIAA.

24. Laves to Robert Redfield, November 3, 1942; Laves to Arthur Jones, September 8, 1942, Records of the OCIAA. Also see the following for a discussion of Mexican political activity surrounding the Sleepy Lagoon case and its use of the wartime rhetoric of democracy: David Gutiérrez, *Walls and Mirrors: Mexican Americans, Mexican Immigrants and the Politics of Ethnicity* (Berkeley: University of California Press, 1995), 126–130.

25. Cranston to Laves, May 28, 1942, and September 17, 1942, Records of the OCIAA.

26. McWilliams, *North from Mexico*, 240–244; Pauline Kibbe, *Latin Americans in Texas* (Albuquerque: University of New Mexico Press, 1946), 252–254.

27. Duplán to Sánchez, April 23, 1943, Coke R. Stevenson Papers, Texas State Library and Archives Commission, Austin, Texas.

28. Cullen W. Briggs to Stevenson, July 8, 1943, Stevenson Papers. According to Luis L. Duplán, the Mexican Consul at Austin, the State Department had unofficially designated Blocker as diplomatic advisor to Governor Stevenson. Duplán credited Blocker with suggesting the idea of a Good Neighbor Commission. Duplán to Ezequiel Padilla, September 29, 1945, Galarza Papers.

29. Messersmith to Stevenson, June 29, 1943, Stevenson Papers. The resolution excluded African Americans despite immediate protestations that pointed to the blatant problem of discrimination against blacks and the apparent inconsistency of the Legislature's action. The following are sample letters of protest received by Governor Stevenson shortly after the passage of Resolution 105: E. H. F. Jones to Stevenson, June 28, 1943; B. E. Howell, President, and G. F. Porter, Secretary, National Association for the Advancement of Colored People, Dallas Branch, to Stevenson, August 3, 1943; Eloísa Galán to Stevenson, September 18, 1943; Stevenson Papers.

30. Stevenson, "Proclamation by the Governor of the State of Texas No. 7039,"

June 25, 1943; Draft of Letter, Stevenson to Padilla, June 25, 1943; Briggs to Stevenson, July 8, 1943; Telegram, Briggs to Ernest Boyette, Governor's Secretary, July 9, 1943; Messersmith to Stevenson, August 12, 1943; "Remarks Made by Licenciado Ezequiel Padilla, Mexican Minister of Foreign Affairs, to the Press on Wednesday Evening, August 11, 1943," Enclosure to Letter, Messersmith to Stevenson, August 12, 1943; Stevenson to Padilla, August 12, 1943, Stevenson Papers.

31. My forthcoming book, "The Politics of Good Neighborliness in Texas during the Second World War," addresses the important role that Mexican leaders played in fighting discrimination and segregation in the schools, in public establishments, and in the workplace. Three available works address aspects of this history: Gutiérrez, *Walls and Mirrors*; Kibbe, *Latin Americans in Texas*; and San Miguel, *Let All of Them Take Heed*.

32. Laves to Rockefeller, December 28, 1942, Records of the OCIAA.

33. Daniel, *Chicano Workers and the Politics of Fairness*, 6–13.

34. John Morton Blum, *V Was for Victory: Politics and American Culture during World War II* (New York: Harcourt Brace Jovanovich, 1976), 198–199; Trimble to Lawrence W. Cramer, Executive Secretary, FEPC, September 1942, Records of the FEPC. Historians agree that the State Department's decision to block the El Paso hearings ultimately undermined the early work of the FEPC in the region. This essay indirectly offers an explanation for the State Department's action. The troubles at Los Angeles which erupted around the time of the planned El Paso hearing and weeks after the Bracero Program had been established left State Department officials nervous about the possibility of added attention to the problem of discrimination. State Department officials had consistently expressed concerns about drawing attention to discrimination as government agencies addressed the problem. This was evident during the first official expressions of interest in discrimination and the need for governmental action evident by December 1941, as well as during the establishment of the OCIAA's Latin American Division and the Spanish-speaking section between March and April 1942. The State Department, however, endorsed these initiatives, including the decision to establish the FEPC office in El Paso. The prospects of a full airing of widespread discrimination in the Southwestern copper region, coming in the wake of the well-publicized troubles in Los Angeles and the understanding associated with the Bracero Program that encouraged Mexico to more actively intervene on behalf of Mexicans in the United States, no doubt made the State Department more concerned about impairing relations with Mexico.

35. The Barelas Community Center, located in Albuquerque, collaborated with government agencies to provide important services including a health clinic, adult education classes, and recreational activities. The center was planning, in cooperation with the University of New Mexico, a training school for Spanish-speaking social workers. The Taos County Project involved the University of New Mexico as well as a number of federal agencies. The project offered its mostly rural constituency assistance in agricultural methods and marketing practices as well as advice and help in diet, schooling, and recreation. The OCIAA sought to establish a Midwest project in Chicago that would be modeled after the work done in New Mexico by the Barelas and Taos projects.

36. Most of the work that the OCIAA supported directly involved "public educational programs," including Spanish-speaking fiestas, or celebrations; exchange programs that brought Mexican intellectuals and artistic talent to local areas; and scholarly conferences. The OCIAA also established a scholarship fund for Spanish-

speaking college students, and promoted radio programs and other media outlets that publicized Spanish-speaking contributions to the war effort. Laves to Wallace K. Harrison, April 14, 1942, Records of the OCIAA.

37. Louis T. Olom, Untitled Report, November 17, 1942; Olom to Laves, November 18, 1942; "Memorandum for Files," November 16, 1942, Records of the OCIAA.

38. Saposs, "Memorandum for the Files," November 17, 1942. Besides the agencies already mentioned, the others that were represented at the November meeting called by the Bureau of the Budget included the War Production Board, the War Labor Board, the Board of Economic Warfare, and the Office of Price Administration.

39. "Second Inter-Agency Meeting on Problems of Spanish Speaking Peoples Held December 10, 1942, in Mr. Walter H. C. Laves' Office," December 11, 1942, Records of the OCIAA. Besides the six agencies already noted, the following had representatives at the December 10 meeting: the WMC, Bureau of the Budget, the War Department, the Office of Civilian Defense, the Office of Defense Health Welfare Services, the Bureau of Public Assistance, and the Labor Department. The following discussion on the December 10 meeting is also based on two other reports by the staff of the Children's Bureau of the Department of Labor: Pauline Miller, "Report on the Meeting Called by the Coordinator of Inter-American Affairs on Problems of Spanish Speaking Peoples," December 11, 1942; Memorandum, "Report of Meeting on Spanish-American Minorities," December 15, 1942, Records of the OCIAA.

40. "Second Inter-Agency Meeting on Problems of Spanish Speaking Peoples"; Emilio Zamora, "The Failed Promise of Wartime Opportunity for Mexicans in the Texas Oil Industry," *Southwestern Historical Quarterly* 95 (January 1992): 323–350. Cramer's report appears disingenuous, since the subsequent history of the FEPC in Texas and the other Southwestern states belies his positive report.

CHAPTER 10

Rosita the Riveter

Welding Tradition with Wartime Transformations

NAOMI QUIÑONEZ

World War II transformed and stimulated the social and economic status of many American women who took jobs in the defense industry. Wartime conditions dispatched women to the workforce, made them heads of households, and distanced them from exclusively domestic traditions creating a suspension of intolerance for women working outside of the home. This era proved to be especially significant for Mexican American women, whose new wage-earning status created a sense of self-sufficiency and intensified issues of self-identity.[1] Although not all Mexican American women participated in the workforce during the war, those who did influenced the changing values and mores of their own and subsequent generations.

This essay explores the social and economic pressures, opportunities, and limitations that expanded the contours of culture, gender relationships, and self-perceptions of many Mexican American women of this period. Their experiences reveal the complex and difficult decisions many made while negotiating the new and uncertain terrain that led to personal transformations set into motion during the war. The various achievements and contradictions that characterized this period are especially poignant considering the "back to normalcy" campaign that artificially forced most female defense plant workers back into the home.[2] Nonetheless, their experiences more than likely planted the seeds for the sociopolitical and economic changes that would influence and launch a generation of Chicanas into the social and political activity that evolved during the era of the social protest movement.

Although the bulk of historical research on the effects of World War II on women covers the experiences of Anglo women, with some comparisons to those of African Americans, little research has been directed at measuring how the lives of Mexican American women were affected.[3] One exception, however, is to be found in the *Rosie the Riveters Special Collection* compiled by Sherna Berger Gluck. This collection of oral histories of female defense plant workers during the war offers insight into the lives of an ethnically diverse selection of women, many of whom are Mexican American. Their words chart their challenges and aspirations and shed light on their rapidly changing roles and shifting cultural traditions.[4]

The following discussion will draw attention to the major thread of the Mexican American women's experience in the larger World War II tapestry by considering the effects of the war on U.S. women in general. Segments of selected oral histories of Mexican American women will help to elaborate on their many actions and perceptions during the war.

Although necessity forced large numbers of married women into the workforce in the early 1940s, they were hampered by a widespread suspicion that they were taking jobs away from men, and that they belonged in the home. For the 11.5 million wage-earning women in 1940, the wartime worker shortage and subsequent media campaign to recruit them into the workforce created a positive change in the national attitude toward women in the workforce. And for Mexican American women, who had been working in low-paying jobs all along, World War II would prove to yield far more significant economic improvements and opportunities than had ever previously been experienced.[5] Because the demands of the labor market dramatically increased the numbers in the workforce, World War II became a watershed era for U.S. women. As the "other half" of the war machine, women took on the business of war while the men were sent to fight it. Women worked in record-breaking numbers and shouldered the responsibilities of heading households.

Between 1940 and 1945, female workers increased by over 50 percent—they enjoyed steady hours, high wages, good working conditions, and, by 1942, day-care centers.[6] According to William Chafe, by the middle of the war, the female workforce reached 6.5 million or 57 percent.[7] In the manufacturing industries their numbers increased to 2.5 million with an additional 2 million in the clerical positions. Chafe notes that due to these dramatic increases women gained recourse to union representation and occupational mobility. The Women's Bureau called the boost in female employment "one of the most fundamental social and economic changes of our time." In addition, the wartime propaganda machine proved so effective in glorifying women's ability to do men's work that the national perception of women as weak and docile seemed temporarily suspended.

But how lasting were the changes? Would progress made during the war continue during peacetime? Chafe concedes that the disruption caused by the war altered patterns and traditions of living, which helped to eradicate "overt" forms of discrimination against women. But a permanent change, he conjectures, "would require a sustained redistribution of sexual roles, a more profound shift in public opinion and a substantial improvement of treatment and opportunities for women workers."[8] The War Department's massive and powerful media campaign used radio, motion pictures, magazines, and billboards to blitz U.S. communities with sensationalized messages of women as workers. Magazines and billboards praised the emergence of the new wartime woman the advertising industry created. "Rosie the Riveter," the strong, confident woman who donned work clothes and gripped an acetylene torch while exposing a slightly muscular arm, became a national heroine.[9]

The campaign's success in changing attitudes is evident in a 1935 poll that showed that 80 percent of Americans thought it was wrong for women to work, particularly if they were married. By 1942 a similar poll indicated that 71 percent felt that more married women should work.[10] More married women were employed than single, and more women over thirty-five years of age were employed than in the past. By the war's end, women comprised a significant number of the twenty million American workers, or 35 percent of the U.S. workforce.[11]

However, despite the apparent gains women made, there were

obstacles to their success. Some of the largest defense plants in the country, including those in Detroit, Seattle, and Maryland, did not implement training for women or begin to hire them in any significant numbers until the end of 1942. Because employers were "skeptical of women's ability to undertake work requiring physical strength or mechanical aptitude," they refused to modify traditional hiring practices.[12] It was only after severe labor shortages began to adversely affect production that employers were forced to hire women in large numbers.

In addition, both government and private industry maintained divisions between the value of women's work and that of men's work.

Not only did employers hesitate to invest in training women for skilled work, they also attempted to lower their wages.[13] Defense plants and industries throughout the country paid women less for their work than men. Men were usually promoted over women, even over the women who trained them. By manipulating job titles to reflect less than their actual workload, employers could justify paying women less. For example, even women who were able to gain management positions were labeled "trainee" or "assistant."[14]

Despite the hard work demanded of them, women were often pressured into maintaining a glamorous and feminine image, even at the risk of work-site safety. Linda Evans suggests that the image of "Rosie the Riveter" as a heroine who could do a man's job was carefully created so as to "in no way undermine [her] traditional femininity."[15] However, for many women, maintaining a glamorous and feminine image often left them vulnerable to the hostility of male blue-collar workers, subjected constantly to catcalls and the general disrespect that typified male sexism.[16]

Nor did women receive the kinds of services they needed to balance eight-hours-a-day, six-days-a-week jobs with child rearing, cooking, cleaning, and shopping. Chafe notes that since war production centers sprung up overnight, many were located in isolated areas away from restaurants, banks, transportation lines, and shopping areas. He attributes the high rate of absenteeism and job turnover to these exhausting routines and the inconvenience involved.[17] The need to tend children was a major cause for absenteeism. Because it affected production, the Federal Works Agency finally funded a day-care center for defense workers. By 1943 more than 44,000 child-care and welfare facilities had been established, but "their efforts paled in comparison to the need." In 1944 a Women's Bureau survey reported that 16 percent of mothers in war industries had no child-care arrangements whatsoever.[18]

Although research by feminist scholars reveals that this "watershed era" for women had definite limitations, nonetheless, the wartime labor shortages created a window of opportunity for ethnic populations, who had been historically restricted from any kind of economic mobility. This presented many ramifications for the economic and political development of Mexican Americans.

In the strong response to wartime opportunities was a simmering desire to fulfill a patriotic duty. Albert Camarillo notes that "the war effort at home and abroad kindled in everyone, and Chicanos were no exception, a sense of patriotism and commitment to American democratic ideals."[19] The promise of belonging to a nation that had rebuffed and exploited them caused many to take on their new roles with hopes of change for a better future. Mexican American defense plant worker Margarita Salazar McSweyne recalls "being involved in that era you figured you were doing something for your country—and at the same time making money."[20] Thus, Mexican American men entered the service with no hesitation, and women entered the labor market to discover that, for the first time, they could obtain higher-skilled jobs for much higher wages than they had ever previously earned.

However, the furor over national unity during the war did not eliminate racial discrimination. Discriminatory practices against Mexicans and Mexican Americans in the Southwest persisted, and racial incidents, such as the Sleepy Lagoon Case and the Zoot Suit Riots in Southern California, typified the kinds of attacks leveled against Mexican American communities.[21] The ability to negotiate the sexism and racism they encountered in their wartime communities also assisted Mexican-origin women workers to develop strategies for survival and success. These skills, along with unprecedented employment opportunities, strengthened their social status and increased their economic mobility.

In her comparative statistical profile of Mexican women in the labor market, Vicki Ruiz notes that the percentage of Mexican American women in clerical and sales positions increased from 10.1 in 1930 to 23.9 in 1950. These white-collar positions were heretofore unattainable by most Mexican American women. Mexican American women's work provided them "a new sense of independence and importance."

This new sense of "independence" among Mexican American women workers at this time is critical to understanding the development of their social agency.[22] Which is to say that even within the most harsh and repressive social frameworks they managed to create strategies of survival and even transcendence for themselves and their families.

The gradual development of their ability to gain some economic and social agency can be attributed to their struggles earlier in the century, between 1910 and 1930. As new immigrants, Mexican women were forced to alter a largely patriarchal social structure in order to adjust to the demands of U.S. industrialization. Their roles as homebound subjects in Mexico changed in the United States, where the need for economic survival took precedence over tradition. Women were forced to enter the workplace in order to help the family survive. Although this did disrupt and change patterns of family and tradition, expectations continued to be foisted on women to fulfill the exclusive roles of wives and mothers. Some abided by the older traditions and others did not. Nonetheless, the new patterns created by the shifting wartime social terrain allowed them more mobility in the public sphere. By World War II, many were ready to partake in the social and economic transformations that made it possible for them to enjoy their work, take pride in themselves, and cultivate self-esteem. They sought not only economic improvement, but also a place in society. As Sherna Gluck emphasizes, the new demands of the war gave many Mexican American women "cultural permission" to step out of their traditions and take on new customs and expand their experiences and ideas of the world.[23]

With World War II, Mexican American women perceived themselves in a new light, so much so that by the war's end they began to question discrimination in all of its forms. The very observation and questioning of their unequal status can be understood as a pre-feminist concern, one with ramifications for the development of Chicana feminism in the following decades.

The next section will build on the oral histories of Mexican American women who worked in defense plant industries in Los Angeles. The *Rosie the Riveters Special Collection* contains nine oral histories of Mexican American women.[24] In this essay I will examine four from that collection. In addition, I conducted a fifth oral history. These oral histories focus primarily on the experiences of women who worked in the aircraft manufacturing industry in Los Angeles. Since Los Angeles had the largest aircraft manufacturing centers in the United States, the sampling represents a wide range of defense-plant work experiences. Furthermore, 42 percent of the workforce in these centers proved to be women. By 1944, one in nine women worked in aircraft-related employment. Gluck adds that in Los Angeles, "the existence of an already resident Mexican population in addition to the newly migrated black population means that the experience of a cross section of working class women can be documented."[25] Thus, although small, this sampling represents a wide range of experiences women encountered in the workplace during the war.

In the original ten interviews with Mexican American women contained in the Rosie the Riveter collection, the age range among the women represents two closely linked generations. Born between 1911 and 1918, six of the women ranged between twenty-three and thirty-one years old at the start of the war. Four were born between 1923 and 1925 and ranged between seventeen and nineteen years old for the same period. This sample can easily reflect the probability of both mother and daughter working in the defense industry at the same time (such as in the case of the seventeen-year-old). With the exception of one woman, all of the interviewees were born in the United States and lived in the Southwest. Three were born in Texas, four in California, two in New Mexico, and one in Mexico. The latter came to the United States as a small child; her family settled in Texas and later moved to California. Educational achievement varies; however, all of the respondents received their education in the United States. A little over half completed high school, while four reached between the eighth and tenth grade. One reached the fifth grade. All of the women belonged to families of the working class.

Although most of the interviewees mentioned their fathers' occupations and listed their mothers as homemakers, the interviews reveal that several of the women's mothers worked in factories and as domestic workers. Their fathers' occupations included agriculture, mining, restaurant, and day-labor work. Two fathers worked in skilled employment—one as a surveyor and the other as a butcher.

Marriage and fertility patterns clearly reflect the strong influence of acculturation and a move beyond traditional expectations. Of the ten interviewees, six divorced; four of those divorced more than once (one divorced three times). The others remained married; two of those became widows and did not remarry. Family size ranged between one and five children (one woman bore one child, while one bore five children). The majority raised between two and three children. Family size tended to be small since the sampling averaged 1.4 children. Again, this group's tendency to have small families represents a move away from traditional expectations of Mexican women.

The following discussion will center on the idea of independence. Independence will be viewed with regard to personal issues of self-esteem, autonomy, reaction or response to tradition, personal change, and transformation, and also with regard to public issues of justice, equality, social change, economic independence, and women's liberation. The respondents' retrospective views of their lives during the war make for a fascinating analysis since they link their experiences during the war to the development of their current attitudes and ideas about contemporary women in the United States.

Since most of the women attended public school with little expectation of obtaining good jobs, many seemed to jump at the initial war-created opportunities to obtain higher-skilled jobs and make good wages. Some entered the workforce during the war by interrupting their public education, while others waited until they graduated from high school. The most common response to their work experience is that it took them out of their world, as defined by Mexican tradition, and "expanded their horizons."

Margarita Salazar McSweyne turned away from a career as a beautician to take a job in the aircraft industry during the war. Originally from New Mexico, Salazar McSweyne's large family moved to the Boyle Heights area of Los Angeles when she was an infant. Shortly after graduating from high school she worked as a beauty operator in her neighborhood. At age twenty-five she saw an opportunity to improve her wages and took a position as an assembler of planes at Lockheed. Her new experiences changed her world.

Raised in a traditional Mexican family, "Margie" Salazar McSweyne and her sisters were closely supervised by family members in their youth. The chaperone system severely limited her ability to know more about life, but she obediently lived within the confines of her family and community. Most of her social networks were tied to the Mexican youth clubs. Salazar McSweyne described how at nineteen she and her sisters began to spread their wings. "We were so sheltered and so kept at home, and we were beginning to make our own friends. . . . Still I didn't go out on a date alone until I was twenty-one." Salazar McSweyne's motivation to leave the beauty parlor and enter the defense industry was colored by a sense of adventure, economic improvement, and patriotism. "I thought it'd be a whole new experience and [I would] find out if it was as lucrative as they said. And then, being that my brothers would talk about going in the Navy, I guess I felt it was something new, why not try it."[26]

At the plant Salazar McSweyne began to extend her social networks. She attended the parties of her new friends, dated, and eventually broke away from the youth clubs because her new social life allowed her to experience "more mixtures with others." Her volunteer work in the Civilian Defense Corps introduced her to servicemen whom she entertained at local USO dances in downtown Los Angeles or Hollywood. Gluck offers a context for the change in family traditions: "GIs were respected and trusted and social activities with them were permissible. The resulting social climate often led to increased independence for young women."[27] Salazar McSweyne recalls that her mother was "so wrapped up in missing her boys that she didn't see anything wrong with the servicemen. In fact, a lot of us had boyfriends in the service and people we'd write to." Salazar McSweyne attributed her mother's acceptance of her new behavior to the fact that her own sons were in uniform.[28]

Because of health problems, Salazar McSweyne transferred to a clerical position with Lockheed which motivated her to take bookkeeping classes at night school. After she married, her wages helped the couple to purchase a home and raise a family. Her skills enabled her to operate a small business with her husband, and she eventually became a bookkeeper in a small local business. With the exceptions of a few interruptions to have children, Salazar McSweyne never stopped working. Gluck comments that Salazar McSweyne's story shows how the war changed the social life of many young women. "Although the protective shell that had surrounded Margarita Salazar was beginning to crack even before the war, the changes brought about during the war hastened the process."[29] Indeed, Vicki Ruiz points out that prior to the war, young women could approach the rules parents laid down for them in three ways. They could accept the rules, rebel against them, or compromise and circumvent them. The fact that some young women rebelled, or found creative approaches to compromise, points to the crack in the protective shell.[30] Salazar McSweyne's experience reflects how the war further relaxed those rules and granted her more freedom.

Perhaps the most telling effects of that era are in the hopes Salazar McSweyne expresses for the future. At the time of the interview, almost twenty-five years after the war, she conveyed a wish to go into public speaking and to "get involved with the public in some way or another, maybe in a political sense, or maybe just organizing things." She also expressed her support of the women's movement. Like that of many other women of her generation, Salazar McSweyne's style of women's rights appears to be rooted in the power of femininity. In one way, she expresses what any feminist would express: "Be a woman. Push for rights." However, she also adds, "be a woman first . . . fix your hair and fight like a woman—but get what the women should have." Margarita Salazar McSweyne's concerns about the importance of femininity reflect her generation's perception about its power in what she perceives to be a "man's world."[31]

The daughter of a field hand and a homemaker, Mary Luna reflected excitedly about how the war "expanded my horizons." Immediately after graduating from Inglewood High School in 1942, Luna circumvented her sheltered upbringing to work in the defense industry. Her position as a riveter at Douglas Aircraft in Burbank, California, benefited her entire family. Critical to the household income, her job helped the family get off welfare. Despite a hectic six-day work week that included attending to chores at home, Luna recalled, "I looked forward to going to work . . . and meeting new friends."[32] For Luna, friendships proved to be extremely important, since they helped expand her social life. She recalls various racial backgrounds among the employees at Douglas, noting that there were a number of Native American women and Mexican girls, blacks, and Anglos.[33]

Like many other women in defense plant work, Luna endured male hostility and sexism on the job. She vividly recalls the gruffness of the men she worked with and how they often yelled at her. She relates how, despite the fact that more women were employed at Douglas than men, the men were almost always promoted over the women. But, she stipulates, "Women were just glad to get a job, so they didn't complain much." On the other hand, she observed how women began to make inroads into higher positions such as supervisors, also known as "leadmen." Luna notes that it was very difficult for women to take on such positions and that "very few made it." She further comments,

> They had to be tough and rough to get that. If you were just a regular worker, when you minded your own business you never got ahead. You had to almost be a very aggressive type. I remember the ones that did make it. They were very aggressive. But the men, being that there weren't so many, as long as they were good workers, they made it.[34]

Luna's comments show how women had to work twice as hard as men in order to get ahead. Even if they did not complain, they were intensely aware of their marginalization.

In addition to making new friends, Luna enjoyed the fact that her earnings enabled her to buy luxury items such as fancy clothes. Like other working women of her time, she loved buying luxuries and extras, the items that seemed out of her reach before the war. However, she also became aware that her financial abilities irritated some of her nonworking women friends since she was "getting ahead." Luna broaches an important difference between working and nonworking women which somewhat reflects the nontraditional and traditional lives of women during that period. Her example to nonworking female friends and family may well have chafed against their own sense of women's place. At the same time, they probably could not have helped but envy her ability to buy the things she loved. Luna and her peers could be seen either as disruptive to traditional women's roles or as examples of independence. Luna noted that a nonworking female cousin's jealousy quickly abated when she decided to go to work and began to buy her own things. For Luna and many like her, "getting ahead" appears to have meant the ability to acquire comfort items.

Because the entire family started working during the war, every member chipped in for expenses and shared the household chores. Luna accumulated a substantial savings, which became problematic for her when she decided to marry. Reluctant to tell her boyfriend of three years and husband-to-be about her savings account, Luna sought advice from a trusted woman friend about whether or not to mention the savings to him. Her friend encouraged her to do so. Luna's trust in a woman, as it superseded that in her husband-to-be, demonstrates the power of women's friendship networks and their importance beyond the workplace. Her economic independence calls attention to the fact that many Mexican American women workers became responsible for the purchase of homes and property, with and without their husbands' contributions. A woman's wages may have allowed her to buy personal extras while she lived with her family, but her savings proved instrumental in major purchases when she married.

After marriage, Luna continued to work and then stopped temporarily to raise her child. During this time she maintained her female friendships. She fondly recalls how she and other neighborhood women would enjoy their social life together. They would get dressed up and go to restaurants or the movies, or play cards at each other's homes. When her daughter reached school age, Luna attempted to return to work, but found that Douglas would not accept her. Luna applied during a period shortly after the aircraft industry laid off thousands of women. Undaunted, she asked a friend at Douglas for help, and got hired within the next few months. However, much to her disappointment, the workplace she remembered no longer existed. Gone were the women who created an environment of enjoyment and friendship. She found only three other women in her work area, and they all complained about the lack of opportunity for promotion. The men worked all the lead positions. Shortly after she left Douglas to work at Honeywell, she became involved in union organizing. Luna remained at Honeywell, where she served as a union steward until her retirement in the 1970s.

Luna was emphatic about how her wartime experience at Douglas changed her life. She met many people and tasted a life outside her neighborhood. She made her own money, traveled, and worked at other jobs. "I think I gained a lot of confidence," she reflected. "It made me feel grown up and mature. At first I was insecure, but I found out I was worth something." Luna used her love for yard work as a metaphor for the sense of independence and enjoyment she attained during the war. "I like yard work. I think that's on account of the aircraft experience that I'm more able to tackle things. Like I did the landscape in the front [of the house]. I just dig them all out and then buy the plants and put them in. I'm not afraid to tackle anything." Luna reflected about the importance of autonomy and independence. "It's good to be happy with yourself. You can go places by yourself. Because I'm telling you, you're going to be alone a lot. If you can't enjoy being by yourself, why that's terrible."

Her ideas about women's independence have been passed to her daughter, who received a degree in bilingual education at UCLA, where she became active in Chicano politics. Like Salazar McSweyn, Luna said she is all for the women's movement, and believes it is long overdue. She said she supports abortion only under certain conditions and thinks that women should have the right to have the number of children they want. "I think it's about time. . . . Isn't it possible in this day and age that we have all these things like equal wages . . . and opportunities? I think we should have had it a long time ago." It is clear that Mary Luna's wartime work experience deeply influenced her life.[35]

One of the more philosophical and descriptive interviews is that of Rose Echeverria Mulligan, a graduate of Garfield High School and a self-described tomboy. Echeverria Mulligan's Protestant parents emigrated from Mexico, where her father worked as a store owner and her mother worked in a factory. Her mother's influence as worker and sole support of her own family in Mexico made Echeverria Mulligan and her two siblings "responsible" at an early age. Consequently, she worked at a local five-and-ten-cent store while in school.

Sixteen years old when the war started, she describes herself as a good student and active in school politics. Answering the call of the war effort, she applied to Douglas Aircraft right after she graduated and began to work as an assembly-line inspector.[36]

Echeverria Mulligan lamented the loss of innocence caused by the war. It appears that during this time she seriously began to question the difference between men's and women's roles. She reflects on how the war robbed men of the ability to relate to women in a positive way:

> We all changed from the giddy young girls and all our dreams went out the window. We didn't expect very much of the fellows that came home. They were so out of it . . . and they were the ones that wanted to go to college.
>
> Certainly the women of my generation wanted marriage, but the men didn't want us women.

Echeverria Mulligan was keenly aware of how the war disrupted the traditional relationships between the sexes. Her confrontations with sexism on the job profoundly affected her. She vividly recalls how sexual exploitation of women at Douglas ruined the reputations of many women. In many cases "a lot of girls ended up getting fired." Her concern centers on how sexual affairs could easily lose women their jobs. "The men didn't [get fired for their sexual liaisons], you know—they went on."

No matter how hard or well women worked, they were subject to the authority and expectations of men. Negative male attitudes affected the most personal and intimate relationships women experienced with others. Typical of her generation, Echeverria Mulligan added, "It's a man's world after all."

There is no doubt that Echeverria Mulligan's intimate and workplace experiences with men affected her perception about a devaluation of women. It is a view that helps her understand some of the motivations of the women's movement, motivations that offer her hope that women will appreciate themselves more, and not stand for second-class status. "I think that probably your generation has picked up on it. I think you understand there's something that made you see this, something along the road."

Even after the war Echeverria Mulligan continued to struggle with her relationships with men. Her own husband returned from the war withdrawn and on edge. Eventually they separated. This painful experience only accentuated her feelings of isolation from men.

Echeverria Mulligan expressed a hope that women will help each other more. With regard to women's liberation she asks: "You think the time will ever come when women can have children and not be married? When that time comes, then, I think, they'll be liberated and so will men."

Echeverria Mulligan's most revealing statement about her own feminist ideas is contained in her wishes for her daughter. It is a statement pivotal to how Mexican American women of the war era imparted their experiences, concerns, ideas, and beliefs to the next generation:

> I think my second daughter is going to go out now and form another kind of life for herself. She may never marry. She may be liberated because she doesn't want children and that is really the true liberation. You cannot be truly liberated with family, not if you want to save your children and [yet] you cannot escape motherhood. Women are going to have to find a way of raising a family and work without guilt.

For the most part, Echeverria Mulligan expresses the views of women who have experienced the injustice of the double standard, recognize it as a part of women's subordination, and yet hold on to hope for a new era of "liberated" women who know their worth.[37]

Beatrice Morales Clifton had left her first husband, borne two children, and remarried by the time the war entered her life. Never having worked before, she was coaxed past her timidity and into the workforce by the needs of her growing family. In 1942, at the age of twenty-seven, she received training and then worked as a riveter for Lockheed Aircraft. Her very traditional husband insisted that she not work. She found it necessary to defy him, and took a job anyway. This represented Morales Clifton's first experience in defying men. There would be others.[38]

Her workplace recollections trace a process of personal development. Initially, Morales Clifton experienced intimidation by male co-workers who displayed hostility toward any woman with whom they worked. Their antagonism and condescension added to her feeling of inadequacy. After her first days on the job she was reduced to tears.

"I was very scared because, like I say, I had never been away like that and I had never been among a lot of men. Actually, I had never been out on my own. Whenever I had gone anyplace, it was with my husband," she said.[39]

Soon enough, Morales Clifton befriended a number of women with whom she enjoyed working. She also joined the union, and her salary, along with her self-esteem, began to improve. "I was just a mother of four kids, that's all. But I felt proud of myself and felt good being that I had never done anything like that . . . and being that it was a war, I felt that I was doing my part."[40] Like many of her peers, she found working to be fulfilling. The fact that her work contributed to the war effort provided an added bonus.

Morales Clifton felt proud about making her own money, but soon realized that money accounted for only a small part of her gradually increasing sense of independence.

> went from 65 cents to $1.05. That was top pay . . . it was my own money. I could do whatever I wanted with it. . . . I used to buy clothes for the kids, buy little things that they needed. I had a bank account and I had a little savings at home where I could get a hold of the money right away if I needed it.[41]

She explains that her husband never asked her about her earnings, although he knew how much she made. "I did what I wanted. . . . I started feeling a little more independent. Just a little, not too much because I was still not on my own that I could do this and that."[42]

Morales Clifton's limits became apparent when her son became ill. Although her husband helped with household chores, he immediately blamed their son's poor health on her time away from home, even though her mother cared for their children. She quit her job and stayed home for a year. That was when she realized her dissatisfaction. "When I quit, I just took over the same as I was before—taking care of my kids. Well, it was kind of quiet and I wasn't too satisfied.

That's why I started looking to go to work. I had already tasted that going-out business and I wasn't too satisfied."[43] By the war's end, she had worked several jobs, but longed to return to Lockheed. In 1950, she went back to the defense industry, and a few years later, in 1953, her husband died. Morales Clifton continued working at Lockheed and married several times, always to men she met at Lockheed. She learned how to drive, traveled, and attended drafting school to study blueprints. She worked as a lead-riveter from 1951 to 1978.[44]

In retrospect, Morales Clifton recognizes the difference work made in her development. "The changes started when I first started working. They started a little bit, and from then on it kept going. Because after I quit the first time at Lockheed, I wasn't satisfied. I started looking for ways of getting out and going to work. See, and before I had never thought of going to work."[45] Morales Clifton's work experience made her aware of the relationship between skilled work, self-esteem, and economic well-being. Involved in buying and selling property since the war, Morales Clifton prospered in real estate. Her hopes for her daughters reflect an understanding about the importance of education and economic well-being. She wishes that she had obtained a better education. Like other interviewees, Morales Clifton supported the women's movement, and believed that abortion should be allowed if necessary. Although she felt positive about women having many career choices, like her peers, she maintained the importance of feminine identity. "I wouldn't want to lose my identity as a women."

For Maria Castellanos, who was seventeen years old when the war broke out, working in the defense plants became a family affair. Castellanos, her sister, and their mother entered the workforce at about the same time. The two sisters stuck together and worked at small defense plants such as Standard Company in Lincoln Heights, and Pacific Chemical, located in downtown Los Angeles. Employment opportunities pushed the family to Los Angeles from El Paso, Texas, just after the Depression. The sisters were raised by their single mother, who worked as a domestic until the war. Castellanos married shortly before the war. "The war made people do crazy things." She recalls, "I got married two weeks before my husband was sent to the Philippines in 1942. I didn't see him again until

1945." In fact, Castellanos and her two sisters all married men who served during the war.[46]

"Being that we were an all-woman family, we took care of everything: We worked six days a week taking care of the house, the yard, all the money matters," reflected Castellanos. Her mother had worked as the sole provider since she and her sisters were toddlers. They learned the responsibilities of work at an early age.

Castellanos recalled that her mother's earnings allowed the family to purchase property. "My mother bought some property, four little houses on a hill in Lincoln Heights, and the plan was that when the boys came back, we would each take a little house, and my mother would have the fourth one." She and her sisters helped to fix the property and managed to maintain it while working ten-hour days, six days a week. Castellanos reminisced about what her earnings allowed her to do. "I loved clothes, and I could buy some of the prettiest clothes, like I had never been able to before. I'd have my sisters take photos of me and then send them to my husband overseas." Castellanos does not fail to mention, however, that despite her earning power, she and her sisters followed strict rules set down by their mother, even as married women. Castellanos was careful to work and play within the parameters set by her mother.

Vicki L. Ruiz's research indicates that working women of this time were very conscious of how their earnings could help broaden their recreational experiences. At the same time, they were careful to respect their culture's expectations of them. "Although enjoying the creature comforts afforded by life in the United States, Mexican immigrants retained their cultural traditions."[47] Ruiz's point can also be applied to the children of Mexican immigrants.

Castellanos recounted how sexual harassment and unequal pay for women forced her and her sister to look for work elsewhere. "The men in the plant could be very mean, and they were always after the women. I'd complain, and if they didn't do anything about it, I'd leave." Castellanos eventually joined a union.

> I was getting tired of fighting all the time for fair pay, and I wasn't shy about it either. I'd just go up to the boss and ask him why so-and-so was making more money than me even though we were doing the same job. If I didn't get a good

answer I'd walk, and sometimes I'd get other women to walk out with me.

Castellanos mentioned that when she joined the union, things improved. She worked as a riveter and assembler in one plant, and loaded DDT into canisters at another.

Recalling her feelings when she realized that she would have to give up her job after the war, Castellanos commented,

> I had mixed feelings about it. I wanted the returning men to have jobs, but I wasn't ready to give up my life. I felt sad and angry sometimes because I really enjoyed working. But I guess I just went along with it because we [women] knew we really didn't have a choice. We didn't talk about our disappointment very much though; most of the talk was about the excitement of marrying and having families and setting up housekeeping. But I never really felt the same way about myself again, like I did during the war.

Castellanos did not return to the workforce until after she raised her children in the 1970s.

Castellanos said she felt that women's rights are long overdue. "You'd think we'd have more fairness for women right now, but it's been almost fifty years and it seems like we've just started." Her hopes for her own future are tied to her hopes for her daughters: "happy family life, good men." And, like so many of the other women interviewed, she feels strongly about the importance for women of maintaining their femininity.

"Does this generation want to be more like men? Or do they want to be women with rights, I really don't know. Personally, I don't want to be like a man—I'd like to be better—really." These views seem to express her generation's hope and the uncertainty about changes for women in the future.

The absence of men during the war created a dramatic contrast for women to see themselves, and each other, as autonomous, independent individuals, capable of doing men's work and earning their own wages, as well as caring for their families. The contrast also drew attention to the pervasiveness of institutionalized sexism. The majority of women interviewed experienced, firsthand, male hostility as they entered nontraditional employment. They also either witnessed, or proved to be victims of, sexual harassment and exploitation in the workplace. Consequently, women drew closer together in the recognition of the male-dominated force that attempted to keep them in a subordinate status. Beatrice Morales Clifton's friendship with women at the plant helped her overcome her terror of men and made the workplace an enjoyable experience. Mary Luna consulted with a good female friend before making a major financial decision that involved her fiancé. As in Ruiz's description of the women of UCA-PAWA (see n. 3), it appears that women at some defense plants also cultivated "social spaces" where workplace friendships continued outside the plants, and caused them to look to each other for both support and recreation. As precursors to "sisterhood" networks, these friendships ensured moral and economic support that crossed racial lines. The workplace became a meeting ground for different races and cultures. Mexican American women interviewees often recounted the diversity of their workplace, and acknowledged that work pulled them out of sheltered cultural enclaves and exposed them to women from other backgrounds, Anglos, blacks, and Native Americans.

It is interesting to note that the interviewees addressed racism as an experience outside the workplace. For example, Beatrice Morales Clifton experienced difficulty securing housing because landlords did not rent to Mexicans in Pasadena. Mary Luna recalled the prevalence of racism against Mexicans at Inglewood High School, and that curfews for blacks in the city of Inglewood continued even after the war.[48] Rose Echeverria Mulligan described Garfield High School as one in which Mexican and white students did not mix. A violent racial experience affected her family so profoundly that she and her brother vowed never to marry Mexicans in order to stave off discrimination. They both married Anglos. Although the women interviewed encountered racism in the larger society, their workplace appears to have provided a temporary refuge from it. In fact, most recounted their friendships with blacks and Anglos in very affectionate terms. Their major obstacle seems to have been sexism.

Workplace friendships, coupled with relaxing dating traditions due to wartime support of G.I.'s, offered Mexican American women a greater degree of sexual freedom and sophistication. There was no longer a need for out-and-out defiance of family values; a Mexican American woman could date several men, attend parties in different parts of the city, and go to nightclubs. As in the case of Margarita Salazar McSweyn, who could go out only with a chaperone before the war, women found themselves liberated from that tradition during the war. Women also acquired the freedom to spend leisure time with women friends, instead of depending on husbands or boyfriends. Their wartime social life offered many Mexican American women the opportunity to enjoy themselves and acquire a sense of worldliness away from male "protection" or scrutiny.

For most of the interviewees, their work experience left them with a heightened self-esteem. It is clear that women took pride in their economic autonomy. As important, they gained confidence in their ability to take on the responsibilities of work and family and enjoyed learning new skills, achieving workplace goals, and contributing to the war effort. These experiences informed some of their comments: "I felt I was worth something," or "I expanded my horizons," or "I felt proud of myself." Many of the interviewees continued to work after the war. No longer content with the traditional role of stay-at-home wife and mother, several clearly expressed their discontent with the old traditions. The ten women shared similar feelings about liking what they had done and become during the war. Some of them expressed a lack of desire to return to old traditions. In looking back, the interviewees recognized their equality to men, and consequently, many years later, could understand and support the idea of women's liberation.

Perhaps the most compelling consequence of the independence that Mexican American women gained is revealed in their attitudes about male/female relationships *after* the war. Echeverria Mulligan's story provides a clue for why so many of the interviewees divorced. Some married several times. She observes that the weariness and uncertainty with which most men returned from the war stood in stark contrast to the attitudes of women who had begun to cultivate a positive sense of confidence and self-esteem. Of the ten interviewees, five divorced, the majority of those having married more than once. When asked what she would do over again if she had the chance, Maria Fierro asserts, "I would never get married." Fierro recalls that she felt better when she wasn't married, "because this way I didn't have to put up with him when I came home from work." She continues, "If I didn't find anybody that was going to help me in any way, I might as well just be by myself."[49] Women's preference for being alone, rather than dealing with or enduring old forms of patriarchal control, must have been directly affected by their knowledge that they could, indeed, do it alone. Mary Luna also expresses this autonomy, or the ease of being alone: "It's good that you can be happy with yourself. You can go places by yourself."[50]

In her study of chaperonage among Mexican and Mexican American women, Vicki Ruiz points out that young women's resistance to chaperonage, fueled by pressures to acculturate, contributed to its decline during the latter half of the interwar period. Chaperonage "could no longer be used as a method of social control, as an instrument for harnessing women's personal autonomy and sexuality."[51]

World War II provided a final push away from such measures of control. Having experienced greater freedom to make decisions about their lives as autonomous individuals, many Mexican American women gained the skills and confidence to manage and negotiate their personal, social, and economic circumstances. Hence the social agency they acquired during the war reinforced a sense of independence that held many implications as they entered the postwar period of the 1950s, when the framework for the Chicana feminism of the 1960s would be constructed.

Although the beneficial effects of World War II were relative to a previous history of social and economic marginalization, it seems clear that many Mexican American women became transformed by their economic improvement, newfound social mobility, and elevation of self-esteem. The media campaigns that profoundly influenced and galvanized American women in general deeply motivated Mexican American women as well. By the decade of the 1940s they sought to fulfill feelings of patriotism. Furthermore, the larger social incentives to shift women's sphere from the home to the workplace proved that Mexican American women were capable of taking advantage of changing social currents and were ready to move out of rigid cultural roles and traditions. In the process they were not only exposed to the reality of institutionalized sexism; many also challenged it and the double standard it created. At the same time, the ability to acquire high-skilled trades and earn high wages gave them a sense of economic power and a can-do attitude about their ability to perform successfully in areas previously off-limits to women. These experiences not only allowed them to see themselves in a new light but also made them readjust their expectations of men. Many changed their ideas and their ideals about marriage and family, which transformed previous notions of gender roles. Their ability to transcend fear or guilt about cultivating personal independence shows how many Mexican American women of the war period were dismantling older social constructions and reconstructing their own identities—identities forged by the extraordinary social and cultural circumstances created by World War II.

Notes

1. For information on worker shortages see Vicki L. Ruiz, "And Miles to Go," in *Western Women, Their Land and Their Lives*, ed. Vicki L. Ruiz and Lillian Schilissel (Albuquerque: University of New Mexico Press, 1989), 72.

2. See Sherna Berger Gluck, *Rosie the Riveter Revisited: Women, the War, and Social Change* (Boston: G. K. Hall/Twayne, 1987); Sara Evans, *Born for Liberty: A History of Women in America* (New York: Free Press, 1989); William Chafe, *The Unfinished Journey: America since World War II* (New York: Oxford University Press, 1986); Glenda Riley, *Inventing the American Woman: A Perspective on Women's History, 1865 to the Present*, Vol. II (Arlington Heights: Harlan Davidson, 1986).

3. Exceptions include Vicki Ruiz's laudable study of Mexican American women cannery workers as members of the United Cannery, Agricultural, Packing and Allied Workers of America (UCAPAWA) during World War II, and some ethnographic references to their lives by Ruth Tuck and Beatrice Griffith.

4. Sherna Berger Gluck, *Rosie the Riveters and the World War II Work Experience*. California State University at Long Beach Special Collections Library.

5. Gluck, *Rosie the Riveter Revisited*, 7.

6. Riley, *Inventing the American Woman*, 113; Karen Anderson, *Wartime Women: Sex Roles, Family Relations, and the Status of Women during World War II* (Westport, Conn.: Greenwood Press, 1981), 20.

7. Chafe, *The Unfinished Journey*, 148.

8. Ibid., 149, 150.

9. Maureen Honey, *Creating Rosie the Riveter: Class, Gender, and Propaganda during World War II* (Amherst: University of Massachusetts Press, 1984), 47; Barbara Sinclair Deckard, *The Women's Movement: Political, Socioeconomic, and Psychological Issues* (New York: Harper and Row, 1983), 299.

10. Chafe, *The Unfinished Journey*, 2.

11. Ibid., 148–151.

12. Anderson, *Wartime Women*, 25.

13. Evans, *Born for Liberty*, 223.

14. Ibid., 156.

15. Ibid., 222.

16. Alice Kessler-Harris, *Out to Work: A History of Wage-Earning Women in the United States* (New York: Oxford University Press, 1982), 288.

17. Chafe, *The Unfinished Journey*, 160–161.

18. Evans, *Born for Liberty*, 224.

19. Albert Camarillo, *Chicanos in California* (San Francisco: Boyd and Fraser, 1984), 69.

20. Gluck, *Rosie the Riveter Revisited*, 85.

21. See Carey McWilliams, *North from Mexico: The Spanish-Speaking People of the United States* (New York: Greenwood Press, 1968), 24; Ruth Tuck, *Not with a Fist* (New York: Harcourt, Brace, 1946), 212–214.

22. Ruiz, "And Miles to Go," 117–119; Camarillo, *Chicanos in California*, 75.

23. Gluck, *Rosie the Riveter Revisited*, 74.

24. Gluck, *Rosie the Riveters*.

25. Gluck, *Rosie the Riveter Revisited*, 3.

26. Ibid., 85.

27. Ibid., 87.

28. Ibid., 87–88.

29. Ibid., 74.

30. Vicki L. Ruiz, "'Star Struck': Acculturation, Adolescence and Mexican American Women, 1920–1950," in *Building with Our Hands: New Directions in Chicana Scholarship*, ed. Adela de la Torre et al. (Los Angeles: University of California Press, 1993), 73.

31. Ibid., 98.

32. Gluck, *Rosie the Riveters*, Vol. 20.

33. Ibid.

34. Ibid.

35. Ibid.

36. Gluck, *Rosie the Riveters*, Vol. 27.

37. Ibid.

38. Gluck, *Rosie the Riveters*, Vol. 8.

39. Gluck, *Rosie the Riveter Revisited*, 209–210.

40. Ibid., 211.

41. Ibid.

42. Ibid., 212.

43. Ibid.

44. Ibid., 214.

45. Ibid., 219.

46. Maria Castellanos, interview by author, tape recording, Los Angeles, September 16, 1996.

47. Ruiz, "Star Struck," 69.

48. Ibid., 55.

49. Gluck, *Rosie the Riveters*, Vol. 8.

50. Gluck, *Rosie the Riveters*, Vol. 20.

51. Vicki L. Ruiz, "The Flapper and the Chaperone: Historical Memory among Mexican-American Women," in *Seeking Common Ground*, ed. Donna Gabbaccia (Westport: Praeger, 1992), 153.

CHAPTER II

On the Nation's Periphery

Mexican Braceros and the Pacific Northwest Railroad Industry, 1943–1946

ERASMO GAMBOA

Employers in the United States have relied on Mexican contract labor for nearly one hundred years. The idea of contracting Mexican workers for short stints began early in the 1900s when the U.S. government called on Mexico to supplant the dwindling number of Asian and European immigrant workers. This essay examines the history of the World War II Bracero Program, which lasted from 1942 until 1947. After the war, the Bracero Program became the classic model in subsequent binational discussions regarding all official transfer of short-term Mexican labor to this country.[1] The focus is on the harsh day-to-day social and work experiences of Mexican railroad bracero laborers.[2] The great majority of the men endured circumstances very different from conditions spelled out in the official work contracts. While agricultural and railroad braceros have always been more critical to the Southwest economy, the Mexican men lent their labor to the entire country during the war. It is to be hoped that the historical references from the "margin" of the Pacific Northwest will serve as a persuasive reminder of this important national contribution.

From the onset of the 1900s, Mexico and the United States, each in its own way, recognized the implications of labor movements across their borders. From the Mexican perspective, political survival inside revolutionary turmoil took precedence over official concerns with emigration. Although President Carranza became alarmed at the loss of potential soldiers to the United States, trepidation over the exodus of persons came largely from political observers and writers.[3]

In the United States, labor shortages, especially in the West, became disconcerting to employers and government officials alike.[4] The agriculture and railroad industries' need for Mexican workers, preferably men, worsened after Congress began to limit the entry of Asian immigrants to the United States.[5]

Mexicans, on the other hand, entered the United States freely, barring a few unenforced restrictions. Once in the United States, or at times in Mexico, labor agents quickly signed quasi-legal contracts, called *enganches*, with immigrants. As the demand escalated for Mexican labor, it spread across the geographical expanse of the country. This swell of Mexican workers led to early binational labor conferences. The first of these negotiations took place in 1909 between President William H. Taft and President Porfirio Díaz of Mexico and resulted in an official agreement to contract jobless men to specific employers.[6] In that year, Mexican contracted workers, the forerunners of the braceros of the first and second world wars, began to arrive in Western and Midwestern sugar-beet fields or at various railroad-company yards. Other contracts delivered Mexican laborers farther north to the Alaskan fish canneries.[7]

The combined flow of free immigrant wage earners and contracted workers constituted a massive exit from Mexico well before World War I. By 1916, the *Los Angeles Times* noted the routine departure of five to six trains per week filled with Mexican men traveling from Laredo, Texas, to locations distant from the international border.[8]

The experiences of José Solano and Juan Salinas typify the character and depth of unrestricted and contracted immigration flows into the United States. A native of Ciudad Durango, twenty-three-year-old Solano left in 1908 for Laredo, Texas, aboard the Mexican Central Railroad. Not obligated to a particular employer, José had little difficulty finding job opportunities in Texas and other Southwestern states. Eventually, he reached the Pacific Northwest. By the beginning of World War I, José settled at Smiths Ferry, Idaho, and felt sufficiently distant from his Mexican culture and family to petition for U.S. citizenship.[9]

About the same time, twenty-nine-year-old Juan Salinas left

Zacatecas for El Paso, Texas, aboard the Mexican Central Railroad. At the time, El Paso, like Laredo, dispatched scores of contract laborers to a range of states for farm and railroad employment. Following stints laying railroad track in Nevada, picking cotton in Arizona, and fishing in California, Juán signed a contract for employment in Alaska's fishing industry. Although Salinas never reached Alaska, he did arrive in Seattle, Washington, in 1907. Years later, and no longer under contract, Salinas brought his wife from Mexico and settled to begin farming in Washington's Yakima Valley.[10]

If Salinas and Solano exemplified the outward ripples of Mexican immigration, the Southwest and Midwest experienced the full weight of unchecked entry from Mexico. The Dillingham Commission, which held hearings on immigration, noted this fact. In these regions, Mexicans, literally available on demand, had substituted for the absent Asian workers and also started replacing upwardly mobile European ethnics. The Dillingham Commission also called attention to the mobility and permanent settlement of the Mexican families a "considerable distance" from the border region.[11]

For the time being, the question of wartime worker shortages and curbs on Mexican immigration proved troublesome. Employers preferred to continue rotating temporary contract workers by legally tying them to specific labor terms, including type of job and wages. The Immigration Act of 1917, however, prohibited further entry of contract labor. As things stood, any solution to the shortage of workers had to balance the labor needs of specific industries and the civic and political concern over both legal and undocumented immigration.

Following extensive lobbying from the railroad and agricultural industries during 1917, the Secretary of Labor granted employers permission to recruit Mexican contract workers. By building on earlier international labor agreements, the United States and Mexico sanctioned the first wartime bracero program, officially called the Temporary Admissions Program. It required employers to file an official request specifying the number of workers, job, wage, and place of employment. Employers electing to contract labor in Mexico were required to comply with any state-imposed housing regulations and cover all transportation costs. The contract, on the other hand, fixed the worker to a particular employer for a specified length of time. To address public anxiety, and as insurance against workers breaking the contract to remain in the United States, employers withheld a percentage of each person's wages until the completion of the work period. In the event that a worker violated the contract, the employer notified the Immigration Bureau to revoke the worker's legal status to remain in the United States. Government officials included these conditions to give the perception of being fair-minded between employer and worker rights. In reality, the stipulations were seldom enforced, favoring the employer.

When the World War I bracero program ended in 1921, the U.S. and Mexican governments, and the workers themselves, declared the Temporary Admission Program a failure.[12] Moreover, and as the following example points out, the Temporary Admission Program had little effect in slowing the ongoing dispersal of Mexican immigrant communities.

During World War I, the Milwaukee and St. Paul Railroad Company began to employ Mexican workers in extra-gang crews on its main line from Minnesota to Washington state. In 1942, twenty-year-old Francísco Soto penned a personal narrative relating how railroad employment initially recruited his father during the Díaz administration. Later the entire family immigrated. In 1908 and after several *enganches*, the family went to work with the Santa Fe Railroad in Holly, Colorado. Additional labor contracts relocated the family farther north to Garden City, Kansas, and later to Montana. In 1918, through the Temporary Admission Program, the male members of the family joined an extra-gang crew of Mexican bracero track laborers employed by the Milwaukee and St. Paul Railroad Company at Elso, Montana. The railroad company soon realized that many Mexican immigrants were not accustomed to working in Montana's frigid winter climate and transferred everyone to Tacoma, Washington. In 1919, the company released the crew when the six-month contract expired. While some of the contracted workers returned to Mexico or the Southwest, the Sotos abandoned railroad work completely and started farming in Washington.

After World War I, the nation's postwar prosperity coincided with increased immigration restrictions on European and Asian labor. This restrictive policy on Asia and Europe meant that Mexican labor, already well entrenched in agriculture and manufacturing, also became vital to the railroads. During congressional debates over Mexican immigration, the General Counsel of the Association of Railway Executives questioned the logic of imposing restrictions. "Are you going to cut off this source of supply?" To persuade Congress, he asked legislators to consider, "What greater calamity could come to a people than to find themselves all of a sudden cut off from labor necessary to carry on their enterprises?"[13] Indeed by the end of the 1920s, railroads as well as agriculture had managed to avoid any meaningful restriction on immigration from Mexico.

For the remainder of the decade, the Atchison, Topeka, and Santa Fe; Chicago, Rock Island, and Pacific; St. Louis and San Francisco; and the Missouri, Kansas, and Texas, and other lines, hired Mexicans until they constituted a majority on section and extra-gang crews.[14] According to Santa Fe officials, Mexicans counted for 85 to 90 percent of the company's track labor in Colorado alone.

In Chicago, a hub of the railroad industry, large Mexican railroad communities grew exponentially when carriers switched to Mexican labor on their track crews.

The Great Northern Railway Company and the Northern Pacific Railway Company, headquartered in the Midwest, similarly began to dispatch Mexican crews to service western track lines. To the dismay of the Brotherhood of Maintenance of Way Employees (BMWE), Mexicans were spreading rapidly along track routes toward Montana and the Pacific Northwest. "There is hardly a place where one does not find them," noted a BMWE spokesperson.[15] The increase became more evident to the BMWE when the Mexican government established a Comisión Honorífica in 1922 in the railroad hub city of Pocatello, Idaho.[16]

The supple movement of Mexican labor away from the Midwest and in the direction of the Pacific Northwest intensified as railroad crews arrived northward from California. By 1929, the convergence of Mexican labor from the Midwest and California represented 59 percent of Pacific Northwest section crews employed by the Union Pacific, Denver and Rio Grande, Northern Pacific, Oregon Short Line, Oregon Railroad and Navigation Company, Southern Pacific, and Great Northern railroads.[17]

By the onset of the Great Depression, Mexican track workers were commonplace in Idaho, Washington, and Oregon communities.

Now the BMWE became more alarmed, charging that railroads favored Mexicans over other workers in the Pacific Northwest. As the union saw it, Mexicans competed for jobs everywhere and were no longer "confined to the Southwestern states, as was the case several years ago."[18] The BMWE reaction echoed a general public distress over the widespread and uncontrolled distribution of Mexican immigrants throughout the nation. Simultaneously and in response, Congress opened hearings regarding Mexican immigration.

When the Depression began in 1929, and authorities decided to repatriate persons of Mexican descent, the anxiety expressed by organized labor and the public became pointless. Now, Mexican immigrants began to leave the Pacific Northwest as the jobs that brought them north quickly evaporated. In Portland, Oregon, the Oregon Bureau of Labor insisted that the Southern Pacific Railroad fire all Mexican employees. Pressured by unemployed whites, the labor bureau argued that Mexicans were less entitled to jobs during the crisis, and if unemployed they would have little choice but to return to Mexico. Even though the Southern Pacific refused to discharge its Mexican track crews, the company created a discriminatory system of racial preference favoring whites over Mexicans in future job vacancies.[19] For the remainder of the Depression, the demand for Mexican immigrant labor virtually disappeared, sending labor agencies, including an Oregon-based commissary with offices in El Paso, Texas, out of business.

At the outset of World War II, agriculture and the railroad industry used the Temporary Admission Program to petition the federal government for assistance in procuring Mexican workers. Unlike in 1917, however, the demand for labor was unusually high. As it stood, farms needed more laborers in order to feed and clothe the nation and the military, as well as our allies. The railroads faced a similar dilemma. Workers were imperative to upgrading the existing track system, which in turn was vital to the movement of nearly all troops, civilians, and the nation's entire agricultural and industrial production. At the same time, these two industries faced a contracting labor market and an increasingly competitive wage structure.

When the federal government and business representatives met in 1941 to address the labor deficiency, they faced issues similar to those faced by the original bracero program twenty years earlier. The enormous demand exerted by the present crisis had the potential of setting uncontrolled immigration in motion. For this reason, a modified World War I–type labor program arranged through another binational agreement seemed the most appropriate method of delivering short-term help. The program had to satisfy three principal objectives. First, solve the labor deficiency. Next, match and hold workers to jobs in certain industries and geographical areas. Last, address the important issue of permanent settlement of immigrants.

In order to satisfy these conditions, the federal government brought the blueprint of the earlier bracero program back to life and adapted separate versions for agriculture and railroads. To win Mexico's cooperation, the World War II Bracero Program contained some safeguards and guarantees concerning wages, housing, and return transportation, as well as against social discrimination. Additionally, the U.S. government permitted Mexican officials to visit the braceros and monitor compliance.[20]

Throughout the life of the bracero programs, railroad 1943–1945 and agriculture 1942–1964, the two industries contracted nearly 5 million Mexican men.[21] During the war, bracero railroaders maintained a good deal of the nation's track system in top condition so trains could operate. Simultaneously, contracted farm laborers produced unprecedented, and similarly essential, levels of agricultural commodities. All along and regardless of the type of work, these laborers became segregated into low-skilled and bottom-level employment through wage levels unacceptable to U.S. workers. Not admitting women split families and created a bachelor society of men; thus it became easier to get workers to leave the United States at the end of their contract periods. In this manner, the government addressed the issue of immigrants becoming permanent residents.

During the war, braceros made a significant national contribution that remains to be publicly acknowledged. After the war, and for almost two more decades, southwestern employers persistently used braceros. Their work, in rich agricultural states like California, Arizona, and Texas, subsidized the nation's food consumption through low prices during an extraordinary period of postwar economic prosperity.

Beyond the outcomes already mentioned, the Bracero Program

treated the men badly, prompting the American Committee for Protection of the Foreign Born to petition the United Nations to intercede on behalf of the braceros. "Our Badge of Infamy," as they called it, is revealed through the experiences of the railroad braceros contracted to Oregon, Washington, and Idaho.[22]

The braceros' contract included provisions to safeguard their general work and living conditions, but their psychological health and social welfare were not taken into account. Family separation was a major issue. The workers departed from their homes for the recruitment center in Mexico City knowing little else than that they were going to work in the United States. Families knew neither where exactly they were going nor how long they would be gone. Once the worker departed, families could not expect to receive any word for weeks.

Better communication between workers and their families would have alleviated anxiety, but phones were scarce in Mexico and simply not available to the braceros in the United States. Letters were the only possibility, but many of the men could not write. Even most letters from those who could write were brief with little detailed information. By the time they were received, the workers had probably moved on to another work site. Often, railroad companies moved their workforce from one area or state to another. The braceros assigned to extra-gang crews continuously moved along the lines, often into very remote areas where passing trains were the only way to send and receive mail.

Return letters were generally also brief. So, with few particulars to go on, both families and braceros tended to imagine the worst. And some letters brought bad news that lowered the workers' morale and hindered their ability to perform well. Some braceros sought emergency leave or terminated their contracts. Others simply became despondent or experienced various traumatic psychological disorders.

The time away from their family increased because after the initial period of 180 days, braceros could exercise an option to renew their contracts for another three, four, five, or six months. One year into the program, nearly 30 percent renewed their contracts; in 1945, over 43 percent opted to stay longer.[23]

During the bracero years, women, both mothers and wives, struggled single-handedly with family matters while the men worked in the United States. On January 28, 1946, María Asunción Juárez wrote directly to President Camacho seeking help to travel to Vancouver, Washington, across the Columbia River from Portland, Oregon. Her husband had enlisted as a bracero with the Great Northern Railroad in April 1945. Hardly three months on the job, he had suffered an accident that sent him to the hospital in Vancouver. By the time María wrote to the president, her husband had been hospitalized for six months and did not expect to be discharged until March. In the meantime, María and her family were "penniless" and suffering in Valle de Santiago, Guanajuato. "Mr. President," she wrote, "I need your help to journey to Vancouver to lend a hand to my husband." Almost defiantly, she added, "I believe I have a right to travel to be with my husband."[24]

The War Manpower Commission (WMC) realized that the family separation issue was detrimental to the success of the labor program, yet little was done. After the war, the WMC concluded that a significant social consequence of the program was workers' dislocation from their families. In a report, the WMC noted that "large numbers of braceros have been secured from isolated districts where there has been little or no movement of population since the days of Cortez, and perhaps centuries before."[25]

The hardship of being away from home increased because 70 percent of the bracero railroad workers were adolescents under twenty-one years old.[26] Many were single and had never been away from home. They became intensely homesick as a result of their solitude and the remote nature of their work. Unlike agricultural braceros, who lived in mobile or permanent camps and could develop a Mexican camp culture and enjoy a social life and recreational activities, railroad braceros often lived and worked with just a few others in rugged areas, miles from any community. Often in the high country of the Pacific Northwest, they had no outside contact except passing trains. Even in the more populated areas, the smallness of a Mexican track crew segregated them not only from their English-speaking surroundings, but also from other braceros.

Workers' homesickness intensified when cold winter weather arrived in the fall and remained for six months or so. Coming from Mexico, these men were not accustomed to the bitter cold, the short days, the impassable roads, the deadlock of deep snowdrifts, and the severity and length of the Northwestern winter.

Housing conditions, too, made the men long for home. Despite workers' contracts stipulating "suitable" lodging, most housing facilities were inadequate. Railroad carriers had for years furnished "company" housing for their Mexican and Mexican American track employees, but they never had to contend with any contractually agreed-upon health and living standards. Well before the Bracero Program started, the Great Northern had a reputation for dreadful worker housing.[27] The war brought even worse housing conditions. Since railroad companies did not have access to the public housing used by farm braceros, they had to locate some sort of temporary housing or hastily construct facilities. In some places, green lumber was used for construction. Once the wood dried out, gaps opened rooms to rodents, insects, and cold air. Satisfactory building and repair materials, as well as other necessary supplies, were in short supply after the start of the war. Further, dilapidated or bare housing that could accommodate the braceros during the summer was wholly inadequate shelter against the winter cold.

Of course, housing conditions varied by place and railroad. The Pacific Fruit Express Railway provided barrack-type facilities shared by the braceros and local workers at Pocatello, Idaho. These bunkhouses had toilet and shower facilities, washtubs and washboards, screened doors and windows, adequate heat and lighting, and even a janitor to clean the premises.[28] In more out-of-the-way places where the carrier did not have its own housing, lodging was arranged with private families, while local restaurants were contracted for board. At Mowich, Oregon, the men had a well-laid-out kitchen with cooking and baking facilities and a large sink with hot water for washing dishes. The kitchen had two large iceboxes for perishable food and screened cupboards for canned and dry goods. Dining tables were covered with oilcloth.[29]

The Portland Division of the Southern Pacific set minimum standards for housing to accommodate groups of three to four braceros. The company provided wood-burning stoves with a top surface suitable for making tortillas, a kitchen table with benches or chairs, a screened cupboard capable of holding a week's supply of food, a house broom, kerosene wall and table lamps, shower facilities, and cots with mattress tick. However, the company did not meet its own standards at every bracero railroad camp. At some tract locations, for example, the workers' only source of water came from overhead tanks that often sat dry, being replenished only by incoming trains.[30]

Braceros working for the Southern Pacific between Corvallis and the Dalles, Oregon, lived in boxcars, barrack-type accommodations, tents, or abandoned car bodies, where they slept on straw mattresses with little else but a stove. Some camps did not even furnish a combination cooking and heating unit without a rental fee. Often, if there was indoor plumbing, there was no hot water.

The WMC knew that substandard housing could jeopardize full compliance with the binational work agreement. To avoid default, the WMC commissioned the Railroad Retirement Board (RRB) to inspect regularly the adequacy of workers' living arrangements and investigate all camp-related complaints. Once the inspection began in earnest, rail companies felt the pressure to improve housing or lose the braceros. Toward the end of 1943, the Southern Pacific ordered 215 new bunk, kitchen, and dining cars to house extra-gang labor. Older facilities were closed and worn-out equipment was sent out for complete overhaul.

Still, considering 147 Southern Pacific camps in Oregon alone, some poor housing units remained. During the winter of 1944, an RRB inspector reported that Southern Pacific braceros stationed at Crescent Lake, Oregon, lived in congested 8 ft. by 24 ft. bunkhouses, rotating living quarters with other workers on twelve-hour shifts. Heating with the small stove provided was impossible because of wide cracks in the walls where green lumber had dried and shrunk. RRB sent a stern warning to the Southern Pacific that winters at Crescent Lake were very severe and it was "necessary that the Mexican nationals have adequate protection from the weather elements."[31]

At the Northern Pacific Railway facilities at Seattle, Washington, an RRB inspector reported appalling sanitary conditions at the Mexican camp. Doors and windows had no screens, and garbage and open cesspool pits posed an endemic health hazard to those living on the premises. The situation was so disgusting that some of the men avoided using the camp privies, aggravating the already deplorable conditions at the camp.[32]

The camps provided by Spokane, Portland, and Seattle were possibly the worst in the Pacific Northwest. At one place, nine men lived in one bunk car with only a small stove for cooking and heating; steel cots without straw ticks, pads, or mattresses; kerosene lamps with no kerosene. Water had to be fetched from a tower a thousand feet away. The only possibility for bathing was in the Columbia River, but RRB officials cautioned that the Columbia "was a rather swift running river at that point and considered dangerous to swim in."[33]

In Vancouver, Washington, fifty-six men employed by the Southern Pacific shared one shower stall and one small washbasin. When RRB inspectors arrived, the braceros had stopped using the shower because it flooded the living quarters. Lack of shower facilities had led to poor hygiene and the quarters were infested with bedbugs. Some companies, to avoid plumbing expense, simply provided galvanized tubs or cut-off wooden barrels. When weather permitted, most braceros preferred to bathe in the rivers and streams.[34]

The amount and quality of food available to the railroad workers was an even more serious issue than housing. Under the contract agreement, workers could either purchase and prepare their own meals or pay a small charge to eat at employer-operated kitchens. The quality of cafeteria services varied, with the larger camps where experienced cooks prepared meals in volume offering the best food and the worst situations occurring when small groups working in remote locations attempted to cook for themselves.

Of course, the quality of the food depended on the cook's proficiency and the availability of food supplies. Partly because agricultural braceros occasionally stopped work for food protests, the WMC stressed quality food and good nutrition for the railroaders. To assure supply and quality, the WMC issued ration books to each bracero, with Spanish instructions on how to use the various food and clothing stamps. Foremen and RRB officials were supposed to offer further directions in the use of ration books, purchasing and ordering food, and preparing balanced meals. But such attempts were complicated by cultural and language difference, male gender roles, and food preferences. Many braceros understood neither the value of the ration books nor the complicated system of redeeming the stamps. They often lost their books or were swindled out of them.[35]

Coming from a culture where women were the cooks or "corn grinders," most of the men, especially the younger ones, simply did not know how to cook. Even those who could were disinclined after a long, physically tiring day of work. But even worse, many Mexican food products were simply not available in the Pacific Northwest.

The RRB directed camp supervisors to try to find stores that sold "food suitable to the Mexican men."[36]

Some companies realized that poor meals brought serious morale problems and searched for Mexican American cooks able to prepare more "traditional" meals. The Southern Pacific located some Spanish-speaking, Chinese Mexican cooks through the Threlkeld Commissary Company, which operated boarding outfits for the railroads. Threlkeld got permission from the Mexican government to contract these cooks, who, in effect, were braceros themselves. By the end of 1943, some 175 of them worked in railroad camp kitchens. Experienced at preparing Mexican cuisine, they provided a valuable service to the national railroad labor program, the railroad braceros, and the companies. But problems remained as braceros had difficulty accepting and appreciating their "chino" cooks. In some instances, the Chinese Mexican cooks simply walked away to avoid the constant ethnic ridicule or scolding for not preparing a particular dish.[37]

At Pocatello, the Great Northern successfully teamed a Chinese Mexican with a Mexican American woman to prepare Mexican food. Also at Pocatello, the Pacific Fruit Express Railway hired an experienced middle-aged Anglo couple able to please the Mexican employees by serving ample quantities of Mexican and American food items.[38]

But even with good cooks, adequate supplies of the right kinds of food were not always available. Braceros demanded certain food items, especially *frijoles*, at nearly every meal. During the war, railroad companies, like everybody else, also had difficulty getting fresh meat. When fresh meat was available, a lack of refrigeration often caused it to spoil.

At the beginning of the program, the railroads assigned braceros exclusively to track labor crews. But as industry-wide labor shortages prevailed, employers sought approval from WMC and BMWE to shift braceros to other types of jobs. By the end of 1943, they were filling jobs on section crews, ripping up track, and performing various roundhouse and store duties. By mid-1945, the WMC qualified braceros for twenty different occupational classifications, including structure helpers, extra-gang foremen, freight handlers, coach cleaners, laundry workers, waiters, camp cooks, kitchen helpers, and motor-car operators.[39] Braceros now held nearly every type of job except those on board the trains or as supervisors. They constructed track beds, laid rail, handled ties, did heavy blasting and leveling, and loaded and unloaded freight. When the winter slowed track repair work, some shifted to yard and shop jobs. For example, at the Northern Pacific roundhouse at Pasco, Washington, the Pacific Fruit Express Car Department at Pocatello, Idaho, and the Great Northern car shops at Spokane, Washington, braceros worked alongside mechanics, cleaning and assembling parts and wiping and oiling locomotives. They also performed nonmaintenance railroad jobs important to keeping troops, civilians, food, and critical supplies moving.[40]

In addition, braceros loaded, unloaded, and iced the cold-storage railcars in job categories ordinarily highly paid and filled according to strict qualifications and seniority. But during wartime, top priority was placed on averting food losses, so even convicts were sometimes used. Using braceros in place of criminals was much less controversial and much more expedient. The Pacific Fruit Express knew that without braceros, it faced "an undetermined loss of needed perishable foodstuffs, both for military and civilian use." At its Wallula, Washington, ice plant, braceros made up 77 percent of the company's ice laborers.[41]

Regardless of the type of job, braceros and other railroad employees worked in an extremely hazardous environment. As the wartime rail volume increased, so did work-related accidents. The total number of accidents rose much faster than the 14 percent increase in employee hours between 1940 and 1942. The Office of Defense estimated that 533 railroad workers were killed and 17,903 suffered some type of job-related injury in 1940. For 1941, the estimates were 749 fatalities and 25,265 injuries; for 1942, 9,451 fatalities and 35,208 injuries.[42]

Especially during wartime, pressure to keep the trains operating resulted in physical and mental strain on the workers, making them more susceptible to mishaps. Braceros were even more vulnerable due to the psychological effect of being in totally foreign work and living environments. Most braceros, even those who had done railroad work in Mexico, were not familiar with safety procedures and precautions in use in the United States. To make matters worse, the railroad carriers sometimes misjudged the severity of occupational hazards and did not sufficiently caution the arriving braceros.

The pressure-filled atmosphere led to many accidents. Frequently, motorized railcars did not have safety rails, and operators were apt to speed with men dangling their feet. Work crews sometimes left tools on the track with disastrous consequences. Fatalities and injuries from passing trains occurred throughout the region and through the life of the program. Others, not using safety lines, fell from bridges. Workers were also injured in the roundhouses and shops where they inhaled poisonous gases, suffered burns, or lost limbs around machinery.

The braceros' work also brought them in contact with carcinogens, such as creosote, asbestos, chromates, lead arsenic, and mercury. And sometimes, more dangerous chemicals were substituted for those in short supply; for example, highly poisonous phosphorous benzol was used as a solvent in roundhouses, in car shops, and in repair shops. The lack of adequate bathing facilities for braceros aggravated contamination.[43]

But many braceros simply were not aware of all the perils associated with their jobs. Mexican workers often neglected to use the readily available protective equipment, such as masks, gloves, and glasses. Thus, they left themselves vulnerable to flying metal and chemical sprays.

Despite U.S. Health Service exams to predetermine workers' physical ability, some braceros simply could not meet the rigorous demands of the job. Widespread malnutrition in Mexico and poor food service in the railroad camps contributed to their overall strain and fatigue. In summary, physical exhaustion, poor nutrition, and the lack of familiarity with the dangers of the job created an environment where braceros were prone to suffer accidents and death. Meanwhile, others died from pneumonia, leukemia, and other illnesses, as well as automobile accidents.[44]

The railroad companies were not officially obligated to return bodies of deceased braceros to Mexico, but they did have a "gentleman's agreement" whereby an employer would pay a death benefit of $150 to heirs. They would also pay up to $130 in funeral expenses for a body that remained in the United States, thereby avoiding the greater expense of transporting the dead back to Mexico.[45]

Regardless of the cause of death, a substantial number of braceros were injured or lost their lives in service to the United States during World War II. Their burial grounds stretch from southern Oregon north to Washington and east to Idaho.

The problem of verbal and physical abuse of braceros prevailed throughout the industry. Much had to do with language and cultural ignorance on both sides. But a good portion derived from the fact that most supervisors belonged to the BMWE, which strongly opposed the Mexican workforce. Supervisors often aggravated a poor work environment through racial and ethnic-based prejudice and discriminatory practices.

Although language difficulties predominated, problems went far beyond the language issue. For example, when RRB investigators found bunkhouses with no running water and general "filth" everywhere, braceros admitted that after their nine-hour shift there was little time or energy to clean up the bunkhouse. The RRB recommended that the company designate one worker to "police the buildings." However, the foreman, considering housecleaning "women's work," refused to permit any member of his section crew to spend a day cleaning quarters when he could be repairing track.[46]

In the course of its investigations and routine inspections, the RRB detected racially based tension between the Caucasian section and extra-gang supervisors and the Mexican workforce. Foremen were found to use explicitly disparaging and racist language to address the Mexicans on a daily basis. This attitude stemmed largely from a perception among Caucasian foremen that Mexicans were intruding in a previously white-predominant occupation. Caucasian railroaders spoke their own language, shared work customs, and enjoyed a special identity developed over generations. They were just not open to braceros' becoming part of their work culture.

Relationships between managers and braceros improved considerably whenever the companies hired bilingual Mexican American supervisors. Mexican American foremen not only had track maintenance experience, but also were well acquainted with both cultures. They tended to empathize with the braceros' own questions of identity, discomfort, feelings of loneliness, distaste for "American" food, and other grievances. Thus, they served as extremely useful intermediaries, resolving potentially serious protests and work stoppages. At

Pocatello, Idaho, the Pacific Fruit Express superintendent allowed a bilingual Mexican American assistant foreman to devote at least 90 percent of his time to nonwork matters, helping the braceros with various personal problems, such as purchasing clothing and money orders. According to the company, the assistant foreman's time was well spent since the braceros were "satisfied and happy."[47]

Throughout the war, Mexico assigned and sent its own labor inspectors to evaluate living and working conditions. However, these inspectors, who were paid per diem plus all travel expenses, were paired with RRB investigators. Their reports tended to praise the railroad program, thereby taking pressure off the railroads to improve conditions for the braceros. They stated that "salaries and their contracts are good," and problems with food were only because the braceros were not used to the kind being served.

The wartime phase of the Bracero Program ended in 1947. After that year, very few braceros came to the Pacific Northwest, whereas the Mexican contract labor program continued elsewhere until 1964.

During its lifetime, the Bracero Program failed to control immigration. Instead, it had the opposite effect, further stimulating Mexican immigration. By the war's end, many immigrants were simply following in the footsteps of an earlier generation of fathers, uncles, or other relatives who had served as braceros.

A surge in interstate migration followed the war as well, as employers sought efficient ways of attracting nonbracero Mexican American labor to areas like the Pacific Northwest. In this way, a Mexican and Mexican American workforce proliferated across the nation as it did during the 1920s.

Recently, two of the leading historians of the Pacific Northwest were asked to name the ten most important events that shaped the region in the past century. Notably, their response included World War II, because it was the single event that contributed most to creating a diverse ethnic population in the region. They commented, "Mexican Americans are recruited as braceros in the fields. By the 1950's Washington State relied on the labor of 15,000 migrant workers, most of them Mexican Americans from Texas."[48]

Without a doubt, the World War II bracero era became the watershed of today's Chicano communities of the Pacific Northwest. During the war, more than one in ten of the farm braceros deserted their contracts with local farmers, but remained in the area. Many more returned to Mexico when their contracts expired, then turned around and returned with their families and as free laborers.[49]

More important after 1947, Pacific Northwest farms recruited and negotiated directly with Mexican American migrant laborers from Texas, themselves mostly first-generation immigrants. Now men, women, and children stepped into the shoes of the braceros. At the other end of the labor circuit, the flood of low-cost bracero laborers made Texas a principal labor-exporting state as entire neighborhoods joined migrant streams north. In Washington's Yakima Valley and Oregon's Willamette Valley, farming communities like Granger and Independence began to develop distinct and vibrant Mexican American neighborhoods. Unmistakable fifty years later for their Rio Grande Valley culture, this generation had roots in San Luís Potosí and Nuevo León, México, but also in Texas localities such as Edinburg, McAllen, and Mercedes.[50]

The Bracero Program of World War II was a defining moment in Chicano social history. During one of its most crucial periods in history, the United States called on Mexico to assist in the war effort by answering the call of desperate employers. By design, the binational accord addressed crucial labor issues on both sides of the border extending to the early 1900s and World War I. In practice, the Bracero Program stimulated immigration, added an additional immigrant population to pre–World War II Chicano neighborhoods, and created new communities altogether distant from the Southwest. Furthermore, employers developed an insatiable desire for easily obtainable Mexican contract labor. All the while, most employers set aside the letter of the binational agreement and inflicted a good deal of physical and emotional abuse on the braceros. In consideration of the long run of the Bracero Program, this outcome cannot be easily dismissed or forgotten. It is an important part of the legacy of Latinos during World War II.

Notes

1. For a discussion of the national emergency see Kitty Clavita, *Inside the State: The Bracero Program, Immigration, and the I.N.S.* (New York: Routledge, 1992),

19–25. Concerning the crisis in the Pacific Northwest see Erasmo Gamboa, *Mexican Labor and World War II: Braceros in the Pacific Northwest, 1942–1947* (Seattle: University of Washington Press, 2000), 22–47.

2. The legislative history of the railroad bracero program is found in Barbara A. Driscoll, *The Tracks North: The Railroad Bracero Program of World War II* (Austin: Center for Mexican American Studies, 1999).

3. Bert Corona describes how El Paso became a refuge for former Mexican soldiers. Mario T. García, *Memories of Chicano History: The Life and Narrative of Bert Corona* (Los Angeles: University of California Press, 1994), 38–40. Also see Ricardo Romo, *East Los Angeles: History of a Barrio* (Austin: University of Texas Press, 1983), 43.

4. James D. Cockcroft, *Outlaws in the Promised Land: Mexican Immigrant Workers and America's Future* (New York: Grove Press, 1986), 56.

5. Legislation against Asian immigration began in 1882 with the passage of the Chinese Exclusion Act. In 1908, the Gentlemen's Agreement virtually stopped Japanese male immigration, and the Tydings McDuffie Act curtailed Filipino immigration after 1935.

6. Cockcroft, *Outlaws in the Promised Land*, 53.

7. Gamboa, *Mexican Labor and World War II*, 10.

8. Carey McWilliams, *North from Mexico: The Spanish-Speaking People of the United States* (New York: Greenwood Press, 1968), 169.

9. District Court Naturalization Records, District of Idaho, Immigration and Naturalization Service, National Archives and Records Center, Seattle, Washington.

10. Interview with Ramon Salinas, Toppenish, Washington, July 26, 1972.

11. U.S. Congress, Senate, Report of the Immigration Commission, Part 25, 1114–1116.

12. The testimony of the Mexican officials on World War I braceros is cited in Arturo Rosales, *Testimonio: A Documentary History of the Mexican American Struggle for Civil Rights* (Houston: Arte Público Press, 2000), 84–85. The lack of U.S. enforcement of the Temporary Admission Program is discussed in Driscoll, *The Tracks North*, 42–43.

13. U.S. Congress, House, Hearings before the Committee on Naturalization, 70th Congress, 391.

14. Ibid., 402–403.

15. U.S. Congress, House, Hearings before the Committee on Immigration and Naturalization, 71st Congress, 355.

16. Gilbert G. Gonzales, *Mexican Consuls and Labor Organizing: Imperial Politics in the American Southwest* (Austin: University of Texas Press, 1999), 49.

17. Gamboa, *Mexican Labor*, 9.

18. Hearings before the Committee on Immigration and Naturalization, 350.

19. Ibid., 369.

20. The effectiveness of these inspectors is discussed in Gamboa, *Mexican Labor*, 75–76.

21. Regarding the number of braceros contracted between 1942 and 1964 see David G. Gutierrez, *Between Two Worlds: Mexican Immigrants in the United States* (Wilmington: Scholarly Resource, 1996), 49–50.

22. American Committee for Protection of the Foreign Born, "Our Badge of Infamy: A Petition to the United Nations on the Treatment of the Mexican Immigrant" (New York: American Committee for Protection of the Foreign Born, 1959).

23. Railroad Retirement Board, *Monthly Review* (May 1945), 3.

24. Letter, María Asunción Juarez to President Manuel Ávila Camacho, January 28, 1946, Ávila Camacho, Box 795, file 546.6/120-10, Archivos de la Nación, Mexico City.

25. Memorandum from Churchill Murray War Manpower Commission, Mexico, to John Dewey Coates, Chief, Foreign Labor Service, Washington, D.C., August 14, 1945, folder, daily life, box 3, entry 196, Mexican Track Labor Program (MTLP) RG 221. All references to the MTLP are found in folders in several boxes dated from 1943 to 1946, Record Group 221. These documents are located at the National Archives and Records Center, College Park, Maryland.

26. Secretaría del Trabajo y Previsión Social, *Los Braceros* (Mexico, D.F.: Dirección de Previsión Social, 1946), 30.

27. William Thomas White, "A History of Railroad Workers in the Pacific Northwest, 1883–1934" (Ph.D. diss., University of Washington, 1980), 173.

28. Memorandum from G. C. Peterson, Field Representative, to E. B. Miller, District Manager, October 27, 1944, folder, RRB Complaints, box 8, entry 191.

29. MTLP, Memorandum on the handling of Mexican nationals employed by the Southern Pacific lines, August 27, 1943, folder, RRB Complaints, box 8, entry 191.

30. MTLP, Report of Inspection Tours on Spokane, Portland and Seattle Railway, folder, RRB Inspector Reports 1943, box 8, entry 191.

31. MTLP, Report of Inspection Tours on Spokane, Seattle, Portland Railway, folder, RRB Inspection Reports, 1943, box 8, entry 191.

32. MTLP, Memorandum from H. L. Carter, Director RRB, to John D. Coates, Chief, Foreign Labor Section, October 17, 1945, folder, RRB Complaints, box 8, entry 191.

33. MTLP, Report of Inspection Tours on Spokane, Portland, Seattle Railway, folder, RRB inspection reports, 1943, box 8, entry 191.

34. MTLP, Report of Inspection Tours on Spokane, Portland, Seattle Railway, folder, RRB Inspection Reports, 1943, RRB, Box 8, entry 191.

35. The federal government translated some of the instructions regarding the ration books into Spanish, and officials tried to explain the system of allocating food and clothing. In spite of these efforts, many men did not understand. MTLP, Memorandum from A. W. Motley to C. La Berten, July 13, 1943, folder, OPA instructions, box 7, entry 196.

36. Ibid.

37. The word *chino* is used in Mexico and among Mexican Americans to refer to most persons of Asian descent, especially Chinese. MTLP, Memorandum from G. C. Peterson, RRB field representative, to E. B. Miller, district manager, October 2, 1944, folder, RRB complaints, box 8, entry 191.

38. An interview with one of these Mexican American cooks is found in Erasmo Gamboa, *Voces Hispanas Hispanic Voices of Idaho: Excerpts from the Idaho Hispanic Oral History Project* (Boise: Idaho Humanities Council, 1992), 9–10.

39. Driscoll, *The Tracks North*, 108–110.

40. MTLP, Memorandum from E. H. Price to W. J. Macklin, August 31, 1943, folder, RRB complaints, box 8, entry 191.

41. MTLP, Letter from E. H. Price, Assistant to General Manager PFE, to W. J. Macklin, Regional Director, RRB, August 31, 1943, folder, RRB complaints, box 8, entry 191.

42. A. Whitney, *Wartime Wages and Railroad Labor: A Report on the 1942–1943*

Wage Movement of the Transportation Brotherhood (Cleveland: Brotherhood of Railroad Trainmen, 1944), 109.

43. Substitution of products in short supply was not limited to the railroad industry but was also common in manufacturing and agriculture.

44. MTLP, Records of WMC, folder, Northern Pacific, box 6, entry 196.

45. Driscoll, *The Tracks North*, 117–118.

46. MTLP, Memorandum from G. C. Peterson to E. B. Miller, February 20, 1945, folder, RRB complaints, box 8, entry 191.

47. MTLP, "Pacific Fruit Express, Pocatello, Idaho, Investigation," folder, RRB, complaints 19045, box 8, entry 191.

48. "New History for a New Millennium," *Seattle Times*, January 21, 1996.

49. The number of deserters varied across regions from 3 percent in the Southwest to 10–12 percent in the Pacific Northwest. W. A. Anglin, "Foreign and Domestic Agricultural Workers, Special Report, March 1, 1946, Southwest Division," USDA Production and Marketing Administration, Labor Branch, table X.

50. The history of Idaho's Mexican American railroad communities is found in Erasmo Gamboa, "Mexican American Railroaders in an American City: Pocatello, Idaho," in Robert McCarl, ed., *Latinos in Idaho: Celebrando Cultura* (Boise: Idaho Humanities Council, 2003).

Selected Readings

Acosta-Belen, Edna. "Puerto Rican Women in Culture, History and Society." In *The Puerto Rican Woman: Perspectives on Culture, History, and Society*, edited by Edna Acosta-Belen. New York: Praeger, 1986.

Acuña, Rodolfo. *Occupied America: A History of Chicanos*, third edition. New York: Harper Collins, 1988.

Allsup, Carl. *The American G.I. Forum: Origins and Evolution.* Austin: Center for Mexican American Studies, 1982.

Bachelor, David L. *Educational Reform in New Mexico: Tireman, San José, and Nambé.* Albuquerque: University of New Mexico Press, 1991.

Balderrama, Francisco E. *In Defense of La Raza: The Los Angeles Mexican Consulate and the Mexican Community, 1929–1936.* Tucson: University of Arizona Press, 1982.

Beck, Warren A. *New Mexico: A History of Four Centuries.* Norman: University of Oklahoma Press, 1962.

Blum, John Morton. *V Was for Victory: Politics and American Culture during World War II.* New York: Harcourt Brace Jovanovich, 1976.

Campbell, Julie A. "Madres y Esposas: Tucson's Spanish-speaking Mothers and Wives Association." *Arizona History* 31, no. 2 (Summer 1990): 161–182.

Carroll, Patrick J. *Felix Longoria's Wake: Bereavement, Racism, and the Rise of Mexican American Activism.* Austin: University of Texas Press, 2003.

Chibnall, Steve. "Whistle and Zoot: The Changing Meaning of a Suit of Clothes." *History Workshop Journal* 20 (Autumn 1985): 56–81.

Clavita, Kitty. *Inside the State: The Bracero Program, Immigration, and the I.N.S.* New York: Routledge, 1992.

Cockcroft, James D. *Outlaws in the Promised Land: Mexican Immigrant Workers and America's Future.* New York: Grove Press, 1986.

Cohen, Richard D. "Schooling Uncle Sam's Children: Education in the USA, 1941–1945." In *Education and the Second World War: Studies in Schooling and Social Change,* edited by Roy Lowe. London: Falmer Press, 1992.

Cooke, Henry W. "The Segregation of Mexican American Children in Southern California." *School and Society* 67 (1948): 417.

Cosgrove, Stuart. "The Zoot-Suit and Style Warfare." *History Workshop Journal* 18 (Autumn 1984): 77–91.

Craig, Richard B. *The Bracero Program.* Austin: University of Texas Press, 1971.

Crocker, Ruth Hutchinson. "Gary Mexicans and 'Christian Americanization.'" In *Forging a Community: The Latino Experience in Northwest Indiana, 1919–1975,* edited by James B. Lane and Edward J. Escobar, 115–134. Chicago: Cattails Press, 1987.

Daniel, Clete. *Chicano Workers and the Politics of Fairness: The FEPC in the Southwest, 1941–1945.* Austin: University of Texas Press, 1991.

De León, Arnoldo. *San Angeleños: Mexican Americans in San Angelo, Texas.* San Angelo, Tex.: Fort Concho Museum Press, 1985.

Deutsch, Sarah. *No Separate Refuge: Culture, Class, and Gender on an Anglo-Hispanic Frontier in the American Southwest, 1880–1940.* New York: Oxford University Press, 1987.

Donato, Rubén. *The Other Struggle for Equal Schools: Mexican Americans during the Civil Rights Era.* Albany: State University of New York Press, 1997.

Dozer, Marquard. *Are We Good Neighbors? Three Decades of Inter-American Relations, 1930–1960.* Gainesville: University Press of Florida, 1959.

Driscoll, Barbara A. *Me voy pa' Pensilvania por no andar en la vaganzia.* México, D.F.: Consejo Nacional para la Cultura y Las Artes y Universidad Nacional Autónoma de México, 1996.

———. *The Tracks North: The Railroad Bracero Program of World*

War II. Austin: Center for Mexican American Studies, 1999.

Escobar, Edward J. *Race, Police, and the Making of a Political Identity: Mexican Americans and the Los Angeles Police Department, 1900–1945*. Berkeley: University of California Press, 1999.

Etulain, Richard W., editor. *Contemporary New Mexico, 1940–1990*. Albuquerque: University of New Mexico Press, 1991.

Foley, Neil. *The White Scourge: Mexicans, Blacks, and Poor Whites in Texas Cotton Culture*. Berkeley: University of California Press, 1997.

Fregoso, Rosa Linda. "Homegirls, Cholas, and Pachucas in Cinema: Taking over the Public Sphere." *California History* 74, no. 3 (1995): 316–327.

Gamboa, Erasmo. *Mexican Labor and World War II: Braceros in the Pacific Northwest, 1942–1947*. Seattle: University of Washington Press, 2000.

Garcia, Juan. *Mexicans in the Midwest: 1900–1932*. Tucson: University of Arizona Press, 1996.

García, Mario T. "Americans All: The Mexican-American Generation and the Politics of Wartime Los Angeles, 1941–1945." *Social Science Quarterly* 65 (June 1984): 278–289.

———. *Memories of Chicano History: The Life and Narrative of Bert Corona*. Los Angeles: University of California Press, 1994.

———. *Mexican Americans: Leadership, Ideology and Identity, 1930–1960*. New Haven, Conn.: Yale University Press, 1989.

Garcia, Richard A. *Rise of the Mexican American Middle Class: San Antonio, 1929–1941*. College Station: Texas A&M University Press, 1991.

Gelder, Ken, and Sarah Thornton, editors. *The Subcultures Reader*. London: Routledge, 1997.

Getz, Lynne Marie. *Schools of Their Own: The Education of Hispanos in New Mexico, 1850–1940*. Albuquerque: University of New Mexico Press, 1997.

Gluck, Sherna Berger. *Rosie the Riveter Revisited: Women, the War, and Social Change*. Boston: G. K. Hall/Twayne, 1987.

Gómez-Quiñones, Juan. "Piedras Contra La Luna, México en Aztlán y Aztlán en México: Chicano-Mexican Relations and the Mexican Consulates, 1900–1920." In *Contemporary Mexico:*

Papers of the Fourth International Congress of Mexican History, edited by James W. Wilkie, Michael C. Meyer, and Edna Monzón de Wilkie. Berkeley: University of California Press, 1976.

Gonzales, Phillip B. "*La Junta de Indignación*: Hispano Repertoire of Collective Protest in New Mexico, 1884–1933." *Western Historical Quarterly* 31 (Summer 2000): 161–186.

Gonzalez, Gilbert G. *Chicano Education in the Era of Segregation.* Philadelphia: Associated University Presses, 1990.

———. *Mexican Consuls and Labor Organizing: Imperial Politics in the American Southwest.* Austin: University of Texas Press, 1999.

González, Nancie L. *The Spanish-Americans of New Mexico: A Heritage of Pride.* Albuquerque: University of New Mexico Press, 1969.

González-Souza, Luis F. "La Política Exterior de México ante la Protección Internacional de los Derechos Humanos." *Foro Internacional* 18 (Julio–Septiembre 1977): 108–138.

Griffith, Beatrice. *American Me: Fierce and Tender Stories of the Mexican-Americans of the Southwest.* New York: Pennant Books, 1954.

Griswold del Castillo, Richard, and Arnoldo De León. *North to Aztlán: A History of Mexican Americans in the United States.* New York: Twayne, 1997.

Gutiérrez, David G. *Between Two Worlds: Mexican Immigrants in the United States.* Wilmington: Scholarly Resource, 1996.

———. *Walls and Mirrors: Mexican Americans, Mexican Immigrants, and the Politics of Ethnicity.* Berkeley: University of California Press, 1995.

Hall, Stuart, and Tony Jefferson, editors. *Resistance through Rituals: Youth Subcultures in Post-War Britain.* London: Routledge, 1993.

Henley, David E., and Mrs. David E. Henley. *Minnesota and Her Migratory Workers: Land of Promises—Partially Fulfilled.* Minneapolis: Minnesota Council of Churches and Home Missions Council, 1950.

Hoddeson, Lillian, Paul W. Henrisken, Roger A. Meade, and Catherine Westfall. *Critical Assembly: A Technical History of Los Alamos during the Oppenheimer Years, 1943–1945.* Cambridge, England: Cambridge University Press, 1993.

Hoffman, Abraham. *Unwanted Mexican Americans in the Great Depression: Repatriation Pressures, 1929–1939.* Tucson: University of Arizona Press, 1974.

Holloway, John, and Eloina Pelaez, editors. *Zapatista! Reinventing Revolution in Mexico.* London: Pluto Press, 1998.

Jones, Solomon James. *The Government Riots of Los Angeles, June 1943.* San Francisco: R and E Research Associates, 1973.

Kennedy, David M. *Freedom from Fear: The American People in Depression and War, 1929–1945.* New York: Oxford University Press, 1999.

Kibbe, Pauline. *Latin Americans in Texas.* Albuquerque: University of New Mexico Press, 1946.

Kingrea, Nellie Ward. *History of the First Ten Years of the Texas Good Neighbor Commission and Discussion of Its Major Problems.* Fort Worth: Texas Christian University Press, 1954.

Kirstein, Peter N. *Anglo over Bracero: A History of the Mexican Worker in the United States from Roosevelt to Nixon.* San Francisco: R and E Research Associates, 1977.

Kliebard, Herbert M. *The Struggle for the American Curriculum: 1893–1958.* New York: Routledge, 1995.

Koppes, Clayton R. "The Good Neighbor Policy and the Nationalization of Mexican Oil: A Reinterpretation." *Journal of American History* 69 (June 1982): 62–81.

Korrol, Virginia E. Sanchez. *From Colonia to Community: The History of Puerto Ricans in New York City.* Berkeley: University of California Press, 1994.

Lopez, Thomas R., Jr. *Prospects for the Spanish American Culture of New Mexico.* San Francisco: R and E Research Associates, 1974.

Lugo, Alejandro, and Bill Maurer, editors. *Gender Matters: Rereading Michelle Z. Rosaldo.* Ann Arbor: University of Michigan Press, 2000.

Lull, James, editor. *Culture in the Age of Communication.* New York: Routledge, 2001.

Madrid-Barela, Arturo. "In Search of the Authentic Pachuco: An Interpretive Essay." *Aztlán* 4, no. 1 (Spring 1973): 31–60.

Mazón, Mauricio. *The Zoot-Suit Riots: The Psychology of Symbolic*

Annihilation. Austin: University of Texas Press, 1984.

McWilliams, Carey. *North from Mexico: The Spanish-Speaking People of the United States.* New York: Greenwood Press, 1968 (first edition, 1949).

Mecham, J. Lloyd. *A Survey of United States–Latin American Relations.* New York: Houghton Mifflin, 1965.

Mexican Congress. Los Presidentes de México ante la Nación, Informes, Manifiestos y Documentos de 1821 a 1966. México, D.F.: XLVI Legislatura de la Camara de Diputados, 1966.

Minnesota Governor's Interracial Commission. *The Mexican in Minnesota.* St. Paul: Governor's Interracial Commission, 1948.

Montejano, David. *Anglos and Mexicans in the Making of Texas, 1836–1986.* Austin: University of Texas Press, 1987.

Moye, J. Todd. "The Tuskegee Airmen Oral History Project and Oral History in the National Park Service." *Journal of American History,* September 2002 <http://www.historycooperative.org/journals/jah/89.2/moye.html> (January 30, 2004).

Nash, Gerald. "Spanish-Speaking Americans in Wartime." Chapter Seven in Nash, *The American West Transformed: The Impact of the Second World War.* Bloomington: Indiana University Press, 1985.

Padilla, Ezequiel. *Free Men of America.* Chicago: Ziff-Davis, 1943.

Perales, Alonso. *Are We Good Neighbors?* San Antonio, Tex.: Artes Gráficas, 1948.

Pike, Fredrick B. *FDR's Good Neighbor Policy: Sixty Years of Gentle Chaos.* Austin: University of Texas Press, 1995.

Plascencia, Luis. "Low Riding in the Southwest: Cultural Symbols in the Mexican Community." In *History, Culture, and Society: Chicano Studies in the 1980s,* edited by Mario T. García and Francisco Lomeli. Ypsilanti, Michigan: Bilingual Press, 1983.

Pycior, Julie Leininger. *LBJ and Mexican Americans: The Paradox of Power.* Austin: University of Texas Press, 1997.

Ramirez, Catherine S. "Crimes of Fashion: The Pachuca and Chicana Style Politics." *Meridians: Feminisms, Race, Transnationalism* 2, no. 2 (2002): 1–35.

Ramos, Henry A. J., *The American GI Forum.* Houston: Arte Público Press, 1998.

Romo, Ricardo. *East Los Angeles: History of a Barrio.* Austin: University of Texas Press, 1983.

Rosales, Arturo. *Testimonio: A Documentary History of the Mexican American Struggle for Civil Rights.* Houston: Arte Público Press, 2000.

Ruiz, Vicki L. "And Miles to Go." In *Western Women, Their Land and Their Lives,* edited by Vicki L. Ruiz and Lillian Schilissel. Albuquerque: University of New Mexico Press, 1989.

———. *Cannery Women, Cannery Lives: Mexican Women, Unionization, and the California Food Processing Industry, 1930–1950.* Albuquerque: University of New Mexico Press, 1987.

———. "Dead Ends or Gold Mines? Using Missionary Records in Mexican-American Women's History." *Frontiers* 12, no. 1 (1992).

Salisbury, Richard V. "Good Neighbors? The United States and Latin America in the Twentieth Century." In Gerald K. Haines and Samuel J. Walker, editors, *American Foreign Relations: A Historiographical Review.* Westport, Conn.: Greenwood Press, 1981.

Sánchez, George I. "Bilingualism and Mental Measures: A Word of Caution." *Journal of Applied Psychology* 17 (1934): 765–772.

———. *Forgotten People: A Study of New Mexicans.* Albuquerque: University of New Mexico Press, 1940.

Sánchez, George J. *Becoming Mexican American: Ethnicity, Culture and Identity in Chicano Los Angeles, 1900–1945.* New York: Oxford University Press, 1993.

———. "Go after the Women: Americanization and the Mexican Immigrant Woman, 1915–1929." In Ellen Carol DuBois and Vicky L. Ruiz, editors, *Unequal Sisters: A Multicultural Reader in U.S. Women's History.* New York: Routledge, 1990.

Sanchez, Thomas. *Zoot-Suit Murders.* New York: Vintage Books, 1991.

San Miguel, Guadalupe, Jr. *Let All of Them Take Heed: Mexican Americans and the Campaign for Educational Equality in Texas, 1910–1981.* Austin: University of Texas Press, 1987.

Santillán, Richard. "Rosita the Riveter: Midwest Mexican American

Women during World War II, 1941–1945." *Perspectives in Mexican American Studies* 2 (1989): 115–147.

Servín, Manuel P. "The Post–World War II Mexican-Americans, 1925–65: A Non-Achieving Minority." In *An Awakened Minority: The Mexican Americans*, second edition, edited by Manuel Servín. Beverly Hills, Calif.: Glencoe Press, 1974.

Skelton, Tracey, and Gill Valentine, editors. *Cool Places: Geographies of Youth Cultures*. London: Routledge, 1998.

Takaki, Ronald. *Double Victory: A Multicultural History of America in World War II*. Boston: Little, Brown, 2000.

Tireman, Loyd S., and Mary Watson. *A Community School in a Spanish-Speaking Village*. Albuquerque: University of New Mexico Press, 1948.

Valdés, Dionício. *Al Norte: Agricultural Workers in the Great Lakes Region, 1917–1970*. Austin: University of Texas Press, 1991.

———. *Barrios Norteños: St. Paul and Midwestern Mexican Communities in the Twentieth Century*. Austin: University of Texas Press, 2000.

Vargas, Zaragosa, editor. *Major Problems in Mexican American History*. New York: Houghton Mifflin, 1999.

Welsh, Michael. "A Prophet without Honor: George I. Sánchez and Bilingualism in New Mexico." *New Mexico Historical Review* 69 (January 1994): 19–34.

Zamora, Emilio. "The Failed Promise of Wartime Opportunity for Mexicans in the Texas Oil Industry." *Southwestern Historical Quarterly* 95 (January 1992): 323–350.

Zoraida Vázquez, Josefina, and Lorenzo Meyer. *México Frente a Estados Unidos (Un Esayo Histórico, 1776–1988)*, second edition. México, D.F.: Fondo de Cultura Económica, 1992.

Zorrilla, Luis G. *Historia de las Relaciones entre México y Los Estados Unidos de America, 1800–1958*, Tomo II. México, D.F.: Editorial Porrua, S.A., 1966.

About the Writers

LUIS ALVAREZ is an assistant professor of history at the University of Houston. He earned his Ph.D. from the University of Texas at Austin; his dissertation was "The Power of the Zoot: Youth Culture, Resistance and Community in the U.S., 1938–1945."

MARIA EVA FLORES was born and reared in Fort Stockton, Texas. She is a member of the Congregation of Divine Providence and has taught high school English and speech and drama in Texas and Louisiana. She has also done community pastoral work in San Antonio. Currently, she serves as the University Archivist and Special Collections Librarian at Our Lady of the Lake University in San Antonio, Texas.

ERASMO GAMBOA is Professor of History in the American Ethnic Studies Department at the University of Washington. His publications include *Mexican Labor during World War II: Braceros in the Pacific Northwest, 1942–1947* (Austin: University of Texas Press, 1990). His publication *Voces hispanas: Excerpts from the Idaho Hispanic Oral History Project* (Boise: Idaho Commission on Hispanic Affairs, 1992) won the 1992 American Library Association Award for Best Local History.

LYNNE MARIE GETZ is Associate Professor of History at Appalachian State University in Boone, North Carolina. Her book, *Schools of Their Own: The Education of Hispanos in New Mexico, 1850–1940*, was published by the University of New Mexico Press in 1987. She is a native of southern Colorado and received her Ph.D. in history from the University of Washington.

DAVID MONTEJANO is Associate Professor in the Department of Ethnic Studies at the University of California, Berkeley. He is a native Texan. His doctorate from Yale University was in sociology. His book, *Anglos and Mexicans in the Making of Texas, 1836–1986* (Austin: University of Texas Press, 1987), won the prestigious Frederick Jackson Turner Award.

JULIO NOBOA is Assistant Professor of Education at the University of Texas at Brownsville. Originally from Chicago, he earned his doctorate in curriculum studies from the University of Texas at Austin. His dissertation was "Leaving Latinos Out: The Teaching of U.S. History in Texas." For over a decade, he has also been a columnist and freelance writer.

NAOMI QUIÑONEZ received her Ph.D. in history with an American-studies specialization from Claremont Graduate University in Pomona, California. An independent scholar, Quiñonez is also an award-winning poet who has written two books of poetry and is anthologized in many books and journals.

MAGGIE RIVAS-RODRIGUEZ is an associate professor at the University of Texas at Austin School of Journalism since 1998. She is the director of the U.S. Latino and Latina WWII Oral History Project and the editor of this book. She is a former journalist with over seventeen years of professional experience at major daily news outlets.

RITA SANCHEZ teaches Chicano Studies at San Diego Mesa College in San Diego, California. She received her master's degree in English from Stanford University, where she was a Ford Foundation Fellow and a Stanford Chicano Fellow. She promotes the study and research of family history. Her book *Cochise Remembers: Our Great-Grandfather Charles Henry* (San Diego: R and R, 2000), is used in the classroom.

DIONICIO VALDÉS is a native of Detroit, Michigan. He is currently a professor in the Department of History at Michigan State University and senior research scholar with the Julian Samora Research Institute at Michigan State. He is the author of *Al Norte:*

Agricultural Workers in the Great Lakes Region, 1917–1970 (University of Texas Press, 1991), and *Barrios Norteños: St. Paul and Midwestern Mexican Communities in the Twentieth Century* (University of Texas Press, 2000). He is also co-editor, with Refugio Rochín, of *Voices of a New Chicana/o History* (Michigan State University Press, 2000).

EMILIO ZAMORA is a historian in the School of Information, with a courtesy appointment in the department of history, at the University of Texas at Austin. His bachelor's and master's degrees are from Texas A&I, Kingsville (now Texas A&M, Kingsville), and his doctorate is from the University of Texas at Austin. His research interests include Mexican American history and the history of Mexican workers in Texas between 1890 and 1945. His book, *The World of the Mexican Worker in Texas* (College Station: Texas A&M University Press, 1993), won the T. R. Fehrenbach Book Award and the H. L. Mitchell Award.

Index